THE

GERMAN SECTARIANS

OF

PENNSYLVANIA

VOLUME I.

BY

JULIUS FRIEDRICH SACHSE

AMS PRESS

NEW YORK

SPECIMEN OF ARTISTIC PEN-WORK MADE AT EPHRATA CLOISTER ABOUT 1

ORIGINAL 12 X 18 INCHES.   PHOTOGRAPHED BY J. F. SACHSE.

THE

GERMAN SECTARIANS

OF

PENNSYLVANIA

1708-1742

A CRITICAL AND LEGENDARY HISTORY

OF THE

Ephrata Cloister

AND THE

Dunkers

BY

JULIUS FRIEDRICH SACHSE

PHILADELPHIA:
PRINTED FOR THE AUTHOR
MDCCCXCIX

Reprinted from the edition of 1899–1900, Philadelphia
First AMS edition published 1971

Manufactured in the United States of America

International Standard Book Number :
Complete Set : 0-404-08340-4
Volume one   :0-404-08341-2

Library of Congress Catalog Card Number:73-134385

AMS PRESS INC.
NEW YORK,N.Y. 10003

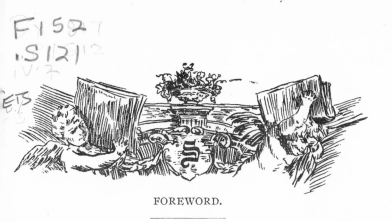

FOREWORD.

In submitting to his readers the present volume of Penn-sylvana local history the writer offers no apology. The universal approval bestowed by both press and public upon

THE GERMAN PIETISTS OF PENNSYLVANIA

has encouraged him to persevere in his labor and research, and he now presents a continuation of the history of the "Sect People" of Pennsylvania in the form of an exhaus-tive account of the EPHRATA CLOISTER and the DUNKERS. Incidentally, the early history of one is that of the other. Later, however, while the Dunkers or German Baptist Brethren became a large and flourishing denomination, the other branch resolved itself into a monastic society composed of both sexes, and was fixed for many years in unique habi-tations upon the banks of the picturesque Cocalico in the county of Lancaster. At last the institution, by a change of the social and political conditions, together with the death of the older members of the society, lapsed into a regular German Seventh-day Baptist congregation.

The members of the original society were the virtual successors to the Society of the Woman in the Wilderness on the Wissahickon, which formed the basis for our first volume of this series. In issuing the same, the hope was expressed that the publication would be the means of bringing to light some further facts and documents bearing upon this interesting phase of our early local history. In this wish the writer was not disappointed. Among the valuable contributions brought to light it is but necessary to mention the following :

(1) *Zwei Stücke aus Pennsylvanien.* Being letters from Pastorius, dated March 7, 1684.

(2) *An Account of the Religious Condition of Pennsylvania.* By Justus Falkner, at Germantown, 1701.

(3) The original MS. of the *Send-Schreiben of Johann Gottfried Selig to Rev. Francke, at Halle.*

(4) Pastorius' *Send-Brieff Offenherziger Liebesbezeugung an die so-genannte Pietisten in Hoch Deutschland.*

(5) Biographical sketch of Magister Zimmermann, showing that he was a student of Rev. M. Tobias Wagner.

(6) Two heretofore unknown English books, by Conrad Beissel and Michael Wohlfarth, printed by Bradford, Philadelphia, 1729.

The more we look into the history and religious condition of the German immigrants who came to these shores in the early years of the eighteenth century, the greater becomes our admiration for the deeds they accomplished. Many were religious enthusiasts of doctrine inimical to the orthodox faiths which flourished under official sanction. Persecuted at home, they left the Fatherland and came either with their families to enjoy the promised religious liberty, only to find that they were the victims of scheming agents, and that many of the representations made to them prior to their departure had but little foundation in fact.

Yet, notwithstanding these drawbacks, we find here at an early date the altars of the various faiths, orthodox and sectarian, mystic and separatist, erected side by side in the sylvan groves of Penn's colony. Though differing upon religious tenets and creeds, these Germans, almost without exception, were of the same moral and industrious class that went so far to make our Commonwealth what is it.

Whether Separatist or Orthodox, Lutheran, Quaker or Moravian, Mennonite or Dunker, New Mooner or Seventh Dayer, all were known for their thrift, industry and religious devotion. Quite a number of them came to these shores, singly or in companies, to seek the peace of mind which they supposed could only be attained by practising their peculiar tenets.

The founder of the Ephrata Community was one of those religious leaders who, in a few years, succeeded in gathering around him a number of men and women, some of considerable erudition; and in less than a decade we had here in Pennsylvania a semi-monastic community, which developed into a religious, educational, commercial and industrial establishment, and at an early date set up here, far away from the chief city of the Province, the third printing-press within the Colony, and the first to print with both German and English types.

The writer not only proposes to trace the peculiar history of this Community from its inception to its decline— recall their legends and chronicle their traditions—but also to present, as nearly as possible, a complete bibliography of the various publications of these people, as well as of all issues of the Ephrata press. Fac-similes of title-pages are given whenever attainable.

Many of the facts and incidents are presented here for the first time, being culled from letters and manuscripts found in possession of descendants of the secular congregation, which was connected with the mystical Community. Others, again, were found in private collections and in various archives abroad, where they had reposed and lain forgotten for over a century, until brought to light by the investigation of the present writer.

It may be said that an undue importance has been awarded to some of the humble characters, who became leaders in these religious sects, and, by force of their surroundings, were thus thrown into prominence. The writer has no desire to elevate any such persons; neither does he wish to detract one iota from the credit due them: his sole aim being to tell the true story of this feature of the German influence in the settlement and development of our Commonwealth. Their influence has extended far beyond the confines of our present State, as is instanced in the general history of the German Baptist Brethren (Dunkers) and the Moravian Church.

In compiling the present story, one of the leading thoughts of the writer has been to preserve every item of interest, both literary and pictorial, connected with our subject or emanating from the mystical society at Ephrata.

Our illustrations are all from original sources; the views of buildings and surroundings are reproductions of photographs made by the writer at various times, from 1886 to 1899. The illustrations printed in the text are mainly selected from a Kloster copy dating prior to 1750, forming a feature in which this work stands unique. The text is also amplified with foot-notes wherever necessary, as a guide to the future student.

The quotations from the _Chronicon Ephretense_, which have been more or less freely used, are mostly from the excellent translation by Rev. J. Max Hark, D.D. (Lancaster, 1889).

Acknowledgments are due to the Hon. Samuel W. Pennypacker for suggestions and the use of his unrivalled collection; to Frank Ried Dieffenderfer, of Lancaster, and Dr. John F. Mentzer, of Ephrata, for assistance in solving some local questions; also to John W. Jordan, of the Historical Society of Pennsylvania, Albert J. Edmunds, and to the many friends who have aided me in various ways toward bringing this work to completion.

J. F. SACHSE.

July, 1899.

CONTENTS.

CHAPTER I.

EPHRATA OF THE PRESENT DAY.

Location. Description. Gross' Hollow. Old Eagle Inn. Paxtang Road. Horseshoe Pike. The Mountain Borough. Social Functions. Ephrata Press of To-day. Mountain Springs. Joseph Konigmacher.

CHAPTER II.

BEYOND THE COCALICO.

Across the Stone Bridge. Grist Mill. Ancient Mile Stone. "29 to T." The Old Stile. The Kloster. Old God's Acre. Tribe of Fahnestocks. Ephrata Academy. Erbs' Corner. Zion Hill. Proposed Monument. Patriot's Day. Kloster Mühle. Trials of the Kloster Officials.

CHAPTER III.

ADVENT OF THE PALATINES.

Trials of Early Settlers. Causes Leading to the Founding of the "Order of the Solitary." Pietists and Enthusiasts. Designing Land Agents. Arrival of Religious Communities. Fears of Quaker Governors. Proclamations Against Palatines. Declaration Signed by Germans. Spread of Sabbatarian Doctrine. Theosophy. Remains of the Community.

CHAPTER IV.

GERMAN PILGRIMS.

Arrival at Boston. Johann Conrad Beissel. Parentage. Youth. Apprenticeship. Travels as Journeyman Baker. Calls Master's Wife Jezebel. Enlightened in Spirit. Heidelberg. Introduced into Rosicrucian Chapter. Banished. Sails for the New World. Arrives in Pennsylvania. Disappointment. Description of Germantown. Schwartzbrod and Pumpernickel. Apprentices himself to a Weaver.

CHAPTER V.

THE WEAVER'S APPRENTICE.

CHAPTER VI.

THE LABADISTS ON THE BOHEMIA MANOR.

CHAPTER VII.

THE HUT IN THE FOREST.

CHAPTER VIII.

THE GERMAN BAPTIST BRETHREN.

CHAPTER IX.

THE NEW DUNKERS ON THE CONESTOGA.

CHAPTER X.

THE CRADLE OF GERMAN LITERATURE.

CHAPTER XI.

ALEXANDER MACK.

CHAPTER XII.

KOCH-HALEKUNG,—THE SERPENTS' DEN.

CHAPTER XXII.

THE WEYRAUCHS HÜGEL.

CHAPTER XXIII.

THE ZIONITIC BROTHERHOOD.

CHAPTER XXIV.

THE AMWELL DUNKERS.

CHAPTER XXV.

THE HOUSE OF PRAYER.

CHAPTER XXXI.

HEBRON.

CHAPTER XXXII.

SARON.

CHAPTER XXXIII.

BETHANIA.

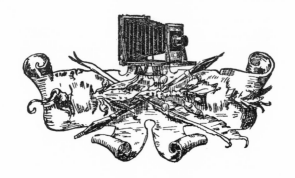

LIST OF PLATES.

(NEGATIVES AND REPRODUCTIONS BY JULIUS F. SACHSE.)

FAC-SIMILE OF TITLE-PAGES.

ILLUSTRATIONS.

CHAPTER I.

EPHRATA OF THE PRESENT DAY.

PHRATA! Of all the words and names in the vocabulary of Pennsylvania none embraces so much of what is mystical and legendary as the word Ephrata, when it is used to denote the old monastic community which once flourished in the valley of the Cocalico in Lancaster county, and whose members lived according to the esoteric teachings, practised the mystic rites, and sought for both physical and spiritual regeneration and perfection according to the secret ritual as taught by the ascetic philosophers of old.

Glancing over any good map of Pennsylvania the searcher will find noted in the northern part of Lancaster county the town of Ephrata,—pronounced Ef-rā-taaw. The exact location, if the map be a modern one, is where the Reading & Columbia railroad crosses a branch of the Cocalico creek; or, if the map be an old one, where the road from Lancaster to Reading intersects with the Brandywine and Paxtang road leading from Downings' to Harris' ferry.

The Ephrata of the present day is a flourishing town or borough of perhaps three thousand inhabitants, support-

ing several banks, hotels and numerous industrial estab-
lishments.

With this modern hive of life and industry we really
have but little to do, except to mention it in a general
way, as it merely takes its name from the old community
of mystic theosophists who once flourished in the vicinity.
So we will pass the modern town after a short description
as it appears at the close of the nineteenth century, and
then lift the veil of the past and study the history and
recall the romance of the devout people who settled here
over a century and a half ago, and flourished and prospered
within this most fertile valley until the increase in population and the changes in the political condition of the
Province, together with other causes which will be fully
set forth, made the monastic feature of the community an
uncongenial one to our republican institutions.

The visitor, as he steps from the train at Ephrata station
on the Reading & Columbia railroad, finds himself in the
midst of a typical modern Pennsylvania-German town.   A
few paces below the railroad is the chief square of the
borough.   Here Main and State streets intersect.   It is an
old cross-roads, where formally stood a provincial tavern
with its necessary outbuildings.   It was known as Gross'
Corner and Gross' Hollow.   This old landmark was the
nucleus for the present town.   Now two large hotels upon
opposite corners and an imposing business block have supplanted the old-time hostelrie, and form what is virtually
the centre of the town.

From this point the fine broad street is a sloping one,
gradually ascending towards the east as it leads up to the
Ephrata mountain, with its erstwhile renowned springs in
the background.   Westward the street descends at an easy
grade until it reaches the Cocalico, which is spanned by
an ancient stone bridge of several arches.   As one leaves
the centre of the town in either direction the business

FROM SKETCH MADE ABOUT 1840.

THE OLD INN FORMERLY AT GROSS' CORNER.

THE GERMAN SECTARIANS OF PENNSYLVANIA.

houses gradually give way to the comfortable homes, neat and tidy, such as are to be found in every Pennsylvania town and village wherever the German element predominates.

The houses, set well back from the street line, are of a style of architecture characteristic to Pennsylvania Germans, mostly two story, having an ample front porch with benches at either side of the door, trellised with sweet-flowering vines. All woodwork and paint is kept scrupulously bright and clean. In summer nearly all the dwellings have neat flower-plats in front, while in the rear there is an ample kitchen-garden, which is invariably attended to by the wife or matron of the home. Another peculiarity is that all houses are built with the gable end towards the side, none facing the street.

The finely shaded main street, originally the Brandywine and Paxtang road, and in later years known officially as the Downingtown, Ephrata and Harrisburg turnpike, but locally as as the "Horseshoe pike," is a highway which,

SOCIAL FUNCTIONS OF THE PAST.

before railroad days, was the connecting link between the Lancaster turnpike and Harrisburg. It diverged from the former highway at Downingtown, and from its peculiar curved course received the name it bears from the teamsters who then toiled over its hills to the Susquehanna. Such part of this old thoroughfare as lies within the borough limits is now Main street of the town.

The chief cross street—State —is such part of the old State road connecting Lancaster and Reading as lies within the borough limits.

Ephrata is laid out on a somewhat irregular plan, the ex-

posure on the hillside being north by west, and on account
of this location it is frequently called the Mountain borough
of Lancaster. Since August 22, 1891, when the town was
incorporated, the streets and footways have been nicely
graded and paved, and a system of electric lighting has
lately been introduced. The town is also provided with
a good supply of water obtained from never-failing springs

THE EPHRATA REVIEW.

THE EPHRATA NEWS.

Ephrata Reporter

THE EPHRATA PRESS AT THE CLOSE OF THE NINETEENTH CENTURY.

upon the mountain side which overlooks the town. There
are also excellent schools, churches of various denominations and ample hotel accommodations for visitors and trav-
ellers. There are also published within the borough three
weekly newspapers,—*The Ephrata Review*, *The Ephrata
News*, and *The Ephrata Reporter*.

Mention has been made of the "Springs." This is a

summer resort some distance up the mountain side, facing upon Main street.   The resort was originally started in the year 1846 by Joseph Konigmacher, a local celebrity, and

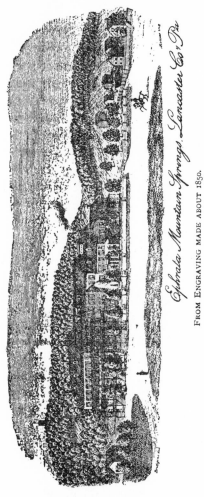

Ephrata Mountain Springs, Lancaster Co., Pa.

FROM ENGRAVING MADE ABOUT 1850.

under his management soon gained considerable reputation as both a pleasure and health resort, being patronized by many men of social and national prominence during the antebellum days.   The resort became known as the "Ephrata Mountain Springs," and in the course of a few years it came into great favor with Philadelphia and Baltimore society folk. Of late years, however, the old resort has lost much of its prestige, and gives the visitor but little idea of what it was under the Konigmacher régime, when the porches and halls were filled with the wit and beauty of the days of Pierce and Buchanan. The elevation of the Springs is reputed to be 1250 feet above tide water, and from the observatory which once stood within the grounds magnificient views, extending far into the neighboring counties, were to be seen.

Within the past few years another fine resort, " The Cocalico," has been built within the town, and offers modern conveniences to visitor and tourist. Such is the modern town of Ephrata.

It is, however, with an older settlement—Old Ephrata, the Ephrata of colonial days—that our interest centers, and which is still recalled by several quaint buildings,—of a style and architecture foreign to this country,—structures which have weathered the storms of over a century and a half, and now stand like silent

JOSEPH KONIGMACHER.

monitors of the past, relics of a by-gone age ; unique structures, second only in interest to the quiet resting-place—the God's acre by the roadside—where repose the actors and characters, pious and God-fearing men and women, who once upon a time lived in these quaint houses, labored to turn the wilderness into a blooming garden, and here erected the altar of mysticism, and kept alive for years the fires of theosophy and the esoteric speculations of the Heavenly Bridegroom and the Celestial Eve. Here they lived as a community, many as celibates, laboring and hoping, until they were laid one by one in the peaceful Kloster cemetery, there to remain until the harbinger should appear in the skies and proclaim the Millennium.

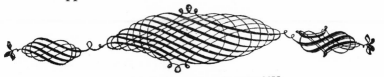

A SPECIMEN FLOURISH, FROM KLOSTER MSS.

CHAPTER II.

BEYOND THE COCALICO.

OR our purpose we will now leave the bustling, modern borough at the foot of Main street, cross the stone bridge which spans the picturesque Cocalico and continue up the old turnpike. A few rods bring us within the borders of the old confine, formerly known as "The Settlement of the Solitary" (*Lager der Einsamen*), locally, as the "Kloster," and on some old records as "Dunkerstown," but properly as "Ephrata."

The first object to attract attention after crossing the creek is a large brick grist-mill of modern construction, its massive chimney forming a prominent feature in the landscape. As the improved methods of milling and growing business demanded increased facilities steam-power and new machinery were introduced; and, to meet further demands, it was rebuilt upon several occasions, until it has now lost all its former identity when it was a typical Pennsylvania water-mill. The only thing giving any clue to its antiquity is an old tablet which was replaced in the new wall. It bears the legend "Aº MDCCLVI" (1756) and

NEGATIVES BY J. F. SACHSE.

TOLL-BOOTH ON TURNPIKE, LOOKING WEST.

MILL BEYOND BRIDGE.

refers to the original mill erected by the Baumann family. Upon the site of the present mill once stood the second paper-mill of the Community. It continued as a paper-mill until about the year 1836, when it was sold to private parties and turned into a grist-mill.

The chief mill-site of the old Community, the original "Kloster Mühle," is situated about a mile further down the creek as it winds its course around Mount Zion. The history of both mills will be fully described in the proper place.

Returning to the highway, which is now known as the

Clay and Hinkeltown turnpike, we pass the miller's dwelling, a modern brick house. Upon the opposite side of the turnpike we have an old mile-stone, set when the Horseshoe pike was first located. It bears the following legend: "29 To T.–59 To P." To the uninitiated these letters are something of a puzzle, especially when told that the upper characters mean 29 miles to Downingtown! an incident which has been seized upon and brought out with avidity by ignorant and biased writers whenever they wish to say anything against the intellectuality of the Pennslyvania-German.

ANCIENT MILE-STONE ON THE HORSESHOE PIKE.

More than one writer has made merry over the Pennsylvania-Dutch who, according to him, publish their ignorance to the world on their mile-stones by spelling Downingtown with a "T."

Now, the fact of the matter is that the shoe is upon the other foot; the "T" does not stand for Downingtown, but for turnpike. It will be recollected that the turnpike between Philadelphia and Lancaster was the first hard road in the United States, and was for years alluded to as "the

Turnpike," and our road led from this turnpike to the Susquehanna. Incidentally it may be mentioned that the construction of this great highway proceeded chiefly from these same Pennsylvania-Dutch, who, with some modern would-be historians, are continually held up as examples of ignorance and boorish stupidity.

Upon the right-hand side of the road as we journey west, just above the ancient mile-stone, there stands an old stone house dating back perhaps to colonial days. Just above it a large brick house faces the road, from which it is now separated by an ornamental fence. This building in former days, when the horn of the stage-driver and the crack of the teamster's whip were familiar music throughout the land, was a public house, where cheer was dispensed to man and beast. The tablet bears the legend: "BUILD by DANIEL BAUMAN & SALLY his WIFE 1819."

Copyright, Century Co., N. Y.
THE OLD STILE.

Just above this former hostelrie is an old toll-booth, No. 2 on the Clay and Hinkeltown pike. Directly opposite, a stile leads over the rail fence into the meadow beyond. Passing over the rude steps and entering the enclosure we are within the Kloster grounds. Several large buildings in the rich green meadow, some distance from the road, attract our notice as they loom up against the sky. In local parlence, the whole of this property or farm is known as the "Kloster." The cluster of houses seen upon the right is prominent from the extreme pitch of the high gabled roof of the chief building. This is known as the

SISTER HOUSE AND SAAL FROM SOUTHWEST.

"Saal" or prayer hall, and stands at right angles with the "Sister House," whose gable end at this point is just visible over the tops of the out-buildings. The peculiar large and rambling building towards the left, standing alone in the meadow, is what remains of the old "Brother House." The chapel or Saal, with the extensive galleries which once adjoined it, has long since been demolished. The *Kloster presse*, or Ephrata printing establishment, is said to have been located in the lower corner of this house.

All these ancient buildings are now occupied as tenements, except the Saal proper, which is still devoted to its original uses, religious services being held upon the scriptural Sabbath by the local Sabbatarian or German Seventh-Day Baptist congregation.

The smaller dwelling among the trees, about equi-distant between the two groups of large buildings, was once the cabin of Father Friedsam, the founder and master-spirit of the Community. The elevation just beyond the buildings is known as Mount Zion, and was formerly the site of several large structures, somewhat similar to those described. They were used for monastic purposes by the Zionitic Brotherhood. At the top of the hill, a flag-pole is seen in the extreme distance. This marks the secular burying-ground of the Community, and it is here that so many Revolutionary soldiers found their last resting-place in the winter of 1777–1778, after the battles of Brandywine and Germantown, when the buildings of the Brotherhood were occupied by the American forces as military hospitals.

Returning once more to the turnpike, a short walk brings us to the lane leading into the Kloster grounds. At this point we reach the old God's acre of the Kloster. It is separated from the road by a low stone wall without ornament or coping. The main entrance to this hallowed spot is from the Kloster side. Standing in the road and looking over the low wall, one is attracted by the peculiar

THE OLD BROTHER HOUSE (SOUTH FRONT).

angle formed by the Sister House and Saal as seen from this point. The small modern house seen just above the main gateway is for the use of the tenant farmer of the Kloster farm.

ENTRANCE TO THE OLD GOD'S ACRE OF THE KLOSTER.

E will now go into the old graveyard with its green hillocks and mossy tombstones, often bearing strange legends and mystic symbols: inscriptions which recall to the local historian and genealogist the various persons of greater and lesser note who once lived and died within the confines of the Community. The most prominent tomb is that of Conrad Beissel (Father Friedsam Gottrecht) the founder of the Community. It is marked with a large marble slab, and is shaded by a tall wild cherry tree, which has sprung up within the last half-century. A few feet away, under the shadow of the same boughs, is to be seen the head-stone of the Reverend Peter Miller (Prior Jabez), while clustered around the graves of these two great leaders are the graves of the different celibates, male and female. Many are marked with quaint inscriptions; others again with stones merely giving the religious name of the occupant of the narrow cell below: characters of whom we shall have much to say in the progress of this history.

Within the bounds of this cemetery there also rest a number of early settlers who belonged to the secular Sabbatarian congregation. These people lived outside the Kloster confine, but were baptized members of the congregation. Many of these old pioneers were the ancestors of some of our prominent families of the present day. As an illustration, it is but necessary to mention old Dietrich Fahnestock who, as set forth upon his modern tombstone, was the " Father of the Tribe of Fahnestocks."

Leaving the old cemetery for the present, and continuing up the turnpike, a few rods bring us to a frame house of modern build. It fronts upon the pike, and is surmounted by a cupola and clock, with hour hand and bell. A large sign under the center window bears the inscription, " EPHRATA ACADEMY Founded 1837—By the Society of—

Seventh-Day Baptists." This building is now used as an unclassified township school.

As we continue our ramble up the thoroughfare, we pass cultivated fields upon either side of the road. These were formerly woodland, from which the inmates of the two houses were supplied with fuel. The woodlands were then known as the Brother and Sister woods respectively; the

THE OLD EPHRATA ACADEMY.

latter being upon the left-hand side of the road. We at last come to the top of the hill—Erb's Corner, as it is locally known.

The massive stone house on the corner opposite the Kloster grounds, during colonial days, was a tavern stand. It was built and kept by Henry Miller, who contracted the deadly camp-fever while ministering to the wounded soldiers in the hospital on Zion Hill. He was buried within sight of his home among the patriots in the cemetery on that hill. The tablets on the old tavern bear the legend: "HENRY MILLER MDCCLXIII & SUSANA MARGAR: his Wife."

The guide-post at the cross-roads informs us that it is thirteen miles to Lancaster and eighteen miles to Reading. The ascent was a gradual and easy one. The country road, which here crosses the turnpike, forms the boundary of the Kloster grounds proper. This road is known as the upper or old Reading road, and dates from Provincial days.

Let us now turn to the left and continue our walk down this old road. As we look towards the Cocalico, the Kloster grounds lie before us. We have here a panoramic view, with the ancient buildings in the distance. The clusters of small cottages, which for a century or more have stood on the slope of Zion Hill, and were formerly utilized for various industrial purposes by the Community, are plainly seen. It was upon the high ground, about half-way up this hill, where stood the original buildings of the Zionitic Brotherhood, which were used for hospital purposes during the Revolution. A short distance further we reach the highest part of the Kloster property. Here, separated from road and field by a neat white-washed pale fence, is the secular graveyard of the old settlement, wherein are buried over two hundred patriot soldiers of the Revolution, whose only epitaph for many years was a plain board upon which was inscribed in German *fractur-schrift*

Hier ruhen die Gebeine von viel Soldaten.

A local tradition tells us that this inscription was placed over the common grave on Zion Hill at the instance of Peter Miller who, as Brother Jabez, succeeded Beissel as leader of the Community.

The prominent feature of this cemetery, the title of which is now vested in the "Ephrata Monument Association," is a tall flag-staff and the base of a projected monument, designed as a tribute to the memory of the many soldiers interred there. The corner-stone was laid by

Governor Francis Shunk so far back as 1845, but after a few courses of stone were put in place the enterprise lapsed until a few years ago, when the Monument Association was revived with every prospect of now carrying the project to an early completion.

Under their auspices September 11th of each year is now celebrated as "Patriots' Day" by patriotic meetings, addresses and processions, thus keeping alive the spirit of patriotism and the interest in the projected monument.

From this spot is obtained a fine view of the country. Beyond the Kloster property is seen the modern town of Ephrata with its industries, the Ephrata mountain forming a

MONUMENT AS PROJECTED IN 1845.

verdant background to the beautiful landscape. Turning to the south, if the day be clear, Akron and Lititz are plainly seen.

Leaving Mount Zion and continuing our ramble down the old road, which now dips towards the Cocalico, a short walk brings us to the mill-seat of the Kloster, where once upon a time stood their five mills, which ground corn, sawed timber, fulled cloth, pressed oil from the linseed raised in the vicinity, and wove much of the paper used in the Province. At the present day there is but a single mill upon this site,—it is a

17TH **PATRIOTS' DAY!** 1845

A HOLIDAY FOR PATRIOTS

The Second Annual Memorial Celebration of
PATRIOTS' DAY,
WILL BE HELD ON
Wednesday, September 11th, 1895,
At MT. ZION, Ephrata, Pa.

In memory of Two Hundred brethren who fought at the Battle of Brandywine, were brought here, nursed, died and were buried. The exercises will begin at 10 o'clock, P. M. with fire a salute of THIRTEEN Guns.

MAJ. RICKSECKER POST, No. 152, G. A. R., of Lincoln, Pa.,
ADDRESSES WILL BE DELIVERED BY

Julius F. Sachse, Esq., of Phila.; Hon. A. C. Seyfert, of Earl; Ex-Attorney General W. U. Hensel, of Lancaster; Hon. Wm. H. Andrews, of Titusville, Pa., Ex-Mayor James B. Kenney, of Reading; and others.

A special feature of the occasion will be music by

100 VOICES, Assisted by the **EPHRATA CORNET BAND.**

A GRAND CONCERT BY THE Ephrata Cornet Band,
PROF S. A. URICH, Leader, will be given IN THE EVENING, on the lot adjoining the Borough school building. Addresses will also be delivered on this occasion by prominent individuals. The exercises will conclude with a

GRAND DISPLAY OF FIREWORKS.
All are Invited.   Admission to Grounds and Concert, (in the Evening,) 10 Cts.
REFRESHMENTS of all kinds, in season, on the Grounds.
1894   GOV. D. H. HASTINGS is expected to be present and preside on the ev ing.   1895

ONE OF THE EFFORTS MADE TO COMPLETE THE MONUMENT.

flour- and grist-mill.   In the present structure the only
feature which recalls the days of yore,—when the mill was
run *pro bono publico* by the cowled brethren of the *Societas Ephratensis*,—is a large stone or tablet bearing a Latin in-

> Deo propitio reftauratiu
> pro bono publico impen-
> fis Societatis Ephratenfis
> Ano MDCCLXXXIV post
> ordinem fundatum Lmo Fun-
> datorisque obitum XVII

scription, which was placed by the Brotherhood in the walls
of their grist-mill when they reconstructed it in 1784.

It is an interesting fact that the flour made in this mill
is still a stone-pressed, ground flour, made in the same
primitive manner as when run by the Brotherhood.

Just below the mill is the old ford over the Cocalico.   It
is now superseded by a wooden bridge.   Crossing this struc-

THE SAAL AND OUTBUILDINGS.

ture, a few rods bring us to the forks of the Reading road.
The branch road is known as the lower Reading road, and
takes its course *via* Gross' Corner (the Ephrata of to-day)
and Reamstown.   At the intersection there is a massive
stone house, which was formerly a tavern stand.   The tablets

in the walls bear the following inscriptions: "JACOB KIM-MEL A. D. 1795.—ESTHER KIMMEL MDCCVC."

Leaving the old mill-site and turning towards the left, passing the dam, we follow the windings of the picturesque Cocalico; a shady foot-path shields us from the sun, and leads us to our starting-point. About half-way down this path, some distance from the mill-dam, the creek widens and deepens perceptibly. Here, tradition states, was the baptistery of the Community. It is directly opposite the Brother House. A short walk further, and we are once more at the old turnpike bridge.

THE OLD TURNPIKE BRIDGE OVER THE COCALICO.

The Kloster of late years has become something of a curiosity for visitors, especially during the summer season, when the grounds are frequently overrun by sight-seers, busybodies and relic-hunters, who know little or nothing of the history of the old Community, and seem to ignore the fact that the grounds are private property and often fail to respect the rights of the residents.

These incursions sometimes lead to encounters between the residents and the visitors, which generally end in the discomfiture of the latter.

An instance of this kind, which came to the notice of the writer, will illustrate the trials of the Kloster people. Several years ago one of Philadelphia's leading divines

visited Ephrata with several members of his flock. During
the stay at the Springs a trip to the Kloster was planned
under his direction. Of course he knew everything about
the Kloster history and the ancient buildings and their
uses, or at least he thought he did,—an opinion shared
by his companions. Well, the party drove up in several
wagons and entered the grounds, walking about as if they
owned the place. The reverend gentlemen aired his
opinions about the old Dutch Dunkers and their religion.
As they were about to enter one of the old buildings they
were accosted by a man in the garb of a plain working
farmer, who stepped up to the Dominie and asked his
business. The haughty reply was that that it was none
of his affair, with the further injunction to go about his
business, as he was not fit to be seen in the presence of
ladies in the costume he was in. One word brought on
another, until the Dominie, drawing himself up to his full
height, told the farmer that he wanted him to understand
that he was the Reverend Doctor ——— of ——— Church
in Philadelphia. The reply was: "I ton't care who you
was; I am de trustee, und I tell you to clear out." The
party did not inspect the buildings.

It is, however, but just to say that when strangers come
properly introduced or accompanied by a resident all
reasonable courtesy is usually extended to them by the
Kloster authorities.

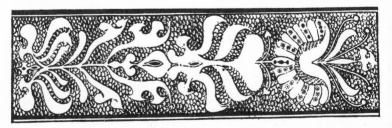

SPECIMEN OF ORNAMENTAL PEN-WORK FROM THE KLOSTER SCHREIB-STUBE.

CHAPTER III.

THE ADVENT OF THE PALATINES.

 COMPARATIVELY few persons in the State of Pennsylvania are familiar with the true history of old Ephrata and its founders, or the causes that led to its existence and dissolution. The plain and unassuming denomination of Christians who chose it as a suitable place for religious retirement, and assembled in the vicinity of its green peaceful valleys for the exercise of their pious devotions, and whose object was more the enjoyment of their Christian privileges than the establishment of a name for the admiration of posterity, have left little from the wreck of time to point out the important services they have rendered to religion and their country.

The traveller who now visits the old Kloster grounds finds nothing but relics of its former greatness. The houses devoted to the purpose of religious services have either disappeared or are fast crumbling into ruin. Every vestige of the place, as originally established, is fading away from the world forever.

At the time when the first settlement was made by these pious pioneers the surrounding country was yet an unbroken wilderness; the wild animals of the forest—such as bears, wolves and foxes—roamed at will, coming from their dens on the mountain to the very doors of the settlers' cabins; creeping reptiles from the swampy lowlands also abounded, and added to the terror of the venturesome colonists; while, as an old letter tells us, "the gloom of the adjacent forests was only broken by the smoke of the wigwam or the occasional gleam of the Indians' council-fire."

Properly to understand the causes which led to the formation of this organization—known to the members as "The Order of the Solitary (*Der Orden der Einsamen*)—and made its existence possible, one must take into consideration the political as well as the religious situation of the settlers at the time in question; nor must the peculiar temperament of these emigrants from the Fatherland be overlooked; then again the newness of the country, the limited means of intercourse, together with the fear of the savage, the distance between the scattered settlements, the differences of nationality and language,— those of each nationality pursuing a different policy, thus engendering local jealousies,

A DENIZEN OF THE FOREST.
(From an old sketch.)

—all these matters tended to act upon the sanguine temperament of the German settlers, the majority of whom had left their native land on account of religious intolerance and persecution, fleeing to this Province here to enjoy the promised liberty.

Many of these people were what were known as Pietists or Enthusiasts. These, together with the followers of Simon Menno, came thither to live in peace with the world and worship the Almighty according to the dictates of their conscience. Others, again, professed Quakerism, and sought within the fold of the Religious Society of Friends that elysium on earth pictured to them in the far-off Fatherland by designing land-agents and speculators.

MONG the Germans who thus came to these shores in the early days of the eighteenth century there were several communities who came, it might be said, in a body; seeking in the New World not only to escape the persecutions to which they had been subjected in the Fatherland, but also to put into practice some of the peculiar religious doctrines in vogue among scholastics at that time,—dogmas which they were prevented from publicly proclaiming or practising by the church authorities in Germany. Notable examples were Kelpius and his band of Pietists, who settled on the banks of the Wissahickon in 1694, and were known as the Society of the Woman in the Wilderness; the Labadists who, in the latter part of the seventeenth century, settled on the Bohemia Manor in Maryland, and there founded a monastic community; the Mennonites and Dunkers, two sects who differed from each other mainly in the fact that while the former administer baptism by sprinkling the latter believe in the necessity of immersion, and in the early part of the eighteenth century formed quite a community in Philadelphia county. To many of these people the fertile valleys of the Conestoga and Pequea, then within the bounds of Chester county, proved particularly attractive, and as they continued to arrive in large numbers they soon attracted the at-

AUTOGRAPH OF WILLIAM PENN.

tention and excited the fears of Governor Keith, who, as

early as 1717, expressed the apprehension that, under the circumstances, the Province might soon become a foreign colony.[1]

To counteract this state of affairs it was ordered in a council held September 17, 1717 :

" That all Masters of Vessels who had lately landed any " of such passengers, to appear before the Board, and render " an account of their number and character."

A proclamation was also issued calling on all such emigrants to appear within the space of one month before some magistrate,—

" Particularly before the Re- " corder of this City to take " such oaths appointed by law " as are necessary to give assur- " ances of their being well affec- " ted to his Majesty and his Gov- " ernment. But because some " of these foreigners are said to " be Mennonists, who cannot for " conscience's sake take any

ARMS OF PENNSYLVANIA.
(From a contemporary proclamation.)

" oaths, that those persons be admitted upon their giving " any equivalent assurances in their own way and manner."

---

[1] The Governour observ'd to the Board that great numbers of fforeigners from Germany, strangers to our Language & Constitutions, having lately been imported into this Province daily dispersed themselves immediately after Landing, without producing any Certificates, from whence they came or what they were ; & as they seemed to have first Landed in Britain, & afterwards to have left it Without any License from the Government, or so much as their knowledge, so in the same manner they behaved here, without making the least application to himself or to any of the magistrates ; That as this practice might be of very dangerous Consequence, since by the same method any number of foreigners from any nation whatever, as well Enemys as friends, might throw themselves upon us ; The Governour, therefore, throught it requisite that this matter should be Considered by the Board.—Col. Rec., vol. iii, p. 29.

SIR WILLIAM KEITH,
LIEUT.-GOV. 1718-1726.

PATRICK GORDON,
LIEUT.-GOV. 1726-1736.

ORIGINAL PORTRAITS IN THE COLLECTION OF THE HISTORICAL SOCIETY OF PENNSYLVANIA

Ten years later, when Patrick Gordon was Governor, at a council held at Philadelphia, September 14, 1727, we read:

"The Governour acquainted the board, that he had called "them together at this time to inform them that there is "lately arrived from Holland, a Ship with four hundred " Palatines, as 'tis said, and that he has information they will " be very soon followed by a much greater Number, who de- "sign to settle in the back parts of this Province ; & as they " transport themselves without any leave obtained from the " Crown of Great Britain, and settle themselves upon the " Proprietors untaken up Lands without any application to "the Proprietor or his Commissioners of property or to the "Government in general, it would be highly necessary to " concert proper measures for the peace and security of the " province, which may be en- "dangered by such numbers "of Strangers daily poured "in, who being ignorant of "our Language & Laws, & " settling in a body together, " make, as it were, a distinct " people from his Majesties " Subjects.

"The Board taking the " same into their serious Con-

"sideration, observe, that as Seal of the Province of Pennsylvania.

"these people pretended at first that they fly hither on the " Score of their religious Liberties, and come under the " Protection of His Majesty, its requisite that in the first " Place they should take the Oath of Allegiance, or some "equivalent to it to His Majesty, and promise Fidelity to "the Proprietor & obedience to our Established Constitu- " tion ; And therefore, until some proper Remedy can be had "from home, to prevent the Importation of such Numbers " of Strangers into this or others of His Majesties Colonies.[2]

---

[2] *Vide* Colonial Records, vol. iii, pp. 282–283.

" 'TIS ORDERED, that the Masters of the Vessells import-
" ing them shall be examined whether they have any Leave
" granted them by the Court of Britain for the Importation
" of these Forreigners, and that a List shall be taken of the
" Names of these People, their several Occupations, and the
" Places from whence they come, and shall be further ex-
" amined touching their Intentions in coming hither ; And
" further, that a Writing be drawn up for them to sign de-
" claring their Allegiance & Subjection to the King of
" Great Britain & Fidelity to the Proprietary of this Prov-
" ince, & that they will demean themselves peaceably to-
" wards all his Majesties Subjects, & strictly observe, and
" conform to the Laws of England and of this Government."

During the week ending September 27, 1727, the following paper was drawn up and presented to the Provincial
Council, wherein it was read and approved. This was a
printed form to be signed by the German emigrants who
came by sea or land from other provinces with an intention
of settling within the bounds of Penn's grant. The
declaration set forth :

ARMS FROM ROYAL PROCLAMATION ANNOUNCING GRANT TO PENN.

" We Subscribers, Natives and late Inhabitants of the
" Palatinate upon the Rhine & Places adjacent, having
" transported ourselves and Families into this Province of

"Pensilvania, a Colony subject to the Crown of Great
"Britain, in hopes and Expectation of finding a Retreat
"& peaceable Settlement therein, Do solemnly promise &
"Engage, that We will be faithful & bear true Allegiance
"to his present Majesty King George the Second, and his
"Successors Kings of Great Britain, and will be faithfull
"to the Proprietor of this Province; And that we will de-
"mean ourselves peaceably to all His said Majesties Sub-
"jects, and strictly observe & conform to the Laws of
"England and of this Province, to the utmost of our
"Power and best of our understanding."

It is an interesting fact that the first person to sign the
above declaration appears to have been Rev. George
Michael Weiss, V. D. M., of the Reformed Church.

N pursuance of the action of the authorities over one
hundred of these German settlers in the Conestoga
and Pequea valleys took the oath of allegiance and
were naturalized.[3]   Although the majority of them
—being engrossed with their domestic and secular
affairs, such as clearing the ground and founding a
homestead—neglected more or less the old religious
questions which had occupied them in the Fatherland for the now more important ones of successful
husbandry; there were some, however, who still
pondered here in the New World over the abstruse dogmas
of mediæval theology.   Nor were the Mennonites and Dunkers as a body all of one opinion; consequently it was not
long before several of these enthusiasts began to formulate
doctrines or conclusions of their own, and caused more or
less dissension, with the ultimate result of several distinct
sects being formed among the settlers on the Conestoga.

Further, a branch of the English Sabbath-keepers of New-

---

[3] For the names of such settlers who qualified under this act see Statutes
at Large of Pennsylvania, vol. iv, 1724-1744, Harrisburg, 1897, pp. 58-59,
149-50, 221, 284-85, 329-30.

town had been formed in 1724 on the French creek, in the adjacent township of Nantmill, which, two years later, by the accession of a large number of seceders from the Great Valley Baptist (first-day) Church became an active organization, vying in importance and numbers with the parent stem at Newtown. Naturally this society had an effect on the Germans in the surrounding townships, many of whom were in reality *Taufgesinte* of the Sabbatarians, and resulted in the formation of a German branch in Coventry township, as well as a small community of Dunkers on the Conestoga who kept the Sabbath. It was not long after the organization of the latter society that a complete severance took place between the Dunkers in this and the adjoining county who kept the First and those who kept the Seventh Day as the day of rest and worship.

PRIMITIVE METHOD OF GRINDING CORN.

This small fraternity on the Conestoga eventually formed the nucleus of our community on the Cocalico. It was through the efforts of one of their members, Conrad Beissel, that the society, after the removal to and permanent establishment at Ephrata, became a peculiar community, different from all other religious bodies in the Province.

Beissel became the acknowledged leader of the German Sabbath-keepers on the Conestoga, and he made certain innovations in the services and engrafted on the simple form of the Sabbatarian worship certain mystic dogmas of the seventeenth century with which he had become more or less imbued before his departure from the Fatherland.

It was here, and here alone, in this secluded valley, in the primitive forest, on the banks of the Cocalico, that there was successfully established for a time in the New World a mystical community under the name of *Ein Orden*

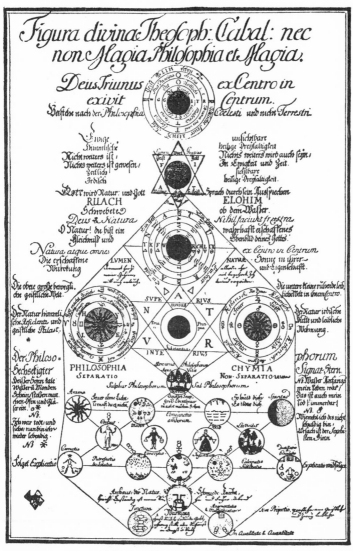

A PAGE OF ROSICRUCIAN THEOSOPHY.

Size of original MSS. 12 x 18 inches.

der Einsamen (the Community of the Solitary), whose chief aim was to attain spiritual and physical regeneration and perfection. Here for over half a century the secret mysteries of this occult philosophy were explained and the sacred rites practised without fear of molestation or official interference, while the votaries lived undisturbed in their voluntary seclusion. Here for years the most profound occult sciences, combined with the simple Sabbatarian tenets, were taught and promulgated, and possibly in no other community in this country was there so complete a renunciation of the world and as much simple Christian faith manifested as there was among the recluse Sabbatarians of Ephrata.

The maintenance of these principles as the prime basis of their life resulted in the adoption of the cloister system together with the rule of the White Friars and the building of a monastery for the members of the Community. Yet even stranger than the unique ceremonial and teachings of this Fraternity is the history of its founder, Conrad Beissel.

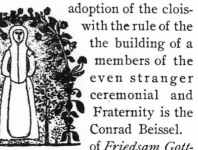

AN EPHRATA SISTER.[4]

He, under the name of *Friedsam Gottrecht*, as a theosophist, preacher, leader, organizer and composer all in one, stands without an equal among the religious leaders in the early days of the Province. How this journeyman baker in a small town in Germany,—ignorant, uneducated, poor, unknown and somewhat inclined to dissipation,—in his twenty-fifth year, while working at his trade, was suddenly chosen by the unseen powers to forsake the bake-trough and become a leader among men, is almost beyond comprehension. However, within a few years we find this heretofore laborer in the wilds of the New World, thousands of miles from his

---

[4] Contemporary sketch made in Kloster, 1748.

THE KLOSTER AT EPHRATA.

(A) VIEW FROM THE MEADOW LOOKING TOWARDS ZION HILL.   (B) VIEW FROM ZION HILL SHOWING EPHRATA MOUNTAIN IN THE DISTANCE.

PHOTOGRAPHS BY JULIUS F. SACHSE.

birth-place, at the head of a mystic community, strangely combining in its teachings the occult philosophy of the Mystics and Cabalists of the Middle Ages with the severely simple Sabbatarian worship and tenets as set forth in their primitive Bible teachings.

Of this mystic Community thus formed in the wilderness there still remains several buildings, now rapidly going into decay through age and neglect, and they, too, will soon be a thing of the past. It is not alone, however,

OLDEST KNOWN PICTURE OF EPHRATA CLOISTER.

by their mystic symbolism, the quaint architecture or interior arrangements of their habitations, or the curious religious ceremonials or rites that this band of Sabbath-keepers will live and go down to posterity for ages to come, but by the fact that from almost the earliest formation of the society they made free use of the printing press, obtaining as early as 1745 a press of their own, the first outside Philadelphia county; the second to print with German characters, and the third in the Province. Imprints from this press are at the present day among the scarcest and most prized specimens of Americana.

MAP OF THE PALATINATE, WHENCE CAME MOST OF THE EARLY EMIGRATION TO PENNSYLVANIA.
(From the German Exodus to England, 1709.)

CHAPTER IV.

THE GERMAN PILGRIMS.

N the fall of the year of grace 1720 there arrived at Boston, the chief city of the Massachusetts Bay colony, a vessel from Europe. Our records fail to give either the name of the vessel, the master or the port whence it came. The stranger part of this arrival was that it brought to that port a number of German emigrants, whose objective point was the "Quaker Valley" (*Quakerthal*) in the Island of Pennsylvania (*Die Insul Pensilvanien*). Among the number was a band of religious enthusiasts from the Palatinate, who had left their native land to escape the religious persecution which had again broken out over the fated Rhine valley upon the accession of Karl Philip as Elector Palatine, who had reintroduced the Catholic religion. A system of oppressing his Protestant subjects was inaugurated and persisted in, notwithstanding the vigorous protests from the Protestant ruler of Prussia and the States General, supported, as they were, by the intercession of King George of England.

The leader of this party was a man aged thirty years, short in stature, with a well-knit frame, high forehead, prominent nose, and a sharp piercing eye—Johann Conrad Beissel—a native of the Palatinate.

ONRAD BEISSEL was born in April, 1690, at Eberbach, a small town on the Neckar, belonging to a sub-bailiwick of the district of Mossbach, in the Palatinate, at present subject to the Grand Dutchy of Baden. He was the son of a dissolute journeyman baker, who died two months prior to the birth of the child, and was therefore a true *Opus-posthumum;* as his biographer states, "by which orphan-birth the Spirit indicated his future lone condition, and that, as one preordained to be a priest after the order of Melchizedek, he should derive little comfort from his natural kindred."

The child received the name of Johann Conrad Beissel; his mother was a pious and devout woman, and with the help of his other brothers raised him until his eighth year when she also died. The boy, thus left an orphan together with his brothers and sisters, lived and grew up in a state of

PALATINATE ARMS.

the most abject want and poverty, thus matters continued until he was old enough to learn a trade. When he reached the requisite age he was apprenticed by the local authorities to a master baker to learn the trade. The selection of this master appears to have been an unfortunate one, as this person is said to have been one of the careless sort of individuals, to be found in every community, who, having a knack for music, would at any time neglect his business for a jolification and rather scrape a dance on the violin than bend over the bake-through.

The apprentice, who also developed a taste for music, learned to play upon the violin and frequently accompanied his master on these occasions, and, being a comely

THE HOOF-POORT AT ROTTERDAM.

GATEWAY THROUGH WHICH THE PALATINES PASSED AS THEY EMBARKED FOR AMERICA.

youth, it was not long before he would rather fiddle at a wedding feast, and turn a buxom damsel in the dance than kneed his dough or rake the oven.

Thus young Conrad grew up unrestrained and neglected. In due course the *lehrbube* (apprentice) became a *geselle* (journeyman) and, as was then the custom of the Fatherland, had to take his knapsack on his back and with staff in hand as a *wandersmann* journey on foot from town to town, working at his trade for a certain period in each place, until at the end of the circuit he again arrived at his native town. If his record should prove correct, as would be shown by the entries in his *wanderbuch*, and he could produce a masterpiece of his art to the satisfaction of the guild-masters, he would be a *bäcker-meister* (master-baker).

While in his twenty-fifth year, and yet a journeyman at his native home, Beissel experienced a change of heart and commenced to long for spiritual regeneration, upon which the Chronicon comments:

" But ere the spirit of penitence came upon him his " reason became so enlightened that he could easily solve " the most intricately involved matters. " He turned his attention to mercantile " calculation, covering the walls of his " back room with his cipherings, and " mastered it without any help. Soon " after, however, the awakening Spirit " knocked so loudly at his conscience that  " his whole being was thrown into the utmost perplexity, " and so the foundation was laid for his conversion, which " followed after, wherein he attained to such superhuman " faithfulness to God that he may well be regarded as a " great miracle of our times."

ARMS OF MANHEIM.

When the journeyman baker finally started upon his professional *wanderschafft*, he came successively to Strasburg, Manheim and Heidelberg, reaching the former city during the excitement caused by the Turkish invasion of Hungary. He at once offered to enlist in a battalion of four hundred journeymen bakers, them forming there to fight the Moslem who menaced the German Empire. The required number of recruits having been obtained, Beissel, much to his chagrin, was forced to forego his purpose.

It was at Strasburg that Beissel was first introduced into Inspirationist and Pietistical circles. The chief spirit of the latter was one Michael Eckerling, a cap-maker by trade, whose four sturdy sons were destined to play so prominent a role in the Ephrata Community.

From Strasburg Beissel journeyed to Manheim, where he entered the service of one Kantebecker, and according to the Chronicon " was temporarily brought low in the spirit." After remaining for a time at Manheim he was forced to leave his master's house on account of some trouble with the latter's wife, whom he called a Jezebel.

According to an old record it was probably more upon this account than to any other that Beissel became a confirmed celibate, and resolved to devote himself to the service of God.

However, be this as it may, from Manheim he came to Heidelberg,[5] and there secured employment with a baker named Prior. Here he experienced an enlightment of the Spirit. At that time religious revival meetings were held

---

[5] Heidelberg, the present town, was founded in 1147 by Conrad von Hohenstaufen, as Duke of Franconia and Count Palatine. The University for which the town is chiefly noted was founded in 1386. During the Reformation Heidelberg bore an important part. In 1562 the celebrated Heidelberg Catechism was printed. During the Thirty Years' War the town was captured by Tilly, August 20, 1620. Eleven years later it was recaptured by the Swedes, and again became an imperial city. It was captured by Turrene and his robber hordes during the French invasion, and in 1693 the beautiful and populous city was turned for a time into an unpopulated desert, the result of French arson and murder. In the division of 1805 Heidelberg became a part of the Grand Dutchy of Baden. It now has about 40,000 inhabitants.

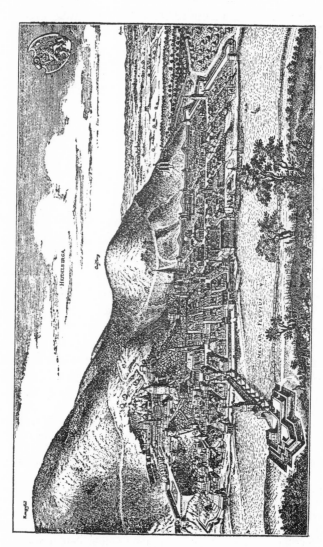

HEIDELBERG BEFORE ITS DEVASTATION BY THE FRENCH.

(MERIAN, 1645.)

in Heidelberg, which Beissel, in common with his companions, attended. One of these services made such an impression on his mind that he forsook the company of his fellow journeymen, and devoted his time and thoughts to the religious truths promulgated at the meetings.

When finally the news arrived from the seat of war that the whole battalion of bakers had been massacred to a man, he recognized in his rejection as a recruit the special hand of Providence, in thus saving him from the cruel fate of his fellows, and, thanking Almighty God for his miraculous deliverance, he at once became an active participant. From the same time he also became a student of religious matters, as well as of subjects relating to his profession. By close application to the latter he soon became the most celebrated baker in the city, and the bread which he baked for his employer achieved so great a reputation as to cause a demand from even the outlying towns and villages, to the great detriment of all the other master-bakers in the vicinity. During this time Beissel devoted all spare moments to study. He also attended the Lutheran church, where he listened to the sound classical discourses of such eminent theologians and servants of God as Rev. Prof. L. Ludwig Christian Mieg, the Rev. Johann Christian Kirchmeir, and others of equal celebrity.

He also made the acquaintance of a learned mystic and theosophist named Haller, who was a friend and correspondent of Gichtel. Through him Beissel obtained an introduction to, or was initiated in, the local Rosicrucian chapter held under the name or guise of a Pietist conventicle, which organization counted many of the most learned and distinguished men in the community among its membership. But, being under the ban of the secular as well as the religious authorities, they were forced to hold their meetings in secrecy, in an almost inaccessible fastness of the forest. Here, within the tiled precincts of the weird rocky chasm (*Felsenschlugt*), by the fitful light of resinous torches, Conrad Beissel followed his guide, was brought to the true Light, taught the first steps of the Brotherhood and received instruction in the rudiments of the secret rites and mysteries of the Fraternity of the Rosy Cross.

The neophyte, whose mind comprehended the teachings, was aided in his studies by some of the best scholars in the fraternity, and it was not long before he was numbered among the adepts of the Order. Although all knowledge of the membership of the Fraternity was guarded from the profane with the greatest care, Beissel's connection with the proscribed society came to the knowledge of one of the master-bakers who had suffered from the excellence of the adept's bread. He was at once informed upon,

ARMS OF THE BAKERS' GUILD.

arrested, fined and given notice to quit the town without any delay, presumably with the loss of his *Wanderbuch*, which would preclude him from obtaining employment at his trade elsewhere.

So, after wandering from place to place, ekeing out a scant existence by wool-spinning and similar precarious employments, he sojourned for a short time among the "Tunkers" at Schwarzenau, where he made the acquaintance of such men as Joh. Jac. Junkerrott, Rev. Joh. Fr. Rock, the celebrated Dr. Carl and others; finally, after much tribulation and persecution, he resolved to leave the Fatherland for the wilds of the New World and affiliate with the Chapter of Perfection established by Kelpius on the Wissahickon. From this his friends attempted in vain to dissuade him; but, notwithstanding the disapproval of Dr. Carl and others of equal prominence, Beissel made preparations to put the plan into execution and sailed for America toward the close of the Summer of 1720.

His companions across the ocean were George Steifel,

THE TRAVELLING JOURNEYMAN'S TOILET.

AN IMPORTANT FUNCTION PRIOR TO ENTERING HIS NEXT APPOINTED TOWN.

IDE P. 86 SUPRA.

Jacob Stuntz, Simon Koenig, Heinrich van Bebber, and others whose names have not come down to us. All those named were destined to become characters of more or less importance in the history of the Sect people of Pennsylvania.

It was stated that these people were religious enthusiasts. In reality they were a band of Pietists, who came to America to join the Community of the "Woman in the Wilderness," established by Kelpius and others on the banks of the Wissahickon in the year 1694, and whose history has been fully set forth in a previous volume.

 EITHER tradition nor records show how this party of devout pilgrims journeyed from Massachusetts Bay to Pennsylvania; whether they went overland by slow stages or came by sea. If they came by the latter route, and the probabilities are all in that direction, it must have been on the sloop "Elizabeth and Hannah," Captain Elias Wiar, which arrived at Philadelphia on October 20th. As this was the only vessel to arrive from Boston in the fall of that year it would seem to settle the date of their landing in Pennsylvania.[6] This assumption is strengthened by the entry in the records, "that the party arrived well and in good spirits at Germantown toward the close of the autumn of the year 1720."

Great was the surprise of these seekers after spiritual perfection and rest when, arriving at the end of their long and weary journey, they learned for the first time that the Community which they sought to join had ceased to exist as an organized body some years prior to their departure from the Fatherland. For some reason this news had not then reached their part of Germany.

Beissel and his companions expected to find here an ideal spiritual community, whose chief interest centered around the Tabernacle in the primitive forest, where the

---

[6] *Vide* Bradford's *Weekly Mercury*, No. 44, October 20, 1720.

time was spent in prayer and a nightly watch was kept to obtain the first glimpse of the harbinger in the skies, who should appear to announce the coming of the celestial bridegroom : a community where the world with its allurements was secondary to the state of spiritual regeneration.

In the place of this expected elysium they found the Tabernacle deserted, the nocturnal watch upon the tower long since abandoned, Magister Kelpius dead, while of the other leaders, Köster had returned to Europe, and the Falkner brothers were itinerating in the adjoining provinces.

Of the other members, most of them were scattered and had again engaged in the every day pursuits of the world, or, as the Ephrata Chronicon states, "After their leader "died the Tempter found occasion to scatter them, as those "who had been most zealous against marrying now betook "themselves to women again, which brought such igno- "miny on the solitary state that the few who still held to "it dared not open their mouths for shame."

Among those who remained true to their tenents and continued in the vicinity of the Tabernacle were Seelig and Matthäi, who, with the remnant of the former Community, lived as hermits or solitaries. Their cabins were close to the romantic glens and gorges of the Wissahickon, where they could, in the primitive forest, commune with nature in silence and speculate over their abtruse dogmas without fear or danger of intrusion.

An even greater surprise for these pilgrims was to find that certain prominent persons, residents of Germantown, who, it was believed at home, were living a life of piety and apostolic simplicity were in reality living here a far different one.

Beissel and his companions found that a number of such persons had enriched themselves by accepting official positions or engaging in worldly pursuits, in some cases at the expense of the German capitalists who had sent them out to develop their holdings.   Brother Agrippa, commenting upon this condition at the time of Beissel's arrival, writes:

" Many who had maintained a very proper walk in Germany had here hung up their holy calling on a nail and, what was worse, would give no one credit for zeal or diligence.   Among these were several who in the Palatinate had let themselves be driven from house and home but here left great wealth behind them after their death.   All this caused him [Beissel] much concern; for he everywhere saw the pious sitting at the helm and exercising magisterial offices."

This allusion evidently refers to Francis Daniel Pastorius and Johann Heinrich Sprögell.   The former had died about a year previous, leaving considerable property; while the other was absent from the Province at that time.

When Beissel learned of the condition of spiritual affairs he concluded to keep quiet as to the true causes of his leaving Germany and as to his projects of a solitary life.   As soon as this determination was reached the party separated for the time being, each going their way.

It may be well at this point to take a retrospective glance at the German metropolis in America, which is so closely connected with our history, and see how it appeared the year following the death of Pastorius.

SEAL OF GERMANTOWN.

Germantown in 1720 was a rambling village of but few houses, extending along a single street, officially known as the North Wales road, a mere dirt lane without paving or kerbing.   The houses were almost without exception plain one-story structures, the ground floor consisting of two rooms.   The front room was generally built of stone, and the back room or kitchen of logs.

This was in reality the living room of the family. The front part of the house was covered with a high-hipped roof, which formed a low bed-chamber; the gables were of clap-boards and pierced for a small window, which gave light and air to the chamber. Many of the roofs were covered with brick tiles after the German fashion; others, again, were of split oak shingles. The front or street doors were all divided in the middle, so as to admit air and at the same time keep out any domestic or other animals. The doors were furnished with a porch and a bench at either side of the door-jamb. The small windows were closed by two-hinged sashes, opening inside and having small panes of glass set in the leaden sash. It was not an unusual thing to find in the rear of the houses thin sheets of horn substituted in lieu of glass, as this had the advantage of being cheaper and unbreakable.

In the street, parallel with the houses, were planted an almost continuous row of fruit-trees, the exception being an occasional pair of poplars which, according to the German custom, were planted in front of a house when a wedding was celebrated.

ERMANTOWN, as originally laid, consisted of 27½ lots upon either side of the main street. These fifty-five lots were drawn for by lot in 1689, in which year the settlers received a charter from Penn, creating the settlement into a borough having its own court of record. The growth of the new settlement as a town, however, failed to come up to the expectations of its projectors, and but few of the many Palatines who came to these shores between the years 1690 and 1720 remained in the "town." Most of the emigrants took up land and went to farming.

While it is true that within the town and vicinity various industrial ventures were established at an early day, it is

equally true that there was but little to attract the emigrant
and insure him a livelihood. Even the great influx of
Germans in the year 1709–1710 failed to make any marked
impression on the town settlement. The few who remained
within the corporate limits were mostly Mennonites, who
cared but little for worldly power or political preferment.
In the year 1708 they built the first church[7] within the
village. Under such adverse conditions the borough government was abandoned after an existence of but fifteen
years, and the projected German metropolis in the New
World became for the time being once more an ordinary
village.

Such was Germantown when Beissel and his fellow-
pilgrims arrived in the fall of 1720. Beissel, who was a
master-baker by trade, soon found that the settlement would
not afford him a livelihood, as every housewife prided
herself as much upon her baking as she did on her
spinning and knitting.

It may be of interest to the present generations to know
just what kind of bread sustained our German ancestors in
the early days of our history. The bread made of rye flour
was of three kinds. These were known as *Schwartzbrod*
(blackbread), *Kümmelbrod* (bread with caraway seed) and
Pumpernickel (Westphalia rye bread). The last was the
favorite, as it was supposed to give the most strength. It
was made of unbolted rye flour into large loaves, often
weighing half a hundredweight. The dough for these
loaves was set without either yeast or leaven, and had to
bake in the oven from twelve to fourteen hours. This
bread was very dark and heavy, with an extremely hard
and thick crust. With persons who had good digestive
organs, the constant use of it proved very nutritious, and
a baking usually lasted a family from two or three weeks.

---

[7] A Quaker Meeting House was built at a much earlier date.

After the separation of the party, Beissel consulted with Conrad Matthäi as to his future course. As he was unwilling to engage in agricultural pursuits, Matthäi advised him to remain in Germantown for the time being and learn the weaver's art, of which he already had some knowledge, as that was virtually the only industry that then afforded any pecuniary reward.

The weaving and knitting *Strumpf-wirker* (frame-work knitter) industry was introduced by the Germans into Eastern Pennsylvania at an early date. It was one of the plans of the Frankfort Company to spin and weave the flax raised upon their lands, as well as card, knit and mill the wool produced in the Province, thus giving employment to the women as well as the men.

So well was this plan carried out that at the first fair held in Philadelphia, the fine linens of Germantown were an important feature, and their prestige was maintained for many years after.

Wool was carded, spun and woven by the Germans in Eastern Pennsylvania even before the seventeenth century had passed. These woollen fabrics were known by the name of druggets, crapes, camblets and serges.

Thus it was that Conrad Beissel acted upon the advice of the Magnus on the Wissahickon, and the German baker indentured himself for the term of a year to one Peter Becker, a master-weaver of Germantown. What were the results from the intercourse of these two men, both of whom were destined to become religious leaders among the German settlers in the Province, will be shown in the subsequent chapters. It will there be seen how, while one of them laid the foundation of the German Baptist Brethren or Dunkards,—one of the most widely diffused and respected Christian denominations in America,—the other established a successful theosophical community on the Cocalico which flourished for many years, and whose legends and records gave the incentive to prepare these pages.

SPECIMEN OF A GERMAN WANDERBUCH.

CHAPTER V.

THE WEAVER'S APPRENTICE.

ETER BECKER, one of the master weavers of Germantown, was born at Dilsheim, Germany, in the year 1687, of Reformed parentage. He was brought up in that faith, but embraced the principles of the Schwarzenau congregation in 1714. He was the leading character of the advance party of German Baptists who reached Pennsylvania in 1719. This contingent consisted of twenty families, of whom several had been members of the original Baptist congregation formed in 1708 at Schwarzenau, on the Eder, in Kreis Wittgenstein, in Westphalia, and who, after leaving the parent stem, settled in the Marienborn district, whence they were driven from place to place by the authorities, as they refused to abstain from public baptism. Three times the congregation changed their situation in the Marienborn district, and finally, in 1715, they found a refuge in Crefeldt.

It appears that the leading members of this congregation were Johann Heinrich Kalckgläser from Frankenthal; Christian Leib (Libe) and Abraham DuBois (Duboy) from Ebstein; Johann Naass, from the north of Germany; Peter Becker, from Dilsheim; the three Trout brothers, Johann Heinrich, Jeremiah and Balser; Stephen Koch and Georg

Balser Gantz, all from Umstadt; and Michael Eckerling
from Strasburg; all of whom, except the last named one,
afterwards came to Pennsylvania, and will appear as more
or less prominent characters in our narrative.

After a few years trouble arose in Crefeld among their
number in reference to the question whether one might
marry out of the fold. This caused a division, and in 1719
ended by a number of them, under the leadership of Peter
Becker, leaving Crefeldt and coming to Pennsylvania.
Although but few in number, it is an historical fact that
from the arrival of these devout pioneers dates the introduction of the Dunkard Brethren or German Baptist
denomination in America.

Conrad Beissel, the new apprentice, was cordially received
into the devout family of his master, and, according to the
custom of the day, became one of their number. Matters
went on well: the apprentice, who had already had some
experience in this craft during his exile in Germany, proved
an apt scholar, and an intimacy was formed between the
two men, which was maintained with more or less intermission in after years. They were of about the same age
and of kindred spirits, and took to heart the forlorn religious condition of their countrymen in the Province, most of
whom, with the exception of the Mennonites, who kept up
a corporate organization, had gradually fallen away from
the faiths of their fathers, and now reached a state of
indifference to all religious teaching that savored of orthodoxy. It is true that many of these Germans professed
Quakerism; this, however, was merely an excuse for their
apathy to all matters spiritual. This unfortunate condition is graphically described in the Missive of Justus
Falkner to Senior Mühlen, where he states: "There is
"here a large number of Germans who, however, have
"partly crawled in among the different sects who use the
"English tongue, which is first learned by all who come

Abdruck
Eines Schreibens
An
Tit. Herrn
D. Henr. Muhlen/

Aus Germanton / in der Ameri-
canischen Province Pensylvania , fonft No-
va Succia , den erften Augufti , im Jahr
unfers Heyls eintaufend fiebenhundert
und eins.

Den Zuftand der Kirchen
in America betreffend.

M DCC II.

" here.   A number are Quakers and Anabaptists ; a portion
" are Freethinkers, and assimilate with no one. * * * In
" short, there are Germans here, and perhaps the majority,
" who despise God's Word and all outward good order ;
" who blaspheme the sacraments and frightfully and pub-
" licly give scandal (for the spirit of errors and sects has
" here erected for itself an asylum)." [8]

Comparatively little effort was made during the first two
decades of the eighteenth century by the German settlers
to propagate in the New World the Lutheran and Reformed
faiths of the Fatherland, the exception being the Lutheran
congregation at Falkner's Swamp.   This was chiefly owing
to the absence of any regularly ordained pastor of those
churches.

Worse than all was the condition of the children of these
settlers, who were growing up without any religious instruction, except such little as was imparted to them at home.
It must be remembered that the German population was
scattered over a wide stretch of primitive country, without
either school or church where German was taught.   Then
there were a number of clerical impostors in the Province,
who sought to formulate notions of their own, inimical to
good morals and religion.   All this tended to unsettle
matters spiritual in the Province, and separate rather than
unite the Germans who had taken up their abode here.
Even the party brought over by Peter Becker came under
this influence, and for a time were estranged and separated
from their leader.   This happened almost immediately
upon their landing in Philadelphia.   Some went to Germantown, some to Conestoga and elsewhere, while others
settled to the northward in Oley, beyond the Schuylkill.
Many of the fellow-passengers of Becker and Beissel had
found homes on the fruitful plains in the extreme northern

---

[8] For a full translation of this Missive see *Penn. Mag. of Hist. and
Biog.*, vol. **xxi**, pp. 216 *et seq*.

part of Chester county, then known as Coventry township. The Schuylkill was here fordable at many places, and thus the German settlers south or west of that river were placed in easy communication with their fellow-countrymen who settled on the Perkiomen and its tributaries.

This dispersion incapacitated them to meet for public worship and, therefore, they too soon began to grow luke-warm in religion. It was this unfortunate condition which gave the two men so great concern that, even while plying their trade, whether throwing the shuttle and the beam or sending home the weft, or while sitting by the flickering firelight after hours, or resting in the moonlight on the porch bench in front of their humble home, their chief thought and aim was how to bring about an awakening of the religious spirit among their misguided countrymen.

Many were the suggestions made in this weaver's shop, and the plans proposed to redeem their kinsfolk and children from spiritual apathy. The Chronicon states the cause of such indifference : " The great freedom of this land was " one cause of their being thus sold under the spirit of this " world, through which all godly influences has been lost, " and each one depended upon himself."

Determined to carry out his original purpose, Beissel, at the expiration or breaking of his indenture, in the fall of 1721, in company with his former companion Stuntz, journeyed to the Conestoga valley ; and there, in a secluded spot, in the primitive forest, beside a fine spring of water, the two wanderers built for themselves a log cabin. This was on the banks of the Mühlbach (Mill creek) a branch of the Conestoga. This branch rises in the Welsh mountain in the eastern end of Lancaster county, and, after an intricate course, empties into that river at the dividing line of Pequea and West Lampeter townships.

The exact situation of this historic spot can, after the

lapse of a century and three-quarters, be given to a certainty, thanks to some old surveys, maps and records, which have been found and located after a long and patient search extending over years of time. The site of Beissel's original cabin in Lancaster county is upon the grounds of Miss Marianna Gibbons, about half a mile north of the Bird-in-Hand Station on the Pennsylvania railroad, and agrees with the old record, which states that it was eight miles from the junction of the Mühlbach with the Conestoga.

At the time when Beissel and Stuntz came into the Conestoga valley, much of the land was unseated, notwithstanding the fact that titles for it were held by owners, many of whom had never even seen their holdings. Such was the case with the land upon which the two recluses settled. It was upon a tract of one thousand acres, originally deeded to Elizabeth Wartnaby.

Towards the northern line of this tract a large fine spring bubbles out of the bank, about one hundred and fifty yards east of the Mühlbach. Tradition tells us that this spring and the grove surrounding it were a famous gathering-place for the Indians long before they were found by our hermits. This tradition seems to be proven by the number of Indian relics which have been found there.

The stretch of land between the head of the spring and the creek, as well as the rising ground, was all primitive forest. Here, in this beautiful situation, the recluse cabin was built. No more ideal spot could be conceived, and if there be truth in the old saying that "the Celestial Intelligences exhibit and explain themselves most freely in silence and the tranquility of solitude,"[9] the conditions were certainly all favorable to that end. No better selection for a "secret chamber" could have been found to tempt the

---

[9] *Les Clavicules de Rabbi Salomon.*

unseen spiritual forces to reveal themselves than this verdant grove on the Mühlbach.

There are still two specimens of this forest left; two tall pines which stand erect, like sentinels of the past, beside the old upping block in front of the Gibbons homestead, and remind us of the time when Beissel, Stuntz and Van Bebber sojourned here and rested under the shadows of their branches.

The stretch of land between the spring-head and the creek still retains much of its former character. The creek, however, is dammed, and the spring flows into it just at the head of the mill dam, and now slack water replaces the purling, rapid current of yore.

The fertile stretches of land between the Conestoga and the Pequea had attracted, at an early day, the attention of the Mennonites, and at the time of Beissel's advent had become their chief settlement in the New World.

There were weighty reasons why Conrad Matthaï advised the two enthusiasts to select a situation on the Mühlbach in the Conestoga country. The dominant one was that, while they were virtually in seclusion, they were at the same time so placed that they could readily engage in revival work among their countrymen. That the selection was not a hap-hazard one is shown by the fact that it was a strategic point of no mean order, from which they could easily reach the Germans who had settled within the radius which included Coventry, Oley, Pequea and Conestoga. Twelve years previously the very first settlement by whites in Lancaster county had been made by Mennonites and Huguenots not more than three miles distant. Then again they were within easy reach of such of the brethren as remained in the vicinity of Germantown and Roxborough, and still occupied their anchorite huts in the fastness of the Wissahickon and the Ridge.

After the two men were well established in their new

abode, they entered upon a life of seclusion and prayer, exhorting their neighbors when opportunity offered and imparting instruction to such of the young as were sent to them. From this evidence we may well assume that in this lovely grove beside the limpid Mühlbach, in the cool shade of the forest trees in summer, or in the rude log-hut in winter, the first free school was held within the bounds of Lancaster county.

The faculty were two or three religious enthusiasts; the pupils, the children of the early German settlers; the curriculum, simple as it was, was strictly religious and moral. The writer doubts whether it went beyond the alphabet, *Vater Unser*, the catechism, and a few *Bibel-sprüch*, such as were in vogue among the early Germans. However, be this as it may, crude as was the instruction imparted in the rude hut on the the Mühlbach, there are evidences that it laid a religious foundation in the pupils to which they remained true to the end. Then again it is well to consider that no charge was ever made for instruction, the work was purely and simply a labor of love and duty with these pious recluses, and the future investigator and historian will undoubtedly join with the present writer and accord to Beissel and his companions the credit due to them as pioneers in the field of education in the valley of the Conestoga and its tributaries.

SPECIMEN OF KLOSTER PEN-WORK.

CHAPTER VI.

THE LABADISTS ON THE BOHEMIA MANOR.

EFORE the year was out the two recluses were joined by Isaac Van Bebber, the younger, the nephew of Heinrich Van Bebber, who had crossed the ocean with the pilgrims. After a short sojourn at the cabin upon the Mühlbach, Van Bebber prevailed on Beissel to accompany him on a visit to the Labadist Community at Bohemia Manor, where had been established, in 1684, the first Protestant mystic community in the New World.

Young Isaac's chief object in this projected trip was evidently to visit his father Isaac Van Bebber and kinsman Matthias Van Bebber, who now, in his advancing years, was clothed with judicial authority, while Beissel's interest lay in the mystical community, founded there by Dankärts and Sluyter almost forty years before.

The Van Bebbers were originally Mennonites, and came to this Province as such at an early date. The first to arrive was Isaac Jacob Van Bebber in 1684. He was a native of Crefeldt on the Rhine. In 1687 he was joined by his father, Jacob Isaac Van Bebber, and his brother Matthias, and later by other members of the family.

They first settled in Germantown, but did not all remain there. The elder removed to Philadelphia in 1698 and engaged in mercantile pursuits. Matthias settled on the Schippach in 1702, and in 1704, together with his elder brother Isaac Jacob, and a number of others from Germantown, removed to the Bohemia Manor.

From the fact that these men are frequently referred to as Isaac Jacobs, Jacob Isaacs and Matthias Jacobs, some writers have assumed that they were German Jews. Such, however, is not the case. They were Mennonites, but, like many others of the early settlers, after their sojourn in the Province, they became somewhat unsettled as to their faith. This is shown by the report sent by Johann Gottfried Seelig, one of the original Pietists, who arrived in 1694, to Spener, wherein, writing of Jacob Isaac Van Bebber, he states : "He was formerly a Mennonite, but he desires to depart with his whole house, to acknowledge and abandon the follies, scandals, shortcomings and stains of his former religion." [10]

PREMIERE APOLOGIE
POVR MONSIEVR

DE LABADIE,

ET POVR LA IVSTICE DE SA
DECLARATION CONTRE LA
nouuelle Eglise Romaine conuaincue par
l'exame de l'Epist.de S.Paul aux Romains,
de n'estre ni de la foi, ni de la conduite
de l'Ancienne ; & n'estre ni Catholique ni Apostolique.

Comme aussi d'error en plusieurs points fondamen
taux de la Religion Chrestienne, & principale
ment en celui du S. Sacrement de l'Euchari
stie, soit qu'ät à laPrestrise & Sacrificature,
dont la nullité lui est prouuée , soit quant
au Sacrifice & à la vraye Messe,
qu'il lui est clairement mon
stré qu'elle n'a pas.

Surquoi le point veritable de la reelle & substantielle
presence & manducation de I. C. en la Sainte
Cene,sans qu'il soit besoin de transubstantiatiō & de sacrifice lui est expliqué,& M. de
Labadie justifié en ses vrais sentimens.
touchant ce mystere.

Par E. Dufes . dit de Blanc-mont repondant à la
Lettre d'Antoine Sabré Hermite , sujet affidé
de M. S. Martineä Euesque de Bazas.

M. DC. LI.

TITLE-PAGE OF ONE OF THE BOOKS OBTAINED
BY BEISSEL FROM PETER SLUYTER.[11]

It was this spiritual unrest which evidently induced the Van Bebbers to remove to the Bohemia Manor, where at that time the Labadist Community was at the height of its development.

---

[10] *Penna. Magazine*, xi, p. 440.
[11] Now in possession of the writer.

There can be but little doubt that, although the Community at the time of Beissel's visit was already in a state of dissolution, it was due to his visit to Bohemia Manor and the conferences with Sluyter, together with a number of books and papers, both printed and in manuscript, of Labadie and Yvon which Beissel obtained, that we owe many of the peculiar features of the Ephrata Community. Not the least important one was the separation of the sexes.

This visit was made none too soon, for soon after the two pilgrims had departed Peter Sluyter died, and, there being none to replace him or wield the necessary authority, the few remaining members separated and the community passed into history. By virtue of lasting impressions made on the mind of Conrad Beissel, thus shaping his course of life in after years, a short review of this mystical community will not be out of place.

HE Community on Bohemia Manor was the outcome of an attempt made by the parent congregation at Waltahouse in Wiewerd to establish a Labadist colony in America, and thus to secure a retreat for their church and to widen its bounds. The first place selected was in Surinam, then recently acquired by the Dutch in exchange for the New Netherlands. Several colonies were sent out, but the climate proving inauspicious, the attempt was abandoned, and the two leading men, Jasper Dankärts and Petrus Sluyter, were sent in 1679–80 to look for a more suitable situation in either New York, the Jerseys, New Sweden or Maryland. They preferred the tract at the head of Chesapeake bay where the Bohemia and Elk rivers emptied into that estuary. This was a Barony known as the Bohemia Manor. It contained over 20,000 acres and was granted by Lord Baltimore, in 1660, to Augustine Herrman or Heerman, born in Bohemia, and a surveyor, who prepared for him a map of Maryland.

Sluyter and Dankärts returned to Holland and made a favorable report to the society at Wiewerd, which at once made extensive preparations to send another colony to the New World. This party arrived at New York on July 27, 1683, and after a short stay in that city journeyed to their new home on the Bohemia river. This spot was selected for two reasons: the chief one is said to have been their belief that it was situated within the bounds of Penn's grant. Then again, the two agents, during their first visit had made several converts, among whom was Ephriam Herrman, and on him and his issue this manor was by his father's will to be entailed. He promised them, on their first visit, that if they would return and establish their church, part of the manor should be given for this object. Through his instrumentality Augustine Herrman contracted to convey an extensive tract of the manor to Sluyter and others, induced by the expectation that he would secure the establishment of a colony. Augustine repented of his agreement, distrusting the other parties to it, and refused for some time to carry it out, but finally, on August 11, 1684, executed a conveyance of the tract therein meted and bounded, containing 3750 acres, part of Bohemia Manor, to Peter Sluyter and Jasper Dankärts, Petrus Bayard, of New York; John Moll and Arnoldus de la Grange, of Delaware. This land contained four necks, and was afterwards called the Labadie tract.

Moll and de la Grange at once released their interest to Sluyter and Dankärts, which makes it probable that their names were inserted merely to deceive Augustine Herrman.[12] Finally Dankärts conveyed his interest to Sluyter by deed executed in Holland in 1693. Augustine Herrman died in 1686. The statement that in his will he

---

[12] Augustine Herrman in his will designates Peter Sluyter, alias Vorsman, and Jasper Dankärts, alias Shilder.

PORTRAIT AND AUTOGRAPH OF AUGUSTINE HERRMAN.

expressed great disapprobation of his son Ephraim's adhesion to the Labadists is not borne out by that document.[13]

Upon the arrival of the party at the Bohemia Manor they at once started to erect several buildings, the chief one being known as the "Great House." Several families soon arrived from Wiewerd followed by Sluyter's wife, who, as abbess, presided over the women. Some converts also came from New York. Thus was founded in North America a branch of the Labadist Community of Waltahouse, of which Sluyter proclaimed himself bishop, under Yvon, Archbishop of Wiewerd.

The settlement at Bohemia never numbered over one hundred, men, women and children all told, mostly novices or probationers, whose faith was to be tried by a very severe system of discipline and mortification. Fire, for example, was not permitted in their cells in the coldest weather, though there was so much wood about them that they were forced to burn it in order to be rid of it. They were to live hidden in Christ. All desires of the flesh were to be subdued. A former minister herded cattle; a young man of good family carted stone or bent over a wash-tub. Food to which they had repugnance must be eaten, and sins confessed in open assembly. There were different grades to be attained in conformity to the principles and discipline of the society. Punishments were the deprivation of clothes, taking a lower seat at the table and expulsion. The highest rank, that of brother, was gained by total separation from the world. They took their meals in silence, so that men ate together for months at the same table without knowing each other's names. The men and women ate at different tables. They slept in different rooms which the head or his substitute might visit at all times for examination or

---

[13] *Vide* facsimile and copy of will in *Penna. Mag. of Hist. and Biog.*, vol. **xv**, p. 321.

instruction. They labored on the land, and at different trades or employments assigned by the head. Their dress was plain, all worldly fashions being prohibited as well as luxuries of all kinds. They worked for the Lord and not for themselves—not to gratify their desires, but merely to sustain life. All property was held as common stock, into which all joining the community put what they owned and left it when they withdrew. They manufactured some linen and cultivated a large plantation of corn, flax and hemp. They often expounded the Scriptures among themselves. They held that both parties must be born again, or marriage was unholy, and that they ought to separate if both were not endowed with grace, but might live together, provided the believer loved Christ more than his earthly partner. Sluyter, head and bishop as he was, was grossly inconsistent with the principles of the society, raising tobacco and dealing in slaves, and he was charged particularly with treating them with extreme cruelty.

The only accounts of this institution, from one who was actually present, known to the writer, are those recorded in the journal of a Samuel Bownas,[14] a public Friend, who made two visits to the Bohemia Manor. The first was when the Labadist Community was yet in a flourishing condition; the other, after a lapse of twenty-four years, four years subsequent to Beissel's visit, when the leader was dead, the community scattered and the great buildings abandoned.

The first entry, under date of August, 1702, notes the following:

" After we had dined we took our leave, and a friend, my guide, went with me to a people called Labadies [*sic*], where we were civily entertained in their way. When supper came

<hr>

[14] An | Account | of the | Life, Travels | and | Christian Experiences | in the | Work of the Ministry | of | Samuel Bownas, | Stanford | re-printed by Daniel Lawrence | for Henry and John F. Hull | MDCCCV.

in it was placed upon a long table in a large room, where, when all things were ready, came in, at a call, about twenty men or upwards, but no woman : we all sat down, they placing me and my companion near the head of the table, and having paused a short space, one pulled off his hat, but not the rest till a short space after, and then one after another they pulled all their hats off, and in that uncovered posture sat silent (uttering no words that we could hear) near half a quarter of an hour ; and as they did not uncover at once, so neither did they cover themselves again at once ; but as they put on their hats fell to eating, not regarding those who were still uncovered, so that it might be about two minutes time or more between the first or last putting of[f]their hats.   I afterwards queried with my companin [*sic*] concerning the reason of their conduct, and he gave this for answer, that they held it unlawful to pray till they felt some inward motion for the same ; and that secret prayer was more acceptable than to utter words ; and that it was most proper for every one to pray, as moved thereto by the spirit in their own minds.

"I likewise queried, if they had no women amongst them ?   He told me they had, but the women eat by themselves and the men by themselves, having all things in common respecting their household affairs, so that none could claim any more than another to any part of their stock, whether in trade or husbandry ; and if any had a mind to join with them, whether rich or poor, they must put what they had in the common stock, and if they had a mind to leave the society, they must likewise leave what they brought and go out empty handed.

"They frequently expounded the scriptures among themselves, and being a very large family, in all upwards of a hundred men, women and children, carried on something of the manufactory of linen, and had a very large plantation of corn, tobacco, flax and hemp, together with cattle of several kinds. But at my last going there [1726] these people were all scattered and gone, and nothing of them remaining of a religious community in that shape."

The geographical position of the Labadist settlement was originally in Baltimore county, now Cecil county, on the north bank of the Bohemia river, embracing several thousands of fertile acres. The Bohemia river empties into the Elk, which flows into Chesapeake bay. The house or mansion of Herrman was detroyed by fire, but the foundations are visible within a few hundred feet of the river. The remains of his deer park can also be seen. His body was removed to the Bayard vault, a short distance from the old mansion, and when this was abandoned for another vault in Wilmington no mark was left of his burial place. An oolite slab in the yard of another house, built after the burning of the first, records the memorial of "Augustine Herrman, Founder and Seater of Bohemia Manor."

An effort was made some years ago by the Maryland Historical Society to obtain this stone, but proved fruitless. It is supposed that the stone became an internal part of a new monument erected upon the ground in Herrman's memory, built and dedicated by a society of Bohemians.

The manor can be reached from Elkton on the north, distant seven miles ; from Middletown, on the east, about the same distance ; and from the Sassafras river, on the south, direct from Baltimore by boat. The road by way of Elkton is probably the best, as the roads thence to the old manor are remarkably pleasant and good.

It has been stated, upon different occasions, that there was some similarity in doctrine between the Labadists and the Quakers ; also that Labadie [15] and William Penn were

---

[15] Jean de Labadie, a noted mystic and theosophist of the seventeenth century, born at Bourg-en-Guienne, February 13, 1610. Died at Altona, Holstein, February 2, 1674. Educated at the Jesuit's College of Bordeaux, he became a member of that society, but left the order in 1639, and in 1650 became a Protestant, joining the Reformed Church. He settled in

friends and associates; further, that it was at the latter's instance that Bohemia Manor was selected by the agents of

MONSIEUR JEAN DE LABADIE, 1610–1674.[16]

the Labadist Community, under the impression that it was

Montauban, and was the means of inducing over three hundred Catholics to adopt a similar course. He was elected pastor of the church and remained in charge for eight years. During which time he continued his mystical speculations, and founded a society somewhat similar to the Quietists of his old communion, this society became known as "Labadists." Being at length banished from Montauban for sedition, he went first to Orange, thence to Geneva. In 1666 he was invited to Middleburg, Holland. Here his followers increased in number and included many persons of rank and education. Among whom was Anna Maria v. Schurman and the Princess Palatine Elizabeth. The heterodoxy and contumacy of Labadie, however, soon led to his deposition by the Synod of Naardon and to his banishment from the Province.

[16] Portrait in Pantheon Anabaptist.

within the bounds of Penn's grant.[17]   The best contemporary witness upon this matter is Gerard Croese,[18] who, in his *Quakeriana* (English edition, London, 1696, pp. 221–4), states :

"To shew what agreement there was between the Quakers " and these Labadists in Doctrine, and what Institution to one " and the same purpose ; and lastly : what intentions they had " to join in Friendships, and contract acquaintances, I will " shortly and in a few words relate it.   As to their Doctrine, "although these Men at first introducing little or nothing " which was different from our Faith, yet, in process of time, "they brought in divers Innovations about the use of the " Holy Scriptures, and the guidance and operations of the " Holy Spirit, and Prayers and the remaining parts of Wor- "ship, and the Sacraments and Discipline of the Church, so " that they came nearer to the Opinions of the Quaker in these " things, than to our Doctrine.[19]   Now it appears that these " men, no less than the Quakers, reprehended and found fault " with many things in our Churches, and those of all Protest- "ants, that they were all so corrupt and depraved that no "effect, no fruit of the Spirit of God appeared amongst them, " nor no Worship of God, but only a carnal and external one ; "no mutual attention, no conjunction of minds, no love, no " will, no endeavours for the good, one of another, or the " common good, that there was to be seen.   Lastly, that no " one's life and Manners answered what they all professed, or "the Example and Precepts of Christ.   And as this was the "complaint and Quarrel of the Quakers, so in like manner " was it of these people too, that with these vices above others " were infected those that were the Prelates and Preachers of " the word, and Steward of the Mysteries of God.

" Finally,—These people thought thus, that they were the " Men from whom the beginning and first Examples of the

---

[17] For letter from William Penn to Herrman and others, dated " London, 16th of 7 Month, 1681," on the subject of his right to territory seated by them and claimed by Lord Baltimore, see *Hazard's Annals*, p. 575.

[18] For sketch of Croese and his *Quakeriana*, see *German Pietists* and *The Fatherland*, Philadelphia, 1897.

[19] Gerard Croese was a clergyman of the Reformed faith.

THE
General Hiſtory
OF THE
QUAKERS:

CONTAINING
The Lives, Tenents, Sufferings, Tryals,
Speeches, and Letters

Of all the moſt

Eminent Quakers,
Both Men and Women;

From the firſt Riſe of that SECT,
down to this preſent Time.

Collected from Manuſcripts, &c.

A Work never attempted before in Engliſh.

Being Written Originally in *Latin*
By *GERARD CROESE.*

To which is added,

A LETTER writ by *George Keith*,
and ſent by him to the Author of this
Book: Containing a Vindication of himſelf, and
ſeveral Remarks on this Hiſtory.

LONDON, Printed for **John Dunton**, at the *Raven*
in *Jewen-ſtreet.* 1696.

TITLE-PAGE OF ENGLISH EDITION CROESE QUAKERIANA.

" Restitution of the Church was to be expected, who also
" were wholly intent upon the famous work of the Reforma-
" tion: Just as the Quakers thought, that this was chiefly re-
" served for them, and that they were in a special manner
" obliged to go on with this work of Reformation.—So great
" was the Fame of this Society, that there was scarce any place
" in these countries where there was not great talk about these
" Teachers and Workers, so that in foreign Countries there
" was scarce anywhere, unless it were among such People, who
" have no regard to what is done abroad who had not heard
" something of them. Therefore when these Reports were
" gone over into England and Scotland ; at first indeed there
" were some of these Men who, being adverse from the State
" of the Church as under the Bishops, contained themselves
" within their own Churches which were more remote from
" external rites and splendor, and a worldly and delicate polite,
" as they call it, and elegant Life and Conversation, who also
" undertook the Ministerial Function. At last, also the
" Quakers, who as soon as they heard of this sort of Men,
" and their plain Religion, and way of Life that they followed,
" they began to think in good earnest of this society of People,
" and to be better acquainted with them, and to consider ways,
" and means amongst themselves how they should come to
" enter into Consultation with them. I know that there was
" one of those Ministers of the Gospel, so averse from the
" Episcopal way, and addicted to Presbyterial Churches, who
" not only himself writes to this Society, but also communi-
" cates his thoughts upon this subject to an eminent Quaker,
" which Man when after that time he foresaw many things
" from the face of the Kingdom, which tho not altogether true
" indeed, yet seeming very probable and likely to come to pass,
" at that time he was not such a fearer of Episcopacy, but that
" one might read in his Countenance, and since he was a Man,
" that one time or another it would come to pass, as afterwards
" it happened that he was made a Bishop. The first of the
" Quakers that came from Scotland to the Labadists to Am-
" sterdam, was George Keith, a Man both very skillful in, and
" much us'd to Controversie and Disputes. After him, comes
" out of England R. Barclay, a Man likewise of great Experi-

"ence, and well seen in the Defence of his Religion, These
" Men, one after another, treat about this matter with Labadie,
"and the rest of them, on whom the Government of the
"Society lay. But when the Quakers open'd their mind
"briefly, and in a common style, but they on the other hand
"us'd such deep and far fetch'd Speeches, and those so round
"about the bush, and turning and winding, and so much
"Eloquence, or endless Talkativeness, that the Quakers knew
"not what these Men would say, or how to know or find out
"and discern their Opinions, Institutions and Intentions, or
"where to have them, (which also had often happened to our
"People enquiring of these men about these things) and now
"began to suspect, that they were not such a pure sort of
"People, and were either bordering upon some errors, or
"privately entertained and bred some Monstrous Opinion.
"And when the Quakers tried again at another time to see
"further if by any means they could bring things to a Consent
"and Agreement, and a conjunction together, that they might
"act in common concert, the Labadists not only drew back,
"but also resented it ill, and were so angry, that they thought
"it would be to no purpose to try any farther Conclusions with
"them. And either upon the occasions of these Meetings
"together, or from the designs of some of their Adversaries to
"reproach them, it came to pass, that from that time the
"Labadists came to be called Quakers, which name followed
"them from Amsterdam to Hereford, and there accompanied
"them, so that Men all abroad not only call'd them by the
"name of Quakers, which to them appeared a horrible Title,
"but also oftentimes us'd to thrown stones at them. To avoid
"which reproach, and withal to shew, how much they hated
"both Name and Thing, they, out of their Printing-Office
"which they carried about with 'em publish'd a Writing by
"the Title, showing what the Argument of the Book was:
  An Examination and Confusion of the Quakers.
" Nevertheless after this, there went to these Labadists in
" Friesland William Penn, that most famous Man Amongst
"the Quakers : a man of such Spirit and wit, as was both
" willing and able to Encounter with all their Adversaries.
" But the end of all was the same."

CONRAD BEISSEL.

THIS ALLEDGED SILHOUETTE OF BEISSEL WAS FOUND IN THE SISTER HOUSE MANY YEARS AGO. IT CAME INTO POSSESSION OF
GEORGE STEINMAN, ESQ., OF LANCASTER, AND BY HIM WAS GIVEN TO THE HISTORICAL SOCIETY OF PENNSYLVANIA.

CHAPTER VII.

THE HUT IN THE FOREST.

HORTLY after the return of Beissel and Van Bebber to the Mühlbach from their pilgrimage to Bohemia Manor, they were joined by George Stiefel, another companion on the voyage to America. The four enthusiasts now determined to enter upon a joint life of probation and seclusion from the world, or, as the original manuscript *Chronicon* stated, "they resolved to dwell together in a brotherly and communal manner."

Religious meetings were henceforth held at regular hours in the small hut in the forest, as well as about the country, whenever the opportunity offered. Instruction was also imparted to such children as were sent to the four recluses. One of these scholars, Barbara Meyer, afterwards known as Sister Jael, was attached to the Community for almost sixty years, as the *Chronicon* states:

"There is still [1786] a person in the Sister's Convent who, in her childhood, had gone to him, and had become so enamored of his [Beissel's] angelic life that she became his steadfast follower, and has now for almost sixty years endured all the hardships of the solitary and communal life."

The peculiar tenets promulgated up to this time by the

four recluses were strictly in accord with the creed and religious views as published by Hochman von Hochenau. Beissel, however, according to an old manuscript, wholly intent upon seeking out the true obligations of the Word of God and the proper observance of the rites and ceremonies it imposes, stripped of human authority, conceived that there was an error among the brethren in the observance of the day for the Sabbath.

This idea was considerably strengthened by his intercourse with the Sabbatarians in Chester county, at Providence and Newtown, upon his return from the visit to the Labadists. He then commenced to question which day was the true Sabbath according to the Scriptures. It was not long before he made the announcement publicly that, as the Seventh Day was the command of the Lord God, and that that day was established and sanctified by the great Jehovah forever, no change ever having been announced to man by any power sufficient to set aside the solemn decree of the Almighty, he felt it to be his duty to contend for the observance of that day. Hence he intended to observe the Scriptural Sabbath, and work and labor upon the remaining six days, as commanded by Divine Writ. This departure caused the first disagreement between the four enthusiasts; they, however, finally acquiesced, and the Sabbath was now kept in the hut on the Mühlbach.

The strange mode of life kept by Beissel and his companions, their earnest exhortations and revival services naturally aroused much attention among the settlers in the Conestoga valley. The meetings became well-attended by people from far and near. Some were attracted by curiosity, but most of them from a desire for spiritual devotion and instruction.

One of the first fruits of the labors of these four exhorters was that a revival or awakening took place among the Mennonites and others in the vicinity. This gradually extended throughout the Conestoga valley, and thence into the Schuylkill valley as far as Falkner swamp. A fervent spirit was especially noticeable among such as had been identified with the *Schwarzenau* movement in Germany.

ESIDES this true revival spirit manifested among the German population in 1722, which was aroused mainly by Beissel's personal efforts, there were also influences at work contrary to all sound religious doctrines, advanced by men who were ignorant visionaries or even worse. This gave rise to several peculiar sects, which flourished for a brief time. The adherents of the most important of these irreligious and visionary sects were known as the "Newborn" (*Neugeborene*), and for a time attracted some attention. Personal efforts were made by the founder of this sect, Matthias Bauman, to inveigle Beissel and his companions into their fold, but these efforts proved unavailing, as Beissel dismissed him with a sound berating. According to the *Chronicon*, in a review of Bauman's visit to the Mühlbach, Beissel "gave him [Baumann] little satisfaction, telling him to smell his own filth, and then consider whether this belonged to the new birth; whereupon they called him a crafty spirit full of subtility, and departed."

THE NEUGEBORENE OR BAUMANITES.

The *Neugeborene*, or *Stille im Lande* or Baumanites, were a sect somewhat similar to the "Inspired" of Germany. The movement in Pennsylvania was the outcome of a religious excitement, started in Oley by one Matthias Bauman. This man was born of humble parentage in the town of Lambsheim, District Frankenthal, in the Rhine Palatinate. He was a poor ignorant day-laborer without any education. In the year 1701 he was stricken with a severe illness. During his delirium he claimed to have been translated to heaven and given the power of prophecy.

Upon his recovery he cried out for several hours, " Repent ! O, ye men, repent ! The Judgement-day is near at hand." After this he again fell into a comatose condition, and de- clared that it was told him : " Men imagine that they are living in the light of day ; but they are all gone wrong in the darkness of night." These trances occurred for fourteen days, the last one continuing for twenty-four hours, so that it was thought he had died and prepara- tions were made for his funeral. When he recovered he went to the minister and told him that God had sent him back into this world to tell men that they should be converted ; but the minister, who thought he was out of his mind, sought by means of a worldly book to drive these notions from his head.

AN OLD EPHRATA DESIGN.

Matthias Bauman came to Am- erica in the year 1719, it is claimed in response to letters showing the neglected condition of the German settlers in the Province.   He settled in Oley, and at once started to preach his doctrine of regeneration and free- dom from all sin.   One of his chief arguments was that, as they were free from sin, they had no further use for Holy Writ, except such parts as would support their dogma.   All sacraments were rejected as useless to the regenerate.   Matrimony was discouraged together with all good counsel, with that peculiar stubborness common to ignorant religious enthusiasts.

Bauman made many converts to his pernicious doctrine, and by his activity he soon came into conflict, not only with the orthodox faiths, but also with the Quakers in Philadelphia. It was his habit frequently to harangue the masses from the court-house steps in the city on market days; and upon one occasion he went so far to prove that his doctrine was true, and that he was a special envoy from God to man, as to propose to walk across the Delaware river at high tide. Bauman, however, failed to prove his faith in this manner.

Among other ridiculous things, this visionary claimed that his followers were free from all sin and could not sin any more. To substantiate his teachings he had printed in Germany a tractate of thirty-five octavo pages: *Ein Ruf an die Unwiedergebohrene Welt* ("A Call to the Unregenerate World"). No copy of this pamphlet is known to the writer, although it was printed for circulation in this Province. Several extracts appear in the *Chronicon Ephretense*, which give an idea of the tenor of the work:

Page 12: " Men say that Christ hath taken away sin ; it is true in my case, and of those who are in the same condition in which Adam was before the fall, as I am." [20]

Page 16: "As Adam was before the fall, so have I become, and even firmer."

Page 12: " With the body one cannot sin before God, but only before men and other creatures, and these the judge can settle."

Personally Matthias Bauman was reputed to have been an upright and honest man. He labored in the Province until his death, which it is claimed took place in 1727. After his death his followers were led by Kuhlwein and Jotter, but the organization soon languished and most of the members were absorbed by the Brethren and Moravians, when the sect passed into history.

[20] Geore Fox makes the same claim in his Journal.

A few of the misguided converts, however, adhered to the pernicious doctrine of Bauman long after the sect ceased to be a distinctive organization. These people for many years proved a disturbing element in the German settlements. Two instances of this kind are quoted by Rev. Mühlenberg, where he came into direct contact with Bauman's followers. The first is in his report to Halle, under date of June 10, 1747,[21] where he states: "Upon " that day, together with Jacob Löser, the schoolmaster of " New Hanover, I called to visit one of the so-called New- " born, who lived about eight miles from New Hanover " [Montgomery county]. This man had married a widow " some twenty years ago. She bore him five children, " whom the mother, without the father's consent, had bap- " tized and sent for instruction to the Lutheran church. " For this she was subjected to much indignity by her " husband.[22] The old man professes that he was born anew " in the Palatinate." In conclusion Mühlenberg states: " The evidences of his regeneration, according to his oft- " repeated assertions, are, that he had withdrawn from the " Reformed church, refused to partake of the holy sacra- " ments, and objected to take the oath of fealty to the new " Count Palatine, on which account he was cited to appear " before the Consistory, and upon refusing to do so was " thrown into prison. Thus, according to his imagination, " he suffered for Christ and the Truth's sake. He refuses to " listen to any convincing evidence or receive the Scripture " in all its parts as proof. Nor will he take any advice or " instruction, and being of a weak intellect, he is self-willed, " turbulent, passionate and abuses the Pennsylvania liberty " he enjoys.

"After arriving in this country he united with the New- " born, a sect so-called. These profess a new birth, which

---

[21] *Hallische Nachrichten*, original edition, 224, 5 ; new ed., p. 346.

[22] For additional particulars see Halle report.

"they have received immediately and instantaneously by
"inspiration, in visions and dreams from Heaven. Having
"thus received this new birth, they imagine they are like
"God and Christ. They say : 'They can neither sin nor
"err—they have attained perfection—hence they need no
"longer to use the means of grace. The Word of God
"they consult only to support their false principles. They
"ridicule the sacraments, speaking scandalously of them.'"

The other case cited by Mühlenberg occurred on May
7, 1753, at the funeral of Philip Bayer, at Oley,[23] about
ten miles from New Hanover. The deceased was an old
house-father, who, after his arrival in the Province, like
many of the settlers, fell away from the faith of his fathers
and became imbued with the Bauman heresy. Upon the
arrival of the regular Lutheran clergy, he, however, renewed his fealty to the faith, and when, in his last sickness,
sent for Mühlenberg to administer the rights of the church.
The Separatists in Oley still claimed him as one of their
own, and upon the day of the funeral a large concourse of
people were present. The services were to be held in a
large meeting-house, and Mühlenberg embraced the opportunity to exhort his hearers in both German and English.
He was not permitted to proceed, however, without interruption, as a number of persons who adhered to the Sectarians organized another gathering outside of the meeting-
house, the leader being an old Newborn, who, by his
shouting, seriously disturbed the services. At last, when
he found that but few people came from the meeting-house
to join his gathering, he got very angry and left.

Mühlenberg states that the gist of his harangue was that
many years ago a light had appeared to him in his chamber while in bed, and revealed to him that he was a child
of God, and that such things as civil authority, Divine
ministry, the Bible, the Sacraments, churches and schools

---

[23] *Vide* burial record, New Hanover Church.

were all from the Devil, and that all persons to be saved must become as he was, etc. Mühlenberg quaintly adds that such would certainly not be in the interest of the community, as he often gets drunk, and then treats his poor wife to an unmerciful beating.[24]

———

Beissel, who was a fluent speaker and earnest exhorter, soon became a power among the Separatists and Mennonites who had scattered throughout the fertile valleys of the Conestoga and Pequea. His teachings at that time were but little tinged with that mysticism and speculative theology which characterised his hymns and writings in after years.

ROM an old manuscript we learn that "almost immediately upon his arrival in the Conestoga country, many persons became attached to him by his attractive and gentle manner. Almost every one judged themselves fortunate when received by him with favor and admitted to his friendship; and all strove for his company, hoping thereby to attain the Divine virtues.

"He proved a marvel to almost every one, and thus it was that the awakened in the Conestoga valley became so heartily enamoured of Conrad Beissel and placed unbounded faith in him.

"We do not say too much, when we state that this our [spiritual] father [Beissel] was the cause of their conversion [awakening] if they were not actually converted by him, which happened shortly before the congregation [in the Conestoga valley] was organized."

The effect of this religious revival among the Germans was widespread, and resulted in quickening Peter Becker

———

[24] *Vide* Halle reports, original edition, pp. 588-9; new edition, pp, 147-8.

and the Dunkers in the vicinity of Germantown into activity. The first practical result was that, in the fall of 1722,
Peter Becker, accompanied by Johannes Gumre, George
Balser Gansz, and one of the Traut brothers, who was also
known by the name of Seckler, made a pilgrimage through
the Province to look up their former brethren who were
now dispersed through the country, and remove, if possible,
all stumbling-blocks in the way of again uniting them.
They wished to induce them to hold meetings and love-
feasts, thereby reviving a religious spirit among them and
their neighbors.

The journey of these missionaries extended through the
Skippack and Perkiomen valleys to Falkner's swamp and
Oley, thence across the Schuylkill to the Conestoga valley,
and returned by way of Coventry and the settlements along
the French creek. This series of meetings was continued
after their return to Germantown, being first held alternately at the homes of Becker at Germantown and Gumre's
on the Ridge, but ultimately they were regularly held
at Peter Becker's. From these weekly services, begun in
the fall of the year 1722, dates the history of the Dunker
denomination or Church of the Brethren in America.

Let us return once more to the cabin on the Mühlbach.
Just when all seemed to be working so well and smoothly,
and the fires of spiritual awakening appeared to glimmer
upon almost every hearth within the German tracts, a
cloud appeared on the horizon which disrupted the party
who made their home in the cabin in the forest. This
was brought about by a curious incident. A close intercourse had all this time been maintained between Beissel
on the one hand, and Matthäi and his fellow recluses on
the other, who lived on the banks of the Wissahickon;
visits were made and returned, and an intimate union
existed between the enthusiasts on the Ridge and in the
Conestoga valley. Among the visitors from the Wissa-

hickon was one whose history in after years became prominently interwoven with that of the Ephrata Community. It was while journeying on foot from Germantown to the valley of Virginia, that this devout revivalist first came to the hut on the Mühlbach, and so pleased was he with the work of the four brethren that he remained with them some time before he again took up his journey southward.

This man, a Pietist from Germantown, journeyed from place to place, exhorting and preaching to his countrymen, and he was even then entering upon a long journey to preach a revival among the Germans in North Carolina, who had settled there as early as 1710, having been influenced and diverted from Pennsylvania by the seductive brochures issued by Kocherthal and others. The name of this visitor to the hut in the wilderness was Michael Wohlfarth, in after years Brother Agonius, of the Ephrata Brotherhood, a firm supporter of Beissel, and an inveterate opposer to the godless teachings of the day. So pleased was Michael Wohlfarth with what he saw and heard during this sojourn on the Mühlbach that he asked Beissel's permission to join the band upon his return from the South.

Shortly after Wohlfarth's departure, in the fall of 1722, a request was made by the Hermits on the Wissahickon for a contribution of some kind. A compliance with this request caused considerable dissension between the four recluses, and ended by Stiefel refusing positively to give his consent to any contribution, especially so, as he considered it an unjust demand, although such requests had repeatedly been complied with by Beissel during his sojourn on the Mühlbach. As Beissel remained firm in his determination to respond to Matthäi's request, Stiefel left the party. [Johann George Stiefel was born at Frankfort-on-the-Mayn. He was awakened when a soldier at Schwarzenau, and joined the inspired. In 1720 he came to America with Beissel. After his departure from the Mühlbach he lived

INDENTED BILL USED IN LIEU OF MONEY IN THE PROVINCE
OF PENNSYLVANIA.

at Oley and Frederick as a recluse.   Becoming acquainted with the Moravians, he moved to Bethlehem in 1746. Two years later, October 15, 1748, he died, and was buried among the single men on the hill.]

N the meantime Van Bebber's health became impaired by the rigorous mode of life pursued by Beissel and his companions, so he, too, felt constrained to leave the cabin on the Mühlbach.   Beissel was loth to lose him, and the parting was a painful one, as noted in the *Chronicon :*

"He took leave of the Superintendent [Beissel] with much love, and protested that it was not possible for him to live in that way.   The former gave him the following counsel to take with him : 'Know that when you are successful in the world, God has forsaken you ; but when all misfortune comes upon you here, then know that God still loves you.'   After many years he froze both hands and feet in a shipwreck and was put under the care of Christopher Witt in Germantown.   There he remembered this farewell, and sent his last greeting to his old friend."

Shortly after the departure of the two hermits, Stuntz, who had been the capitalist of the party, during the temporary absence of Beissel, sold the cabin on the Mühlbach to Joseph Gibbons, a son of James Gibbons, who in the meantime had purchased the Wartnaby tract [25] upon which the cabin was built. [26]   Stuntz's excuse for this act was that he

---

[25] Elizabeth Wartnaby's original deed was dated 1715 ; her indenture to James Gibbon's was dated September 20 (O. S.), 1727.   In 1733 the title was confirmed by John, Richard and Thomas Penn to Joseph Gibbons ; his father, James, having died in the meantime.   This Joseph Gibbons was the great-great-grandfather of the present owners.

[26] *Vide* p. 54, *ante.*

was thus in part repaying himself for money and travelling expenses advanced to Beissel.

This unprincipled act left Beissel again homeless and alone.[27]   He, however, was far from being disheartened, and, making a vow "never again to borrow from men on God's account," he once more started out to build for himself a habitation in the quietude of the forest.   With his axe upon his shoulder and his books and papers in his knapsack (*feleisen*), he journeyed a mile further into the heart of the woods, and settled besides a fine spring of water known as *Die Schwedenquelle* (the Swedes' spring). There, in the summer of 1723, he built with his own hands a small log cabin, wherein he intended to live a life of solitary seclusion, "not knowing what God had ordained for him."

No effort has been spared to identify this spring, aided by the best local authorities the terrain was carefully gone over; the difficulty of identification was greatly enhanced by the fact that the name *Schwedenquelle* (Swedes' spring) was a mere local one, and excepting the *Chronicon Ephretense*, does not appear upon any of the early records, surveys or conveyances.

After a diligent inquiry and a careful comparison of notes, all indications point to the fine spring upon the farm owned by Elam H. Denlinger.   This was originally known as the Evans' tract, and in later years as the "Whitehill" property.   It is located in East Lampeter township, south of the Philadelphia and Lancaster turnpike, and is about equal distance between the Mühlbach and the Pequea. The spring is the source of a run which empties into the Mill creek.

His solitary condition was, however, but of short dura-

---

[27] Beissel in reality had but little cause to complain of his companion's act ; his brethren had no legal claim to the ground, as they were merely squatters.

tion, as no sooner was it known to the brethren on the Wissahickon, than he was visited by some of the recluses from that locality, and almost immediately upon the completion of the cabin he was joined by Michael Wohlfarth, who had just returned from his missionary tour among the Germans in North Carolina. Henceforth they became friends and companions until death separated them. Thus the two hermits (for such they were for a time) lived a life of silent contemplation in the seclusion of the forest, without anything to mar their equanimity or devotions.

Early in the following year (1724) a new trial awaited them. They were visited by an erratic visionary, Johannes Stumpf, who asked to be received as one of their number. His request was granted, but on account of his unsettled mind he caused them much trouble.

We will now leave Beissel and his companions in their solitude for a short time, and see what efforts at religious revival were made by Peter Becker and others at Germantown, spurned on as it were by the awakenings at Conestoga.

ENGRAVED ON TYPE METAL AT EPHRATA ABOUT 1745.

MEETING HOUSE OF THE KEITHIAN QUAKERS, 1692-1731.

FORMERLY ON LAGRANGE PLACE, WEST OF SECOND STREET, PHILADELPHIA.

CHAPTER VIII.

THE GERMAN BAPTIST BRETHREN.

ENTION was made in the previous chapter that Peter Becker held weekly services in Germantown and the vicinity during the fall of the year 1722. This active spirit was continued during the next year. Religious meetings were held in different houses and localities, and every effort was made to bring about a spiritual awakening among the indifferent Germans scattered through this part of the Province, and who for a number of years had lived here without the services of any regular ordained pastor of either the Lutheran or Reformed faith, notwithstanding the repeated requests sent to Germany for spiritual advisors.

The individual efforts of Peter Becker, seconded by a few other earnest men and women, resulted in a revival spirit, and the organization of a regular congregation founded upon scriptural truths as interpreted by them. Here they evidently followed the example set by the Keithian Quakers, who, after their leader had left them, and being unwilling again to unite with the Quakers, met together, searched the Scriptures, and determined to resign themselves entirely to the guidance of Holy Writ and to live a life of primitive Christian simplicity,—a movement from which arose the denomination of Baptists in Pennsylvania who kept the Seventh Day holy.

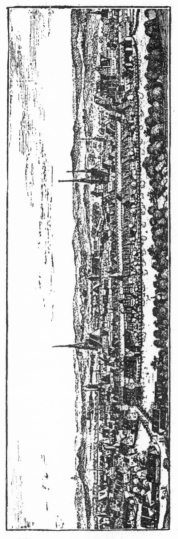

ZWICKAU, IN SAXONY, WHERE THE FIRST BAPTIST CONGREGATION WAS FORMED.

The small gatherings in the weaver's shop on the outskirts of th straggling village of Germantown were also destined to form the nucleus for so large and respectable a denomination of Christians as the German Baptists or Dunkers, whose organizations now extend throughout many, if not all, of the States forming the American Union.

Officially this denomination is known as the *Brethren*, a name assumed for themselves, on account of what Christ said to his disciples, Matt. xxiii, 8: " One is your Master, even Christ, and all ye are brethren." Locally the members are known as German Baptists or Dunkers (Täufer, Tunker). The latter term was originally one of derision, from the manner in which they administered the sacred rite of baptism.

The Baptist Brethren movement in Germany dates back to the year 1521, when the so-called Zwickau prophets,

Nicholas Storch, Marcus Stubner and Thomas Münzer arose in Saxony and preached the doctrine of adult baptism and the coming millennium. The latter prophet subsequently spread the doctrine throughout Switzerland, Franconia and Thuringia. His adherents took an active part in the peasants' war, and suffered an overwhelming defeat at Frankenhausen, May 15, 1525. In 1528 the Emperor Charles V. issued an edict crushing the sect wherever found within his dominions. Notwithstanding this persecution, the doctrine spread from Bavaria to Holland. The members were known by different names, such as *Stäbler* (*Baculares*, *Stablarii*), because they taught that a Christian should not bear arms, but defend himself merely with a staff; *Clanucalarii*, because they refused to publish any creed; *Gartenbrüder* (*Hortularii*), because they held their assemblies in the open fields or woods; *Heftler* or *Knöpfler*, because they eschewed buttons as a luxury,[28] and substituted hooks and eyes on their clothing,—a peculiarity still prevalent among one branch of the Mennonite Brethren in Pennsylvania, locally known as "Hookers."

ARMS OF ZWICKAU.

Glancing over the subsequent history of the Anabaptists, during the next two centuries, and casting the veil of charity over the frightful excesses of the Knipperdolling episode at Münster, we find a slow but gradual spread of the faith over Europe, in spite of the efforts made by the civil and ecclesiastical authorities to crush the various con-

---

[28] In some parts of South Germany and the Rhine Palatinate rows of silver and metal buttons were used on men's vests and coats, as a matter of ornament. This is still the case among some of the German peasantry. The Baptist movement was against this excessive use of buttons as an adornment. Plain dress, similar to the Quaker garb, was adopted at an early day as a sign of the renunciation of this world's vanities. The use of hooks and eyes on the male garb was confined to such localities where the use of buttons was what may be called a national feature.

gregations. A number of independent movements tended to keep the doctrine alive, chiefly in northern Germany, Holland and Switzerland. The most important of these is to be found in the history of Simon Menno and his followers. The Schwarzenau gathering in 1708 was but another of these independent mov _nents. Its origin is more or less vague as to detail, from the fact that no regular records were kept in the early days of the movement, or if so, they were evidently lost or destroyed during the persecution instituted by the authorities, who drove the members from place to place.

Fortunately Brother Timotheus [29] of the Ephrata Community (Alexander Mack the younger) made some attempt, after the death of his father, to gather and preserve what remained of the records and accounts of the original congregation. For this purpose he searched the remaining papers of his father and those of Peter Becker with the following result.

It appears there were originally eight persons who met at Mack's house or mill at Schwarzenau for religious conference ; they were five men and three women :

(1) George Grebi, from Hesse Cassel.

(2) Lucas Vetter, from Hessenland.

(3) Alexander Mack, from Schriesheim, between Mannheim and Heidelberg in the Palatinate.

(4) Andreas Bone, from Basel, in Switzerland.

(5) Johannes Kipping, from Bariet, in Würtemberg.

(6) Johanna Nöthigerin or Bonisin (wife of Andreas Bone).

(7) Anna Margretha Mack (wife of Alexander Mack).

(8) Johanna Kippinger.

This little company met together regularly to examine carefully and impartially the doctrines of the New Testa-

---

[29] In some of his later writings he calls himself Br. Theophilus. He was also known as Br. Sander, the latter a corruption of Alexander.

SPECIMEN OF EARLY PENNSYLVANIA ENGRAVING (XVIII CENTURY).

THE BAPTISM OF CHRIST ON A DUNKER BAPTISMAL CERTIFICATE.

COLLECTION OF JULIUS F. SACHSE.

DESIGNED AND ENGRAVED BY C. F. EGELMANN.

ment, and to ascertain what are the obligations it imposes upon professing Christians; determining to lay aside all preconceived opinions and traditional observances. After a time, when they felt themselves spiritually prepared, it was determined to put their teachings into practice; as Theophilus quaintly says:

"As they were now prepared thereunto, so they went into the solitude in the morning. Even eight went out unto the water called *Aeder*. And the brother upon whom fell the lot baptized first the brother whom the congregation of Christ wanted baptized, and after he was baptized he immersed him who had baptized him and the remaining three brothers and three sisters; and so all eight were baptized in the early morning hour.

"This was accomplished in the above-named year, 1708. But of the month of the year, or the day of the month or the week, they have left no account."

Two of the original members of the Schwarzenau concongregation subsequently came to this province, and ended their days here, viz., Alexander Mack and Andreas Bone.

ETURNING once more to our story, it was on the morning of Wednesday, December 25, 1723 (Christmas Day), that a number of German settlers, who had located within the bounds of the German township, wended their way towards the humble weaver's shop where Conrad Beissel had served his apprenticeship, at the extreme end of the borough limits in what was known as Van Bebberstown. History has unfortunately failed to preserve for posterity the exact location of Becker's humble abode. This, however, is but of secondary importance. We know that it was in Van Bebber's township on the North Wales road. Tradition strongly points to the vicinity of the present church, where the earliest meetings were held. However, be this as it

"AFTER THE LAPSE OF TWO CENTURIES."

ADMINISTRATION OF THE ORDINANCE OF BAPTISM IN A GERMAN RIVER DURING THE CLOSING YEARS OF THE XIX CENTURY.

FROM A SKETCH MADE AT THE TIME.

may, upon the day in question the solemn scenes which took place on the Eder in Germany fifteen years before were to be repeated here in the western world, and the foundation laid for a new Christian denomination. The seed sown in Germany was to be transplanted into our virgin land, where it was destined to take root and flourish far beyond any expectation of the devout band on either the Eder or the Wissahickon.

It was a typical winter's day, the air crisp and cold, the sky clear, the ground hard and frozen, with a thin covering of snow. Many were the sad memories of the Fatherland that came into the minds of these pilgrims in a far-off land, as they plodded over the frozen ground, separated, as it were, from both kin and church, they thought of the joyous *Christmesse* at home.

The day was a well-chosen one for their object,—the fervent desire to organize a church home for themselves to found a new Christian sect in the New World. The series of devotional meetings held by Peter Becker and his helpers was about to become the grain of seed which was to bring forth a mighty tree with wide-spreading root and branches. Their aim was to form a *Gemeinde* or commune of their own,—to give them the benefit of religious instruction and at the same time emancipate them from what Falkner calls "the melancholy, saturnine Quaker spirit" which then prevailed in the Province.

It was well nigh noon when the party assembled and devotional exercises were commenced. After these were over it was found that there were present seventeen persons who had been baptized in Europe, viz., Peter Becker, Johann Heinrich Traut, Jeremias Traut, Balser Traut, Heinrich Holzappel, Johannes Gumre, Stephan Koch, Jacob Koch, Johannes Hildebrand, Daniel Ritter, Georg Balser Gansz, Johannes Preisz,[30] Johannes Kämpfer, Magdalena Traut,

[30] According to Isaac N. Urner, Esq., Johannes Preisz was a son of

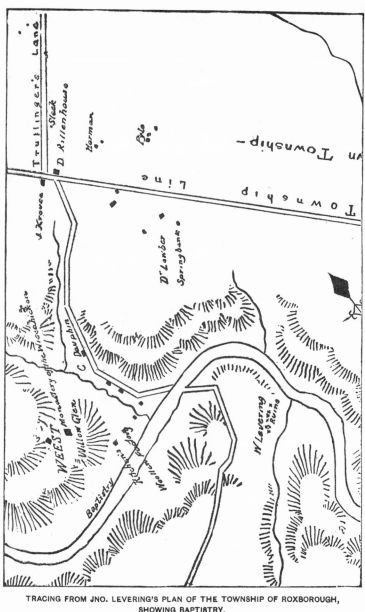

TRACING FROM JNO. LEVERING'S PLAN OF THE TOWNSHIP OF ROXBOROUGH,
SHOWING BAPTISTRY.

Anna Gumre, Maria Hildebrand, and Johanna Gansz. These persons proceeded formally to organize themselves into a congregation, and constituted Peter Becker their elder.

Six postulants now presented themselves and asked to be baptized as by Scripture ordained, and then received into fellowship, viz., Martin Urner, his wife Catherina Urner ; Heinrich Landes and his wife ; Friedrich Lang and Jan (Johannes) Mayle. Thus they became the first Anabaptists among the High Germans in America. In the church records this band of converts is always referred to as the " First Fruits." The immersion took place the same day. After a noonday meal had been served the party went in solemn procession down the old Indian trail, which led from the North Wales road to a ford on the Wissahickon, and thence beyond the ridge towards the Schuylkill. This trail, which long since has become a public highway, was known north of the township line successively as Morgan's and Trull-inger's lane, now Carpenter street. South of the dividing line the trail was successively known as Gorgas', Milner's Garseed's and Kitchen's lane. The course of the creek at this point makes a sharp turn and here comes nearest to Germantown. The distance from Bebberstown, or the upper part of Germantown, to the Wissahickon is but a short one. The distance traversed by the party was about one and one-half miles ; it was a short journey for the sturdy Germans of that day. The objective point of the party was a level bank, or strip of land on the estate of Johannes Gumre, adjacent to the creek, where easy access could be had to flowing water. The ravine of the Wissahickon is a rugged one, with towering rocks upon either bank, making the shore inaccessible, except in a few places.

Jacob Preisz, who came from Prussia to America in 1719. The family first settled at Indian creek, Montgomery county, Pa. In later years the above-named Johannes and his children became prominent among the Coventry Brethren.

The strip of land in question is about two hundred yards north of Kitchen's lane. There the recession of the rocky ravine forms a space large enough to accommodate quite a respectable number of people. While the rocks are covered with evergreens, the alluvial soil on the bank has fostered the growth of the catalpa and other deciduous forest trees. In former days, at the time of the scene we are now describing, when the country was as yet covered with a fine forest growth, a rivulet broke over the rocky wall in the background and formed a picturesque waterfall as it leaped from rock to crag in its wild flight down to the bottom of the ravine.

When the party reached the banks of the Wissahickon the afternoon was already well advanced, so little time was lost. After a fervent invocation to the throne of grace and the reading of a passage from Luke xiv, the newly constituted elder entered the water through the thin ice leading by the hand the first candidate. This was Martin Urner,[31] a native of Alsace, who had been brought up in the Reformed faith, and who, together with his two brothers, for a short time had been members of the Hermits on the Ridge.

The scene was a solemn one. The small procession on their way to the creek was rein forced by some of the Hermits from the heights on the other side of the stream, and some others who were attracted out of curiosity, so that by the time the party arrived at the banks of the frozen stream the company was quite a goodly one—wit nesses who were to

ARMS OF CANTON URI.

assist by their presence at what was to be the founding of a new Christian denomination in America.

---

[31] The Urner family is said to have belonged to the Canton of Uri in Switzerland, as the name unmistakably shows. *Vide* History of the Coventry Church, by Isaac N. Urner, LL.D., Phila., 1898, p. 30.

THE BAPTISTRY ON THE WISSAHICKON.

LEVEL BANK AND POOL, ABOVE KITCHEN'S LANE, WHERE THE FIRST DUNKER BAPTISM WAS ADMINISTERED IN AMERICA.

Clear above the sound of the rushing waters and the rustle of leafless branches rose the solemn German invocation and the singing of the baptismal hymn composed by Alexander Mack, *Ueberschlag die Kost, Spricht Jesu Christ, wann du den Grund wilt legen.*[32] Numerous as had been the mystic rites and occult incantations held on the rugged ravine and valley of this stream since the gentle Kelpius and his band settled there thirty years before, none were more fervent or brought so great and lasting results as this solemn rite upon the narrow strip of rock-bound land on the shore of the Wissahickon. There stood the administrator deep in the cold water, before him knelt the rugged Alsatian, thrice was he immersed under the icy flood. As he arose the last time the *Segenspruch* was pronounced and Martin Urner once more entered the material world to become a factor in the religious development of his adopted country. His wife, Catharina Reist, was the next candidate, followed by the other four persons, the same scenes being repeated in each case.

LONG before the solemn rite was ended the winter sun was well down over the Schuylkill hills and the sky covered with leaden clouds. The party now proceeded to the house of Johannes Gumre where dry clothing was provided. In the evening a love-feast was held, the rite of footwashing was observed, at which the newly constituted elder officiated as a token of his humility. This was followed by the breaking of the bread and the administration of the Holy Communion, and was partaken of by the seventeen constituents and the six newly baptised converts, making twenty-three members in all.

Thus was perfected the organization of the first " Congregation of the Brethren in America."

---

[32] " Count the cost, says Jesus Christ, when the foundations thou wouldst lay."

As the party separated two bright lights were seen in the distance, and attracted attention as the flames leaped high up in the winter air far above the tree-tops. One of these fires was some distance down the creek ; the other, almost opposite Gumre's house, upon the high ground where now rises the tall spire of the Roxboro Baptist church. At first it was feared that some house or stable was on fire. But when the party crossed the stream and climbed up the hill, it was soon found that the flames were nothing but the lighting of the sacred fires of the winter solstice, typifying the growing power of the sun which set in upon this day. This was according to an old Saxon custom, perhaps connected with the older Mithraic cult. It is a custom which, with some modifications, has came down to the present day, and is perpetuated in the Christmas tree with its burning tapers.

The two fires were lit with certain mystic rites by the remaining Hermits on the Ridge twice every year as the two natal days came.[33] The difference in their observance was that, while the fires upon the night of December 25th were built so that the flame shot high up in the air, those upon St. John's Day, June 24th, were built to burn low, and when well ablaze were scattered down the hillsides. The rite opposite Gumre's was observed by Johann Selig[34] and his companions, while the fire further down the stream was the tribute of Conrad Matthäi and other Hermits, who had assisted at the baptism in the afternoon, and who now lit the sacred fire upon the the highest bluff near their cabins. This was not only typical of the coming spring, but was also an omen for the new sect of Christians, who had organized but a few hours before nightfall on the banks of their beloved stream,—the Wissahickon.

---

[33] *Vide* German Pietists, p. 34.

[34] Johann Selig was then living in a cabin on the Wigert Levering plantation, east of the present Baptist church.

The proceedings just recited naturally created considerable stir among the German people in the neighborhood,—a condition of which Peter Becker did not fail to avail himself. The winter, however, proved to be an exceedingly hard and stormy one, and the meetings were discontinued until spring. They were resumed early in May, and continued with great success. Efforts were also made to reach and influence the youth and to educate them in matters spiritual. Many were attracted to the services and "taught to walk in the fear of the Lord and to love the Brethren." As the fame of this awakening spread abroad there was such an increase of attendance that no room could be found large enough to accommodate the worshipers; so, whenever the weather permitted, the assembly was held in the open air.

During the summer love-feasts were held, and many felt impelled to join the congregation. The *Chronicon Ephratense* further tells us: "Under these circumstances they deemed it well to make a detailed report of this new awakening to their brethren in Germany. Therefore they prepared in common a writing addressed to them, in which they informed them that they had become re-united in Pennsylvania, and that hereupon a great awakening had resulted in the land, which was still daily increasing; that of the awakened, several had joined their communion, to which they had to consent, as they dared not withstand the counsels of God."

One of the results of these communications was that Alexander Mack, his family and others of the original Schwarzenau congregation, eventually emigrated to Pennsylvania.

It may be well to state at this time that the romantic spot on the Wissahickon where the first baptism was held by the German Baptist Brethren has now been restored to almost the same primitive condition as it was upon that memorable Christmas Day in 1723.

The only material change that the spot underwent in

the course of years was when the first Gorgas, after his purchase from the younger Gumre, built a dam across the creek for his mill-seat. The breast of the dam and the head of the mill-race were at this spot. The building of the dam deepened the water for some distance up the stream, and covered the low sloping bank at the shore. This, however, did not deter the German Baptists of Germantown from holding their successive baptisms at this now historic spot. So usual did this custom become, that upon nearly all the old township and local maps the spot is noted as the *Baptistrion* or Baptistry.[35]

Within the past two years the Park Commission of Philadelphia has acquired title to such portion of the old Gumre tract as borders on the Wissahickon, and the historic spot is now within the Park limits. When the old mill was removed by the Park Commissioners, the dam-breast was also opened, and the creek now, after the lapse of many years, again flows free and unharnessed as it did when Peter Becker entered the water with his first converts.

A visit to the spot will show at a glance how appropriate was the selection, and suitable it was for the practice of a solemn religious rite. Secluded and romantic, it seems to be hidden from the material world and its allurements. Shaded with a growth of forest with a circular rocky wall in the background, the rapid stream is as clear as crystal, when not clouded by a sudden rain, while the opposite bank, towering high above it, is still clad with its original covering of pine and hemlock. A more quiet and restful spot can hardly be pictured; even now, though within Park limits and just opposite to the Wissahickon drive, with its constant stream of horses and bicycles, the peaceful silence of the old Baptistry is only broken by the rippling of the creek, the rustle of the leaves, or the shrill note of a feathered songster as he calls to his mate.

---

[35] *Vide* map on page 92 *supra.*

EFORE the summer of 1724 was over a new crusade was projected, being intended to reach the Germans in outlying districts, where some of the original members and " First Fruits " had gone to get cheaper or more fertile lands. For this purpose a company was organized, under the leadership of Elder Peter Becker, to go on an extended pilgrimage, which was to include the Pequea and Conestoga valleys. The party, consisting of fourteen persons, and of whom seven were mounted, journeyed forth from Germantown on Wednesday, October 23, 1725. A strange sight it was, as these devout enthusiasts, part on horseback and part on foot, started out upon the highway, then hardly worthy of the name of a road, towards the Perkiomen.

The first stop was made in the beautiful Skippach valley, where a number of Germans had settled. Here several meetings were held with much success; thence they went northward, crossed the Perkiomen and continued on through Providence to Falkner swamp, where a halt was made at the house of one Albertus, who, it appears, was in communion with the party. Here revival meetings were held, which closed with a *Liebesmahl* in the evening, followed by the breaking of the bread; thence they journeyed to Oley, in Berks county, near Douglassville, where similar work was done with the same results. From Oley the party went southward and crossed the Schuylkill, going direct to the house of Martin Urner, one of the " First Fruits," who, since his baptism, had permanently settled in Coventry,[36] Chester county, immediately opposite the present town of Pottstown.

Martin Urner, from the time he came to Coventry, ex-

[36] It appears that Martin Urner had purchased four hundred and fifty acres of land in Coventry township of the Penns as early as 1718, and the names of the three Urner brothers appear in the assessment lists of "Scoolkill," Chester county, as early as 1719-22. *Vide* history of the Coventry Brethren Church, by Isaac N. Urner, LL. D., Phila., 1898.

horted his neighbors whenever opportunity offered, besides holding meetings at his own house on Sundays with more or less regularity. One of the results of his labors was that when Peter Becker and his party reached there they found two persons prepared for baptism in addition to the settlers who were ready to form a congregation.

On the next day, Saturday, November 7, 1724, being the Scriptural Sabbath, a meeting was held in Urner's house, at which Elder Becker presided. The two candidates were baptized in the Schuylkill, and the ceremony was followed by the usual love-feast and bread-breaking in the evening.

Upon this occasion was organized the Coventry Brethren Church, of which Martin Urner was made preacher. The following nine persons were the constituent members: Martin Urner, his wife, Catherine Reist Urner; Daniel Eicher and wife, Henrich Landes and wife, Peter Höffly, Owen Longacre (sic.) and Andrew Sell.

From Coventry the revivalists journeyed towards the Conestoga country, as the western part of Chester county was then known. Upon leaving Urner's the party divided, the mounted men keeping to the road and passing the night of Monday, November 9th, at the house of Jacob Weber, who then lived in the Conestoga valley, evidently near the present Weberstown, in Leacock township. Those on foot took a shorter route, probably over the Welsh mountain, and stopped at the house of Johannes Graff. This was in Earl township, at what is now known as Graffsdale, at the lower end of Earl township. The original tract of 1419 acres was situated on Graff's run, a branch of the Mühlbach (Mill creek). Johannes Graff was the earliest and wealthiest settler in the vicinity. The foundation-stones of the cabin which he built in 1718 are yet to be seen upon the property of a lineal descendant.[37]

---

[37] "The Three Earls," an historical sketch and proceedings of the centennial jubilee held at New Holland, Pa., July 4 1876, by Frank Ried Diffenderffer, Esq.

The footmen passed the night under the hospitable roof of Johannes Graff, and on the next day journeyed to the house of Hans Rudolph Nägele, a Mennonite preacher, where both horse and footmen again united. Fortunately the exact situation of Nägele's house can now be definitely determined, by aid of the original surveys, as will be seen by the facsimile of this draft.

URING the day Peter Becker, Henrich Traut and several others visited Beissel and his companion at their cabin beside the *Schwendenquelle* to enlist their sympathy and assistance in their own efforts toward an awakening among the Germans in the Conestoga country. The two recluses readily acceded to the wishes of Becker and his companions, and assured them of their hearty support.

The night was passed at the house of Stephen Galliond. Early upon the next day, Wednesday, November 11th, the party retraced their steps and journeyed towards the valley of the Pequea to bring about an awakening among the Mennonites, who had settled there, many of whom had become followers of the seductive Bauman and his noxious "Newborn" teaching. A large gathering was held at the house of Heinrich Höhn on Thursday, November 12th, at which Beissel was present.

At this meeting, according to the old records, extraordinary revival powers were manifested. The evangelists spoke with such force concerning apostolic baptism and the Divine purpose concerning fallen man involved therein, that after the close of the meeting five persons felt convinced and applied for baptism. These candidates were Heinrich Höhn and his wife, at whose house the revival was held; Johann Mayer and wife and Joseph Schäffer. The party at once proceeded to the Pequea, and the ordinance was administered to them by Peter Becker. Before the rite was concluded, another person, Veronica Friedrichs, the wife of a local miller, presented herself as a candidate and was accepted.   During this service on the banks of the placid Pequea, much fervent spirit manifested itself among all present, and no one was more impressed than Conrad Beissel.   He had felt for some time past that longer to withstand the ordinance of God was presumption.   To overcome this craving and ease his conscience, Beissel, some time previous to this pilgrimage, attempted to baptise himself.   This questionable act, however, failed to convince him, and the uncertainty of its efficacy left him in a very unenviable state of mind.   Yet he considered his old master and the others present so far beneath him in every respect, that it would be too great a humiliation for his proud spirit to receive baptism at their hands.

The stepping forth of Veronica Friedrichs, the fervent

THE OLDEST KNOWN REPRESENTATION OF A CHRISTIAN BAPTISM.[38]

prayers and pious ejaculations, all tended to increase the excitement of Beissel; well may it be assumed that it reached a fever heat, and that his mental conflict was a fearful one.   He, too, longed to enter the water and be

[38] Original in crypt of St. Lucina in Cömeterium of Callistus, dating from the third century.

plunged beneath the flood, and through it again enter the material world cleansed from all taint and sin. While he felt himself called to fulfill a mission to preach the Gospel among his fellow-men, yet his pride forbade him to humble himself, as he considered, to bow to his old master and receive the rite at his hands.

While Veronica was being baptized the excitement rose still higher. Suddenly, in the very midst of the solemn rite, Beissel remembered how it was recorded in Scripture that even Christ had humbled himself to be baptized by so lowly a person as John. The scene on the banks of the Pequea upon that November day was certainly an impressive one; religious enthusiasm was wrought to a high pitch and reached its culmination when Conrad Beissel announced his intention to be baptized in "apostolicwise," and importuned Peter Becker to administer the rite. No preparations were made, but as Veronica Friedrichs was led up the slippery bank, Beissel humbly entered the freezing water and knelt before the elder who, after a short invocation, immersed the candidate thrice, face forward, under the cold flood.

The old record, commenting upon Beissel's baptism, states: "It was thus that Wisdom brought him into her net: he received the seed of his heavenly virginity at his first awakening; but now a field was prepared for him in America into which he might sow this seed again."

The scene of this baptism, Pequea creek, a typical Pennsylvania mill-stream, has its source in Salisbury township, Lancaster county, and in West Caln township, Chester county, flows in a southwesterly course of about thirty miles, and empties into the Susquehanna river, dividing Leacock and Lampeter townships from Strasburg, and Conestoga from Martic township. In its course it formerly furnished power for numerous mills.

If we except the immersion in the Wissahickon on the

previous Christmas Day, this baptism in the Pequea was the most noteworty one in the history of the sect-people of Pennsylvania. While the former one laid the foundation of the German Baptist Brethren church in America, the immersion of Beissel virtually created the first schism within that fold, from which may be traced the beginnings of the German Seventh-day Baptists in the Province: an organization which, though small in number, still exists in different parts of our State.

After Peter Becker's work was finished, a procession was formed, and the party, amid the singing of a hymn, proceeded to the house of Heinrich Höhn, where dry and warm garments were provided for the newly baptised, while the rest of the day was spent in edifying conversation. In the evening a *Liebesmahl* was given at the house of their host, at the close of which fervent supplications were again offered for the success of the new religious movement in the Conestoga valley.

Early on the next day, November 13th, the party went to Isaac Friedrich's house on Mill creek, where they attempted to hold a religious meeting. A disagreement, however, arose among the party, as some insisted upon returning home; others, again, wanted to continue the evangelizing work. Among the latter was the elder, Peter Becker, who insisted on holding a religious meeting at the house of Sigmund Landert on the coming Sunday. This meeting did not prove a success, either in power or in spirit. During the day the quarrels of the previous week were renewed. The first broke out among the women, and then Michael Wohlfarth and Simon König began to argue about the questions which had divided the Baptist congregation at Crefeldt.

After peace was restored, Sigmund Landert and his wife asked to be baptized and received into communion. Peter Becker, before he would grant their request, spoke as follows:

" These two persons have applied to us for baptism ; but
" as they are unknown to us in their walk and conversa-
" tion, we make this announcement of the fact to all men
" here present, especially to their neighbours.   If you can
" bear favorable witness concerning their lives, it is well,
" and we can baptize them with the greater assurance ;
" but if you have any complaints to bring against them,
" we will not do it."

But even this baptism failed to prove a success.   The
pool selected was a small dam in a tributary of Mill creek,
within the bounds of the farm of the candidates.   Here, it
appears, that the water was shallow, stagnant and muddy,
and after the immersion the two candidates were in so
filthy a plight that they had to be washed off.   Before the
Germantown pilgrims finally departed for home, they consulted with the newly baptized converts from the Conestoga and Pequea valleys, and told them that henceforth
they would have to shift for themselves and arrange their
own affairs according to their circumstances and ability,
without expecting any help from the parent stem at Germantown.

The kiss of peace and charity was then given and passed,
and the pilgrims, on November 14th, started upon their
homeward journey east of the Schuylkill.

The new converts were not slow in acting upon the suggestions of Peter Becker to arrange their own affairs ; the
twelve persons, six brothers and six sisters, proceeded
forthwith to form themselves into a regular Baptist congregation.   This became known as the Conestoga Church
or *Gemeinde*.   It consisted of Conrad Beissel, Joseph
Schäffer, Johannes Meyer, Henrich Höhn, Sigmund Landert and Jonadab ; Sisters Migtonia, Christina, Veronica
[Friedrichs], Maria, Elizabeth and Franzina.   Beissel was
by common consent acknowledged as the leader of the
new congregation.   He accepted the charge and promised

THE INSTITUTION OF THE LORD'S SUPPER.

CARTOON BY MRITIS OF CLIENT AT VIENNA NO. 6 BY THE

COLLECTION OF JULIUS F. SACHSE.

henceforth to emulate Christ and live a holy and godly life.

It may be well at this point to define what is meant by a love-feast or *Liebesmahl* among the German Baptist Brethren, as it differs materially from what is understood by a love-feast among other denominations. With the Moravians and others it is a symbolical service, at which coffee or chocolate and a small cake or bunn are served in church during the singing of hymns and the reading of suitable selections from Scripture. With the Brethren the love-feast is patterned after that of the early Christian church, being a regular full meal, partaken in silence before the communion, similar to the supper eaten by Christ and the Apostles, and it serves as an introduction to the more solemn part of the evening's service.

THE ORDER OF THE LOVE-FEAST.

HE order of the love-feast, as observed at the present time in the Brethren church, differs but little from the service instituted by Peter Becker. It is as follows:

Upon the day set for the observance preparatory services are held during the afternoon. If there are candidates for baptism present the service is usually held after the administration of the ordinance. This is what is known as a "self-examination" service, where is read 1 Cor. xi, special stress being laid upon verses 27, 28, etc. In the evening the services are opened by prayer and congregational singing. The members seat themselves at tables, the sexes separate; all men (brothers) on one side, with heads uncovered, women (sisters) on the other side with heads bedecked with the prayer covering, usually a neat lace cap with strings tied beneath the chin. At large gatherings separate tables are arranged for the sexes at opposite sides of the room or *Saal*.

When all are properly seated, the elder present designates some one to read John xiii, and comment upon it. The men and women then turn on the benches, so that they sit back to back, with the table between them. The ceremony of feet washing is then performed, each sex attending to themselves, the act being performed separately but simultaneously, accompanied by the singing of appropriate hymns.

The present writer has witnessed the observance of this service in two ways, viz.: where it was performed by the elder on the male side and by the oldest sister on the female side. In the other method, which is the recognized custom and rule with the Brethren meeting in the old church at Germantown, the elder merely washes the feet of the first brother on the right, who in turn did the same for his neighbor, and so on until the service was performed. The same was done on the women's side. The commencement in both methods was the same. Small tubs of tepid water were brought into the *Saal* for the use of each sex. The elder and eldest sister then proceeded to gird themselves with a large linen towel or apron, using this to dry the feet of the worshipers after the ablution. As the worshiper's feet are dried hands are shaken and the kiss of love and charity is given. This service is a solemn ceremony instituted by Christ as a token of humility, and upon that account is scrupulously adhered to by the Brethren.

When the pedelavium is completed, the members, having resumed the covering of their feet, face inwards on the benches, and the evening meal or love-feast is brought on the table.

This consists of a full meal. The viands of which are varied according to the custom of the congregation; at some places a large mug of coffee and wheat biscuits are served; at others, chiefly in the rural districts, lamb soup is the chief dish for the repast of the Brethren, while bread and apple butter are served the strangers and visitors. A blessing is invoked upon the meal, which is then eaten in absolute silence, the partakers, solemnly looking forward by faith to the time when Christ shall come again to serve us. When all have eaten, thanks are returned. After this comes the passing of the salutation of the holy kiss. When all have received and passed it, the communion emblems are brought forward and uncovered. This service commences with the reading of John xix, to call to mind the passion of Jesus. Then follows the breaking of the bread, which is unleavened and baked so that it may be broken into strips; and as the members stand at the table the blessing of Almighty God is invoked upon the emblem.

A strip of bread is then passed to both sexes, with this difference: As the pieces are handed from man to man, each brother breaks off a morsel for the one next to him, and repeats, " Beloved brother, this bread which we break is the communion of the body of Christ." For the sisters, on the other hand, the elder breaks a piece for each woman, and as he hands it to her repeats the above sentence, substituting the word "sister" for "brother." This difference in the administration of the Sacrament is partly founded upon the belief that, as the weaker sex had no part in the breaking of Christ's body, so even now they should have no part in breaking the emblem which typifies it.

When all are served the bread is eaten simultaneously and in silence. After the bread is partaken the cup with unfermented wine is taken up, and as the members stand it is carried to the Lord in prayer. The elder then passes the cup to the nearest brother, saying: " Beloved brother, this cup of the New Testament is the communion of the blood of Christ." The brother in turn passes it to his neighbor. The same rule is used in serving the sisters as in the distribution of the bread ; the elder passes the cup to each sister in turn, who returns it to him after she has partaken.

The versicles used are based upon 1 Cor. xv., 23–26.

When all have communed, prayer is offered and the services closed with the singing of a hymn, according to Mark xiv, 26.

In the observance of this service the German Seventh-day Baptists of the present day, at both Ephrata and Snow Hill, have of late years made a radical departure from the time-honored custom of their fathers.

The service as now administered is celebrated by candle-light as of old, but is opened with the reading of such parts of Scripture as bear upon the service of foot-washing. This act is then observed ; as in years gone by the elder or oldest brother girding himself and washing the feet of the brother to his right, who in turn does the same for his neighbor. When this service is finished, the bread is broken and the cup passed, after suitable selections of Holy Writ have been read.

It will be observed that in this instance the meal has been abolished. This change was brought about by Elder Andrew Fahnstock, a former preacher, who served the congregation prior to 1863. A cold colation is, however, almost in every instance prepared for such members as come from a distance.

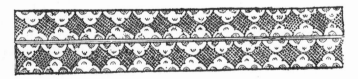

BORDER FROM THE KLOSTER COPY-BOOK.

OR some time previous to the occurrences narrated in the last chapter Beissel and Wohlfarth had made a practice of keeping the Sabbath or the Seventh Day at their cabin in the forest without, however, making any effort to promulgate the doctrine. This was an important feature which was overlooked by Peter Becker and his party in the excitement incident to the great revival. But no sooner had the party returned to Germantown than the fear was expressed that Beissel might attempt to introduce his convictions as to the true Sabbath. To counteract any such movement it was proposed to send Johannes Kemper, who was endowed with the gift of prayer, as superintendent of the Conestoga congregation. There is, however, no record to be found that this proposition was carried into execution. The Sabbath question, together with Beissel's future course, gave the Germantown congregation much concern, and Elder Becker was publicly charged with having "left too much in the hands of the new converts."

Notwithstanding these forbodings at Germantown, the meetings of the Conestoga congregation were held at regular intervals at the house of Simon Landert, and at all of them Conrad Beissel presided. After the baptism of

Beissel in the icy flood of the Pequea, a great change came over our religious enthusiast; he appeared to realize that a large measure of the spirit rested upon him. Our old chronicler states that "he conducted all meetings with astonishing strength of spirit, and used so little reflection over it that even in the beginning he was not suffered to use a Bible, so that the testimony in its delivery might not be weakened by written knowledge. He began his discourse with closed eyes before a large crowd of hearers, and when he opened his eyes again most of them were gone, not being able to endure the spirit's keenness. On such occasions wonderful mysteries of eternity were often revealed through him, of which he himself had before been ignorant; but these were soon sealed up again, and then he would say: "The Spirit retires again into his secret chamber." He was a born orator, and could carry out a proposition to great lengths, especially if he had rationalistic persons before him, for which his opponents blamed him very much. In his delivery, however, he was too fast, because he had to hurry after the spirit, when he often concerned himself but little about the rules of language.

At one of the meetings at Sigmund Landert's during the month of December, the question was broached as to the advisability of obtaining a regular teacher, or, in other words: Who should be their spiritual leader? At this juncture Hans Mayer, a neighbor of Landert's, and one of the converts baptized on November 12, 1724, rose in the meeting, and pointing to Conrad Beissel, solemnly proclaimed him to be the man-elect, chosen by God, to be their leader, and asked that he be accepted accordingly,— a proposition which was unanimously acceded to. Beissel, who again saw the hand of Providence in the direction of his course, accepted the trust and became their leader, or, as he modestly states, "the teacher of the new Dunkers on the Conestoga." According to the *Chronicon*, "his ordination to this office he received from the same one who had bestowed it upon Elijah, John the Baptist and other reformers, who were awakened specially and directly to come to the help of a church fallen asunder."

At either this or the following meeting a *Liebesmahl* was held, where the kiss of charity was passed, the bread broken and the rite of feet-washing observed, at all of which Conrad Beissel officiated for the first time. From this time (December, 1724) the Conestoga congregation was a regular corporate body of the German Baptist Brethren.

This wave of religious excitement among the German settlers in the Conestoga valley and adjacent country increased rather than diminished during the winter. It was the season when farm work was out of the question, and the pioneer in these western wilds really had but two topics for thought or conversation during the long winter nights,—politics and religion. In the former the Germans were but little interested, as they had no part in the government, nor newspapers to advise them of legislative action. This left them with the single topic of religion, of which most of them knew even less than of the political questions of the day. Thus it was that new questions arose at almost every meeting. Many of these were based upon the true Sabbath, which was strictly observed by Beissel. These discussions caused some of the members to refer to the Scriptures and advance the argument, that if it was obligatory to obey Holy Writ in the question of the Sabbath, they must also conform in other matters, both ordained and forbidden.

Several of these enthusiasts argued that if they were to emulate primitive Christians, who kept the Sabbath, they should also discriminate as to clean and unclean food. These extremists now proposed henceforth to eschew the use of pork, in which determination they were at first encouraged by Beissel.

As pork or *Pökelfleisch* (pickled salted meat, chiefly pork) was really the chief nitrogenous food of the early settlers during the winter season, this resolve led to some amusing experiences, and upon more than one occasion caused an involuntary fast upon the part of the devotees.

ARLY in the year 1725, Beissel and several of the congregation went on a visit to the Baptists in Coventry and Germantown, thus returning the visit of the Becker party.   Among the number from Conestoga were two of the brethren who had strictly determined to eschew unclean food as set forth by the Mosaic law.   This led to no end of trouble during the trip, as the two men not only refused to partake of pork, but also absolutely objected to any food being prepared for them in any vessel in which pork had ever been kept or prepared.   It was soon found that but few families had such culinary appliances as were absolutely free from any taint of the hog or his products.   Others again refused to listen to the scruples of the two visionaries who, as a consequence, were doomed to fast while their companions regaled themselves with such viands as were set before them by the thrifty housewife.   They then modified their objections so far as that, before such vessels were used, they were permitted thoroughly to scour and cleanse them after the manner of their own.

These two brethren, whose names unfortunately have not come down to us, went to even greater extremes before they returned from this journey as they also raised scruples against geese.

According to one account, their argument was that as these animals supply man with feathers which are used for his luxurious indulgence, the bird itself should be eschewed in every form by the true believer.

The true reason, however, was that as in Jewish law the swan was classed among the unclean birds (Lev. xi, 17, 18), the goose, both wild and domestic, from its similarity to that bird, should also be rejected as food by the strict adherent to the law.

How largely the goose entered into the domestic economy of the early Germans is shown by the following : To begin with, the feathers and down, which were plucked at regular intervals, furnished the bedding, and when sold were supposed to clothe the women. The eggs were a spring-time delicacy. Each egg was supposed to contain as much nutriment as a pound of beef. In the winter, after the goose had been crammed, it was prepared in different ways. One of the favorite methods was to boil it down in a spiced jelly (*zitter ganz*). The giblets, feet and neck were used for soup-stock, while the abnormal liver was utilized for a tasty Christmas pie (*Gänse-leber pastete*). Lastly, the goose-grease (*gänsefett*) was carefully preserved for its medicinal qualities. No housewife or mother would ever be without this panacea. No matter how sore the throat or bad the cold, an outward application of goose-grease was always depended upon to work a cure.

Then again the great dish among the early Germans, upon high days and holidays, was a roast goose, usually stuffed with apples and chestnuts. This was roasted by hanging on a spit over live coals on the hearth, great care being over the wood used, as the meat was apt to partake of its flavor. This was a delicacy prepared only upon feast-days or upon special occasions, such as an official visitation. To refuse to partake of the dish was not only a great breach of civility, but was also taken as a mark of disrespect to the housewife.

These peculiar actions of some of Beissel's party gave rise to the report that Beissel and his adherents were really attempting to revive Judaism. Owing to these unfavorable impressions the party returned to the Conestoga without having accomplished anything of value to the Brethren.

This attempt at Judaizing forms one of the strangest

episodes in our early history, and, stranger yet, it was not brought about entirely by a search of the Scriptures upon the part of the settlers.

Among the earliest settlers in the Tulpehocken country we find traces of Jewish Indian-traders, who had sojourned in the vicinity of the present Schaffertown, as far back as 1720, to better drive their barter with the Indians. Whether they drifted down from New York or came by way of Philadelphia is immaterial. Certain it is that they were here, prospered and eventually settled permanently in this valley. It is not supposed that any of these early pioneers had their families with them when they first came to these wilds, or that they were numerous enough to form a distinctive settlement or congregation. The presumption is against this theory : their object was to barter and trade for peltries, not to found a home and live by agricultural pursuits.

That they were successful is shown by the fact that, as the settlers gradually increased in numbers,—coming down the Susquehanna from New York and overland from Philadelphia,—we soon find traces of a few of these Jewish traders married and settled down. Whether they were married before they came here or took their wives from among the German settlers is an open question. It is certain, however, that they strictly adhered to the ancient customs of their fathers.

It was from intercourse with these Jewish traders, who adhered as strictly as they could to the requirements of their faith, that the Mosaic ceremonies and customs were derived and practiced by the German settlers, whose reason was almost dethroned with religious excitement and vagaries. Some even went so far as to circumcise each other and blaspheme against Paul because he did away with that rite. The Ephrata chronicles quote several such cases, notably one A—— W——, of Oley, and one D—— C——.

The result of this was that several German families in

AN OLD PENNSYLVANIA POST-ROAD.

SCHAEFFERSTOWN, LEBANON CO., PENNA., SHOWING LOCATION OF SYNAGOGUE.

the old township of Heidelberg actually returned to the old dispensation, and with these accessions quite a Jewish community was formed in Lancaster county.

It was not long before a house of prayer was built by them for the worship of the great Jehovah: it was the first synagogue in the American desert. It was built on the old Indian trail leading from the Conestoga to the Swatara. The place where this synagogue stood—the first in Pennsylvania for many years—is still pointed out by old residents. It was a rude log-house, locally known as the *Schul;* yet here the law was elevated and the *shophar* blown long before it was done in the chief town of the Province.

Our view of the old post-road shows the site of the *Schul*, now occupied by a modern house. Tradition tells us that the ancient log-house in the foreground was formerly the home of the *Hazan* or reader, who in later years served the congregation, which at one time was the most distinctive and populous one of the ancient faith in the Colonies.

THE SHOPHAR, OR SACRED TRUMPET.

The claim that this Jewish congregation was recruited by proselytes from among the early settlers is strengthened by the fact that but few Jewish names —such as Isaac Miranda —appear among those of the settlers in the vicinity. Nor do either the Ephrata records or those sent to Holland by Boehm make reference to any number of Jews in the vicinity. The same is true of the Lutheran and Reformed reports; they all, however, make reference to

ARMS OF THE BÜHLER FAMILY AS AUGMENTED BY THE EMPEROR CHARLES V, MAY, 1521.

the fact that Judaizing influences were rampant among the early settlers.[39]

Then, again, a majority of names, whose owners are known to have been members of the congregation and rest upon the hill, were originally of the Reformed faith.

How firm the hold of these Jewish customs became engrafted upon the early Germans in Pennsylvania is shown by the fact that traces of them still linger among us, as even down to the present day there are families in Berks, Lebanon and Lancaster counties who refuse to use milk in connection with meat dishes, such as frizzled chipped beef, etc., as they had learned from their parents or grand-parents that this was against Divine command.

Another illustration was the practice of offering special

SEAL OF DAVID.

supplications at the advent of each successive new light (new moon), traces of which may still occasionally be found in the rural communities, and which, toward the close the third decade of the Eighteenth Century, culminated in the formation of a distinctive sect, in the vicinity of Ephrata, known as the "New Mooners," a full account of which is given in a subsequent chapter.

This Judaizing movement in Pennsylvania was but a repetition of what had taken place upon a much larger scale in Germany, during the early days of the Reformation, when a number of fanatics with their families went over to Judaism.[40]   For a time these influences and acces-

---

[39] *Vide* Mühlenburg, *Hallische Nachrichten.*

[40] There are still evidences of the above movement to be found in Germany, where families, who at that time returned to Judaism, have remained true to that ancient faith down to the present time.   An interesting illustration is that of the Bühler (von Bühl) family, an old Frankish race, which at the time of the Reformation became Protestant.   One

sions increased to such an extent that three of the Rabbis ventured so far as to go to Luther and argue with him,[41] and actually hoped to proselyte and carry him over with them and thus bring about the millennium by uniting all peoples under the old dispensation.

Luther naturally opposed this movement in his own rugged way, and after taking the leaders as well as the Rabbis sharply to task, he published, in 1542, a pamphlet, which went through several editions, *Concerning the Jews and their Lies.* He requested the German nobility to take notice of these attempts at Judaizing and to suppress them.

However, be this as it may, the German Jewish congregation of Heidelberg township, in the absence of documentary information, will always remain one of the most interesting problems for the student of Pennsylvania-German history.

Upon the high hill, about one-fourth of a mile south of Schafferstown, is what remains of their burial-place; it is the oldest Jewish cemetery in the State, and is now unfortunately almost obliterated..

A revival was held at the house of Johannes Landes, early in May, 1725, upon which occasion Beissel for the first time publicly administered the ordinance of baptism. There were seven candidates, Hans Meyle and his wife, Johannes Landes and his wife, Rudolph Nägele and his wife, and Michael Wohlfarth, the fellow-mystic and companion of Beissel, who was the most important of the number.

---

branch, however, according to family traditions, during this agitation accepted Judaism, since which time the descendants have adhered strictly to that faith, and by intermarriage with others now show a strong pronounced Semitic type, while the other branch of the Bühler family, from which the writer and the Pennsylvania Bühlers are descended, and whose members remained true to the faith of the Reformation, show fair Saxon features. No representative of the Jewish branch of this family is known to the writer to be in this country.

[41] See *Lutheran Church Review*, vol. xvii, p. 148 *seq. ;* also *Martin Luther, the Hero of the Reformation*, by Rev. Henry Eyster Jacobs, D.D. (New York, 1898.)

MMEDIATELY after their baptism, Wohlfarth, accompanied by Rudolph Nägele, started on a proselyting tour throughout the country, mainly through Oley and the country north of the Schuylkill, where the revival of old Jewish and biblical ceremonies had also received much consideration during the past winter. This called forth a sharp rebuke from Beissel. It was a epistle to these few visionaries in Oley wherein he counsels them to leave off their folly. The efforts of the two evangelists awakened but few, as most of their hearers disregarded the message.

A prominent German Baptist, known in the records as Brother Lamech, who had settled in the Conestoga valley, also joined the congregation about this time, and became a staunch supporter of Beissel. It was this same Lamech who kept the diary of the congregation, and later of the Ephrata Community, extracts of which were published and are known as the *Chronicon Ephratense.* His proper name does not appear in any records known to the present writer, and he is one of the few prominent actors in our history whose identity has not been discovered.

The Conestoga congregation increased rapidly, and in the spring of 1725 numbered twenty-two regular members. The growing demands of his flock now made it imperative that Beissel should be nearer to them. He, therefore, left his cabin at the *Schwedenquelle* in charge of Stumpf, and went into a cabin which was erected for him on the land of Rudolph Nägele. The example of the leader was quickly followed by other members of the congregation, and in a few months the land in the vicinity of Nägele's house was dotted with the small log-cabins of persons who wished to live in closer communion with the new leader. The record states : "In this region wonderful influences came down upon him [Beissel] from eternity, of which the least ever became known."

Beissel in his addresses now frequently introduced some of the mystic speculations of occult theosophy, which most of his simple-minded hearers failed to comprehend. The effect of this was that, while some of them deemed him inspired, others shook their heads sadly and thought him demented. Thus matters went on until it became imperative for him to sacrifice his beloved solitude and take up an abode among his people.

The regular meetings were still held in the houses of different members. No effort appears to have been made to build a separate house of worship for the uses of the congregation. At these house-services, the question of the Sabbath became more or less prominent as the time progressed.

This stimulus came from a source entirely distinct from the movement of Conrad Beissel. It was brought about by the English Sabbatarians who had settled on the borders of Conestoga and Coventry townships and there established a community of their own faith. It was about the same time as the German revival movement, which has just been described, that the English Sabbath-keepers in Newtown, Providence, Easttown and Tredyffrin townships of Chester county became more or less restless, on account of persecutions from their more orthodox neighbors, and migrated to the upper end of the county, where they took up land at the falls of French creek in Nantmill township, and there founded a settlement and congregation, destined for years to be the largest and most influential body of Seventh-Day Baptists in the Province. Among the list of names of these early pioneers, who were mainly Welsh, are to be found quite a few who in later years appear in the Ephrata register, and whose remains await the general call in the old God's-acre at Ephrata.

Following is a partial list of these early Sabbatarians: Owen Roberts, William Iddings [Hiddings], Richard,

Jeremiah, and John Piercell [Piersoll], John Williams, William David, Philip Roger [Rogers], Lewis David, Simon Meredith.

Abel Noble,[41] who is called the Apostle of Sabbatarianism in Pennsylvania, made frequent visits to this settlement on the French creek, upon which occasions he extended his visits to his old friends, Beissel and Wohlfarth, who in turn attended the meetings of the Sabbath-keepers in Nantmill.   It was this intercourse which strengthened our mystics—Beissel and Wohlfarth—of the correctness of the doctrine of the Sabbath.   Thomas Rutter, of Philadelphia, who had been baptized by Bernhard Köster[42] in 1697, also accompanied Noble on several of his visits to our two enthusiasts.   The result was that Beissel and Wohlfarth eventually became the apostles of Sabbatarianism among the German-speaking population in the Province.

The year 1725 passed without any special incident worthy of notice.   The congregation continued to grow in numbers and influence, and the *Chronicon* states : " The Spirit awakened many free souls of both sexes, who began to strive for the knightly crown."   Any amount of controversy was indulged in between the stronger members, mainly on the question of infant baptism and the Sabbath, but this merely added zest to the meetings without impairing their usefulness.

During the year a number of immigrants arrived in the Province who in after years became identified with the Brethren movement in Pennsylvania.   These persons were formerly attached to the Baptist congregation at Crefeldt, and among their number were Abraham Dubois, ————— Luy (*sic*), the widow Becker and her children, and lastly the Eckerling family, consisting of the widow and four stalwart sons, who were destined to prove, next to Beissel,

---

[41] *Vide* German Pietists, p. 126.

[42] *Vide* German Pietists, p. 275.

the most prominent characters in the mystic Camp of the Solitary on the banks of the Cocalico.

The first record we have for the year 1726 is the an-

TYPE AND COSTUME OF EARLY PALATINES.

nouncement that persons of both sexes flocked to hear Beissel. Among the fairer sex were two young women,— Anna and Maria Eicher,—who left their father's house and placed themselves under his guidance. This new departure caused much gossip throughout the community. To prevent any possible scandal the members built a cabin on Mill creek for the two sisters, who were the first to assume a solitary life, and they lived there under the care of Brother Lamech.

The English congregation near the forks of French creek, in Nantmill, also increased in membership and importance. Early in the year 1728 they were joined by a number of seceders from the Great Valley Baptist Church. The leading persons in this migration were: Philip Davis, Lewis Williams, Richard Edwards, Griffy (Griffith) Griffiths and William James. Further accessions followed, and the Nantmill congregation became numerically the strongest in the Province. The intercourse between the Germans in the Conestoga valley, who were inclined towards keeping the Seventh-day, and their English-speaking brethren in Nantmill, was cordial and intimate, and was the means of spreading the doctrine of the Sabbath still more among the Germans south of the Schuylkill.

On Easter Sunday, 1726, a *Liebesmahl* was held at Nägele's, at which a controversy was started upon original sin and purgatory, or, as the account states, the judgments of God. Be this as it may, a heated discussion was indulged in, wherein Daniel Eicher and Heinrich Landes, from Schuylkill, and Hans Meyer took an active part. This controversy caused great trouble among the Brethren, and so affected Heinrich Landes that he soon after died.

During the year 1726, Simon König, who will be remembered as Beissel's companion across the ocean, had surveyed, for himself and two friends, 500 acres of land adjoining that of Hans Graff, so that they might be near the new congregation. It was bought from John Estaugh, attorney for the London Company.[43] The tract was located in Leacock township, and was watered by Mill creek.

---

[43] The tract of land in Lancaster belonging to the London Company, which was laid out about 1727, is described as containing 5571 acres. It extended from the northeast corner of Lancaster Town eastward across both Conestoga and Mill creeks.

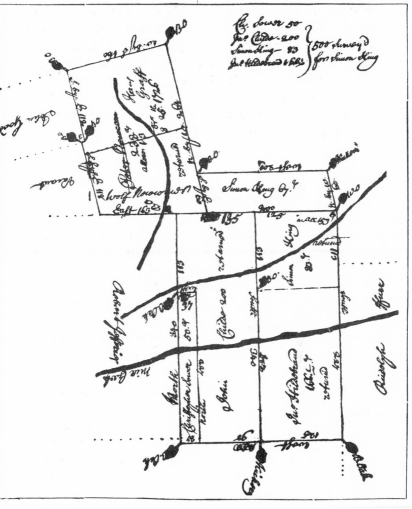

COPY OF TAYLOR'S ORIGINAL PLAN SHOWING 50-ACRE TRACT SURVEYED IN 1726 FOR CHRISTOPHER SAUER, IN MILL CREEK VALLEY, LANCASTER COUNTY.

(Original in collection of the Historical Society of Pennsylvania.)

König at once proceeded to divide his land, as is shown by the original survey, which is still in existence.[44]   Two hundred acres went to Jno. Childs, of whom we have no record.   Johannes Hildebrand, a Baptist from Germantown, got 168½ acres.   König retained eighty-three acres. The remaining fifty were sold to a German tailor who came to this Province in the fall of 1724, and who, after failing to obtain any encouragement at his trade in Germantown, bought a small farm from Simon König and resigned himself to agricultural pursuits.

The name of this humble settler, who came here to the Conestoga valley with his wife and five-year-old son, was Christopher Sauer, who, though unknown to fame at this time, was destined to become a prominent character in both the political and religious sphere of the Germans in Pennsylvania.

His sojourn in the Conestoga valley was undoubtedly the turning-point of his career.   It was due to his intercourse with Conrad Beissel and his associates that this humble journeyman tailor from Laasphe, in Wittgenstein, became the first German printer in America, and through his press wielded an influence among the Sectarians in the Province greater than that of any other person or organization.

He also has the credit of being the second person who made an attempt to publish a German newspaper in America, and the first to be printed with German type and prove a permanent success.   Such parts of his history as come within the scope of this our narrative will often read more like a romance than reality.

Hildebrand, König and Sauer, who settled on their plan-

---

[44] A facsimile is shown on page 125.

tations during the summer, proved a valuable accession, not only to their countrymen in the Conestoga valley, but to the Baptist congregation as well. All were Separatists from Germany, and the differences and discussions which arose among them in this country tended to intensify, if possible, their feelings toward the orthodox forms of worship. This was especially the case with Sauer. Of the three men, Hildebrand, who was a man of more than ordinary education, character and mental strength, was perhaps the most important and influential, and as he had been somewhat of a leader among the Baptists in Germantown, he forthwith assumed an active part in the direction of the Conestoga congregation.

Revival services were held at his house during the fall and winter, and culminated in a love-feast on Christmas Day, to which the whole community were invited. During the afternoon a baptism was held, when six persons,—three brothers and three sisters,—were immersed by Beissel in the icy waters of Mill creek. Among the number were the sisters Anna and Maria Eicher, the two maidens who had left their home and settled on Mill creek to live a life of seclusion and prayer. An apparently well-founded tradition states that on this occasion Christopher Sauer's wife, Maria Christina, was also numbered among the converts who received baptism at the hands of Conrad Beissel.

The year 1727 dawned propitiously and witnessed an increase of membership. There is, however, but little to relate. New differences seemed to arise at almost every revival meeting, but still the work of evangelizing went on. The intercourse with the English Sabbatarian Baptists had its natural effect of leading many of the Germans toward that doctrine, and led to far-reaching results.

The most important event of the year was undoubtedly the meeting held on Whitsunday (May 21, 1727) at the house of Martin Urner at Coventry, which all the congre-

gations within the Province were invited to attend.   This
was really the first general meeting or conference of the
Brethren Church held in America, and was evidently
largely attended.   In the absence of Elder Becker, who
was detained by sickness, Conrad Beissel was obliged to
officiate.

PON this occasion great enthusiasm was manifested.   The multitude was exhorted by Beissel, Hildebrand, Wohlfarth and other revivalists.   Deep impressions were made upon
the hearers, and many were converted.   According to the *Chronicon*: "On this occasion quite extraordinary powers of eternity manifested themselves, such as
were never known before or after, so that it was called the
congregation's Pentecost."   In the afternoon eleven converts were immersed in the Schuylkill by Beissel.   This
was followed in the evening with a love-feast and breaking
of bread.   The meetings were continued during the next
day (*Pfingst-Montag*) with equal success.

This revival, the most important one thus far held in the
Province, is noteworthy for two special features.   First, it
was upon this occasion that Beissel first proved his great
power as an exhorter and independent religious leader.   It
was here that the Germantown Brethren commenced to
realize that Beissel was far stronger as a leader than Elder
Peter Becker, and would soon dispute with him the leadership of the Brethren.   The other feature was the introduction of antiphonal or choral singing into the services of the
simple worship of the Brethren.   Here was the inception
of the music and hymnology which, fostered by Conrad
Beissel, proved in after years so important a feature in the
Ephrata Community as to attract the attention of the
musical critics of the Old World.   Our record states:
"The singing was pentecostal and heavenly; yea, some
declared that they heard angel voices mingling with it."

But the chronicler naively adds : "Of which the reader has liberty to judge for himself." However, the hymnology of both the Brethren and Sabbatarians dates from this meeting and developed rapidly in the Western World, where it now numbers hundreds of hymns and melodies.

The religious activity among the German settlers at this eventful period was not confined alone to the German Baptists. Strenuous efforts were being made by those of the Orthodox faiths to obtain regular pastors from Germany. Even the Mennonites—recognizing the new condition of things in the Province and the necessity for providing for the coming generations and to spread their peculiar doctrines among their English-speaking neighbors—had printed an English translation of their confession of faith. A collation of this title reads :

" *THE | CHRISTIAN | Confession | Of the Faith of the harmless | Christians, in the Ne | therlands, known by | the name of Mennonites. | Amsterdam | Printed, and Reprinted and Sold by | Andrew Bradford in Philadelphia, | in the year 1727.*"

Collation : Title, 1 leaf ; Preface, pp. (2) ; Confession, pp. 5-40. 16mo.

This book was supplemented by another, somewhat of a historical nature, of 44 pages, under following title :

"*An—Appendix | to the | Confession of Faith | Of the Christians, called, | Mennonists. | Giving | A short and full Account of them ; because | of the Immagination of the Newness of | our Religion, the Weapon and Revenge | less Christendom, and its being. | Published formerly in Low-Dutch, and translated | out of the same into High-Dutch, and out | of that into the English Language, 1725 | Philadelphia : Printed by Andrew Bradford in the Year | 1727.*"

Upon the reverse of the title page appears the curious note :

The

Chriſtian

CONFESSION

Of the Faith of the harmleſs
Chriſtians, in the *Ne-
therlands*, known by
the name of

MENNONISTS.

A M S T E R D A M:
Printed, and Re-printed and Sold by
Andrew Bradford in *Philadelphia*,
in the Year, 1727.

TITLE-PAGE OF MENNONITE CONFESSION.

(Original in Historical Society of Pennsylvania.)

AN
APPENDIX
TO THE
CONFESSION of FAITH

Of the Christians, called,

MENNONISTS:
GIVING

A short and full Account of them; because
of the Immagination of the Newness of
our Religion, the Weapon and Revenge-
less Christendom, and its being.

Published

Formerly in the *Low-Dutch*, and translated
out of the same into *High-Dutch*, and out
of that into the *English* Language, 1725.

PHILADELPHIA:
Printed by *Andrew Bradford*, in the Year
1727.

"TO THE CHRISTIAN READER.

" We lovingly desire thee, not to look so much on the
" meanness of the wording of this little Book ; because we
" are of Dutch Extraction, and therefore willingly will
" own, that we are not exquisete in the English Language ;
" but to look on the Grounds and Truths therein : And
" also kindly desire thee to Read the Same without Parti-
" ality ; and consider the Exhortation of the Apostle Paul,
" 1 Thes. 5.21.   Prove all things, hold fast that which is
" good."

At the end of the book is printed the statement :

" We the hereunder written Servants of the Word of
" God, and Elders in the Congregation of the People
" called, *Mennonists*, in the Province of *Pennsylvania*, do
" acknowledge, and herewith make known, That we do
" own the afore-going *Confession*, *Appendix* and Menno's
" Excusation, to be according to Our Opinion ; and also,
" have took the same to be wholly ours.   In Testimony
" whereof, and that we believe the same to be good, we
" have hereunto Subscribed our Names.

" SHIPACK	" CANASTOGE
" Jacob Gaedtschalck	" Hans Burgholtzer
" Henry Kolb	" Christian Heer
" Martin Kolb	" Benedict Hirchi
" Claes Jansen	" Martin Bear
" Michael Ziegler	" Johannes Bowman
" GERMANTOWN	" GREAT-SWAMP
" John Gorgas	" Velte Clemer
" John Conerads	" MANATANY
" Glaes Rittinghausen	" Daniel Langenecker
	" Jacob Beghtly.

The two books were issued in separate form, as well as
bound in one.   They are now extremely rare and afford us
a valuable insight to what straights our German ancestors
were placed to set themselves in the proper light before

MENNONITE MEETING HOUSE, GERMANTOWN.

the community. The special object of the Mennonites in publishing these books in the English language was to show the Quakers that they were in accord with them as a peaceful body of Christians. Further, that they had no affiliation with the other sects, which were then organizing active revivals throughout the three counties. A fac-simile of the title-pages of these extremely rare books are given upon opposite pages (130, 131).

At this time (1727) the chief question which agitated the leaders of the Conestoga congregation was that in reference to the Sabbath. A movement by which they antagonized the Mennonites, as well as those of the Ortho-dox faiths. While Beissel, Wohlfarth and several others adhered strictly to the Sabbath, others decided in favor of the Lord's Day, while some favored the observance of both days. Among the latter was Johannes Hildebrand, who held that Christians should remain passive on the Sabbath, abstaining from all labor and communing with God in spirit. Upon the Lord's Day the public religious services should be held. These propositions did not meet with the approval of Beissel and his adherents, and eventually wrought a temporary rupture between the two leaders.

Three months after the above occurrences (it was after the harvest was gathered, August, 1727) a grand visitation was made by the Germantown congregation to the Brethren of Conestoga. A series of general meetings was projected, to be held at the house of Heinrich Höhn, but they proved anything but harmonious. The disturbing circumstances were as follows : On the journey to Conestoga two of the Brethren, Stephen Koch and Heinrich Traut, went to see Stumpf, who, it will be remembered, occupied the cabin of Beissel at the *Schwedenquelle*. After the latter's departure Stumpf married his cousin, for which act he was disowned by the congregation. The two German revivalists, how-ever, extended to him the hand of fellowship and the kiss of charity, and urged him to accompany them to the meeting at Höhn's. Here Stumpf, who was mentally unbalanced, caused great excitement by imitating the action of various animals and shrieking amidst terrible contortions, and as he could not be pacified he had to be restrained.

At the meeting upon the following day Beissel preached a sermon against the unrighteousness of Christians who kept persons in servitude, fortifying his statements with quotations from the New Testament. This was evidently aimed at Peter Becker, to whom Beissel had formerly indentured himself, and who, it appears, forced Beissel to indemnify him for some unexpired time before he would cancel the indenture. This berating so affected Peter Becker that he became sick and was taken to Hildebrand's house, where he remained for some time.

The result of this meeting was to widen the breach already existing between the Germantown Baptists and the Conestoga congregation, which in turn divided itself into two factions: one under Beissel, who kept the Sabbath; the other, of such as adhered to the Lord's Day or Sunday, who acknowledged Johannes Hildebrand as their elder. Numerically the Sabbatarians were the stronger in the Conestoga congregation. Messengers or evangelists were now sent out by the *Beisselianer*, as they were called by their opponents, to the various German settlements to preach the doctrine of the Sabbath,—an aggressive course which had been decided by Beissel, and was at once put into execution.

The most successful of these missions began in the fall of 1727, and it extended from Falkner swamp to Oley. It was under the leadership of Michael Wohlfarth, assisted by three other brethren. So successful was this mission that Beissel was sent for to baptize the converts. The first immersion took place on March 8, 1728, when eleven candidates were baptized, among whom was Andreas Frey, who was appointed elder of the new congregation. Five more were added toward the end of May.

The year 1728 was designed to be an important one for the German Sabbatarian congregation, as it brought about a complete severance from the parent stem, and the foundation was laid for the future community of the Cocalico.

Among the noteworthy occurrences was the conversion of one of the four Eckerling brothers, who in later years all became leading spirits in the Ephrata community. It was upon the advice of Michael Wohlfarth that the widow Eckerling sold her plantation at Germantown, and of Conrad Matthäi that two or three of the sturdy sons came to the Conestoga valley in August, 1727, where at least one of the brothers, Israel, hired himself to Christopher Sauer as an ordinary farm hand. It was Sauer who first introduced the Eckerlings to Beissel and the meetings presided over by him. The result was that on the following Whitsunday (June 9, 1728) Israel Eckerling, his master, Christian Sauer, and Jacob Gass were baptized by Beissel and admitted into the congregation.[45] An extended notice of the Eckerling family will be given in its proper place.

The strict observance of the Sabbath amongst the congregation, together with the obedience to the command, " Six days shalt thou labor," soon led to some friction with the civil authorities, who were either English Quakers or Churchmen, and had little sympathy with the revivals or awakenings among the German population. The intercourse with the English Brethren on French creek and Newtown became more frequent, and Abel Noble, Thomas Rutter and ———— Welsh were welcome visitors to Beissel's cabin on the Mühlbach. The tenets of the Seventh-day advocates were further spread by the use of that powerful aid of civilization, the printing-press. An

---

[45] *Chronicon Ephratense*, original edition, chap. vi, p. 34.

extended account of this departure of Beissel will form the basis for the next chapter.

During the year German emigration to the Province had assumed proportions so large as to again excite the fears of the government and cause Governor Gordon to appeal to the home authorities for protection against this influx of Palatines. The result of this appeal was made known in his speech at the opening of the Provincial House of Representatives, December 17, 1728, wherein he states :

" What relates to the necessary Provision for the Exigen-
"cies of the Government, with other matters that may
"require your Attention, I shall leave to your own Con-
"sideration, and as any thing further occurs, it shall be
"communicated to you by Messages. Only I must make
"use of this first Opportunity to acquaint you, that I have
"now positive Orders from Britain to provide by a proper
"Law against those Crowds of Forreigners, who are yearly
"powr'd in upon us, of which the late Assembly took
"Notice, in a Message to me of the 18th of *April* last :
"Nor does this arise, as I conceive, from any Dislike to
"the People themselves, many of whom we know are
"peaceable, industrious and well affected, but it seems
"principally intended to prevent an English Plantation
"being turned into a Colony of Aliens. It may also re-
"quire our Thoughts to prevent the Importation of *Irish*
"*Papists* and *Convicts*, of whom some of the most notori-
"ous, I am credibly informed, have of late been landed in
"the River."

This speech was printed and scattered as a broadside throughout the Province. Nothing, however, could stop the influx of the steady stream of sturdy German bone and muscle : Acts of Assembly, proclamations, speeches and broadsides were equally impotent ; and even before the expiration of Gov. Gordon's term German influence be-

The S P E E C H

Of the Honourable

PATRICK GORDON, Eſq;

Lieut. Governour of the Province of

PENNSYLVANIA,

And Counties of *New-Caſtle Kent* and *Suſſex,* upon *Delaware,*

**To the Repreſentatives of the Freemen of the ſaid Province
met at *Philadelphia, December* 17th, 1728.**

came an important factor in the settlement and development of the Province.

The closing months of the year 1728 were turbulent ones for the Brethren in the Conestoga valley. Johannes Hildebrand and his followers, Hans Landes, Heinrich Höhn, Daniel Eicher, Hans Rolande and Luis, encouraged by Elder Becker, became quite aggressive in their opposition to the Beissel party, who kept the Seventh-day. This animosity tended to widen the breach between the parent congregation and its daughter, until within a few months it ended in a complete rupture. The *Chronicon*, in commenting upon affairs in the month of December, 1728, states :

"About this time the power of God manifested itself "palpably in the meetings, witnessing against the old " Adam and his many false sanctuaries ; whereat many were " offended and separated themselves from the congregation. " These Separatists, like men sick with the plague, finally " banded together and set up a meeting of their own ; so " that in those times there were more apostles than there " were righteous ones, which, however, by no means con- " founded the superintendent, for he had reckoned on all " these, and yet worse quarreling, when he left his beloved " solitary state and waded into the sea of humanity."

The Germantown Baptists now reproached Beissel for his ingratitude toward them, as it was at their hands that he had received baptism. This, instead of rallying him, only tended to increase his vehemence against his former friends. At the same time he was forced to acknowledge the truth of their argument. How to overcome this dilemma was a serious question. At last, however, a way was found out of the difficulty, which was worked to their own satisfaction. This was the novel proposition to renounce the Becker baptism and return it to the old congregation, and then to have such of the *Beisselianer* as had been immersed by Becker rebaptized. This strange scene was enacted toward the close of December, evidently in the Mühlbach or the Conestoga. Upon the appointed day a general meeting of the Sabbatarians was held, during which three brothers and four sisters were selected for the chief ceremony. It had been decided that it was proper for the Sabbatical number to be the foundation of the re-baptized congregation. The number seven and the two sexes were therefore chosen. According to the teachings of the Rosicrucians the number seven represents the union of the square and the triad, and is considered the Divine number, in the same sense in which forty is the perfect numeral. Jan Meyle and Beissel were the first to enter the icy water; special hymns were sung, and after an invocation, in which both men renounced their former baptism, Meyle immersed Beissel thrice backwards, and immediately afterwards repeated the operation thrice forwards, thus baptizing the candidate. Beissel then repeated the same ceremony upon Meyle and the others in turn. This act completed the separation between the Germantown and Conestoga Baptists.

An incident which happened during the same month closes our record for the year. Peter Beller,[46] a German or Swiss settler near the Pequea, had a very sick daughter, who had heard of Beissel and the religious revivals held in the vicinity. At the request of the girl the parents were induced to send for him. This was during the night, and when the messenger arrived at Beissel's cabin he was at his devotions, praying for the entire Christian church. Beissel at once went to Beller's house and prayed with the sick girl, who was rapidly failing and desired baptism before she died. Beissel was willing to accede to her wish, night though it was, as he felt that not only her soul, but

---

[46] Peter Beller was an early settler in the Conestoga country. His name appears among the list of taxables as early as 1718.

her life as well, might be saved thereby.   But to be effective the immersion would have to be in flowing water.   To this the parents objected, yet the condition of the patient was such that no time was to be lost.   So Beissel bowed to the wishes of the parents, but expressed his doubts as to the efficacy of the rite thus administered.

Preparations were now made without delay.   It was a scene worthy of the pencil of a Teniers : the small chamber, with its rude furnishings, furtively lit by a few dripping candles, which threw their fitful shadows over the scene ; the bed in the corner with its pallid patient ; the weeping family, and the austere figure of Beissel, with a few sympathetic neighbors in the background.   During Beissel's fervent prayer a scalding-tub, such as is used upon a farm in butchering swine, was rolled into the room, and then filled with cold water.   When full the sick girl was lifted from her bed into the tub, wherein she kneeled. Thrice were buckets full of water thrown over her head, as she could not be entirely immersed in the tub.   She was then again lifted into her bed and carefully covered with a feather bed.   A hymn closed the services, which had extended well into the next day.

The young girl after her baptism requested that a religious meeting be held in her presence at the house upon the next Sabbath.   This request was acceded to by Beissel. Upon the next Sabbath a large congregation assembled at Peter Beller's humble house, the meeting was opened at the appointed time, and the young girl was present, but in her coffin.   The meeting was a funeral.   The circumstances attending her death so deeply moved the parents that they both asked to be baptized.

CHAPTER X.

THE CRADLE OF GERMAN LITERATURE.

ERETOFORE we have known Conrad Beissel and Michael Wohlfarth merely as two religious enthusiasts, erratic and peculiar, —often, it may be said, visionary schemers; yet, with all their shortcomings and the delusions of their followers, it is a remarkable and strange fact that German printing in America was ushered in by these same pious evangelists; call them erratic visionaries if you will, but the fact remains the same.

While credit is undoubtedly due to the Pietists—headed by Kelpius, Köster, Selig and the Falkner brothers who settled on the Wissahickon—for the sporadic attempts made to use the printing-press in their descriptive and controversial literature in Dutch, German and English, it was left to their legitimate successors—headed by Conrad Beissel—to inaugurate a new era of Christianity and to use the local printing-press in disseminating the views and doctrine of the congregation. The attempt ended in the establishment of a press of their own at Ephrata,—the first in the western world to print with the accustomed type of both the English and German language.

How early Beissel sought to obtain the use of a printing-press for the purpose of spreading his peculiar views is shown by the imprint upon the title-pages here reproduced. To him is due the credit of issuing the second original American book which was printed in both the German and English languages.[47b]

The early works—controversial, mystical and poetical— were Pennsylvania products in the fullest sense of the word, as they were composed and translated here in the Conestoga valley ; or, coming down still closer, we may designate the valley of the Mühlbach, in Lancaster county, as the cradle of German literature in America.   How intimately this fertile valley is connected with the German-American press will be further recognized by the fact that from it, after a sojourn of some five years, emerged the German tailor-farmer Christopher Sauer, and started his press in Germantown, the first in America to print with German characters.

Considerable credit is evidently due to both Beissel and Wohlfarth in bringing about the determination of Sauer to engage in a trade then entirely foreign to him, yet in which he became so prominent in after years.   Then, again, the first substantial encouragement received by the Germantown printer was a commission from Conrad Beissel for a hymn-book of some eight hundred pages.

The first work issued by Conrad Beissel was, according to the *Chronicon*, *Das Büchlein von Sabbath* (a book on the Sabbath).   It was an octavo in German, printed with Roman type by Andrew Bradford in Philadelphia, 1728.

Strange as it will appear, the above may not have been the first or original edition of this curious work, as Dr. William M. Fahnestock, in a communication made to the Seventh-day Baptist Publication Society,[47] at Plainfield, N. J., December, 1852, mentions a German copy of the *Mystyrion Anomias* in his possession, and distinctly states that

---

[47b] Vide *German Pietists*, pp. 266, 296–97.

[47] Reply to Elder James Bailey.

it was written and published by Beissel in the year 1725, while he still belonged to the regular Dunker congregation and lived in his cabin on the Mühlbach, and that it was the publication of this "truly forcible and truly remarkable" tract which caused his separation from that body.

No copy of either of the above versions are known to exist, although there is a bare possibility that Dr. Fahnestock's copy may still be preserved by some member of that family. The German title was: [48]

MYSTYRION ANOMIAS. | *Das* | *GEHEIMNISS der UNGERECHTIGKEIT* | *oder der* | *BOSSHAF-TIGE WIDER–CHRIST* | *Entdeckt u Enthüllt* | *Bezeu-gend dass alle diegenigen zu dem* | *Gottlosen Wider-Christ angehören, die* | *bereitwillig die Gebothe Gottes verwerfen* | *unter welchen ist sein heiliges, und* | *von ihn selbst eingesetzer SIEBEN–Täger SABBATH* | *oder seine heilige Ruhe von welcher derselbe* | *ein Vorbild ist.* | *DEN SO SPRICHT DER HERR. Exod. xx. v. 10* | *Der Sie-bende Tag ist der SABBATH der Herrn* | *deines GOTTES.* | *Geschrieben zu der Ehre des Grossen GOT-TES* | *und seine Heilige Gebothe* | *von* | *CONRAD BEISSEL* | *Gedruckt im Jahr 1728.*

This book caused a great sensation among the Germans in the rural districts, and was eventually translated into English by Beissel's trusty companion, Michael Wohlfarth, Beissel being but an indifferent English scholar. The English version, printed in 1729, was also done by Andrew Bradford at Philadelphia It was an octavo of thirty-two pages. One of these was the title; one, scriptural texts; three, *to the Reader;* twenty-six, text.

Mystyrion Anomias | *the* | *Mystery of Lawlesness:* | *or,* | *Lawless ANTICHRIST* | *discover'd and Disclos'd,* | *Shewing that all those do belong to that* | *Lawless Antichrist, who wilfully reject* | *the Commandments of God, amongst* |

---

[48] Title from an old German manuscript.

MYSTYRION ANOMIAS

THE

Myſtery of Lawleſneſs:

OR,

Lawleſs *ANTICHRIST*

DISCOVER'D and DISCLOS'D

Shewing that ALL thoſe do belong to that Lawleſs *Antichriſt*, who wilfully reject the Commandments of GOD, amongſt which, is his holy, and by himſelf bleſſed *Seventh-Day-Sabbath*, or his holy Reſt, of which the ſame is a Type.

For thus ſaith the Lord, *Exod.* xx. ver. 10.

The Seventh Day is the Sabbath of the Lord thy God.

Written to the Honour of the Great GOD and his Holy Commands.

By *CUNRAD BETSELL.*

Tranſlated out of the High-Dutch, *by* M. W.

Printed in the Year 1729

TITLE-PAGE OF THE ENGLISH VERSION OF BEISSEL'S SABBATH-BOOK.

(Original in collection of Julius F. Sachse, Philadelphia.)

which, is his holy, and by himself blessed | Seventh-Day-Sabbath, or his holy Rest, | of which the same is a Type. | For thus saith the Lord, Exod. xx. ver. 10. | The Seventh Day is the Sabbath of the | Lord thy God. | Written to the Honour of the Great God | and his Holy Commands. | By Cunrad Beysell. | Translated out of the High-Dutch, by M. W. | Printed in the Year 1729.

The chief part of the title of this curious work was taken from Martin Luther's annotations to the second chapter of Second Thessalonians, verse seven. To this was added a part of the tenth verse of the twentieth chapter of Exodus. The reverse of the title-page contained six scriptural texts: Psalm 119–126; Psalm 89 : 30–34; Isa. 24 : 15; Rom. 2 : 12; Psalm 110 : 96. Then follows the preface. There is a very curious feature in this introduction "To the Reader," as in it Beissel sets forth that, in order to conform strictly to apostolic usage, all truth to be proclaimed to the world must first be made known unto men by word of mouth, and after its delivery may then be written or printed. This plan Beissel adhered to throughout his whole career, all his epistles and *Lectionen* having been first delivered in public. The body of the book is written in a colloquial style as a spiritual dialogue between a father and son. Its whole trend is an exposition of the true Sabbath, which here gets sharply mixed with the anti-Christ.

However curious the work appears to us at the present day, it seems to have been successful in its mission in both tongues. Our records tell us that it was "so effective that the congregations now publickly adopted the Sabbath as the day for divine services."

The editions of the *Sabbath Book* are the scarcest among the issues of the American press. They are so rare that they are not enumerated in any catalogue or list of American imprints. In fact, they were absolutely unknown to bibliographers until the present copy was brought to their notice by the writer.

This copy, of which the title-page is reproduced in fac-simile, was found bound up in a volume of tracts upon the Sabbath by R. Cornthwaite, of London, and bears the book-plate of Henry Gurney, Esq., of Philadelphia.

Beissel's preface *To the Reader* is here reproduced in full, as it conveys the best idea of his rhetoric and style at the outset of his eventful career :

"To the Reader.

" Kind Reader, Whosoever thou art, thou must know, that according to the Mind of the Spirit, it is not Apostolical to publish any Truth to the World, before it is made known unto Men by Word of Mouth, as it is to be seen by the Apostles. Wherefore we have followed them in this ; and that knowledge of Truth in us, (bestowed by God,) concerning the Rest of God, typifyed in the Seventh-Day-Sabbath, together with other Truths to us made known in the Light of God, seriously and with that Ability which God bestoweth, have laid open some Years before Men : Whilst we do and know, that the Time is near at Hand, wherein God the Truth, in which the first Christians did live in, will set on the Candlestick again, and that Whore, which has long bore the Name of Christ's Bride, shall be destroyed, together with her false Doctrine and Commandments of Men. And because many Contradictions and Gainsayings have appeared against the Truth, and espe-cially against the Seventh-Day-Sabbath, or the Rest of God, and that mostly by them who do pretend to be clear of the Whore and her Cup, whereby the Truth is often dreadfully wronged: For which Reason now, we have found it neces-sary, to write this Truth, and deliver it to the Press, so that we may not hide God's Work nor Council, neither draw any Judgment of silence upon us, since the time draweth near, that God will glorify his Rest.

" We do not seek for Contention, nor to quarrel with any Body; for Christendom (so called) is filled with it already. We do therefore say, If any Body has a Mind to quarrel, let him know, that the Church of God never hath that Custom. Neither do we want to fight with Letters, for we know very well, that the sharp and subtil Reason of Men, can magisterially pervert God's holy and simple Truth, and explain the Words of God after her crooked Serpentine Will. But we lay open the divine Truths (as we know them in the Light of God) before Men. He that can and may perceive, let him perceive; but he that will not, has it to himself; but let such a one know, that God in his own Time shall defend his Honour, and take Vengeance on his Enemies, and on the Enemies of his holy rest.

" Furthermore, we find it very necessary to mention this yet, that by no means any body take us, or understand us after this Manner, as if we were of such Mind, to believe, that every body is a Christian, that doth but keep the Seventh-Day ; far be it, for we have not learned Christ after such a Manner : For we do believe that this Commandment of the Sabbath doth not touch an unconverted Heathen, or Nominal Christian, because he doth not stand in the Rest or in the Peace with God. Wherefore we do testify, that, if any body will be Partaker of the true Rest and Peace with God, and also take Rest here with the People of God on the Seventh-Day, as a Type of Eternal Rest, that the same must truly repent, and withdraw with all his Heart and whole Mind from all Vanity, and Love of Creatures, and from all Worldly and carnal or fleshly Desire whatsoever, and turn with his whole Heart and Mind to God, to enter totally in that simple or mean, (and before the World,) despised Doctrine of Jesus Christ, to give himself over with perfect Obedience into the same, in denying of the World, yea, of himself, and of all his own Will and seeking; to live wholly and solely up to Jesus Christ, and thus he shall obtain Peace with God in Christ Jesus. Then and no sooner he shall taste and experience what it is to love God, and then that Love of God will constrain him to love God's Commandments, and to keep them with Christ and his Apostles, and with all true Believers. Then the Seventh-Day shall be called a delightful Sabbath unto the Lord, when he shall do with Love and Delight all the same things that are demanded of a true Sabbath-keeper, Esa. 58. ver. 1, &c.

" Here now, thou canst perceive our whole Mind briefly. Be

thou recommended unto the Grace of the Almighty. May the Lord be pleased, according to his Promises, to pour out of his Spirit upon all Flesh, that many, many may come to the Knowledge of Truth, which is in Christ Jesus, and that the Whore together with Antichrist, may soon be destroyed, that not so many poor Souls may be deceived any longer, whom the false Teachers make believe, that themselves and they also are Christians, whereas they do live worse than Moral Jews or Gentiles,

'' Read and Consider.''

ICHAEL WOHLFARTH also published at this time, upon his own account, the pamphlet in both German and English, having for its theme the "Lord's Seventh Day." The immediate motive for its issue was the result of a series of political changes in the Province.

In the year 1729 Lancaster county was formed from a part of Chester county. This new division included the Conestoga and Pequea valleys, while Nantmill and Coventry remained part of Chester county. The officials of the new county were no sooner installed than they began what might be called a crusade against the Sabbath-keepers, who not only obeyed the scriptural injunction to keep the Seventh Day holy, but also complied with the remainder of the command, "Six days shalt thou labor." This resulted in a number of the Sabbatarians being arrested and imprisoned, upon their refusal to pay the imposed fine. This persecution, however, had an effect contrary to what was intended by the authorities, as the Sabbatarians were only urged thereby to more firmly uphold their religious principles, all being ready to suffer for their faith.

In consequence of this unwarranted action of the civil authorities, Beissel, Wohlfarth and another brother made a pilgrimage afoot, staff in hand, to Philadelphia to in-

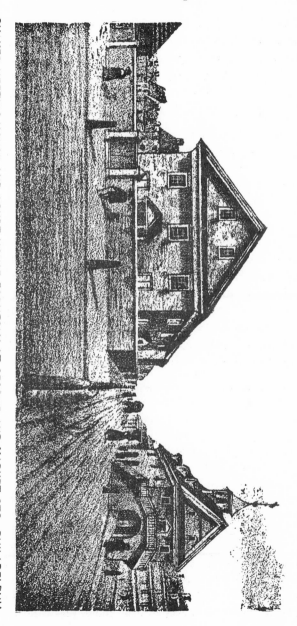

QUAKER MEETING-HOUSE AND COURT-HOUSE FORMERLY AT SECOND AND MARKET STS., PHILADELPHIA.

SHOWING BALCONY FROM WHICH THE GERMAN REVIVALISTS ADDRESSED THE POPULACE.

tercede for their brethren.   While upon this mission they
attended a Quaker meeting on the 19th of October, and
after listening to a long testimony from a woman Friend,
Wohlfarth, who was the best English scholar among the
German Sabbatarians, arose and delivered a lengthy exhortation after the following introduction :

" My friends,—I beseech you that you listen to me, for I
have a message to you from the Lord.   Therefore I demand
that you listen to me, for I shall not leave this spot until I
have delivered the message with which I have been sent unto
you, so that I may appear without blame before my Lord, and
may thus go hence in peace."

This was spoken with earnestness ; the quaint gestures
and appearance of the speaker from the first commanded
close attention.   In the lengthy address which followed,
Wohlfarth earnestly and forcibly called attention to the
necessity of keeping the Seventh Day holy, prophesying
dire troubles in case his pleadings and message from the
Lord were left unheeded.   He closed his earnest harangue
with the following exhortation :

" O therefore! All ye People, Tongues and Nations, that
hear these Words, turn to the true God ; worship no longer
Gods which are the Works of Man's Hands, and of human in-
vention; be not longer deceived; the Light of God shineth very
clear in these latter Days wherein God maketh known his
Truth again, which has been many Years hidden, viz., the low,
mean and despised Doctrine of Jesus, and of his holy, and of the
World rejected Life, which has been hitherto desolate, having
very few Followers, it being a very narrow Path to walk in,
and a straight Gate to enter at; therefore all the World doth
despise it, as a poor Widow that hath no Husband, and is
desolate, nor no body to defend and protect it; but the Children of this World have Protection enough, and are well fed and
maintained, and defended in their vain Worship.   But let me
tell you, the Time is very near at Hand, that God will destroy

the Worshippers of Images, and break in Pieces the Strength of the *Chemarims*, and black Money-Priests, and send out true Labourers into his Harvest. O happy are they that take Notice of the Signs of these Times, and draw back their Ears from Lying, and turn to the low and despised Truth; for it begins to shine forth very bright and clear, and I hope will be enflamed more and more by the Spirit of Jesus Christ, that all Gentiles and Nominal Christians shall clearly see it, and give Glory to the Lord. Therefore repent truly, with all your Hearts; come to the right Fear of God; begin to love him, and keep his Commands with all your Souls, Mind and Strength; enter into the holy Doctrine and Life of Jesus Christ; follow him, and learn of him to obey God, and to do his Will; forsake the World; deny your selves; take the Cross of Jesus upon you, and learn of him to become meek and lowly of Heart; strive and labour hard in the Grace of God, to overcome your old Nature, and become new Men, spiritually minded, and Partakers of the divine Nature; for except being thus renewed, it is in vain for you to imagine that you be Christians. This I tell you as a Word of Truth; then you shall find Rest for your Souls. Now I wish every one of you that is willing to forsake the Vanity of this World, both spiritual and natural, and to serve God in Purity of Heart, Grace, Love and Peace from the only God, the Father of our Lord Jesus Christ, remaining a Lover of all Mankind, desiring your Welfare and Happiness.''

This address, which was immediately put into print in both the German and English languages, caused much discussion, and brought forth several pamphlets *pro* and *con* in both languages, two of which fortunately have come down to us. We have a single copy of Wohlfarth's address (English version) and an answer by John Meredith, also unique. The full titles of the German and English versions are :

Die | ENTBLÖSTE WAHRHEIT | Widerstehend alle Geschminkte und | verkleidete | LÜGEN,—BETRUG u FALSCHHEIT | oder des | HERRN SIEBEN | TÄGER–SABBATH—Stehend wie ein Fels unbeweglig

THR

NAKED TRUTH,

Standing againſt all Painted and Diſguiſed

Lies, Deceit and *Ealſhood.*

OR THE

Lord's Seventh-Day-Sabbath

Standing as a MOUNTAIN immove-
able for ever.

*Proved by Three WITNESSES which
cannot Lie.*

By M. W.

Printed in the Year, 1729,

A SHORT

DISCOURSE,

Proving that the

Jewish or *Seventh-Day Sabbath*

Is Abrogated and Repealed.

By *JOHN MEREDITH.*

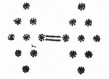

PHILADELPHIA:

Printed and Sold at the New PRINTING-OFFICE,
in *High-Street*, near the Market. **1729.**

TITLE-PAGE OF MEREDITH'S REPLY TO THE SABBATARIAN TRACTS OF BEISSEL
AND WOHLFARTH,

(Original in Lenox Library, New York.)

*für Ewig | Bewiesen durch DREI Zeugen wo nicht |
Lügen können | von M. W. | Gedruckt zu im Jahr 1729.*

*The | Naked Truth, | Standing against all Painted and
Disguised | Lies, Deceit and Falshood, | or the | Lord's
Seventh-Day-Sabbath | Standing as a Mountain immove- |
able for ever. | Proved by Three Witnesses which | cannot
Lie. | By M. W. | Printed in the year, 1729.*

The remarks about Beissel's *Sabbath Book* apply to this
also.   Both works stand unique in the list of American
imprints and bibliography.

During the remainder of their stay in Philadelphia,
Wohlfarth and Beissel, together with Abel Noble, addressed
the populace from the Court House steps, the three men
joining in giving their testimony as to the truth of the
Sabbatarian doctrine, and at the same time calling upon
them to repent and change their ways ere it would be too
late.

Among those attracted to the meetings held by the three
evangelists was the young printer, Benjamin Franklin.
Conrad Beissel, with quick perception and knowledge of
mankind, at once surmised that Franklin would be of
great service to him, provided he could be induced to join
them in their movement of evangelization.   A means of
communication between the two men was soon found, and
resulted in business relations, which were maintained until
the German presses were set up at Germantown and
Ephrata.

The printing of the *Book on the Sabbath* by Bradford
had been unsatisfactory, and Keimer, the other printer,
was cranky and even more impecunious.   In Franklin,
Conrad Beissel found an intelligent assistant, willing to
print his works and issue them in a creditable manner, both
as to typography and proof-reading.   Upon the other hand,
the young printer was vouchsafed encouragement of a substantial character.

DER
IN DER AMERICANI-
SCHEN WILDNUSZ
Inter Menschen von verschiedenen

Nationen und Religionen

Hin und wieder herum Wandelte

Und verschiedentlich Angefochtene

PREDIGER,
Abgemahlet und vorgestellet

In einem Gespraech mit Einem

Politico und *Neubevarenen,*

Verschiedene Stuck insonderheit

Die *Neugeburt* betreffende,

Verfertiget, und zu Beforderung der Ehr

JESU
Selbst aus eigener Erfahrung an das

Licht gebracht

Von Georg. Michael Weiss V. D. M.

Zu *PHILADELPHIA.*
Gedruckt bey *Andrew Bradfordt,* 1729.

TITLE-PAGE OF THE FIRST GERMAN REFORMED BOOK PRINTED IN AMERICA.

(Original in Library of Congress, Washington, D. C.)

Strange as it may appear, it is an undeniable fact that the German mystic and enthusiast, Conrad Beissel, was among the earliest, if not the first, patron of the Franklin press, as well as of Christopher Sauer's.

Beissel and Wohlfarth, in the early day, it appears, were not alone in the field of German literature; there was another pioneer in the field, who in point of time was but a trifling distance behind the two enthusiastic pioneers. This was Rev. George Michael Weiss, the Reformed minister, who in 1729 published a pamphlet against the Separatists,; it was chiefly aimed against Bauman and his followers, the Newborn, of whom we have already spoken.[49]

Like many of the religious books of that period it was written in the colloquial style. This, too, is one of the rarest of our American imprints, a single specimen only being known.[50]

It has the additional distinction of being, so far as we know at present, the first German Reformed book printed in America in the German language.[51]

The little book is a duodecimo, and contains, beside the title, four pages of introduction and twenty-nine pages of text. The title reads:

Der | In Der Americani- | Schen Wildnusz | Inter Menchen von verschiedenen | Nationen uud Religionen | Hin und wieder herum Wandelte | Und verschiedentlich Angefochtene | Prediger, | Abgemahlet und vorgestellet | In einem Gespraech mit Einen | Politico und Neugeborenen | Verschiedene Stuck insonderlich | Die Neugebirt betreffende, | Verfertiget, und zu Beforderung der Ehr | Jesu | Selbst aus eigener Erfahrung an das | Licht

---

[49] See chapter vii *supra.*

[50] For an account of the efforts made by Rev. W. J. Hinke to locate this copy see *Reformed Church Messenger*, March 9-16, 1899.

[51] A book written in the Dutch language by Rev. John Lydius, a Dutch Reformed minister, was published at Albany as early as the year 1700. The only known copy is in the collection of Hon. Samuel W. Pennypacker.

DUNKER MEETING HOUSE, GERMANTOWN.

OLD MEETING HOUSE BUILT 1770.   NEW CHURCH DEDICATED MAY, 1897,

PHOTO. BY J. F. SACHSE, APRIL, 1899.

gebracht | Von Georg Michael Weiss V. D. M. | Zu Phila-
delphia : | Gedruckt bey Andrew Bradfordt, 1729.

Translation :

The | in the Ameri- | can Wilderness | Among People of
Divers | Nationalities and Religions | Hither and Thither
Wandering | And Variously Tempted | Minister | Por-
trayed & Presented | In a Dialogue with one | Politician
and Newborn | Various Subjects Particularly | Concerning
the Newborn | Drawn up, and to the Furtherance of the
Honor of | Jesus | Personally from our Experience now
Brought to the Light. | By Georg Michael Weiss V. D. M.
| at Philadelphia. | Printed by Andrew Bradford, 1729.

From this curious booklet we get a further insight into
the peculiar teachings of the New Born or Baumanites.

The introduction is in the form of a poem, which, according to Mr. Hinke,[51] who made a careful study of the book,
does not possess a very high poetical merit and contains
some very harsh passages, but upon the whole reveals a
fine Christian spirit, as it emphasizes our dependence upon
and consequent obligation to God and submission to His
word. Following is a translation of the closing stanza :

> " For if you wish, O man, to find
> The Lord most merciful and kind,
> And on that awful judgment day
> To meet the Judge without dismay,
> Then to the words of God give ear
> And follow them while you are here,
> Regard them as of highest worth,
> Place them above all things on earth."

It is a strange coincidence that both Boehm and Bauman
came to Pennsylvania about the same time from Lambsheim, in the Palatinate.

" The first five pages form a conversation with a politician. The subject
of their conversation is religious toleration, which soon leads them to
speak of its opposite intolerance. Weiss points out that this intolerance

[52] Rev. W. J. Hinke in *Reformed Church Messenger*, March 16, 1899.

is noticeable especially among the sects of Pennsylvania, where toleration ought to be unlimited, especially among the New Born, and when he
expresses the wish to meet one of this sect, the politician is quite ready
to introduce him to one, with whom he is acquainted.

"They go to his house, and Weiss begins the conversation. He com-
pliments the man on his nice farm, and tells him that he has good reason
to thank God. 'Well,' the New Born answers, 'I have worked hard
and that is the result, but I do not see any reason why I should thank
God.' This leads to a discussion of the *first false doctrine* of the New
Born, the rejection of prayer. Weiss proves from the blessings of God,
which he had received and the help he had enjoyed, but especially from
the Lord's Prayer and the direct injunctions of the Bible that he ought to
pray. When he has exhausted every proof, the New Born replies to him:
'I do not need all that, for I am a New Born. I am perfectly without
sin. God is in me and I am in God.'

"Then Weiss asks him to answer three questions: 1. What do you understand by the new birth? 2. What are the proofs that you are new born?
3. What are the fruits of the new birth? The first question the New Born
answers quite readily by saying that new birth is a communion and union
with God, closing with his favorite formula: God is in me and I am in
God. But Weiss shows him that this question is not as simple and easy
as he had supposed ; in fact, that God could be in men in four different
ways. He could be in us as He was in Christ by a personal union, or as
He was in the prophets by a special illumination and power, or as He is
in the children of God by a renewal of their whole man, or as He is in all
men by His general providence. The New Born then claims without
hesitation that He is in him in the most perfect way, because He is perfectly sinless. This is the *second* false *doctrine* of the New Born, perfect
sinlessness. But Weiss proves to him that he shows no likeness to Christ.
He can neither perform miracles nor preach as Christ did, and, moreover,
he contradicts the plain teaching of the Bible. But the New Born is not
daunted. He answers by denying the authority of the Bible. This is the
third false *doctrine* of the sect, the rejection of Holy Scripture. If God
speaks in and through them, of course Scripture is superfluous. The discussion of the divine origin and authority of the Bible is very interesting.
It reveals the fact that Weiss is a good theological thinker. He presents
three main arguments for its divine origin. In the first place, he points
to the fulfilled prophecies; then he argues from the character of the Bible,
that as there is no better nor more perfect book than the Bible, it must be
of different origin than all other books. And, lastly, he argues its divinity
from the character of its authors. They were good and holy men who
for that very reason could not deceive us when they claim to deliver
divine revelations. Lastly, the objection that the Bible contains contradictions he traces to two causes. Men study the Bible without divine
guidance and enlightenment, and, again, they have no knowledge of the

original languages, the geography, chronology of the Bible and the customs of Bible lands. The discussion then turns to the second question: How do you know that you are new born? The answer is ready imme. diately: 'I feel it within me by a peculiar illumination of God's Spirit.' Weiss warns him against the danger of self-deception, especially since the fruits of regeneration must agree with our consciousness of it. He then defines the fruits to be all spiritual gifts as enumerated in Gal. v, 22; moreover, a Christian life and conduct, prayer, the desire to read the Word of God, to worship God both in public and private, to follow the teachings of faithful ministers, whom God has placed over us. The New Born answers him that he has all the inner fruits, but he declares he can see no use for such outward things as have been mentioned. Especially does he object to divine worship in a church and to ministers. He has absolutely no use for them. With these two peculiarities Weiss has reached the *fourth* and *fifth* peculiar *doctrines* of this sect. They reject the ministry and divine worship, together with everything connected with them, as, *e. g.*, the sacraments. The necessity of the ministry Weiss proves by a large number of arguments. After all these sound and solid arguments, the New Born concludes by saying: 'All your words and arguments are in vain. It is all the same whether you talk or don't talk.'"

HE first result of the acquaintance between Beissel and Franklin was the publication of a duodecimo volume of thirty-two pages. It was printed in the German language with Roman type. It was of a theosophical character, and bears the imprint 1730. The title reads:

Mystische | Und sehr geheyme | Sprueche, | Welche in der Himlischen schule des | heiligen geistes erlernet. | Und dan folgens, einige | Poetischen Gedichte. | Auffgesetzt. | Den liebhabern und schülern der | Göttlichen und Himmlischen | weisheit zum dienst. | Vor | Die aüf dieser welt aber, haben wir keine | speise, werden ihnen auch wohl ein | verschlossener garden, und | versiegelter brun- | nen bleiben. | Zu Philadelphia: | Gedruckt bey B. Franklin in Jahr 1730.

A fac-simile of the title of this rare work is shown upon the opposite page. There appears to be something of a discrepancy between the date upon the title-page and the

MYSTISCHE

Und fehr geheyme

SPRUECHE.

Welche in der Himlifchen fchule des
heiligen geiftes erlernet.

Und dan folgens, einige

POETISCHE GEDICHTE.

AUFFGESETZT.

Den liebhabern und fchüllern der
Göttlichen und Himmlifchen
weifzheit zum dienft.

VOR

Die fäu diefer welt aber, haben wir keine
fpeife, werden ihnen auch wohl ein
verfchloffener garden, und
verfiegelter brun-
nen bleiben.

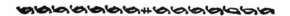

Zu *PHILADELPHIA:*
Gedruckt bey B. *FRANKLIN* in Jahr 1730.

notice of its publication in the *Chronicon*, which places the issue in the year 1729. This may be explained from the reckoning then in vogue. It was late in the fall of 1729 when the arrangements for printing were made with Franklin, and the book was evidently printed within the next five months. This, according to the Old Style, would still be in 1729. According to the popular reckoning, the three months, January, February and March would be in 1730. If this is the case, the imprints should have been 1729-30. Books printed during the over-lapping months, however, usually bore the date of the coming year, which, no doubt, was the case in the present instance.

Another piece of evidence which would seem to establish the correctness of the above, if not of the actual date given in the *Chronicon*, is the fact that no mention whatever of the printing of either this book or of the *Göttliche Liebes und Lobes Gethöne* appear in Franklin's journal and day-book, which he begun July 4, 1730, and which has lately been found in the collection of the American Philosophical Society. Consequently the book was printed, delivered and paid for prior to that date, and ranks among the very earliest of the Franklin imprints, if not the first.

In connection with this interesting subject it may be asked why no mention of any of these German imprints is to be found in his autobiography or other writings. The answer is a simple one; it was due to Franklin's supreme contempt in which he held anything that savored of the German. He took the money of his German patrons, but his private entries were simply as " Dutch." If we were to accept the *Chronicon* literally the discovery of the Franklin imprint would lead to the possibility of a previous edition, probably by Keimer or Bradford.

In regard to this pamphlet the *Chronicon* states : " When " a learned scholar named Gulde saw them he traveled to " him, and asked him [Beissel] why he had made 99 of "them, and not 100. Beissel's answer was that when the "number 99 was reached he stopped in the spirit."

[Rev. Samuel Guldin, a Swiss clergyman, was the first regular ordained minister of the Reformed faith to settle permanently in Pennsylvania. While in Europe he became imbued with the teachings of mystical theosophy, and came to the Province early in the century to join the Kelpius Community on the Wissahickon. From a letter written two years after the death of Kelpius (December 1, 1710), it would appear that he was then living as a recluse in the cabin of Kelpius, and was acting as Magister of the Society of the Woman in the Wilderness. He afterwards became a landowner in Roxborough township and lived there for some years].

As a matter of fact, according to Rosicrucian theosophy, the figure 1 stands for the finite or man, while the 0 represents the infinite, and to make the number 100 would have been to place the finite before the infinite. Therefore 99 was selected, because the figure 9 embodied the symbol of the infinite above the finite. This same question again arose, as will be seen in our account of the building of Bethania, where the symbolism will be explained at still greater length. As an introduction to this book Beissel prints two Scripture texts :

Prov. iii, 13–14.—" Happy is the man that findeth wisdom, and the man that getteth understanding. For it is better than the merchandise of silver, and the gain thereof than fine gold."

Wisdom, vii, 3–8.—[Citation in original is a misprint, it should be Sapi. viii, 4–8.]—For she is privy to the mysteries of the knowledge of God, and a lover of his works.

" If a man desire much experience, she knoweth things of old, and conjectureth aright what is to come, etc."

Then follow the " Mystical and very Secret " sentences, etc., ninety-nine in number. *A specimen page is produced in fac-simile on opposite page.*

MYSTISCHE

Und fehr geheyme

SPRUECHE, &c.

1.

ICH felber recht erkennen ift die höchfte vollkommenheit, und den e..i-gen, Ewigen, und unfichtbahren Gott in Chrifto Jefu recht verehren und an-beten, ift das Ewige leben.

2. Alle untugend ift fünde, aber doch ift keine fo, grofz als die; von Gott gefchieden fein.

3. Wer Gott liebet, der ift von Gott, und hat den eingebohrnen fohn in ihm bleibend, dann derfelbe ift aufgegangen und kommen von Gott.

4. Die höchfte weifzheit ift, keine weifzheit ha-ben: doch ift der der höchfte, der Gott befitzet, dann Er ift allein weifz.

A 2

5. Alle

A careful examination of these sentences will show that they are simply moral proverbs, orthodox in the fullest sense, and are but little imbued with any of the mystical teachings which would be implied with the title.

The ninety-nine proverbs are followed by sixty-two original poetical compositions, sixty-one varying in length from two to twenty-four lines. The sixty-second or last one is an independent composition of twelve lines, with a continuation of twenty-two lines. Then follows: "*A Lesson for a Christian, given unto him to learn by his Taskmaster.*" This consists of eighteen rules for self-examination, and is followed with a two-page prayer, closing with the couplet:

> "To be dead to the world translates the soul unto God,
>   And brings celestial air, releasing from distress and death."

In conclusion we have another *Lection* or section : " Very serviceable and useful for the followers and scholars of Jesus Christ."

The next commission given by Beissel to Franklin was a hymn-book for the uses of the awakened Germans in the Province. This was also a duodecimo of ninety-six pages, and bears the Franklin imprint of 1730. The same remarks as to the time of printing made in regard to the previous volume on page 161 apply to this hymn book. No mention of it is to be found in either Franklin's journal nor ledger subsequent to July 4, 1730. It was the largest work issued thus far by the Franklin press, and it was also printed in German with Roman type. It contains sixty-two hymns, all of which appear to be original compositions written by Beissel and his associates during their sojourn in the Mühlbach valley. Beissel was the author of thirty-one of these hymns, in which mystic exultation revels in rhythmic measure, and free use is made of the vocabulary of sensual love to symbolize religious ecstasy. Beissel and his associates followed in the wake of men like F. Spee,

J. Scheffler and Gottfried Arnold, who took the song of Solomon to be a sacred pattern of style.[53]

The full title of this book reads :

Göttliche | Liebes und Lobes gethöne | Welche in den hertzen der kinder | der weiszheit zusammen ein. | Und von da wieder auszgeflossen | Zum Lob Gottes, | Und nun denen schülern der himlischen | weiszheit zur erweckung und auf- | munterung in ihrem Creutz und | leiden aus hertzlicher lie- | be mitgetheilet. | Dann | Mit lieb erfüllet sein, brin'gt Gott den besten Preisz | Und giebt zum singen uns, die allerschönste weisz. | Zu Philadelphia : Gedruckt bey Benjamin | Franklin in der Marck-strass, 1730.[54]

Upon the reverse of the title-page we find the following curious announcement ; it is introduced as it sets forth the peculiar religious feeling with which these people were then imbued, viz. (translation) :

Necessary Observation.

There are here presented, to such as have been summoned from the world, and souls purchased from mankind [by the blood of the Lamb], divers continual sounding songs of Love and Praise, to extol and glorify their God and the Lamb, who hath redeemed them.

But

For the world with its rabble,
Who only scoff at God's children,
Here find no meat,
As they, living in their sins,
Against God's truth strive
In the most outrageous way.

---

[53] Seidensticker, in the *First Century of German Printing.*

[54] This book has been frequently mentioned as the first German book printed in America. That this is a gross error is shown by the titles here reproduced. The same is true of the claim that Beissel and his associates were the pioneer publishers of German literature in America. This honor belongs strictly to Henry Bernhard Köster and Johannes Kelpius, as is fully shown in the *German Pietists*, pp. 100–108, 166, 278–80.

GOTTLICHE

Liebes und Lobes gethöne

Welche in den hertzen der kinder
der weiſzheit zuſammen ein.

Und von da wieder auſzgefloſſen

ZUM LOB GOTTES,

Und nun denen ſchülern der himliſchen
weiſzheit zur erweckung und aufmunterung in ihrem Creutz und
leiden aus hertzlicher liebe mitgetheilet.

D A N N

Mit lieb erfüllet ſein, bring't Gott den beſten Preiſs
Und giebt zum ſingen uns, die allerſchönſte weiſz.

Zu *Philadelphia:* Gedruckt bey Benjamin
Franklin in der March-ſtraſs. 1730,

Only such as here earnestly strive
God and his commands to revere,
And follow Christ's path to the Cross,—
On such we bestow this :
That they continually to God's Glory
May sing songs of Praise.

VEN to students of Amercan bibliography it is
a fact but little known that to Conrad Beissel, the Rosicrucian recluse in the wilds of
Conestoga, belongs the honor of being the
author and publisher of the first book of
German poetry written in America.[55]

During the same year (1730) Beissel published his *Ehebüchlein* [Book on Matri-
mony], *Die Ehe das Zuchthaus fleischlicher
Menschen.* This book was also printed by
Franklin, and was written in the interest of
celibacy. Matrimony is declared therein to be
the penitentiary of carnal man, and the abom-

INITIAL BY
JOHN PHILIP BOEHM.

inations committed therein under the appearance of right
are fully exposed. The writer has never succeeded in tracing
a copy of this curious work, but has reason to believe that at
least one copy is still in existence among the Moravian Archives at either Bethlehem or Hernnhut, as it was seen and
quoted in a private letter by the late Rev. Wm. C. Reichel.

The distribution of Beissel's *Büchlein von Sabbath*, as it
was called for short, as well as the *Ehe büchlein* among the
German settlers, at once attracted the notice of Johann
Philip Boehm,   at that time had sole charge of the
Reformed congr ations in the Province, Rev. Weiss
having returned to Germany.

Boehm not only opposed the doctrine set forth in these
two books before his people, but he also sent a copy of each
to the Classis of Amsterdam invoking their aid to counteract

---

[55] The Kelpius hymns remained in manuscript. So far as known they
were not printed at the time.

the dissemination of such literature.   Boehm's request was acted upon by the Classis, June 4, 1731, and the two books were referred to the Committee on Foreign Affairs to examine and report.

September 3, 1731. The Committee reports that the one is a dissertation on the Sabbath, wherein the writer asks that Saturday shall be kept in place of Sunday.   As to the other book the following Classis will report.

October 1, 1731. Dominie Alstein reports that the other book has been examined; it treats of marriage, and is not worthy of any further notice.[56]

There is a strong possibility that these two early American imprints, in the German language, are still preserved in some library or archive in the land of dykes and windmills, and it is hoped that this extended notice may attract attention and lead to the finding of the books.

---

[56] Extracts from Acts of Classis of Amsterdam :

June 4, 1731.—Uit Pensilvanien syn overgesonden, twee bocken, die overgegeven zyn aen de Gecommitteerde tot de buitlandse saeken om die te ondersocken en daervan rapport te doen.

September 3, 1731.—Aangaande de twee bockjes uyt Pensilvanien overgesonden, is gerapporteerd, dat twee behelst een vertoog van de Sabbath, wiliende de schrÿver dat deselve gevoegelyker op den Saturdag als op de Sondag gehoude soude worden, en dat van 't tweede bockje op de volgende Classis worde rapport gedaan.

October 1, 1731.—De zaake, Aangaande de twee bockjes uit Pensilvanien voergesonden waarvan in vorige Acten, rapporteerd D°Alstein, 't 2de bockje, handelnde over huwelÿk, niet waerdig is om verder op gelet te worden.

AUTOGRAPH OF REV. JOHN PHILIP BOEHM AS A REFORMED SCHOOLMASTER.

CHAPTER XI.

ALEXANDER MACK.

ETURNING once more to Lancaster county we find, at the opening of the year 1729, two distinct organizations of German Baptists in the Conestoga valley, who are divided chiefly on the question of the Sabbath. The year proved an eventful one for the German Baptists at large, as well as for the congregations on the Conestoga.

The chief event of general interest was the arrival of the venerable Alexander Mack, the patriarch of the denomination, who came to Pennsylvania with his family and a number of Baptists from Germany.

The event of special interest to the local organizations was a political one—the forming of Lancaster county from a part of Chester county. This act brought about a new set of officials, who had but little sympathy with the Germans and their religious movements, and resulted in a series of persecutions against those of them who persisted in keeping the Sabbath and working upon the Lord's Day. This annoyance the English Sabbatarians on French creek, in Nantmill, fortunately escaped, as they were not affected by the political division, and remained within the bounds of Chester county.

Notwithstanding these tribulations the German congregations continued to increase, obtaining their additions chiefly from among the Mennonites and Separatists. To afford temporary accommodations for the new-comers, Beissel and others of his followers, who lived in separate cabins, now gave up their habitations to such families as wished to unite with the congregation and settle here, and either built new cabins for themselves or took up temporary abodes with some of the resident members. Thus

BUILDING A HOME IN THE NEW WORLD.

Beissel went to Rudolph Nägele's; Michael Wohlfarth to Caspar Walter's; Jan Meyle to Hans Friedrich's; Peter Bucher to Hansil Landis', etc. Israel Eckerling and Jacob Gast joined Jan Meyle, and lived together for one year.[57]

From the *Tage-buch* (diary) of one of these pious enthusiasts we learn that all these cabins were built according to a uniform rule, viz.: length, twenty-five feet; breadth, twenty feet; height under joist, eight feet, six

[57] See survey map, p. 92.

inches. Wherever possible the door opened toward the south, with a small porch over it six feet in the clear from floor to ceiling (overhead piece).

An interesting account has come down to us descriptive of the building of these humble cabins. First, four large stones were laid at the corners, so as to be about a foot above the level of the ground. These served as a foundation. Upon these stones the ground-logs were laid; they were notched at the ends and fastened with hickory pins. Smaller logs were inserted at regular distances to form floor-joists. In most cases, however, a solid log floor was laid. Upon the ground-joists the cabin was raised, the logs were run upon skids by the help of wooden forks and the corners were notched so as to bring them as close together as possible. This work was done by the most experienced men, who were known as axe or corner-men. The others carried the logs and ran them up. The door and windows were not cut until all the logs were in place. The interstices between the logs were then filled with loam, the latter being mixed with dry grass. The roof was usually of split oak shingles; the rafters were formed of chestnut saplings, hewn flat on the top. It often happened, when a cabin was built in a hurry, before all the necessary material was prepared, that a temporary thatch or sod roof was put on to shelter the settler. Chimneys and fireplaces for these cabins were an after consideration, and were usually built of loam and stones outside, at one end of the cabin. Another curious feature of these humble dwellings was that many were built without the use of a single pound of iron.

The time of the "Single" or "Solitary" brethren was by no means spent in idle speculations; they betook themselves to various kinds of manual labor, chiefly carpentry, and refused their services to no one who asked their assistance in building a home in the wilderness.

The harnessing of the printing-press in their behalf by Beissel and Wohlfarth proved a powerful factor in the spread of the Sabbatarian doctrine among the English, as well as among the Germans.   An extended account of these publications will form the theme for our next chapter.

With the advent of spring renewed efforts were made by Beissel to extend his doctrines of the Sabbath and baptism among the Germans throughout the country beyond the Schuylkill.   This included the territory from Falkner Swamp to Oley, to which Jan Meyle and Israel Eckerling were sent to assist Andreas Frey.

These efforts at revival tended to increase the feeling between the Germantown Baptists and the *Beisselianer*, as the Sabbatarians were called in derision.   More or less friction was engendered between the individual members, which gradually extended to the leaders.   A similar condition existed on the Conestoga and Mühlbach, with the exception that, as individual differences arose, the aggrieved member would join the rival congregation, for a time at least.   Thus the changing back and forth was a common practice.   This resulted in making the condition of the German Separatists in the Province one of spiritual unrest and uncertainty.

It was at this juncture that Alexander Mack and his party arrived on the good ship *Allen*, James Craige master, from Rotterdam, September 5, 1729.   He was accompanied by his family and a number of German Baptists, among whom were Andreas Bony, the Kalckgläessers, Kriebels, Pettikoffers and other prominent Separatists.   It was fondly hoped by the Germantown party that the arrival of Alexander Mack in Pennsylvania would once more quiet the factions and again unite them upon the common basis of the Schwarzenau movement, of which the venerable Mack was the patriarch.   These expectations, however, failed to be realized as the two leaders, evidently uncertain as to each other's strength, kept aloof ; as it was not until the following year that Beissel and Mack stood face to face, a meeting which did not prove conducive to a union of the two parties.

The *Chronicon*, in speaking of the arrival of Alexander Mack, says : " This reverend man would have well-deserved "to be received with arms of love by all the pious in com- "mon, after all that he had had to suffer in Germany, "especially from his own people. But he was no sooner "arrived among his fellow-believers than they filled his "ears with heavy accusations against them of Conestoga,

"namely, how they had "separated from them, "had written them abu- "sive letters and had "treated them very un- "lovingly with judgments "and condemnations, yea, "and over and above all "this they had yet done "a terrible thing, where- "by not only they, but "even their dead, had been "condemned and put un-

SEAL (ENLARGED) OF ALEXANDER MACK.

"der the ban. . . . Now the good man should, at least "until he had made himself thoroughly acquainted with "the matter, have suspended his judgment. But prejudices "so overpowered his mind that he was not capable of passing "a sound judgment, nor of counteracting the separation."

Another noteworthy incident of the year was the arrival, some time during the summer, of the widow Eckerling with her youngest son Gabriel. She came to Lancaster county, and for a time lived with two of her other sons in in the house of Jan Meyle. She did not remain long with the congregation, as she died within a month or two after her arrival, and was buried beside Landert's wife and Beller's daughter in the family graveyard on Sigmund Landert's farm. This was the first graveyard of the Conestoga congregation.

USPICIOUSLY the year 1730 opened for the Sabbatarians. The diarist of the congregation states that the new congregation, " impelled by holy zeal, grows as the sweet savor of its walk and conversation is spread abroad." Then referring to their leader, he says : " First of all we are to be reminded that the superintendent, who had before his baptism led an angelic life hidden in God, now by baptism had consecrated himself to the lowly humanity of Jesus Christ."

Notwithstanding the bright outlook when the year opened, it was doomed to be a turbulent one. The first trouble was brought about by some gossip in the neighborhood, affecting the young women who had elected to live a spiritual life, and for the purpose of being nearer to the elder, had lived under the protection of Lamech. This gossip, like the story of the three black crows, increased until it became a tale of scandal, in which Beissel and the two daughters of Daniel Eicher were involved. When this came to the knowledge of a local Justice of the Peace, Samuel Jones, he issued a King's warrant for the two girls, and later one for Conrad Beissel. At the hearing Beissel acted as counsel for the defense. The result is thus given in the record :

" To the question whether they were guilty, Beissel demanded the witnesses, and they not being forthcoming, administered a sharp rebuke to the justice, and went his way ; for he had interfered with his office, as it was the

Sabbath. Thereupon the justice sent out the constable after witnesses, who brought together all the old women in the township. Each one of these referred to the other, until at last the accusation was traced back to one. Then the misunderstanding was disclosed; for this one had said it concerning a sister, who, after the flesh of the accused sister, who had a husband; it had been understood, however, of the latter, who was single. The justice thereupon begged pardon of the accused sister and let her go in peace."

This case so incensed Beissel that he published his *Ehebüchlein* (Matrimony the Penitentiary of Carnal Man.) One of the immediate results of this persecution and the issue of the pamphlet was that two married women of the congregation deserted their husbands and joined the two sisters in their retirement. One of these matrons was Maria Christina Sauer, wife of Christopher Sauer, and the other was Maria (Weidenbacher) Hanselmann. Both were rebaptized into the congregation during the summer, and eventually entered the sisterhood at Ephrata.

This act of the two women tended to still further incense those settlers who were not in harmony with the new movements against the leader and his followers. Yet, despite these trials and annoyances, the Sabbatarians gained in both number and importance, and during the summer issued, for the uses of the congregation, a hymn-book, the first German hymn-book printed in America. This book was fully described in the last chapter.

We now come to the meeting of Beissel and Alexander Mack, the patriarch of the German Baptists. Two accounts have come down to us of this interview; one of these is the story in the *Chronicon*, the other is a contemporary manuscript; from these two sources the following is gleaned: In October, 1730, Beissel and a number of his followers planned a visitation to Falkner Swamp. After

their arrival there meetings were held at different houses.
As soon as news of this incursion came to Germantown a
number of the Becker party, headed by Alexander Mack and
Becker, started for Falkner Swamp.   A meeting had been
called at the house of Johann Senseman, and when it was
well under way, while the worshippers were at silent
prayer, the door was suddenly opened, and the Germantown party, headed by Mack, rushed into the room.   The
latter exclaimed : "The peace of God the Lord be with
you."   A voice answered the salutation, saying : "We
have that peace."   Mack now commenced a spirited
harangue, demanding to know why the Conestoga people
had placed the Germantown congregation under the ban
of non-intercourse.   In conclusion, he proposed that both
parties should now betake themselves to prayer, so that
God might reveal unto them which party was guilty of
separation.   Accordingly they fell upon their knees, each
taking hold of his pilgrim-staff with both hands, resting
their bearded heads upon their wrists.   There was a difference in their mode of prayer; while the Beissel party
offered up their invocation in silence, Alexander Mack, as
leader of the Germantown party, broke out in a loud and
fervent prayer, raising his voice as he proceeded.   As his
voice grew louder he was interrupted by Michael Wohlfarth, who shouted : "Cry aloud; shout louder, perhaps
your God is asleep," and similar derisive remarks.   After
order was restored, Mack asked whether Beissel was present.
Upon his being pointed out, Mack failed to identify him,
and requested him to come forward and speak to him, as
he was a stranger to him.   Conrad Beissel then stepped
forward, and said : "I am the man after whom you ask."
Mack then took Beissel to task in a somewhat rough manner.   The latter merely answered with the query : "Why
came he here, in so unseemly and improper a manner, to
raise a disturbance ?"   Before Mack could answer, Wohlfarth

took up the word and overwhelmed both Mack and Becker with denunciations. This precipitated a general wrangle, in which Peter Becker, Alexander Mack, Jacob Weiss, Valentine Leslie, David Gemähle and Michael Wohlfarth took an active part. While the *Chronicon* contents itself with the entry: "Then things became lively," our manuscript account says: "Upon both sides many words were spoken which it is best not to record."

The discussion ended with the discomfiture of the Germantown party, who left the meeting without having accomplished their object. Alexander Mack shortly afterwards wrote and published a small tract bearing upon the controversy,[58] and giving his version of the affair. No copy of this brochure is known. There can be but little doubt that Mack and Beissel, as well as Becker, were pained at heart and deeply regretted the differences which had divided the various congregations of German Baptists in the Province. Beissel, in one of his Theosophical Epistles directed to Becker, writes: "I am well-disposed toward you all in those matters on which the spirits can unite in God; but in those which concern your mode of divine worship I can take no part."[59]

During the next year or two several meetings were arranged between the two leaders, always, however, without result. The insurmountable objection upon the part of the Mack faction was the system of re-baptism practised by Beissel and his followers, as they contended that there was no Scriptural foundation for such procedure. Beissel, in turn, challenged his opponents to show him a single verse in the whole of the New Testament wherein re-baptism was forbidden. In support of his own opposition he further claimed that many of the persons baptized by John

---

[58] Ein Tractälein, darin Er ihner erwiesen, dass sich ein jeder Stamm, müsse zu seinen Pannier halten, *Chr. Eph.*, p. 41, original edition.

[59] Epistle xvii.

the Baptist were again baptized by the Apostles. It was settled, however, that such re-baptisms could not be made an article of faith. Therefore, when in later times some of the old congregation went over to the new, and some wanted them re-baptized, wise men arose among them and hindered it.[60]

How Beissel, Wohlfarth and Meyle went to Philadelphia, and the immediate results of their journey is told in the next chapter.

Among the curious superstitions of this time was the belief among the Germans in lucky and unlucky days. This was an outcome of the neglected spiritual condition of the German settlers, as the lack of regular orthodox pastors tended to foster these and other superstitions. Many of these traditions were brought from the Fatherland, and to them were added such as were current among Irish and English neighbors. The German, being of a sanguine temperament, was especially prone to foster a belief in celestial signs, traditional superstition and unlucky days (*Unglückstage*).

Another belief was that of hexing or bewitching. Whenever anything appeared to be wrong with any person or animal, which could not be accounted for by the local *Bader*, it was at once assumed that the person or thing was *behext* or bewitched. An old manuscript in possession of the writer gives the following "infallible" remedy:

When a human being or animal is *behext* or *bezaubert*, take equal parts of cinquefoil, fennel flower seed, a piece of a human skull (*Todenbein*), water-soaked wood.

These ingredients are to be pulverized. Dose: For a child, as much as will go on the point of a knife; for an adult, a drachm; for a horse, one ounce; for cattle, one-half ounce, to be mixed with vinegar.

Our old MS. records that when the year 1731 was ushered

[60] *Ch. Eph.*, p. 42.

in Satan became more active than ever, causing great tribulation for the Elder. The first cause for trouble came when several other matrons followed the example set by Sauer's wife, and deserted their husbands and families to live a life of Christian retirement. Beissel was blamed by the irate husbands, and several turbulent scenes were enacted at the public meetings.

Beissel and Wohlfarth, however, continued in their activity by organizing revivals and preaching the Sabbatarian gospel. Success crowned their efforts to so great an extent that they again attracted the attention of the civil authorities, who feared that in time they might change the day of worship in the Province and, if not promptly checked, might soon obtain the upper hand if their present rate of increase continued. So they again began to fine and imprison all such persons as were informed against for performing manual labor on the first day of the week. Their action was taken under the Act of 1705, viz.:

AN ACT TO RESTRAIN PEOPLE FROM LABOR ON THE FIRST
DAY OF THE WEEK.

To the end that all people within this Province may with the greater freedom devote themselves to religious and pious exercises :

[Section 1.] Be it enacted by John Evans, Esquire, by the Queen's royal approbation Lieutenant-Governor under William Penn, Esquire, absolute Proprietary and Governor-in-Chief of the Province of Pennsylvania and Territories, by and with advice & consent of the freemen of the Province in General Assembly met, and by the authority of the same, That according to the example of the primitive Christians and for the ease of the creation, every First day of the week commonly called Sunday, all people shall abstain from toil and labor; that whether masters, parents, children, servants or others, they may the better dispose themselves to read & hear the Holy Scriptures of Truth at home, & frequent such meetings of religious worship abroad as may best suit their respective persuasions. And that no tradesman, artificer, workman, laborer or other person whatsoever shall do or exercise any worldly business or work of their ordinary callings on the First day or any part thereof (works of necessity and charity only excepted) upon pain that every person so offending shall, for every offense, forfeit the sum of twenty shillings, to the use of the poor of the place where the offense was committed; being thereof convicted before any justice (either upon his view, confession of the party, or proof of one or more witnesses) and the said justice shall give a warrant, under his hand and seal to the next constable where such offense shall be committed, to levy the said forfeiture or penalty by distress and sale of the offenders goods and chattels, rendering to the said offender the overplus of the moneys raised thereby—

Among the victims of this crusade were two of the brethren, Beno and Samuel Eckerling, who were arrested under the above Act in the fall of 1731 for working upon the Lord's day (Sunday), and were imprisoned in the county jail at Lancaster. But, as they persisted in their convictions, and to quiet the clamor of the populace, the fine was remitted and they were discharged. This ended the prosecution for a time.

With the growth of the congregation and the rapid increase of settlers who flocked into the Conestoga valley, a serious problem presented itself. This was the question of the ownership of the land. It was further aggravated by the increase of solitary brethren and spiritual virgins. Numerous cabins for both solitary and householders now dotted the land, both settled and vacant, between the Conestoga and the Mühlbach. The separate orders of religious enthusiasts looked upon Beissel as their spiritual director, and refused to obey any mandate, either civil or judicial, unless approved by him. They further demanded of him ministrations different from those of the secular congregation, which was made up of the various householders or regular settlers.

This peculiar state of affairs, civil and religious, soon brought on a conflict of authority between the settlers and Henry Hodge, Esq., the attorney for the London Company that owned a large part of the Conestoga valley. In the spring of the year (1730) Attorney Hodge determined to dispossess the German squatters by force, and an application to that effect was made to the court at Lancaster. Before proceeding to extreme measures a hand-bill was distributed throughout the Conestoga valley, as a final notice to all concerned. A copy of this notice also appeared in Franklin's *Pennsylvania Gazette :*

Philadelphia, 20th of the *6th Month,* 1730.

WHEREAS divers Perſons have (illegally) ſettled themſelves and Families on ſeveral Tracts of Land, known by the Name of *The London Company's Land,* and that to the Damage of the Owners thereof:

THESE are therefore to give Notice to all ſuch Perſons, that if they (within one Month after the Date hereof) ſhall refuſe or neglect to make Satisfaction for the Damages already done, and ſhall preſume hereafter to cut any Timber-Trees or Underwood, &c. they may expect to be proceeded againſt according to a Law of this Province, made and provided in that Caſe.   *Henry Hodge,* Attorney.

This notice evidently had the desired effect, and amicable settlements were undoubtedly made, as no records are to be found of either evictions or prosecutions.

In view of these complications and differences the suggestion was made to Beissel that he retire with all the solitary of both sexes and, after the precept of the holy forefathers, begin a household in the wilderness. This suggestion Beissel refused to entertain at the time, and stated that the secular, or congregation at large, had the greater claim upon him. Thus matters continued until February, 1732, when he called a general meeting at which a fervent exhortation was delivered upon the " comforting state of God's kingdom." At the close of the discourse he appointed

Sigmund Landert and another brother as Elders to preside over the congregation in the wilderness. Maria Christina Sauer was designated as matron over the single women of the fold. These three persons were bound by a most solemn promise (at the same time giving to each a Testament) to govern strictly according to the rules of the book. Beissel charged them to regard the Holy Writ as their sole guide, and not to be misled from the straight path therein indicated. He earnestly impressed upon the members of the congregation at large the necessity of remaining steadfast in their faith and convictions.

When this ceremony was at an end Beissel, to the surprise of all present, with tears coursing down his cheeks, impressively laid down his office and resigned his position as *Vorsteher* or teacher of the congregation. Then he stepped down from the prayer-bench an humble member of the congregation.

That this unexpected action of Beissel threw the members into consternation, is not to be wondered at. Henceforth Sigmund Landert assumed charge, but the meetings proved far from harmonious, and from the frequent judicial questions asked and argued, the general gatherings of the Conestoga congregation appeared more like court sessions than religious meetings.

What became of Conrad Beissel and the congregation will appear in a subsequent chapter.

A FRAGMENT FROM AN OLD SAMPLER.

THE GERMAN SECTARIANS OF PENNSYLVANIA.

AN ANCIENT EPHRATA CABIN.

HEN Conrad Beissel bade his dramatic adieu to the congregation, it was evidently part of a preconceived scheme to throw off the care of them and once more retire to the solitude of the forest, there to devote himself to a life of self-contemplation.

Whether he had well considered the effect of the desertion of his followers is a question not to be answered at this late day. However, he gathered up his books and papers and once again, winter though it was, journeyed, staff in hand, deeper into the unbroken forest. His goal lay eight miles north by west. Here, upon the banks of a romantic stream, beside a never-failing spring of limpid water, a cabin had been previously built, far away from any human habitation, by Emanuel Eckerling. The situation was a somewhat peculiar one: the bottom or meadow wherein the cabin stood was one avoided even by the Indians on account of the numberless snakes with which the meadow and the banks of the creek were infested. They called it *Hoch-Halekung*, or the Den of Serpents. The new settlers kept the word, which in time was spelled as pronounced, —Cocalico.

Emanuel Eckerling evidently expected the coming of the late leader. He received him with open arms, and gave up his cabin in part to him until a separate one could be finished for his use. The situation of this cabin was in the meadow or *schwam* beside a spring of pure water, which bubbled out of the ground, sparkling and bright, winter and summer, and thence found its way into the

AN IDEAL HERMIT.

creek, which here makes quite a bend. This spring, at which the two hermits were wont to refresh themselves, is the one still used by the inmates of the old Brother-house. The water is just as clear and refreshing as it was a century and three-quarters ago, and upon more than one hot summer day has served to quench the thirst of the writer.

Conrad Beissel lost no time in clearing a piece of land for seeding when spring opened. This he cultivated entirely by manual labor. At the same time he hewed the necessary timber to build a cabin. He completed this habitation during the summer months. His time henceforth was divided between cultivating his garden and the wooing of the celestial Sophia, passing his hours alternately in study and labor, and living on the simplest fare. He was once more in his beloved solitude; just what the state of his mind was may best be judged from the beautiful hymn, composed during the early days of his sojourn on the Cocalico:

"O blessed solitary life,
    Where all creation silence keeps!
    Who thus himself to God can yield
    That he ne'er from him strays,
    Hath to the highest goal attained,
    And can without vexation live.
    Faith, toleration, love and hope,
    These all have come to his support."

During the spring and summer, when not at prayer or labor, he devoted all spare moments toward perfecting the hymn-book which he had printed for the congregation. His labors culminated in an enlarged collection of hymns, printed by Franklin, with a new title.

Vorspiel | der | Neuen-Welt. | Welches sich in der letzten Abendroethe | als ein paradisischer Lichtes-glantz | unter den Kindern Gottes | hervor gethan. | in | Liebes, Lobes, Leidens, Krafft, | und Erfahrungs liedern abgebildet, die | gedrückte, gebückte und Creutz- | tragende Kirche auf Erden. | Und wie inzwischen sich | Die obere und Triumphirende Kirche | als eine Paradiesische vorkost her- | vor thut und offenbahret. | Und daneben, als | Ernstliche und zuruffende wächterstimmen | an alle annoch zerstreuete Kinder Gottes, das sie | sich sammlen und bereit machen auf den | baldigen ; Ja bald herein brechen- | den Hochzeit-Tag der braut | des Lamms. | Zu Philadelphia : Gedruckt bey Benjamin | Francklin, in der Marck-strass, 1732.

The main part of this title sets forth that it is a "Prelude to the new World, which in the last rosy sunset has appeared as a paradisal refulgence unto the children of God. Illustrated in Songs of Love, Praise, Suffering, Power, and Experience—the crushed, cringing and cross-bearing Church on Earth," etc. The title-page is reproduced upon the opposite page. An appendix, *Zum Beschluss*, a mystical A, B, C, consists of twenty-four sentences, after the order of Beissel's book of 99 proverbs.

VORSPIEL

DER

NEUEN-WELT.

Welches sich in der letzten Abendroethe
als ein paradisischer Lichtes-glantz
unter den Kindern Gottes
hervor gethan.

IN

LIEBES, LOBES, LEIDENS, KRAFFT
und Erfahrungs liedern abgebildet, die
gedrückte, gebückte und Creutz-
tragende Kirche auf Erden.

Und wie inzwischen sich

Die obere und Triumphirende Kirche
als eine Paradiesische vorkost hervor thut und offenbahret.

Und daneben, als

Ernstliche und zuruffende wächterstimmen
an alle annoch zerstreuete Kinder Gottes, das sie
sich sammlen und bereit machen auf den
baldigen ; Ja bald herein brechen-
den Hochzeit-Tag der braut
des Lämms.

Zu *Philadelphia :* Gedruckt bey *Benjamin*
Francklin, in der *Marck-strass.* 1732.

TITLE-PAGE OF HYMN-BOOK PRINTED BY BENJAMIN FRANKLIN, 1732.

Original in Historical Society of Pennsylvania.

This book, a small octavo of two hundred pages, of which only a few copies have been found, contains all the hymns of the *Göttliche Liebes und Lobesgethöne* (1730) with the addition of fifty-five new ones, of which twenty-four were written by Beissel, the rest by Michael Wohlfarth, Martin Bremer and others.

The business part of the publication of this new hymnbook was evidently attended to by Samuel Eckerling. This fact is inferred from three entries in Franklin's Commercial Journal, now in possession of the American Philo-

Benj Franklin Journal, began July 4 1730

sophical Society. This shows that, with the usual German thrift and honesty, the venture was a cash transaction ; in fact, a portion of the money was paid before the work was even begun. These entries even offer another illustration of the contemptuous antagonism entertained by Franklin against the German race.

1731–1	March 20.	Saml. Ackerling [sic] Cr. for Cash towards printing his book of Dutch	£ 10. 00. 0.
1732	May 8.	Received of Samuel Eckerling Cash toward printing the Book	£ 10. 00. 00.
	October 6.	Last week I finished the Dutch for Samuel Eckerling, and received of him as much Cash as made all even between us.	

As this account merely calls for printing, the sheets were evidently bound either at Germantown or in Lancaster

Last Week I finished the Dutch for Samuel Eckerling and receiv'd of him as much Cash as made all even between us . ——— (settled)

county.   Further, it being a cash transaction, no ledger account was opened by Franklin with his German patron.

Beissel had no sooner left the Conestoga valley than discord and dissensions arose among the persons composing the congregation, which was now left without a *Vorsteher* who had the requisite firmness and executive ability to guide its affairs.   Factious and vexatious questions arose among the different parties, and harmony ceased to prevail in their councils.   Upon one point, however, they were unanimous ; this was to recall Beissel from his seclusion and induce him to return to them, or at least to come and give judgment upon their distracting questions.   The consequence of this was that on September 4, 1732, just seven months after his withdrawal from the *Vorsteher Amt*, Conrad Beissel again presided at an *Agapas* or love-feast of his former congregation, which was held at Brother Landert's house.

At the conclusion of the meeting, Beissel stated that, notwithstanding their earnest prayers for him to remain in their midst, he felt it his duty to adhere to his original resolve, and return to his cabin in the wilderness.   This he did after giving them a final admonition to be faithful and to keep the Sabbath and other ordinances of Scripture. Returning to the Cocalico, he was not permitted, however, to enjoy his retirement, as not a week passed without some of the members of the congregation making a pilgrimage to his cabin for advice or instruction.

During the winter (1732–33) the little settlement was increased by the arrival of three more single brethren, Jacob Gast, Martin Bremer and Samuel Eckerling, whose wife Catharina had died a few months before. These three built for themselves another cabin on the banks of the Cocalico, so as to be near their spiritual master. This was the third house in the settlement.

The next arrivals were the two sisters, Anna and Maria Eicher, who clamored for permission to pass their time in seclusion and silent contemplation, and receive further spiritual instruction from their former teacher. Their demand was not received with favor by the resident brethren, but all attempts to dissuade them proved futile. After a long consultation it was concluded that the hand of Providence was in the matter, and, such being the case, they had no right to object. So a house was at once erected on the opposite side of the stream for the exclusive use of the two sisters. This house was completed in May, 1733, and was occupied by the two girls until the erection of the first community-house at Ephrata.

Beissel throughout this trying period took for his prototype Pachomius, a soldier in Constantine's Legion, who, it is said, saw the flaming cross in the skies surrounded by the legend, *In Hoc Signo Vincis*, as it appeared to his leader. Converted to Christianity, Pachomius retired to the Theban desert, and for a time lived the life of a hermit. A few years later he built a hut on Tabenna, an island in the river Nile. Here he founded the nucleus of a large monastic institution with separate buildings for the male and female members. When the two sisters were questioned as to their course, they were wont to answer that they merely followed in the footsteps of St. Paula.

An English contemporary account states: "But he [Beissel] had not been long in the place before the society found him out and repaired to his little cot; the brethren settling with him on the west banks of the Cocalico, and the sisters on the east, all in sight of one another, with the river running between them."

During the middle of October (1733) Michael Wohlfarth made another of his periodical pilgrimages to Philadelphia. He was accompanied by a single brother, whose identity is hidden under the monastic name of Jonadab. The two enthusiasts went into the Yearly Meeting then in session and began to harangue the assembly on the iniquity of their ways. Their violent language, which was heightened by their strange appearance, with long hair and flowing beards, caused some excitement among the Friends, and ended in the two strangers being unceremoniously hustled out of the meeting-house. This, however, was no new experience for Wohlfarth, and, nothing

A CONESTOGA PILGRIM.

daunted, he and his companion mounted the court-house steps, then at Second and Market streets, and spoke to such of the multitude as would give attention.

Toward the close of 1733 a steady stream of German settlers set in, who flocked into the fertile fields and bottoms of this end of Lancaster county. Wherever a fine spring of water was to be found there a German family settled. The vacant lands were rapidly taken up and surveyed for the purchasers, who soon turned the wilderness into a blooming garden. Most of these settlers were Lutheran and Reformed. Accessions also came from among the various German Sabbatarians who were scattered through Falkner Swamp, Coventry in Chester county and elsewhere. These latter, many of whom were poor and without means, clustered around the settlement of their leader. Philadelphia and the surrounding country also furnished some representatives of them. So great was this movement that when the year 1734 opened the country, within a radius of three or four miles from Beissel's cabin, was all in possession of his followers.

According to the *Chronicon*, "Wherever there was a spring of water, no matter how unfertile the soil might be, there lived some household that was waiting for the Lord's salvation."

The country was now divided into four parts or settlements, named respectively, Massa, Zoar, Hebron and Kadesh. The site of only one of these settlements can be definitely located at the present day, viz., Zoar. This was the present Reamstown in East Cocalico township. Kadesh is believed to have been the original settlement on the Cocalico, now the Kloster grounds.

At the opening of the year 1734 the first entry of interest is the record of the death of one of the brethren, Peter Lessly by name, who died of consumption on the last day of the first month. Another cabin was added to the number on the west bank of the creek early in the spring. This was for the use of Israel and Gabriel Eckerling.

It is at this time that we find the first traces and mention of distinctive clothing. Heretofore both men and women had worn plain dress similar to that of the Friends. Now, however, still more radical innovations were introduced, which eventually resulted in the adoption by some of the most austere members of a costume somewhat similar to that of the pilgrims of old.

This action caused reports to be circulated that the brethren living separately on the Cocalico were in reality Jesuits who were here to seduce the populace. It was even reported by some of their enemies that they were sent here from Mexico, and were amply supplied with Spanish gold.

These and many like tales were believed by the common people, and some, whom the *Chronicon* designates as "degenerate Mennonites and partly spoiled church people," became so wrought up by these reports that it was determined to burn down the entire settlement and thus rid the community of the religious celibates. With this object in view, fire was set to the dry leaves and brush in the forest on a night when the wind blew strongly from the west. After the fire was fairly started and began to gain headway, the wind providentially changed, the course of the fire turned, and actually burned the barn and buildings of the chief instigator of the scheme.

To alleviate the wants of the many poor settlers who were attracted to the vicinity (and many of these were found among the number who vilified and denounced the brethren) a granary (*Korn-magazin*) was erected for the storage of rye and corn, which was raised by the single brethren or contributed by the more prosperous secular members. It was a grand and charitable scheme for the assistance of poor German emigrants, the first organization of its kind in the Western World. Several large brick bake-ovens were also built to supply *Pumpernickel* to the indigent settlers. The bread thus baked was distributed to the needy without charge. These ovens were all under one roof and opened into a large room with troughs for the mixing of the dough. A cabin was built between these two offices for Samuel Eckerling who was in charge of both granary and bake-house.

Among those who came to the settlement during the summer (July, 1734) and joined the solitary brethren, was an erratic French Switzer, Jean François Régnier, a native of Vivres. This man, brought up in the Reformed faith, was now a visionary fanatic, and claimed to have been awakened in his seventh year. He professed great holiness, and began to formulate his strange notions whenever opportunity offered. A number of the people, among whom were two of the Eckerlings, became impressed with his apparent earnestness. Beissel, however, with his cool judgment, warned his followers against the new-comer, and cautioned them to beware of him, as his reason was certainly unbalanced.

Some of the ridiculous ravings of this fanatic led to strange extravagances. Among others he asked his followers to bind themselves with him not to eat any more bread made from cereal grain ; so, when fall came, *Pumpernickel* and *Schwartzbrod* were eschewed for a time ; and as a substitute the woods were scoured and acorns gathered and brought to the common granary for their use. All this was done under a supposed spiritual guidance. Régnier also taught that it was consistant with holiness to follow the example of Elijah and other saints, and not to dwell in any house.

Beissel now ordered the brethren to build a rude hut in the woods for the visionary ascetic, and that he be fed upon his scriptural diet (*eichel-kost*) prepared from acorns. As the season progressed the stored acorns became wormy and spoiled, and the Swiss prophet was forced again to beg for plain *Pumpernickel.* This so worried Régnier that his reason became seriously affected, and for a time he ceased to be a factor in the settlement.

[From a fragment of an old manuscript bearing on the Régnier episode, it is shown that there was considerable method in his madness, so far as the acorn diet is concerned. It was not original with him, but was really a revival of a belief which dates back into the dim ages of the long-forgotten past, when the oak furnished the first food for man, both meat and drink, and contained all that was necessary for man's existence. From this manuscript it appears that Régnier not only suggested acorns as a sub-stitute for rye and wheat in making bread, but also for other dishes, such as cereal food (*mehl-speise*), coffee, and lastly as a basis for making an excellent *schnapps* (whiskey). For making bread the acorns were first soaked in water or steamed, to eliminate the bitter principle (*entbittert*); they were then dried and ground into meal, which was baked in the usual manner. The bread, *Eichelbrod*, was about as palatable as *Pumpernickel*, but much less digestible.

As a substitute for coffee the largest and soundest acorns were selected. Only thoroughly ripe ones were to be used. The acorns were then hulled or taken out of their cups, cut into quarters and scalded with boiling water, after which they were drained and allowed to cool. Then they were placed in a bake-oven until thoroughly dry, and finally were roasted in the same way as ordinary coffee beans, and ground for use. To make coffee, about a drachm of the ground acorns was taken for every three cups of boiling water, which was poured over the powder and boiled for about ten minutes. The taste and stimu-lating action of this decoction were entirely different from regular coffee, as it lacked both the *caffèine* and essential oils of the latter.

This coffee substitute was supposed to have peculiar properties, both medicinal and mystical, and was also used to drive all hereditary taint or disease from the system. Thus, down to the present day throughout the farming districts of Pennsylvania, it is frequently given to children who are affected with scrofula. Régnier also made a mash from acorns, which not only furnished a good vinegar, but an excellent whiskey as well. Lastly, there appears a receipt for an *Analeptikum* or tonic, to be used after any serious illness. For this purpose the acorns were to be buried when the moon was in a certain quarter, until they had lost their bitterness, then dried, roasted, powdered and mixed with sugar and certain aromatic herbs.

In the teachings of the Rosicrucian mystics it was stated that the oak furnished the first food for mankind, the acorn as meat and the honey-dew (*honigmeth*) as drink. The rustle of the foliage denoted the presence of the Deity. Even at Ephrata the Zionitic brotherhood would wander into the forest and appeal to this supposed oracle. It was further firmly believed that when the time of Philadelphian restitution should come, it would once more bring about the primeval simplicity when the oak would furnish unto man his entire sustenance.]

Régnier, after his expulsion from the community, had himself baptized by David Gemaehle, one of the seceders from the Sabbatarian congregation, after which the two men went through the country as apostles, paying especial attention to such of the German settlers as had accepted Judaism,[61] who were scattered throughout the eastern part of the Province. Eventually they drifted to New York, where they spoke in the synagogue and aroused much attention. From thence Régnier made a pilgrimage, on foot and bareheaded, to Georgia, where he joined the Moravians.

---

[61] *Vide* chapter ix, *supra*.

CHAPTER XIII.

A RETROSPECT.

ROPERLY to present the spiritual condition of the German settlers within the Province during the time of Beissel's activity in the Conestoga country, it will be necessary at this point to make a slight digression in our narrative and take a retrospect of the whole religious condition from the time of Pastorius' arrival in 1683 down to the time when the Conestoga Sabbatarians were left without a leader by the voluntary retirement of Beissel.

Many of the earliest German emigrants prior to their departure from the Fatherland were for a time dazzled with the doctrines of Quakerism. Few of their number, however, actually joined their meetings after coming to this country, and even these few exceptions at heart still clung in secret to some of the good old ordinances of the Lutheran and Reformed faiths.

As a prominent example of this kind may be named the Germantown pioneer, Francis Daniel Pastorius, who,

Francis Daniel Pastorius.

though to all outward appearances in full fellowship with the Quakers and conformed to their usages, yet had his two sons baptized in the Lutheran Church. Who officiated, who the sponsors were, or where the ordinance was administered neither history nor tradition tells us. That it was done, however, is shown by the published letter to his father, dated June 1, 1693:

" My wife brought to the world, March 30, 1690, unto me a son, named Johann Samuel, and then April 1, 1692, a second one. The name of Heinrich was given him by holy baptism.'' [62]

During the earliest days of Penn's proprietorship there was but little German emigration, and such as sought the shelter of our promised religious toleration were mostly of the Mennonite faith, and in the course of a few decades became one of the most important sects which aided in the making of our Commonwealth. It is a fact worthy of note, that during the whole of the first decade following the landing of Penn there was no place of religious worship for the Germans who adhered to the Lutheran or other orthodox faiths. Pastorius, in a letter written to his father in 1686, states:

" We have here in Germantown, Anno 1686, built a church for the congregation, but have not cultivated outward appearances by erecting a great stone edifice, that the temple of God (which we believers are ourselves) may the rather be erected.'' [63]

---

[62] (" Welches mein Eheweib mir Anno 1690 den 30 Martii ein Söhnlein namens Johann Samuel zur welt gebohren. Und dann Anno 1692 den 1, Aprilis das zweite, deme der name Heinrich bey der heiligen Tauffe gegeben worden. *Umständige Beschreibung*, p. 60.'')

[63] (" Wir haben allhier zu Germanton Anno 1686 ein Kirchlein für die Gemeinde gebauet, darbey aber nicht auf ein äuserliches, grosses Stein, Gebäude gesehen, sondern dass der Temple Gottes (welcher wir Gläubigen selbst sind) gebauet werden, und allesamt heilig und unbefleck seÿn mögen.'')

How the first orthodox services were introduced by Heinrich Bernhard Köster, who came to Pennsylvania with Johann Kelpius, in 1694, and how a tabernacle was erected on the rocky banks of the Wissahickon has been fully told in the preceding volume.[64] The ministrations of Daniel Falkner, in the territory which still bears his name, "Falkner Swamp," are also fully described. It was here that, during the earliest years of the eighteenth century, was built the first German Lutheran house of worship in North America of which any definite record exists.[64]

It is unnecessary to say that it was an unpretentious log-house, without any outward sign denoting its sacred uses. It sufficed, however, for the few Lutherans and Reformed in the vicinity until 1721, the very year that Beissel commenced his ministrations, when it was replaced by a more solid structure to accommodate the increased number of worshipers who flocked there under the pastorate of Rev. Gerhard Henkel.

Returning to the close of the seventeenth century and the earliest years of the next one, we have an occasional arrival of vessels bearing a few German emigrants. These, as stated, were chiefly followers of Simon Menno, and settled in the vicinity of Germantown, and by the year 1708 were strong enough numerically to erect a meeting-house within the bounds of the corporate limits of the town, with Wilhelm Rittighausen as their first preacher.

This meeting-house, also a plain log-house, was the first congregational house dedicated to the worship of Almighty God within the bounds of the German township of which we have any definite record. This house, supplanted in 1770 by the present stone structure, is still used for its

[64] *The German Pietists of Provincial Pennsylvania*, Philadelphia, 1894.
[64] Gloria Die, at Wicacoa, was a Swedish Lutheran church, see *German Pietists*.

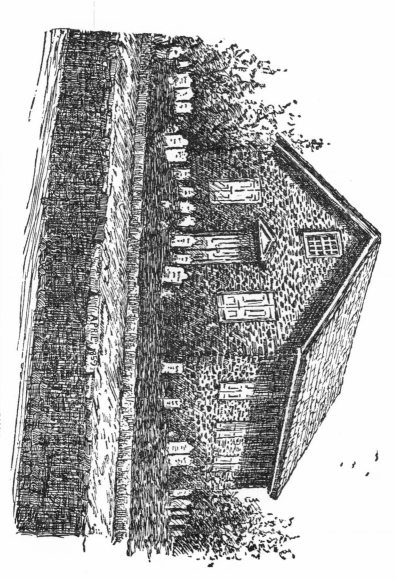

THE OLD MENNONITE CHURCH AT GERMANTOWN.

original purposes by descendants of the early German pioneers who built it.

It was not until the commencement of the second decade of the century that the great wave of German emigration struck the shores of the American colonies, and Pennsylvania received the greater share. Among these emigrants there were many Lutherans and Reformed, as well as Mennonites, Baptists and other non-orthodox sects. It was from the latter that Becker and Beissel gained nearly all their converts. None were thus far gathered from the Lutherans, and but few from the Reformed.

The lack of any number of regular ordained German pastors of the Lutheran and Reformed faiths at this period (1715–1725) was an unfortunate one, and led to a number of both these faiths joining other churches and sects, both German and English.

A situation of which some of the dissenting English clergymen quickly availed themselves, and taken together with the fact that the Quaker tenets were making little or no headway among the laboring classes, and that the Church of England, from its peculiar organization and its relation to the State, failed to appeal to the masses, proved to be the opportunity for both Presbyterian and Baptist clergymen in the Province, one by which their congregations might be increased and the churches placed upon a better financial footing.

There was, however, an important factor which gave the leaders of the above two denominations great concern. This was the Sabbatarian movement, which was then steadily gaining strength among the English settlers in Chester and Philadelphia counties, owing to the distribution of the English tracts of Beissel and Wohlfarth. Numerous attempts were made to counteract the arguments of the two German evangelists, and this eventually brought about the re-publication of the Westminster Shorter Catechism in Pennsylvania.

Among the leading clergymen of the county of Chester was David Evans, pastor of the Presbyterian congregation at Tredyffryn in the Great Chester valley. David Evans was a bold, fearless and aggressive man, who, when finding that the English Sabbatarian publications of the German enthusiasts were being distributed in his territory, and the question of the true Sabbath was even agitated among the staunch members of his own flock, he determined to issue a book, which was not only to refute the doctrines of the Quakers, counteract the arguments of the Sabbatarians, but at the same time supply the long-felt want of an orthodox book of primary instruction, and by reaching the youth would thereby ensure a healthy growth, not only of his own congregation, but of the church at large as well. To accomplish his object he, too, made a journey to Philadelphia and visited the "New Printing Office" lately set up by Benjamin Franklin. Thus far all that was known of this venture was an advertisement, which appeared in the *Pennsylvania Gazette*, No. 174, March 30, 1731–32, setting forth :

"JUST PUBLISHED.

"A Help for Parents and the Heads of Families, to instruct those under their Care, in the first Principles of Religion : Being a short plain Catechism, grounded upon God's Word, and agreeable to the Westminster Assembly's excellent Catechism.

' By David Evans, a Labourer in the Gospel at Tredyffryn in Pennsilvania. Philadelphia : Printed and sold by B. Franklin. Price 9*d*."

No copy of this Catechism seems to have come down to us, and with the exception of the above advertisement, the book appears to be entirely unknown to bibliographers. Nor was it even known that the book was ever printed.

Now at the close of the nineteenth century light has been unexpectedly shed upon the subject; the veil of uncertainty is lifted as it were, and although no copy is known to have survived at the present writing, we are able here to present positive information as to its printing and distribution of what was the first edition of the Westminster Shorter Catechism printed in the Middle Colonies.

From the personal entries of Benjamin Franklin in his journal or day book, commencing July 4, 1730, it appears that Rev. David Evans had printed in 1732, an edition of over four hundred of these "Helps" or Catechisms, viz:

REV. Mr. EVANS DR,

1732
February

3 Reams paper		£2. 5. 0.
Printing 3 sheets & a quarter		
of Catechisms a 25s.		£4. 1. 3.
Stitching 100		5.
Binding 1 doz.		6.

The size of the edition is arrived at by the following calculation: as there were three and a quarter sheets to a book, the three reams of paper would call for about four hundred and forty books, provided none were spoiled in the printing.

Two entries made upon May 8th and June 3d, following, call for cash credits of five and three pounds respectively. Five months later, November 9th, Franklin writes:

"Settled with Mr. Evans and his Dr. to balance £5.8.9." This appears to have closed the transaction so far as the first edition was concerned.

The majority of these "Helps" and "Catechisms" were chiefly distributed among the settlers in Chester and the adjoining counties. A number, however, were sent to parts far from the beautiful valley of Chester; again referring to Franklin's Journal we find that on June 20, 1732, he consigns 50 catechisms to Thomas Whitemarsh, of Charleston,

South Carolina. April 22, 1733, he sends by Captain Watkins to his brother James, at Boston, Massachusetts, 50 catechisms.

During the year 1735 a second edition was printed, in the absence of any specimen of this book it is impossible to tell how near it conformed to the previously quoted one, the only knowledge we have of it being an advertisement in Franklin's paper of March 21, 1733.

"Lately printed, and sold by the Printer thereof. The Shorter Catechism of the Assembly of Divines, with the Proofs at large. Price 4s. per Doz. or 6d. single.[65]

This was evidently a private venture of Franklin, based upon the success of David Evans' edition.

Following interesting entries relating to this second edition, are copied from Franklin's Journal:

Mr. Thomas Evans of Welsh Tract for 100 Catechisms
     bound a 3d. 8d.

Sent to Mr. Timothee by Robert Stevenson
     100 Catechisms

Sent to Brother James by Brother Peter
     100 Catechisms

Returning once more to our retrospect, as German emigrants continued to come to the Province in large numbers, both by sea and from other provinces, the various evangelists and enthusiasts for a time had the field to themselves, of which they did not fail avail themselves.

Among the many letters and missives sent to Germany giving an account of the various "awakenings" and the religious condition of Pennsylvania, written by the participants in these movements, accounts wherein they describe the situation from their own point of view, none is more interesting than the letter dated October 28, 1730, and sent by

---

[65] *Pennsylvania Gazette*, No. 277.

John Adam Gruber, of Germantown to Berleburg, which was
then the veriest hotbed of sectarianism in the Fatherland.

An extract of this missive was published in the *Geistliche
Fama* for 1731.   Gruber was a Separatist, who in Germany
belonged to what were known as the Inspired (*Inspirirten*)
and after his arrival in America remained in hearty sympathy with them, both here and at home.   A fact to be
taken into consideration when passing in judgment upon
this letter.   After a short introduction he states :

" In this vicinity all is dead, and the living spark in those of
good conscience, is being completely extinguished by the tumult
of the world.

"About the well-known companions of our voyages, one
could mention enough to fill a great register of sin and scandal.
The Lord look into it and save such as are willing to be saved,
and such as labor and groan under corruption, so that the enemy
does not completely engulph them.

"At Conestoga, some twenty miles from here, a new awakening has appeared among some of the new Dunkers.   The leader
is the well-known baker Conrad Beissel.   They have a grand
opening among the disposing minds, and urge strongly upon
the rejection of the world and self.   Their clothing and food
is limited to the extreme necessities, and they dispose of all
superfluous chattels and cattle.   They salute no one whom
they meet upon the street, but go straight ahead.   To all outward appearances they live in great harmony.   Both sexes,
almost daily, practice the breaking of bread.   They sanctify
the seventh day, and testify by the rest of their demeanor, that
their aim has been taken with great power and zeal, towards
an irreproachable life, and a constant communion with God.
They have offered some weighty testimonies toward a reawake-
ning of other members, chiefly Schwarzenau Dunkers, from
whom they went out, and who now offer them much opposition.   They have also given them in the meeting-houses of
the now declining Quaker sect.

" How it will go with them in the future time alone will
tell.   I wish them a true Spirit and the help and assistance of

Geiſtliche
FAMA,

mitbringend
verſchiedene
Nachrichten
und
Geſchichte

von
göttlichen Erweckungen und Füh-
rungen/Wercken/Wegen
und Gerichten/
allgemeinen nnd beſonderen Begebenheiten/
die zum Reich Gottes gehören.
Erſtes Stück.

Der Nahme des HErrn wandelt auf der Erden.

Geſammlet und gedruckt
in Philadelphia
1730.

TITLE PAGE OF THE GEISTLICHE FAMA.

Original in collection of Historical Society of Pennsylvania.

the Lord. At least some in these places and land look upon them as a sign of the time. A. Mack has a literary controversy with them about the sanctification of the seventh day.

" Here and there, *Socianism*, *Naturalism* and *Atheism* spread themselves mightily. Therefore I have often wished that one of the elder brethren from home were here : or that I could be amongst them, so that we could quicken our faith in the Lord amongst ourselves. Alas ! my wife will not let herself be disposed unto this. So one must exercise patience until the Lord disposes otherwise.

" I certainly promised to compile a medical history of the Indians. But the knowing ones, who are the best natural scientists, live from 50 to 100 miles from hence, so that I cannot get to talk with them. The most frequent diseases among us are cold and burning fevers, epileptic fits, small-pox and stomach troubles. The root of the wild Spikenard, boiled in milk, is used by the Indians as an antidote for snake-bites. It is taken inwardly, and applied outwardly as well. The *Bibernell* essence with which I supplied myself, has thus far served my house well. Children with us grow fast but have no stamina. In summer the heat is great and in winter it is cold. Sudden changes also occur, all of which ruins our nature.

" The most good natured of the accompanying friends, intend to join the new B[rethren] congregation. They desire Hymnbooks. In case any friends are found who wish to do a pious act, let them send us a couple of hundred."

In the same volume of the *Geistliche Fama* is to be found a reprint of Matthias Bauman's Newborn pamphlet, quoted on page 75 of this work. This was not known to the writer when the previous chapter (VII) was put into print. On account of its extreme rarity a specimen page has been reproduced.

The imprint " Philadelphia" upon the title of the Magazine, called the *Geistliche Fama*, is a false one. The books were printed at Berleburg, Germany, and contain some important contributions from Pennsylvania by different leading sectarians in the Province. Another of these pseudo-

50 **IV. Pensylvanisches Christenthum.**

Extract-Schreiben aus J. A. Gr.
**Brief aus Germantovvn in Pensylvani-
en vom 28. Oct. 1730. empfangen
in B. 1731. den 12. Febr.**

Dessen Geliebtes hat mich sehr erfreuet,
ein Andencken von ihm zu sehen. Ich
wünsche nur, daß solches stäts vor dem HErrn
in seiner Treue vor einander seyn und stehen
möge. Denn bey diesen Zertrennungs- und
Zerstreuungs-vollen Zeiten, da ieder in das
Seinige sich wendet, es sehr nöthig ist, vor die
Risse zu stehen, und das, was schwach und müde
werden will, zu stärcken.

Jn hiesiger Gegend ist alles wie todt, und der
gute Funcken der guten Wisser wird in dem
Welt-Getümmel vollends erstickt. Von unserr
bekannten Reyß-Gefährten wäre manches gro-
bes Sünden-und Aergerniß- Register zu mel-
den. Der HErr sehe darein, und rette, was sich
will retten lassen, und die unter dem Verder-
ben seufzen und stöhnen, daß der Feind nicht alles vollends verschlinge.

Zu Conastoba, etliche 20 Meil von hier,
thut sich eine neue Erweckung hervor unter einigen neuen Täuffern. Der Anführer ist der be-
kannte Becker, Conrad Binsel. Sie haben
grosen Eingang bey denen Gemüthern, dringen
sehr auf eine Welt-und Selbst-Verschmähung,

imprints, which circulated among the German sectarians in Pennsylvania was *Gespräche Im Reich der Geistlichen Todten*, etc. It was a small quarto of forty-eight pages ; a copy is in possession of the writer.

The beginning of the second quarter of the century, however, brought about a change in the unsettled spiritual condition of the German settlers. The arrival of Johann Philip Boehm, a devout schoolmaster, Rev. George Michael Weiss and Peter Miller, upon the Reformed side, and the two Stoevers and others of the Lutheran faith brought order out of chaos.

Gespräche
Im Reich
der
Geistlich Todten
und
Geistlich Lebendigen,
Worinnen
Der Unterscheid/ zwischen denen in Jenatschen Waysen-Hause jüngsthin entdeckten enthusiastisch-und fanatischen Schwärmereyen, wie auch häßlichen Schand-Thaten, und zwischen ungeheuchelter Frömmigkeit, und einen Christen anständigen Wandel gezeiget wird:
gehalten
Von *DEMAS* und *EPAPHRAS.*

Philadelphia/ 1729.

While Boehm, Weiss and Stoever proved sturdy, faithful yeomen in their respective fields, Miller, who was probably the most learned German in the Province, after a few years' labor in the orthodox bounds of the Reformed

I.

Ein Ruf von GOtt
an die unwiedergebohrne Welt
beschrieben
von
Mattheis Baumann.

Ich Mattheis Baumann (anietzo in America) war in Europa in der Chur-Pfaltz
in der Stadt Lamsheim ein armer Taglöhner
und Beysaß. Anno 1701. in dem Junio ist mich
ein Schauer oder Frieren ankomien, wie einen Menschen eine harte Kranckheit ankommt,
und ich übergab mich GOtt, und war recht
los von der Welt, daß ich zu GOtt sagte, ich
wollte gern sterben. Als ich mich in das Bett
legte, da wußte ich gleich nichts von mir selber,
und war wie einer der gleich sterben wollt: wie-
wol ich das nicht weiß, mein Weib sagte es
also. An dem 5ten Tag kam aus mir selber,
und war verzuckt in den Himmel, und hatte
Wort von GOtt, daß ich a) denen Menschen sagen sollte, sie sollten sich bekehren, der jüngste
Tag würde kommen. Und da hab ich gerufen wol
bey einer Stunde einen Ruf über den andern.

FIRST PAGE OF BAUMAN'S CALL TO THE UNREGENERATE WORLD.

FAC-SIMILE TITLE-PAGE (REDUCED) OF STOEVER'S PHILADELPHIA RECORD.

church, left his charges, threw his fortunes into the balance with Beissel and entered the Ephrata Community, where, after the *vorsteher's* death, he became the leading spirit. It is a curious coincidence that nearly all the leading spirits of the mystic movement at Ephrata were recruited from the Reformed church.

Among all the early clergy who labored within the Province of Penn, none were so active in their ministrations or as organizers of congregations as Johann Caspar Stoever. He not only disputed the field with the various Separatists, but entered their very strongholds and organized Lutheran congregations in their midst. It was Stoever's ceaseless activity which proved the greatest check to the spread of the rationalistic ideas among the Germans brought about by their intercourse with the Quakers, and the subsequent abandonment of all regular church forms and discipline, to say nothing of such sporadic movements as that of the New Born and others. If it had not been for the zeal of Stoever and a few others in organizing and protecting the Germans from the inroads being made among them, it is more than probable that a majority of the German and Swiss settlers would have come under the baneful influence of the spiritual lethargy known in German as *Freigeisterey*.

Of all the orthodox clergy then within the Province, Stoever, more than any other, foresaw this danger, and fortunately was prompt to act in the premises. It may be said that at almost every cross-road, wherever there were any number of Germans, Johann Caspar Stoever organized an Evangelical Lutheran congregation, and started a church-book for them; upon the title of which is found his autograph with the addition: "*dermahligen Evangelisch-Lutherischen Pfarrherrn daselbst.*"

A reference to his record of ministerial acts shows that he organized congregations or ministered at the following

places: Coventry, French Creek and Nantmill, in Chester
county; Maxatawney, Oley, Manatany, Conewago, Falk-
ner Swamp (New Hanover), Trappe (New Providence),
Schifenthal, Schuylkill Valley, Colebrookdale, Merion,
Wissahickon (on the Ridge), Skippack, Chestnut Hill,
Germantown, Hosensack, Perkiomen, Leacock, Earltown,
Lancaster, Cocalico, Tulpehocken, Macungie, Quitaphila
(Lebanon), Philadelphia and elsewhere.

Many of these congregations are still flourishing churches,
whose members now point with justifiable pride to the fact
that their earliest records are in the peculiar and unmis-
takable handwriting of Johann Caspar Stoever.

The beginning of the third decade of the century was
evidently the critical period in the religious history of the
Province. The rapid strides made by some of the visionary
and unscrupulous agitators for a time threatened to drag
the German settlers into rationalism and spiritual anarchy.
The activity of the Lutheran and Reformed pastors, with
the shaping of the German Baptists (of which the Sabbatarians may be called the strict Scriptural branch) into a
regular denomination of the Christian church, and the
closer organization of the Mennonites, turned what threatened to be a tide of infidelity and once more brought the
Germans into regular paths of worship.

Another factor in this direction—one which is not to be
overlooked—is, that during these years (1730–1733) we
find the earliest traces of German Roman Catholic missionaries, who proved important agents in combating the
wave of indifference. They were evidently attracted by
the fact that, among the many German settlers who had
located here of late years, a considerable number were of
their faith, and now, owing to the total absence of any
services of their church and the intercourse with the various
Separatists were lapsing into a state of heterodoxy.

Thus it was that several priests itinerated through the

Province and labored among the Germans of their faith, scattered as they were, in the hope of gathering and keep ing them steadfast in the traditions of their fathers. There does not appear to be any evidence or record that these missionaries made any attempt at proselyting, or that they labored among any but their own faith.

Such was the spiritual condition among the Germans in the Province at the time when Conrad Beissel resigned the leadership of the Conestoga congregation, and took the step which led to the establishment of the Mystic Community on the Cocalico.

ORIGINAL TAIL PIECE FROM KLOSTER TYPE FONT.

Bild vnd Contrafactur/
des Edlen vnd Gottsgelehrten HErren Caspar Schwenckfeldts von Ossing/Liebhabers
vnd zeugen der warheit.

PORTRAIT OF CASPER SCHWENCKFELDT.

Original in collection of Hon. S. W. Pennypacker.

CHAPTER XIV.

AN EVENTFUL YEAR.

I N the latter months of the year 1734 several incidents are chronicled which had an important bearing on the Germans in the Province. The most important one was the arrival of the Schwenkfelders during September and October. These peaceful Christians settled principally on the branches of the Skippack and Perkiomen.

Upon their first arrival in Pennsylvania they held a "festival in grateful memory of all mercies and divine favors manifested towards them by the Father of Mercies." This commemorative festival has, since 1734, been annually observed by their descendants. The arrival of these people added another Christian sect to the numerous divisions of the Germans in Pennsylvania.

When Beissel heard that they had come, he, with several of the solitary brethren, made a pilgrimage to the region north and east of the Cocalico, giving especial attention to the Perkiomen country. His efforts among the Schwenkfelders were, however, without effect, for they adhered strictly to their faith.

One of these revival meetings was held at the house of

Leonard Heidt at Oley.   His daughter Maria, a beautiful young girl, just budding into womanhood, became so affected by Beissel's preaching about the "spiritual solitary life," that, when the evangelists left the house, she followed them to the Cocalico and joined with other women living on the east banks of the stream.   This was the more strange as she was betrothed to a young swain in the neighborhood of her father's home.   The day for her marriage had been set and her *Aussteur* (dower) already prepared.   She subsequently entered the Sisterhood, withstanding all the appeals of her parents and fiancé to return to him and the world.   She was also the first of that devout band to change her temporal state for that of immortality.

In September of this year (1734) Michael Wohlfarth made his usual pilgrimage to Philadelphia to harangue the Quakers at their general meeting.   He was accompanied by Jacob Eicher, a son of old Daniel Eicher.   The Friends, advised of their coming, refused to admit them ; so nothing was left for the two pilgrims but to take their usual station on the court-house steps and deliver their testimony to the people as they came from the meeting.

The following notice of this incident appeared in the next issue of Franklin's *Pennsylvania Gazette :*

" Yesterday Morning Michael Wellfare, one of the Christian Philosophers of Conestogoe, appeared in full Market in the Habit of a Pilgrim, his Hat of Linnen, his Beard at full Length, and a long Staff in his Hand.   He declared himself sent by Almighty God, to denounce Vengeance against the Iniquity and Wickedness of the Inhabitants of this City and Province, without speedy Repentance.   The Earnestness of his Discourse, which continu'd near a quarter of an Hour; the Vehemence of his Action, and the Importance of what he delivered, commanded the Attention of a Multitude of People.   And when he had finished, he went away unmolested."

The subject of Wohlfarth's discourse was " *The wisdom of*

God crying and calling to the sons and daughters of men for repentance." This was published by Franklin some three years later (January, 1736–37) together with some additional "*remarks on the present state of Christianity in Pennsylvania.*" It was sold at four pence. No copy of this curious work is known to exist.

Another incident of the autumn of this year was the strange death of Caspar Walter, one of the first members of the Conestoga congregation. He was married and a house-holder. The troubles of the congregation, after the resignation of Beissel and his refusal to return, so affected this devout brother that he sickened and died of a broken heart. The *Chronicon* states that he was "an earnest housefather, went out of time to eternity in deep sorrow of heart on account of the sad schisms in Zion."

N January, 31, 1735, a sad bereavement overtook the German Baptist Brethren in America. This was the death of Alexander Mack, the organizer of the Schwarzenau branch of the denomination. This patriarch of German Baptists was born at Schriesheim in 1679; educated in the Reformed faith, and was by profession a master miller. He embraced the Baptist principles in 1708, came to America in 1729, and acted as chief elder or bishop of the Brethren until his death.

He lived in a log-house which stood in front of the present meeting-house, and was used for the meetings of the Brethren as well as a dwelling of the elder.

This house was built upon half an acre of ground in Van Bebber township, donated August 4, 1731, by Peter Shoemaker to Johannes Pettikoffer, who is said to have procured the necessary funds and material for building by asking gifts therefor from the inhabitants. It was one of the earliest houses built on that part of the highway from Germantown to North Wales. This little settlement became known as Bebberstown after the original owner of the land. Owing to the similarity of the name and the humble condition of the German settlers in the little village, the place in derision was soon corrupted into Beggarstown (*Bettel-*

SIGNATURE TO DEED OF SHOEMAKER TO PETᵔ KOFFER.

hausen in German). The story, so oft told, that the name was due to Pettikoffer soliciting funds and material towards building his house is not warranted by the facts, as the name *Bebberhausen* or Bebberstown appears prior to the arrival of Pettikoffer.

Here in this humble habitation died the patriarch of the great body of German Brethren now distributed over this broad land as a denomination having over 100,000 communicant members, and enjoying the respect of all Christian bodies.

Alexander Mack was buried in what is known as the upper burying-ground of Germantown. A small tomb-stone was placed over the body in the centre of the grave bearing the inscription :

Hier Ruhen | die gebeine | A. M. | geboren 1679. | gestorben 1735. | Alt 56 Yahr.

Here the remains rested until the year 1894, when they were carefully removed to the God's acre in the rear of the Brethren church, where they now repose beside those of his son, Alexander, and family.   The inscription upon his new tombstone reads:

Alexander Mack Sr. | the first minister | and organizer of the | Church of " The Brethren" | in the year 1708 | Born at Schriesheim | Germany, 1679. | Came to Germantown | 1729, died 1735 | Removed from | Axe's Burying Ground | 1894.

Let us now lift the veil of the past for a few moments and picture to ourselves and the generations of the future the scenes enacted at the burial of this venerable patriarch and warrior in Christ.

No sooner had the soul taken its flight upon that bleak winter night, than the *Einlader* or *Anzeiger* (notifier) was sent out towards Germantown, Ephrata, Coventry, Oley and the Swamp.   Wherever there were Brethren they went from house to house, advising them of the death of the patriarch and inviting them to the funeral.   This was a peculiar custom in vogue among the Germans and existed down to the early years of the present century.

Other brethren again took charge of the obsequies.   The *schreiner* (cabinet-maker) was sent for to measure for the coffin.   This was a shaped wooden box made of unpainted cherry wood, as it was believed that the grave-worm could easiest penetrate this wood, and thus the body would be devoured most quickly.   In making the coffin great care was taken that no shaving escaped.   These, as well as all particles of sawdust, were carefully gathered up and placed in the bottom of the coffin, and then covered with a linen cloth, upon which the body was placed.   The reason for this great care was the belief that, if any particle escaped, whatever house it blew into the next death would occur therein in the near future. Then, when the coffin was carried into the house of mourning, it was always brought in head first, or else another funeral would soon follow. Care was also taken to have the foot always towards the door and the lid hidden from view behind the outer door.

There were two peculiarities about this coffin. Owing to the prominence of the deceased, eight metal handles were procured, a species of extravagance rarely indulged in by the Germans of that early day. The other was that the lid was a peaked one, giving the body ample room. The ordinary coffin of that day had a flat lid, and was commonly known as a *nasenquetcher*, from the fact that it often flattened the nose of the deceased.

REAT indeed was the company that assembled on the day of the funeral; the humble cabin in *Bettelhausen*, wherein reposed the mortal remains of the patriarch, was much too small for the multitude who had journeyed from all quarters over the snow-capped hills to bear tribute to the character and pure life of the founder of the German Baptist Brethren in America. A man who was once in affluence, while in the Fatherland gave up his all for the cause, came to the wilds of America for conscience sake, and here ended his days in a cabin built for him with contributions of the charitable.

Upon this occasion were gathered the Brethren from Germantown, prominent among whom were Peter Becker, Christopher Sauer, Heinrich Kalkgläser, Heinrich Pastorius and others, young and old. Then came the solitary from the Cocalico, who, led by Beissel, Wohlfarth and the Eckerling brothers, all in their picturesque Pilgrim garb, had walked the whole distance from Lancaster over the frozen ground in silence and Indian file. There were brethren from Coventry and Chester county with Martin Urner, who had but a short time before been consecrated by the deceased as his successor and bishop of the denomination in Pennsylvania. There was also a deputation of the Sabbatarian Brethren from the French creek. Lastly, there came from the Ridge on the heights of the Wissahickon those of the Pietists of the Kelpius Community who still lived there as hermits. Among these recluses were Conrad Matthäi, Johann Gottfried Selig, Daniel Geissler, Christopher Witt, Andreas Bony and others; all to perform the last homage to the religious leader who now reposed cold and inanimate in the lowly cabin by the roadside.

The obsequies commenced, as was then the custom, about noon with a funeral feast, of which gamon, cakes, cheese and punch were important features. This was followed by religious services, lasting until the sun had set, and when darkness had fairly set in a cortège was formed. First came flambeau-bearers; then the carriers, four of whom bore the coffin upon their shoulders; then followed the Wissahickon Brotherhood, chanting the *De Profundus* alternately with the Ephrata contingent, who sang a hymn specially composed for the occasion. The rear was brought up by the relatives, friends and Germantown Brethren.

It was an impressive and weird sight as the cortège, with its burden and flickering torches, filed with slow and solemn step down the old North Wales road. A walk of about a quarter of a mile brought them to a graveyard. It was merely a small field, half an acre in extent, which was divided from the road by a low stone wall and partly fenced off from the other fields by a rail fence. This ground was known as *Der obere gemein Kirchhoff* (the upper common burying-ground), and was free to all residents who had contributed towards the wall and fence, or such respectable white residents as paid a certain sum for opening the grave. The ground belonged to no particular congregation, nor was it consecrated ground in the usual sense of the word. When the procession arrived at the grave the sight was an inspiring one, worthy of the artist's brush:—the hermits and brethren in their peculiar garb, with uncovered heads and long flowing beards, chanting their requiem; the snow-covered ground; the flickering torches; the coffin upon its rude bier; the black, yawning grave, and the star-lit canopy above. As the mourners surrounded the grave another dirge was sung while the body was lowered into its resting-place. Three clods were then thrown into the grave, a hollow sound reverberating in the night air as they struck the coffin. This ceremony was typical of the return of the body to dust, whence it came. A number of Brethren then seized spades and filled in the grave. When it was about half full the torches were extinguished and thrown into the tomb and the filling proceeded with. After this the company dispersed, and the body of Alexander Mack, founder of the Dunker denomination in America, was left to repose in its narrow cell until after a lapse of a century and a half, when the remaining dust was tenderly removed to consecrated ground in the rear of the church of which he was the patriarch. Well may it be said that he now rests with his own people.

IS wife was Anna Margretha Kling, who died in Germany. He left four children, three sons and one daughter, Alexander, Valentin, Johannes and Elizabeth, all of whom became more or less identified with the Ephrata Community. Valentin, his wife Maria [Hildebrand] and daughter, and the sister, Elizabeth, ended their days therein. Alexander (b. 1712, baptized 1728), for a time Brother Timotheus [Theophilus], married Elizabeth Nice, was ordained by the

IN THE DUNKER GRAVEYARD AT GERMANTOWN.

GRAVE OF ALEXANDER MACK THE PATRIARCH,
(BROTHER THEOPHILUS)
SHOWING OLD AND NEW GRAVESTONES.

GRAVE OF ALEXANDER MACK.
(BROTHER THEOPHILUS)

PHOTO, BY JULIUS F. SACHSE.

Brethren at Germantown in 1749, and ended his days in their service. Heinrich Klackglässer succeeded Alexander Mack, the elder, as elder of the Germantown Brethren, but the death of the patriarch so unsettled the members that seventeen, both men and women, eventually joined the *Beisselianer.*

At this period the hymn-book of the Ephrata congregation was again enlarged. For some reason this edition was not printed upon a press, but laboriously executed during the long winter nights in the cabins on the Cocalico with the pen by the men and women who lived as solitary. The title of this curious work is as follows:

Paradisische Nachts Tropffen | Die sich in der Stille zu Zion als | ein Lieblicher Morgentau | uber die Kinder Gottes | Ausgebreitet | in | Die Sonderheit | Denen zu den füssen Jesu Sitzenden Kindern | Ihrer inwendigen erweck-ung und | Wahren herzens andacht | als | Ein rechte und Göttliche Schulübung um | Die wahre und geheime, ja im | Geist hier verborgen | legende | Sing-Kunst zu lernen | mitgetheilt | und | ans licht gegeben | Im Jahr | 1734.

The *Paradisische Nachts Tropffen* contains 136 pages, viz., title one; text, consisting of 213 hymns, 132 pages; register, two pages. An appendix of thirteen pages, containing sixteen hymns, was afterwards added; this was paged separately, and bore the following heading:

Einfältige-Gemüths bewegungen, Welche aus der inwendigen | Geistes-Stille in Wahrer-Hertzens Andacht heraus | gestossen, und zum Täglichen übung ge | sangs weise in reimen ge | bracht.

Translation: [Simple commotions of the Spirit, emanating from the secret spiritual quietude of true inward devotion. Rendered hymn-like into rhymes for daily practice.]

Specimens of this book are exceedingly rare. Fac-simile of both the *Nachts Tropffen* and the appendix are here reproduced from the copy in the possession of the Historical Society of Pennsylvania.

Paradiesische Nachts Tropffen
Die Sich in der Stille zu Zion als
ein lieblicher morgen tau
über die Kinder Gottes
aus gebreitet.

und

Jn Sonderheit

Denen zu den Füssen Jesu Sitzenden Kindern
Jhrer inwendigen erweckung und
wahren hertzens andacht

als

Eine rechte und Göttliche Schulübung um
die wahre und geheime Ja im
Grist hier verborgen
liegende
Sing-Kunst zu lernen

mitgetheilet
und

das Licht gegeben

Jm Jahr 1 7 3 4

TITLE-PAGE TO BEISSEL'S MANUSCRIPT HYMN-BOOK OF 1734.

Original in collection of Historical Society of Pennsylvania.

FAC-SIMILE OF THE FIRST PAGE OF BEISSEL'S MS. EINFÄLTIGE GEMÜTHS BEWEGUNG.

The year 1735 opened with a great religious revival, which assumed large proportions, extending to nearly all the German settlements in the adjoining counties.

In addition to the accessions from Germantown subsequent to the death of Alexander Mack, all the converts from Falkner Swamp came in a body to the Cocalico during the first and second months of the year.

In the third month (May) Biessel organized a pilgrimage to the Tulpehocken region, preaching a crusade against sin and Satan with so great an effect, that a number of prominent members of the Reformed congregation longed henceforth to live a spiritual life and woo the celestial Sophia.

A FRAGMENT OF EPHRATA MUSIC.

CHAPTER XV.

THE AWAKENING ON THE TULPEHOCKEN.

F all the various movements chronicled in connection with the history of the Ephrata Community none is harder to explain than the outcome of this revival preached by Conrad Beissel in the month of May, 1735.

We have here several organized Lutheran and Reformed congregations, the latter in charge of two pastors, one of whom was ranked among the most devout and learned theologians in the Province. Educated in one of the best universities of Europe, he was ordained to the ministry and for four years faithfully served his charges. Of his church officers, there was one of the clearest headed men in the Province, who for years was consulted by both civil and military authorities in times of need and danger, and at the same time was the official Indian interpreter of the government. Yet both of these men were so carried away by the arguments, sophistry or eloquence of Conrad Beissel, that they, together with several officers of the congregation, left their faith, went to Ephrata and entered there as humble postulants, and, with the exception of a single family, ended their days in the Community.

What these convincing arguments were it is difficult at this late day even to surmise.   The fact, however, remains that we have a regularly ordained minister of the Reformed faith leaving his church and following the footsteps of one who but a few years before had been a humble, uneducated and unknown journeyman baker; but now as an evangelist is spreading the Sabbatarian gospel, combined with mystic theosophy.

In following the course of Conrad Beissel, from the time he first settled on the Mühlbach, we are first of all struck by his peculiarities, and then astonished beyond measure at the wonderful power whereby he induced other people to imitate them.   He has been rather irreverently compared with the Pied Piper of Hamelin, who tuned his pipes and a great multitude followed him wherever he went.   In these days it is hard to understand how it was that when Beissel established his hermitage in what was then a desolate region, men and women came from distant parts to put themselves under his direction.   They voluntarily submitted to hardships, bearing burdens—themselves drawing the plow—and sleeping at night on a rude bench with a billet of wood for a pillow.   Similar phenomena were witnessed in the third quarter of the nineteenth century, when Thomas Lake Harris, an ex-Baptist preacher, induced an accomplished diplomatist, known in every capital of Europe, to endure like privations at Brocton, N. Y.

Perhaps the best illustration of this strange infatuation is instanced by the Tulpehocken awakening, which forms the subject of this chapter and introduces such important personages as Rev. Peter Miller and Conrad Weiser.

Johann Peter Miller (Müller), son of a Reformed minister, under the inspection of *Kreis Kaiserslautern*, was born early in the year 1710, at Altzborn (Alsenborn) Oberamt Kaiserslautern in the Palatinate. He studied at Heidelberg, and matriculated December 29, 1725, at the University while yet in his teens. In his twentieth year the young deacon volunteered in response to the urgent calls for clergy from Pennsylvania.

In the summer of 1730 he floated down the Rhine to Rotterdam, and embarked at that port for America on the good ship *Thistle*, of Glasgow, Calvin Dunlap, master. He arrived safely at Philadelphia, August 28, 1730, and took the oath of allegiance on the following day.[66]

Almost immediately upon his arrival he applied for ordination to Rev. Jedediah Andrews, pastor of the First Presbyterian church in Philadelphia. After a personal examination that clergyman advised the candidate to apply to the Synod. That this advice was acted upon without delay is shown by the following extract from the minutes of that august body, and is dated just three weeks after his arrival in this country :

" 1730, 19th day [September], at seven o'clock A. M.
" *Post precis sederunt qui supra.*

" It is agreed by the Synod that Mr. John Peter Miller, " a Dutch probationer lately come over, be left to the care " of the Presbytery of Philadelphia to settle him in the " work of the Ministry."

The subsequent proceedings were as follows : In accordance with the above resolution the Presbytery appointed three ministers to make the necessary examination of the candidate for holy orders. The latter was now summoned before them and questioned, at the close of which the committee note that they " do appoint him for part of his Tryals " to make an Exegesis in latine on ye Question of Justifi-

---

[66] *Vide* Penna. Archives, Second Series, vol. **xvii**, p. 21 ; also Hazard's *Register*, vol. **xvi**, p. 254.

"OLD BUTTONWOOD MEETING-HOUSE."

THE FIRST PRESBYTERIA. CHURCH IN PHILADELPHIA, CORNER OF HIGH STREET AND BANK ALLEY, BUILT 1704.

" cation, and Yt he prepare a Sermon to be delivered before them." [67]

A week or so later (October 13, 1730)[68] the parties again met, as shown by another minute, where the candidate "came under Tryals, and after a previous Test of his "ability in Prayer, Examining him in the Languages, he "read his sermon and Exegesis on ye Justification and "Various suitable questions on ye Arts and Sciences, "officially [*sic*] Theology and out of Scripture."

So well did the young probationer acquit himself that Rev. Jedediah Andrews, writing to Rev. Thomas Prince, at Boston, 8th month, 14, 1730, says : " He is an extraordinary person for sense and learning. We gave him a question to discuss about justification, and he has answered it, in a whole sheet of paper, in a very notable manner. His name is John Peter Miller, and he speaks Latin as we do our vernacular tongue." [69]

The old manuscript further tells us that the candidate, " having preached a popular sermon on ye day and ye place appointed, and now having delivered his Exegesis upon ye question of Justification, to our satisfaction, ye Presbytery did license him as a Candidate of the sacred ministry to preach the Gospel where Providence may give him opportunity and call." [70]

The young candidate now, after his " Tryals " were passed, expected that his ordination would take place during the week following. In this, however, he was doomed to disappointment, as, for some reason, the service was delayed, and did not take place until after the twentieth of November.[71]

---

[67] *Vide* unpublished manuscript minutes of the Philadelphia Presbytery, case of Charles Tennant and others of the same period.

[68] Date from Boehm's report to Amsterdam Synod, November, 1730.

[69] Hazard's *Register*, vol. xv, p. 201.

[70] *Vide* foot-note 67.

[71] Boehm: reports to Amsterdam Synod.

HEN, finally, arrangements were completed, Peter Miller was ordained in the old Buttonwood meeting-house, as the Presbyterian church was called, which then stood at the south-east corner of Market street and Bank alley, the officiating ministers being Rev. Jedediah Andrews, Rev. William Tennant and Rev. John Boyd.[72]

From the day of his arrival the young minister officiated among the Germans in Philadelphia and Germantown, and to such of the Reformed in the Skippack valley as refused to accept the ministrations of Johann Philip Boehm, and promised to supply them until the return of Rev. George Michael Weiss,[73] who had gone to Germany in in May, 1730, for the purpose of collecting funds for the struggling congregations in Pennsylvania.

From this intercourse with the Skippack congregation Miller came into conflict with Boehm, and disputed the latter's right to exercise ministerial functions because of his lack of any regular ordination. Some of this correspondence is said to be still in existence. Upon the other hand, Boehm seems to have doubted Miller's orthodoxy and cautioned his people against the new arrival.

Rev. Peter Miller is described as being a man of good stature, with a kindly face and friendly manner. He was open-hearted toward those to whom he took a liking, and was modest and genial, upon which account strangers always tried to get an introduction to him and sought his society.[74]

He was a man of much learning and had a good theological training. His disposition, in addition to the simplicity and kindness of his character, was open, affable, familiar,

---

[72] *Vide* Hazard's *Register*, vol. xvi, p. 254.

[73] Boehm's reports to Amsterdam Synod.

[74] *Vide* Acrelius: *New Sweden*, p. 374.

easy of access and agreeable in conversation. A British officer, who visited Ephrata after the Revolution, describes Peter Miller as " a judicious, sensible, intelligent man : he " had none of that stiffness which might naturally have " been expected from his retired manner of life, but seemed " easy, cheerful, and exceedingly desirous to render us " every information in his power." [75]

Almost immediately after his ordination Peter Miller visited the scattered congregations in the Province, and was called upon to take regular charge of the Tulpehocken

SIGNATURE TO A LETTER WRITTEN TO BENJAMIN FRANKLIN.
Original in American Philosophical Society.

church, together with the union congregation of Lutheran and Reformed, which had been formed by the Germans living in the valley of the Cocalico and the Bucherthal. This congregation was known as *Die Evangelische Gemeinde an der Gogallico* (the evangelical congregation on the Cocalico). Both of these charges—viz., the Tulpehocken and the Cocalico—were organized into congregations by Johann Philip Boehm, a devout schoolmaster of the Reformed faith, as early as October, 1727, the Tulpehocken church having thirty-two communicants and the Cocalico congregation thirty-nine communicants on their list,[76] while the same service was done for the Lutherans a

---

[75] *Edinburgh Magazine;* also *American Museum*, Vol. vi, pp. 35–40.

[76] Boehm's Report to the Synod of Holland. Unfortunately the names of these communicants were not given.

year or two later by Rev. Caspar Stöver. When Johann Miller came into this territory Boehm strenuously objected to his invading his field of labor. His protests proved without avail, as they had two years previously, when George Michael Weiss had taken the congregation away from Boehm. This action of Miller opened up the old feud,[77] which, however, ended in the discomfiture of Boehm, and the new-comer was installed in the circuit[78] consisting of the following congregations: Tulpehocken, Cocalico (Muddy Creek), Weisseichenland (White Oak)[79] and Lancaster city. This circuit was then known as the Conestoga Churches.[80]

It must be rembered that the Tulpehocken region, as well as the upper end of the Conestoga valley, was settled almost entirely by Germans of the Lutheran and Reformed faiths.

ENTION has been made of the Evangelical congregation on the Cocalico. When it was determined to build a church for their uses a site was selected about six and a half miles northeast of Ephrata, and a log church was raised on a commanding knoll in what is now Brecknock township, beyond the Bucherthal. This congregation, in church annals, is known as the Muddy Creek (*Moden creek*, *Mode crik*, etc.) church, and is still a union church where Lutherans and Reformed worship upon alternate Sundays. The Lutheran pastor at present writing (May, 1899) is Rev. G. B. Welder; the Reformed minister is Rev. S. Schweitzer.

The old record book of this congregation, like nearly all

---

[77] Boehm: Reports, November 5, 1730.

[78] There were seven churches in the Conestoga circuit; the other three were known as Quittaphilla (*Berg-kirch*), Swatara and Donegal; these were served by Mr. Conrad Templemann.

[79] In Penn township, Lancaster county.

[80] Boehm: Reports, February 13, 1733.

the early Lutheran church registers in Eastern Pennsylvania, was started by Pastor Johann Casper Stöver. The title-page, in his peculiar chirography, bears the date of 1733, and sets forth that this " Church book and Protocol for the Evangelical Lutheran congregation on the Cocalico" was started by him, and that the early records were partly extracted and copied by him from other books and then continued by him. A fac-simile of this title-page appears upon the following page. It is in this register that we find the earliest evidences of Rev. Peter Miller's parochial acts. Thus, upon the first page, under date of January 20, 1730 (O. S.), we find that he baptized a daughter of George Wendel Bügle. This entry further shows that soon after his ordination the young pastor itinerated in the rural districts. Another entry, dated February, 1733, notes the baptism of a daughter of Leonhardt Müller.

The same folio notes acts performed by Rev. Johann Casper Stöver, Rev. Johann Christian Schultz and schoolmaster Zartmann. A reduced fac-simile of this interesting folio is shown on page 237.

As the Reformed element increased in the vicinity a new congregation was formed [81] within the valley of the Conestoga, and had its place of worship about a mile and a quarter southeast of the Ephrata settlement.[82] The church became known as the *Reformirte Gemeinde Cocallico in Conestoken*,[83] and is still a flourishing congregation within

---

[81] The earliest entry in its register is the baptism of Henry Kaftroth, son of Gerhard Kattroth and his wife Mary, baptized December 7, 1738, and their daughter, Mary Elizabeth, baptized October 4, 1740.

[82] The present church is a building of unhewn stone. It stands, as it were, in the midst of the old God's acre. It was erected in the year 1817, supplanting the first church. This primitive building was a log structure with a dirt floor. The material of the old building was purchased by a man named Fasnacht, who carted it to about one mile east of Greenville and converted it into a dwelling house, for which purpose it is still used. —Rev. D. C. Tobias, *History of Bethany Charge*.

[83] Title from the old *Kirchen Protocoll*.

TITLE-PAGE OF THE COCALICO (MUDDY CREEK) CHURCH REGISTER.

FAC-SIMILE OF COCALICO (MUDDY CREEK) CHURCH REGISTER SHOWING EARLIEST
PAROCHIAL ACTS OF REV. PETER MILLER.

the bounds of Ephrata borough, under the name of Bethany church.[84]

This congregation and church were established several years after the building of the Muddy-creek church. The movement was stimulated by the fear that the religious enthusiasm manifested in the valley would tend to lead more of the Germans of the Reformed faith into the fold of the *Beisselianer*. This congregation was always a strictly Reformed church; it was never what was known as a union church.

Rev. Peter Miller ministered to this congregation in addition to his charges at Tulpehocken, Muddy-creek, White Oak and Lancaster. His name appears among the list of early pastors who served the congregation, and from some of these entries we should infer that he occasionally preached for them even long after he entered the Ephrata community, for the entries read: " Peter Miller Jaibetz" (Jabez), the latter being his monastic name as prior.[85]

These congregations, together with several others within that part of the old county of Lancaster, were evidently served with fidelity by the young pastor until his strange conversion to the Sabbatarian doctrine as advanced by Conrad Beissel. It was while the young pastor was itinerating among the people of his faith that Beissel's attention was first drawn to him.

Pastor Miller, who is said to have shown a leaning towards the Separatist movement before he left Germany, and he naturally became interested in the activity of Beissel, who had settled, as it were, within the bounds of one of his parishes. The study of the situation by these two religious leaders—one impetuous, the other of a retiring disposition

---

[84] The corporate name of the church, under the present charter granted November 21, 1861, is " The German Reformed Bethany Church of Ephrata township."

[85] Extract from records, through kindness of Rev. J. C. Hüllhorst, pastor.

—must have been a mutual one, each from his own standpoint. The sequel of our story discloses the victor.

According to Brother Lamech, "the Superintendent "[Beissel] after he had heard that two young preachers "had come into the country, who stood in good repute as "to their character, and also thought well of his work, "aware of his own inability, in view of the important "work before him, thought in his foolishness [*Albernheit*] "that his work would be better carried out if God would "provide one of these young preachers for him, for which "also he often bowed his knees before God. This led to "important matters. For the Superintendent soon after "found occasion to make a visit to Tulpehocken with "several of his disciples, where he was received by the "teacher and elders with the consideration due to him as "an ambassador of God; while on his return the teacher "and C[onrad]W[eiser] an elder accompanied him over "the mountain for six miles. The result of their visit to "Tulpehocken was that the teacher, the elders, and several "others withdrew from the church; whereupon a vener- "able Pietist, by the name of Caspar Leibbecker [Leut- "becker], took the teacher's place in the church."

Of Conrad Weiser the *Chronicon* states that he was "a man who had received from God remarkable natural gifts and sound judgment, and therefore carried great weight with him into whatever sphere he might turn, whether that of nature or of the church. He was the teacher's [Rev. Peter Miller's] main stay, for they were on intimate terms together, which death itself did not destroy."

In the meantime Conrad Weiser again visited the Superintendent in his solitude in the settlement. According to the records, "during this visit he was so enmeshed by the Philadelphian 'little strength' that wisdom finally drew him into her net." The allusion here made refers to the eighth verse of the third chapter of Revelation.

The result of this conference was that before the month of May was over Beissel went again to the Tulpehocken, and with Weiser's aid removed all remaining objections as to re-baptism from the minds of the clergyman and others of his flock.   The culmination was reached upon the last Sabbath in the month of May.   It was a beautiful spring day; all nature was clad in its pristine verdure and seemed to smile a blessing on the sacred rite which was enacted in the valley.

Local tradition mentions both the Tulpehocken and Mill Run [86] as the scene of this remarkable ceremony, where the pastor, schoolmaster, three elders with their families, and several members of a Reformed church voluntarily entered a Sectarian body.

The pastor, Rev. Peter Miller, has left the following explanation of what was perhaps the most important step in his long life :

" Having officiated among the Germans several years, I " quitted the ministry and returned to a private life.   About " that time our small state [the Ephrata Community] was " in its infancy : I never had any inclination to join with it, " because of the contempt and reproach which lay on the " same ; but my inward conductor brought me to that criti- " cal dilemma, either to be a member of this new institution, " or consent to my own damnation, and so I was forced to " chose the first.   We were incorporated with said congre- " gation in May, 1735, by holy baptism.   When we were " conducted to the water, I did not much differ from a poor " criminal under sentence of death.   However, the Lord " our God did strengthen me, when I came into the water ; " and then I, in a solemn manner, renounced my life with " all its prerogatives without reservation, and I found by " experience in subsequent times that all this was put into " the divine records ; for God never failed in his promise " to assist me in time of need."

---

[86] Mill Run, a tributary to Tulpehocken creek, in Lebanon county.

HAT this hejira caused considerable tumult in the infant communities in the Tulpehocken valley, as well as at Muddy Creek and the Conestoga country, may well be imagined, and much feeling was engendered against the seceders. Some laid the delusion of their pastor and church officers to witchcraft and sorcery upon the part of the *Beisselianer;* others went still further, and suggested demonology or the direct intervention of the Evil One. The most cool-headed of the Reformed congregations who had remained steadfast proposed civil prosecution against the Sabbatarians for hetrodoxy and for invading their territory.

In this effort they were seconded by the members of the Cocalico [Bethania?] and Muddy Creek congregations, who had also lost their pastor by Miller's defection. No local magistrate, however, could be found to take action, as all charges apparently fell as soon as it was learned that Conrad Weiser, the official Indian interpreter, was a leader among the seceders.

The faithful members of the Reformed congregation forthwith sent for Pastor Boehm to take charge again of the churches abandoned by Miller, congregations which he had founded. Upon receiving the message of Miller's defection, Boehm immediately returned to his old charges and held his first service at Muddy Creek church on May 11, 1735.

Boehm, in his reports of this period to the Amsterdam Synod, writes:[87]

---

[87] "Und hat dieser Miller Tulpehocken an selbiger Zeit (1730) an sich gezogen, für welchen falschen Geist ich sie öfters gawarnet. Sie blieben aber, als verfürte einfältige Menschen an ihn hängen. Bis endlich der betrug wofür ich sie forthin so geträulich gewarnet an den Tag gekommen, und dieser Miller zu der wüsten siebentäger Tumpler Secten öffentlich übergegangen ist, und sich zu Canestoka in monat April, 1735, hat Tumpeltaufen lassen, und hat bei zehn Familien Reformirt und Lutherisch aus der Gemeinde Tulpehocken mit sich genomen, die thäten wie er."

"And this Miller at the same time (1730) drew [the] Tulpehocken [church] to himself, against whose false spirit I frequently warned them; but they continued to adhere to him like misguided silly people.

"Finally, the fraud against which I warned them so honestly and continuously has come to light, and this Miller publicly went over to the dissolute Seventh-day Tumpler sect and had himself baptized Tumplerwise in the Canestoka, in the month of April, 1735. He took out ten families, Reformed and Lutheran, from the Tulpehocken congregation, who did as he did."

That Miller's conversion to the Sabbatarian fold was not a matter of sudden impulse would be inferred from another of Boehm's reports, dated October 18, 1734.[88] He there states:

"About two years ago[89] he [Miller] together with one of his elders, whom he had installed at Goschenhoppen, went into the house of one of the Seventh-day Tumplers, where they were received as brothers and permitted the host to wash their feet. And this," adds Boehm, "is the truth."

The most curious incident connected with the Tulpehocken revival took place a day or two after the immersion of the converts. It was an act which stands unique in our Pennsylvania church history. This was nothing more or less than a solemn *auto-da-fé*, held within our grand Pennsylvania-German county of Lebanon. Nothing could be more foreign to our thoughts, and yet such is the fact. Who the Inquisitor-General was upon this occasion tradition fails to record. Conrad Weiser, however, appears to have been the chief familiar, while his assistants with torch and forks

---

[88] Ungefähr vor zwei jahr ist er mit einen seinen Eldesten, den er in der Gemeinde zu Goschenhoppen eingesetzt hat in ein haus von einen siebentäger Tumpler gegangen, und sie liesen sich als Brüder grüssen, und von ihn die füsse waschen, und dass ist die Wahrheit.

[89] 1732.

(*mist-gabeln*) were made up of plain every-day German settlers of the beautiful Tulpehocken.   It is true there was no
human victim with *San Benito* and *Caroza;* but the *scheiterhaufen* burned just as brightly and was fed by the same
fuel as if it had been in Seville under a Torquemada of
days gone by.

The scene was in front of Godfrey Fiedler's house,[90] and
was brought about as follows: After the baptism of the
converts, it was proposed to destroy, as heretical, all devotional literature of the old faith which was not in accord

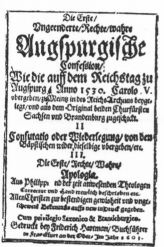

with the new departure.   To accomplish this act of temporary aberration, all the German devotional books in possession of the various families were gathered and taken to
Fiedler's house, and among them were a number, if not all,
from Peter Miller's little library.

It appears that upon the appointed day, Peter Miller,
Conrad Weiser and others assembled at this lowly cabin,
and there solemnly condemned the books and ordered
them to be burned upon the *scheiterhaufen*.   These *libri*

---

[90] At or near Womelsdorf.

heretici consisted of the Heidelberg Catechism ; Luther's Catechism, both the larger and smaller; the Psalter, and a number of time-honored devotional books which for ages had been held sacred in the Fatherland.

Among the proscribed books was a copy of Arndt's *Paradies Gärtlein*, a noted German devotional book.[91] This, according to the belief of the peasantry, was protected by divine interposition from both fire and flood. Many cases are quoted in print, as well as in oral tradition, of the miraculous preservation of this book ; and some persons present objected to its being included, as the Lord would not allow it to be consumed. They were, however, overruled, and our *Paradies Gärtlein* was thrown with the others to be destroyed. A heap of dry brush was prepared in front of Fiedler's house, all ready to ignite when the proper time arrived for it to feed upon the sacred literature.

It was a strange procession that filed out of the humble cabin of Godfrey Fiedler, headed as it was by the late pastor and chief elder of the Tulpehocken congregation. Next followed the *Schulmeister*, carrying an armful of the condemned books, as did others of the participants. When they arrived at the improvised pyre the kindlings were lit and the dry brush was soon ablaze. At the proper moment the various books were solemnly consigned to the flames by Weiser, the schoolmaster and others, with the invocation : "Thus perish all priestcraft."

When the fire had died down the ashes were scattered to

---

[91] For a description of this book see *German Pietists*, pp. 3, 4.

the four winds, and the party, who now considered themselves entirely cut off from the faith of their forefathers, returned to the cabin. Thus ended the first solemn *auto-da-fé* in Pennsylvania of which we have any record. That it was not the last one will appear in the course of our story.

In connection with this burning of the devotional books, there is yet another tradition which relates to the copy of *Paradies Gärtlein.* On the morning after the ceremony, it is said that a member of Fiedler's family passing the ash-heap and partly consumed boughs saw a square block among the embers. On picking it up it proved to be the identical *Paradies Gärtlein* thrown into the pyre on the day before, and which had been under discussion before the ceremony.

There it was, unscathed, while all others were consumed. It is true it was charred on the edges ; the leather cover was shrivelled and black, and the clasps almost burned to a crisp ; yet they held the leaves together, and not a page of the print was destroyed. It was but another instance of the miraculous preservation of this remarkable prayer-book.

When this fact became noised about the country, the simple-minded settlers at once attributed its preservation to Divine interposition, and it was soon quoted with the other remarkable instances of preservation from fire and flood—tales which were prevalent in the Fatherland.

Be this as it may, the book was evidently clasped when thrown into the blazing heap, and by some means it fell short or was diverted, so that instead of falling into the vortex of the fire, it fell among the embers forming the outer circle of the pyre, and was thus saved from destruction. Among the peasantry, however, the miracle story was believed, and the demand for the book in after years became so great that an American edition was printed by Christopher Sauer. For some reason the Germantown printer was never able to immune his output from fire and flood, as was claimed for the German edition.

As the reports of the Tulpehocken awakening, with the defection of so many prominent churchmen and the destruction of the devotional literature spread over the country, they aroused the greatest indignation among the clergy of the diferent denominations.   Several highly colored accounts of the occurrence were sent to Germany, where certain pastorals were issued, warning candidates who contemplated emigration against going to this country: a policy both short-sighted and erroneous, as it was just the want of such regular clergy that led to the peculiar condition in Pennsylvania.

Letters were also written to various pastors in the Province not to concern themselves about the matter, as it was only a *Strohfeuer*.   At the same time the fear was expressed in Germany of a possible introduction into Pennsylvania of the Ellerian heresy (*die Ellerianischen Secte zu Ronsdorff im Herzogthum Berg*).   How groundless this fear was is shown by the fact that no trace of this sect appears in the history of our State.

 FEW weeks after the *auto-da-fé*, Beissel made another visit to Tulpehocken, with the intention of forming the converts into a new congregation, with Peter Miller as elder.   When this proposition was made to Miller, he requested a night's time for reflection and prayer.   On the next morning he declined the offer and made the announcement that he intended to withdraw into the solitude and live the life of a religious ascetic.   This determination of the late pastor was evidently to Beissel's liking, and Michael Wohlfarth was at once appointed as teacher or elder of the congregation.   We will here leave the congregation for a while and follow the course of the late incumbent.

Peter Miller selected as a place for his voluntary retirement a secluded spot on Mill Run, a tributary of the Tulpehocken.   As nearly as can be judged at the present time it was either at or near what is now known as Illig's Mill, and it may be that the spot still known as Dunker's Spring designates the place where the Tulpehocken Brethren were immersed.

The chosen situation was an ideal one. The valley of Mill Run, the *Mühlbach* of Lebanon county, is a romantic dale within the Lebanon valley. The little stream, clear, cold and sparkling as it courses, now turns burr after burr. Every way one looks romantic bits of scenery meet the eye. A century and a half ago this was yet a primitive wilderness. No sound but the purling stream and the plaintive note of the feathered songster broke the silence, while the balsam fir and sweet-scented shrubbery filled the air with heavy perfume. Such was the spot selected by the pious recluse for his probation and retirement. A cabin was quickly built for him chiefly by his own labor. Aided as he was by the other converts, he soon cleared and planted a piece of ground as well as a number of fruit-trees in the coming fall. Here Peter Miller, who now became known as "Peter the Hermit," lived during the summer and fall of 1735. In November he joined the Society on the Cocalico, which was then being organized into a monastic community. In his own account of this period of his life he says:

"At that time (May, 1735) the solitary brethren and sisters lived dispersed in the wilderness of Canestogues, each for himself, as hermits; and I, following that same way, did set up my hermitage in Dulpehakin at the foot of a mountain on a limpid spring. The house is still (December 5, 1790) extant there, with an old orchard. There did I lay the foundation of solitary life, but the melancholy temptations which did trouble me every day did prognosticate to me misery and afflictions. However, I had not lived there half a year when a great change happened; for a camp was laid out for all solitary persons at the very spot where now Ephrata stands, and where at that time the president [Beissel] lived with some hermits. And now, when all hermits were called in, I also quitted my solitude and exchanged the same for a monastic life, which was judged to be more subservient to sanctification than the life of a hermit, where many, under a pretence of holiness, did nothing but nourish their own selfishness. For, as the brethren now received their prior, and the sisters their matron, we were by necessity compelled to learn obedience, and to be refractory was judged a crime little inferior to high treason."

While the devout recluse in his cabin on Mill Run was communing in solitude with God and nature, matters were not running smoothly with the new congregation on the Tulpehocken. Michael Wohlfarth failed to prove himself an acceptable teacher; his violent way of exhorting, with his austere manners, did not suit Weiser and his fellow-members. Consequently he was soon recalled, as Lamech states, "in shame and disgrace." He was at once succeeded by Emanuel Eckerling, who could preach by the hour. He, too, proved unacceptable to the congregation. Where Wohlfarth was aggressive and violent, his successor proved too prosy and suave. So, ere the summer was over, we again find the congregation without any teacher. The outcome may explain the cause for opposition to the two evangelists sent to preside over the congregation by Conrad Beissel.

After the retirement of Emanuel Eckerling, Conrad Weiser assumed the priestly *rôle* and installed himself as teacher of the congregation. Weiser and Beissel at this time were in full accord. He assumed the pilgrim garb, grew a full beard, and mortified his flesh so that even his former associates failed to recognize him. While these events were happening in the Tulpehocken region, a vital change was working on the Cocalico. Accessions were coming to the settlement from various quarters. No less

than seventeen members of the Germantown Dunkers
eventually came to the Cocalico after the death of Patriarch
Mack and joined the Community. Among these persons
were three children of the dead patriarch : Alexander, Valentine and Elizabeth. Others came from Falkner Swamp,
Oley and elsewhere. Thus the settlement assumed quite
large proportions, with no cabin or house in the vicinity
large enough to accommodate the congregation for worship.
With the increase of membership it was evident that some
other system of worship had to be devised, as the little habitations on the Cocalico were all too small to hold a general
meeting. The largest structure then within the bounds of
the *Lager* was a cabin built against the hillside. This was
known as the *Berghaus*, and on account of its roominess
was the favorite place for holding the love-feasts and meetings. But even this now failed to accommodate the people.

To overcome these difficulties it was resolved to erect a
large building for religious and devotional purposes. A
commencement was made in July, 1735, and so rapidly was
the work prosecuted by the united efforts of the brethren,
both solitary and householders, who willingly contributed
their share, that by fall a fine structure was ready for occupation. This house, known to us as *Kedar*[92] and erected to
God's glory, contained besides the hall for meetings large
halls furnished for holding the *agapae* or love-feasts. In
addition there were also a number of small rooms or *kammern*, intended for the solitary, after the manner of the
primitive Greek church.

Before this house was entirely finished the Tulpehocken
brethren, with Miller and Weiser at their head, came to the
settlement. Among this party were five families or households. The names of three are: Peter Klopf, Conrad Weiser
and Hans Michael Miller. In addition there were several

---

[92] In an old MSS. *Kedar das haus der traurigkeit*, i. e., the house of
sorrowfulness.

single men and women who kept to the solitary state. Of the former, Peter Miller, Jemini and another brother, supposed to be Rufinus, have been identified. Of the women, several joined the Sisterhood, but only one remained steadfast. This was sister Thecla,[93] daughter of Peter Klopf.[94] Henceforth the Tulpehocken converts became an integral part of the community on the Cocalico.

Before passing this episode, so pertinent to the Ephrata movement as it was to the Reformed church, it may be well to state that the members of the local Cocalico (Bethania) congregation never forgave Peter Miller for his defection. No opportunity was neglected, either in public or private, to show their disapprobation of the Prior's course; and it was a common occurrence for them, when any of the church officers or members met the devout Prior in road or field, to express their contempt by spitting before or upon him. A local family tradition of one of these Reformed householders states that, upon such occasions, the Prior would never resent the insult, but, merely crossing his hands over his bosom, would utter a short prayer or blessing for his tormentors.

No one could have shown more of a true Christian spirit under such trying circumstances than did Peter Miller. No matter how persistent his tormentor, if at any time the latter got into any trouble no one was more ready to extend a helping hand than this same meek enthusiast, Johann Peter Miller.

The same resentful spirit, only in a somewhat less degree, was evinced toward Conrad Weiser, and whenever an opportunity offered, neither the Conestoga nor the Tulpehocken people hesitated to give vent to their disapproval,—a course in which the aggressors did not always go unpunished,—as their opponent lacked the meekness of the Prior, and was

---

[93] Died October 6, 1748.

[94] Died, 1753.

apt to resent any attempt at insult. An interesting illustration of this is given in a story current early in the present century among the older people. It was that upon a certain occasion, shortly after Weiser had left the Kloster to accept the commission offered him by Governor Thomas, he was riding over the old *Bergstrasse* towards Downing's Mill, and when near the Reading road he met the Reformed pastor of the Cocalico (Bethania) congregation riding upon a horse, Weiser, thinking it a good opportunity to repay the dominie for some previous insults, accosted him with the greeting that he (the pastor) evidently thought himself above the Lord whom he professed to serve. The dominie asked for an explanation. Weiser's answer was that where an ass was good enough for the Saviour it should be good enough for him. The quick-witted dominie replied, that he knew perfectly well that that was true; but as the Governor had appointed all the asses as justices he was forced to ride upon a horse.

TAIL-PIECE FROM KLOSTER FONT.

CHAPTER XVI.

KEDAR.

S the new house of worship neared completion the various Solitary of both sexes, who had dwelt as settlers scattered through the country, gradually moved to the settlement. After the arrival of the Tulpehocken Brethren, four—Peter Miller, Johann Heinrich Kalckgläser, and the two Eckerlings, Israel and Gabriel—as the most important in the Community were quartered in the *Berghaus*.

Kedar, the new house of worship, was of a peculiar construction, different from anything then existing in the New World. The material was of wood, the interstices between the frame-work and floor joists were filled in with wet clay and cut grass, and the sides were then coated with a thin layer of lime. This filling was a peculiarity of all the larger Ephrata structures, and made a house warm in winter and cool in summer, as well as impervious to vermin.

The structure was of three stories, of which the middle one was the chief. This contained the Saal or meeting-room, besides the rooms necessary for holding the Agapæ or love-feasts. The upper story, as well as the ground-floor, was divided off into small rooms or *kammern* for the Solitary.

Even before Kedar was finished, *nacht-metten* were instituted by the Solitary of the settlement. These gatherings were religious watch-meetings held every day at midnight, as at that hour the great Judge was expected. At first they lasted four hours. This time was, however, soon reduced to two hours, as it left but little time for the necessary rest.

When the house was advanced enough for dedication to its pious uses, preparations were made for a general love-feast, the expense of which was contributed by the house-holders to the glory of God who, as the record adds, "had made known His wonders in these heathen lands."

Einlader or inviters were sent out through the Prov-ince among all German Baptists and English Sabbatarians, asking them to participate in the dedicatory services. As the day approached ample preparations were made for a great multitude. In the matter of numbers, however, Beissel was doomed to disappointment, as but few strangers were present, the exception being a strong contingent of English Sabbatarians from the French Creek settlement.

Then again Beissel had rather an exciting experience upon the night preceding the great love-feast, which almost prevented him from assuming his usual place at the meet-ing, and which, it was given out and firmly believed, was an act of the Prince of Darkness. Upon the night in ques-tion it was dark and cloudy ; several human forms entered the settlement and silently picked their way to the cabin occupied by Beissel. It was just before midnight, and all was still and quiet in the Lager, as the time had not yet arrived for the watch-meeting. Two of the intruders lifted the latch and entered the cabin. The anchorite reposed in slumber upon his hard pallet of wood, with a block of the same under his head for a pillow. Not a sound was to be heard but the breathing of the sleeper and the rustle of the wind without. The two men, now beside the cot, without saying a word proceeded to belabor Beissel with a knotted rope and leather throngs. With the first stroke the sleeper awoke with a howl of pain. The blows, however, fell thick

and fast as the intruders followed him about the little room.
At last he gained the door and escaped to the next cabin,
where he fell with fright and covered with bruises.   During
this scene not a word was spoken, the only sounds being the
shrieks of the victim and the swish of the lashes.   After the
escape of Beissel, those who inflicted them departed as mys-
teriously as they had come.

While Beissel and his followers may have firmly believed
that this flagellation was administered by familiar spirits of
the Evil One, so as to prevent the leader from making further
inroads in his kingdom within the Province, the facts are
that the unseen spirits were plain matter-of-fact Germans
of the German Reformed congregation, who thus punished
Beissel for inducing one of their wives to leave her family
and join his society.

 NDER such adverse circumstances the great
love-feast and dedication services proved
somewhat of a disappointment from two
causes.   The first was that so few of the
invited guests came to the meeting.   The
other was an unfortunate break made by one of the brethren
during the sacred rite, by which the strangers present
were more offended than edified.   During the Pedelavium
the brother who washed the feet of Beissel reverently
kissed them and said : " These feet have made many a
step for our welfare."

With the completion of Kedar, one of the house-fathers,
Hans Meyer, the same who first named Conrad Beissel as
Elder of the Conestoga congregation, handed over to Beissel
his daughter Barbara, a young girl of twenty-two summers,
with the request that he " should bring her up to the glory
of God."   Beissel regarded this matter as a providential
leading and, as the *Chronicon* states, " received her, and
had her serve him for the purpose, namely, of founding
the Order of Spiritual Virgins."   The first of these Spiri-

tual Virgins were Maria Hildebrand, Barbara Meyer, Maria Stattler and Maria Heidt, who now bound themselves by a pledge to a communal life. The upper story of Kedar was given to them as their retreat from the world. Shortly afterwards the lower or ground-floor was handed over to the strictest of the single brethren for a similar purpose. These were Michael Wohlfarth, Jan Meyle, Just and Theonis. The arrangement was that the brethren first held their devotions; then, after they had filed out of the Saal, the sisters entered for their hour of prayer. This was soon afterwards changed so that the midnight prayers (*nacht-metten*) were held jointly—an arrangement which gave renewed cause for scandal and gossip among the enemies of the Community.

DRAWING BY AN EPHRATA SISTER.

Beissel, who at first presided over the joint services, taught them on both sides "as a priestly generation to lift up hands unto God on behalf of the domestic household, which was so sorely bound under the yoke of the world; and that this was the continual service of God." The prayers of the pious, however, failed to conciliate the tongues of Dame Rumor; so, after these joint meetings had continued for some months, Sigmund Landert, now a widower, who had disposed of his plantation on the Mühlbach to good advantage, proposed to Beissel that Kedar should be kept exclusively as a Sister-house, in which event he would build out of the wealth which God had vouchsafed him a large house adjoining Kedar to be used exclusively for assembly purposes, provided that he and his two daughters be received into the settlement.

Beissel at first objected to the scheme, but eventually, when Landert offered in addition to build a separate house for him, his consent was given. So popular was the proposal, that Hermann Zinn, a householder, also sold his plantation and offered the proceeds towards the proposed house of prayer.

Plans were at once laid for a large edifice on the hillside,

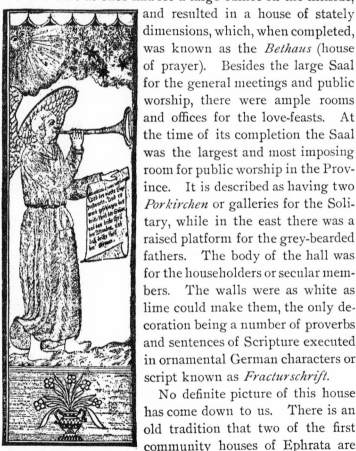

AN OLD EPHRATA DESIGN.

and resulted in a house of stately dimensions, which, when completed, was known as the *Bethaus* (house of prayer). Besides the large Saal for the general meetings and public worship, there were ample rooms and offices for the love-feasts. At the time of its completion the Saal was the largest and most imposing room for public worship in the Province. It is described as having two *Porkirchen* or galleries for the Solitary, while in the east there was a raised platform for the grey-bearded fathers. The body of the hall was for the householders or secular members. The walls were as white as lime could make them, the only decoration being a number of proverbs and sentences of Scripture executed in ornamental German characters or script known as *Fracturschrift*.

No definite picture of this house has come down to us. There is an old tradition that two of the first community houses of Ephrata are pictured on the old symbol *Arbeite und Hoffe* which appears upon the title-page of the Martyr book, printed in 1748. An enlarged reproduction of this symbol is presented on opposite page, and though somewhat vague and indistinct, it may perchance convey to us an aspect of the former Kloster on Zion hill.

AN EPHRATA SYMBOL.[95]

The solitary brethren who were quartered upon the ground-floor of Kedar were again relegated to the cabins

---

[95] The only known picture of the houses on Zion hill. The indistinct one in the foreground is intended for the Hill house (*Berghaus*), above it are Kedar, Zion and others, used as hospitals during the Revolution, 1777–78.

the settlement, and henceforth Kedar was handed over to the Sisterhood. The Saal upon the second floor now became the chapel of the Order of Spiritual Virgins.

Several additional young women were installed and became Spiritual Virgins. Among the number were the two daughters of Sigmund Landert, one of whom, Maria, as Sister Rahel, ended her days in the Kloster. The foundation for a communal life was also laid at this time. Accordingly all provisions were delivered to the Sisters in their kitchen, who daily prepared a supper for the entire settlement in a large dining-hall, they being separated from them by a dividing screen. As Lamech states : " Everything withal was done in order and reverently, according to the leading of the Holy Ghost, and under the supervision of the superintendent, so that the powers of the New World were markedly manifested."

There appears to have been no record kept of any special dedicatory services of the great Saal, except that upon this occasion the camp of the Solitary (*Lager der Einsamen*) received a name to which was attributed a mystical interpretation by the Sophists of the Community. This was taken from Ruth iv, 11, and used in connection with Ruth i, 2, and Genesis xxxv, 16–19. This name has since become historic, viz. :

EPHRATA.

[Ephratah or Ephrath : Hebrew, fruitful, אֶפְרָתָה ; Greek, *Εφραθά Εφράθ.*

1. Name of second wife of Caleb the son of Hezron, mother of Hur and grandmother of Caleb the Spy.

2. Ancient name of Bethlehem-Judah (Gen. xxxv, 16, 19; xlviii, 7). So called in Jacob's time.

Some say that Ephratah may have been the name given to a daughter of Benjamin to commemorate his brother's death near to Ephrath. This would receive some support, because Rachel's son Joseph was called Ephraim, a word of identical etymology, as appears from Ruth i, 1, 2, and I Sam. i, 1.

It is, perhaps, impossible to come to any certainty on the subject.

In Genesis, or perhaps in Chronicles, the name is called *Ephrath* or *Ephrata;* in Ruth, *Bethlehem Judah,* but the inhabitants, *Ephrathites;* in Micah, *Bethlehem Ephratah;* in St. Matt. ii, 6, *Bethlehem in the land of Judah.* Jerome, and after him Kalisch, observes that Ephratah, *fruitful,* has the same meaning as Bethlehem, *house of bread,*—a view which is favored by Stanley's description of the neighboring cornfields. In Psalms cxxxii, 6, we have Ephratah, meaning perhaps Ephraim.] [95b]

[95b] *Smith's Dictionary of the Bible,* London, 1893.

SPECIMEN OF ORNAMENTAL PEN-WORK FROM THE SISTERS' MS. HYMNAL.

(Size one-fourth of original.)

CHAPTER XVII.

JACOB'S KAMPFF UND RITTER-PLATZ.

HE setttlement now became the rallying-point for all the German Baptists, both First- and Seventh-day, within a wide circuit; the meetings were also largely attended by many Mennonites of the surrounding country, and by such of the German settlers as were either lukewarm in their fealty to their orthodox faiths or were debarred by distance from attending the services of any organized congregation of their particular order.

Again, the introduction of mystic theology, combined with some of the esoteric teachings of the Rosicrucian cultus and a closer form of organization with stricter discipline, added to the strength of the new community by attracting a number of kindred spirits who had been imbued with such speculations in the Fatherland.

Among the new arrivals about this time may be mentioned the Thoma family, from Viedendorf, in the Canton of Basel, province of Wallenberg, Switzerland. It consisted of the father, Durst [Theodorus] Thoma, his wife, Catharina, three sons, Theodore, Hans Jacob and Martin, and two daughters, Catharina and Anna.

This family came to Pennsylvania in the ship *Princess Augustus*, Samuel Merchant, master, landing at Philadelphia, September 15, 1736. They had been among the awakened in Switzerland, and upon their arrival at once joined the Ephrata Community, in which they all filled positions more or less prominent. The family, with the single exception of the daughter Anna, sleep in the old "God's acre" by the roadside.

Anna, who was for years a "Rose of Sharon," became the wife of Johannes Wüster [Wister] the Philadelphia merchant, and sleeps in an unmarked grave in the Quaker ground at the corner of Fourth and Arch streets.

With the rapid increase of membership, additional efforts were put forth by Beissel and his supporters to still further extend the scope and usefulness of the new institution on the Cocalico, which was rapidly gaining a reputation for the holiness and aceticism of its people.

The first of these efforts was a decided innovation, it was the introduction and public reading of confessional papers known as *lectiones*. It was ordered that weekly, on the evening of the sixth day, every one should examine his heart before God in his own cell, and then hand in a writen statement of his spiritual condition to the Superintendent, which was to be read at the meeting of the congregation on the following Sabbath. A number of these papers were afterward collected and published in a printed form (a specimen in fac-simile is shown upon the opposite page). It is remarkable that the most unlearned and simple-mined stated their condition so artlessly, unreservedly and simply that one cannot but be astonished at their guile-lessness.

The second new departure of the year was a missionary movement, the object of which was to influence the Germans in West Jersey, where a number of Baptists were settled in Amwell. For this purpose a pilgrimage upon a large scale was undertaken, in which twelve fathers of the congregation joined, prominent among whom was Conrad Weiser. This

Die XLIII Lection.

Auchzet, ihr Himmel, und du Erde ſey frölich, auch das
gantze auserwehlte Geſchlecht der Kinder GOttes, die
wir hoffen auf den Troſt Iſraels, freuet euch, dann die
Zeit unſerer Erlöſung nahet herbey.   Ob wir ſchon jetzt oft
müſſen unſere Saat mit Thränen und Schmertzen ſaen, und
die Schmach der Wittwenſchafft tragen, daß es oft ſcheinet,
als ob der Troſt unſerer Seelen von uns gewichen und uns
verlaſſen hätte: ſo haben wir ihn dennoch lieb, und können
und werden nicht von ihm weichen in Zeit und Ewigkeit.
Und ob wir ihn ſchon empfindlicher Weiſe nicht ſehen noch
ſpühren: ſo wiſſen wir doch gewiß, daß er in unſere Hertzen
an = und aufgenommen iſt und daß er uns unſere Beylage
wohl bewahren wird auf den Tag der Offenbarung und Er-
ſcheinung JEſu Chriſti, da alle Gefangene und Traurige zu
Zion ſollen erlöſet werden, und mit Freuden aus ihrem Ker-
cker gehen.   Darum werden wir nicht müde, auf die herrli-
che Zukunfft unſers himmliſchen Bräutigams zu warten,
der ſo nahe vor der Thür iſt, und zu ſeiner Zeit wird herein
brechen mit ſeinem Pracht und Herrlichkeit, und wird den
Erd Krantz richten mit Recht und Gerechtigkeit.   Darum
erdulten wir auch unſere Anfechtungen mit Freuden, weil wir
ſpühren, daß das Gericht auf Erden einen Anfang mit uns
machet. Dann das Gericht muß zuerſt an dem Hauſe GOttes
anfangen, ehe es weiter gehen kan, Amen. GOTT und dem
Lamm gebühret allein die Ehre.

Die XLIV Lection.

SPECIMEN OF CONFESSIONAL PAPERS READ AT THE EPHRATA MEETINGS, *vide* p. 261.

pilgrimage was under the personal leadership of Conrad Beissel and his trusty lieutenant Wohlfarth. All were clad in the coarse garb of the pilgrims of old, the habit reaching the feet and being secured with a rope and girdle around the waist. This band of missioners, with their full beards and sharp features, their broad-brimmed hats, sandaled feet, and long *Pilgerstab*, walking in silence in single file and head bowed down, could not fail to attract attention wherever they appeared. Their journey led through Nantmill and Coventry in Chester county, and after visiting and exhorting their English brethren in the former and their German brethren in the latter place, they crossed the Schuylkill at Parker's Ford, proceeding over the hill and down the Reading road, through the German settlements —Lutheran, Reformed and Mennonite—to Germantown, where another halt of a few days was made with the recluse on the Wissahickon, then under the leadership of " Sehlee" [*sic*] (Selig) and Matthäi, after which they proceeded to Philadelphia, where they again held forth from the court-house steps, admonishing the populace and advancing the truths of Sabbatarianism. After a somewhat lengthened stay the party finally crossed the Delaware river and journeyed into New Jersey. Here, too, their austere aspect and humble deportment greatly impressed the onlookers. Wherever a German settlement was to be found there they went, preaching and admonishing, and exhorting the settlers to repentance. Thus they pursued their journey until they arrived at Amwell, where, as already stated, there existed a congregation of German Baptists. There the pilgrims met with a cordial welcome, and an awakening or revival of religion at once took place, and as a result preparation were begun to form a congregation similar to the one on the Cocalico—an attempt which proved but a partial success, as will be shown in a subsequent chapter.

The most important event of the year (1736), however, was the issuing of an enlarged edition of the hymn-book of 1732, to which was appended a work of fifty-two pages.

The abstruse title sets forth that it was "Jacob's Tournament and wrestling place, where, the spirit, longing after its origin, in its *sophiam* enamoured soul, wrestling with God for the new name, and came off victorius. Devised in various hymns of faith and pathos, and expressions of the mind, wherein there are set forth, upon the part of God, his unceasing work to cleanse such souls as trust his leadership.

"As upon the part of Man, the eagerness of the Spirit is to preserve and the process of refining and dissolving sin from Man, and the continuous sounds of praise emanating therefrom. For the genial awakening of such as love the welfare of Jerusalem [this book is], published by a lover of the Truth, who lives as a recluse.

"At Philadelphia, Printed by B. F., 1736."

The original German title-page, as printed by Franklin, is shown in fac-simile upon the opposite page.

This consists of thirty-two mystic hymns, of which twenty-eight were written by Conrad Beissel, the final one containing no less than forty-three stanzas. Upon the reverse of the title-page is a motto which, translated, reads: "God gives the Spirit not according to measure; the mystery is great; reason cannot fathom it." The very abstruse preface is dated:

Ephratha in der gegend Canestoges, den 27. April, 1736. This is the earliest public mention of the name Ephrata in connection with the settlement.

It must not be assumed that the religious recluse on the Cocalico spent all their time in mystical speculation and religious devotion. That manual and physical labor was not neglected is shown by the following note by Peter Miller: "At that time works of Charity hath been our chief occupation; Canestogues was then a great wilderness

JACOBS
Kampff- und Ritter-Platz.
ALLWO
Der nach feinem urfprung fich fehnende
geift der in Sophiam verliebten feele
mit Gott um den neuen namen
gerungen, und den Sieg
davon getragen.
ENTWORFFEN
IN UNTERSCHIDLICHEN GLAUBENS-
u. leidens-liedern, u. erfahrungs vollen aus-
truckungen des gemuths, darinnen fich
dar ftellet, fo wol auff feiten Gottes
feine unermuedete arbeit zur rei-
nigung folcher feelen, die fich
feiner fuerung anvertraut.
ALS AUCH
Auff feiten des Menfchen der ernft des
geiftes im aus halten unter dem procefs
der läuterung und abfchmeltzung
des Menfchen der Sünden famt
dem daraus entfpringen-
den lobes-gethön.
ZUR
Gemüthlichen erweckung derer die das heil
Jerufalems lieb haben.
VERLEGET
Von einem liebhaber der wahrheit die im ver-
borgenen wohnt.

Zu *Philadelphia,* gedruckt bey B.F. 1736.

TITLE-PAGE OF HYMN-BOOK PRINTED BY FRANKLIN, 1736.

Original in collection of Historical Society of Pennsylvania.

and began to be settled by poor Germans, which desired our assistance in building houses for them ; which not only kept us employed several summers in hard carpenters work, but also increased our poverty so much that we wanted even things necessary for life."

In addition to these labors the ground was tilled and contributions of grain were secured which were stored to supply the wants of the poor.   Substantial assistance was never refused to such as needed it, and a sweet spirit of charity pervaded the settlement; the solitary of both sexes freely responded to all calls of mercy or humanity.   Works of charity and benevolence indeed occupied most of the time of the solitary when not engaged at their devotions, which, however, were so regulated as not to interfere with their daily labor, and upon that account were mainly held after nightfall.   This unselfish activity was carried to such an extent that they frequently lacked even the supplies necessary for their own daily wants.

OWEVER, this primitive mode of life on the part of the Solitary was not without its tribulations ; there were a number of persons who failed to appreciate their works of charity, or to sympathize with their austere piety.   Prominent among these persons was the township constable, who in the performance of his duties entered the settlement and demanded payment of what was known as the "single men's tax."   This levy was made under an Act originally passed February 22, 1717–18, supplemented March 20, 1724–25, which stated: "Those single men whose estates shall not be rated at fifty pounds, they shall be assessed after the rate of three shillings a head upon a tax of one penny per pound, both for poor rates and city and county levies." [96]

---

[96] *Statutes at Large*, vol. iii, pp. 14-15.

This invasion by the constable caused a great commotion in the camp. Beissel at once summoned all the Solitary Brethren to the Saal to ascertain in consultation the views of all concerned. Nothing, however, was accomplished at the meeting held, as there was a difference of opinion resulting in a division.

One party argued that it was but just and right to pay unto Cæsar his tribute as commanded by Scripture, and counseled that the tax be paid and thus all trouble and annoyance be avoided. The opposing party, headed by Peter Miller, were of contrary opinion, refusing to pay the assessment and claiming personal immunity. Their argument was largely from the history of the Eastern countries; they instanced the fact that the monks and hermits collected by their labor every harvest so much grain as to regularly supply all the prisons in Alexandria with bread, wherefore Theodisius Magnus and other Christian emperors declared them free from all taxes. Considering that they were in no wise inferior to the ancient hermits they urged that the same immunity should be allowed in their case.

The constable, however, who was a plain matter-of-fact person, refused to receive early Church history as a precedent. Summoning some of the neighbors who were antagonistic to the Sabbatarians, without more ado he seized six of the latter party and marched them off to Lancaster. These brethren were Peter Miller, the four Eckerling brothers and Martin Bremmer. The troubles of the constable and his posse were by no means over when the arrest was made, as the prisoners positively refused either to furnish or to enter any conveyance, even if one were provided by the constable. They, however, offered to go peacefully in their usual mode of travel; nothing else, therefore, was to be done by the officer and his deputies than to walk with their prisoners over hill and dale to the county seat. Upon their arrival they were arraigned, and in default of taxes or bail they were committed to the county prison.

Here ten days elapsed, the six brethren subsisting, without a murmur, on the coarse prison fare supplied to them. Not a word of complaint was heard; their time was passed in prayer for their persecutors, in the firm hope that deliverance would come from above, and that in due time their prison doors would be thrown open. At last, no one having come forward to enter bail for them, Tobias Hendricks, a venerable old man and himself a justice of the peace, offered bail for the prisoners, taking their bare word for their appearance in court when wanted. So they were released from captivity, and upon the twelfth day the six brethren once more filed into the camp on the Cocalico.

When the the next court convened the six brethren duly put in their appearance according to promise. The only account we have of this interesting trial, or of the arguments advanced, is the short account in the *Chronicon :*

"At the following May Court of the year 1737 (1736?), they were brought up for a hearing before the Commissioners and Assessors of Taxes, over whom, when they saw before them the men who in the bloom of youth had raised such a warfare against the world, the fear of the Lord came so that they did not speak to them otherwise than friendly, and offered them every favor. The first question was, Whether they would be loyal subjects of the King? To which they answered respectfully, 'that they had already pledged allegiance to another King, and therefore could obey the King only in so far as his rights agreed with those of their King.' The other question was, Whether they would pay the taxes? Answer: 'Not the head-tax; because they acknowledged no worldly authority's right over their bodies, since they had been redeemed from the world and men. Moreover, they considered it unjust that, as they were pledged to spend their lives in their present condition, they should be measured by the same standard as vagabonds, and be made to pay the same tax as these. If they would consider them as a spiritual family, however, they would be willing to pay of their earthly possessions according to what was just.' All this was granted them, and remains unchanged to the present day."

The final result of the trial is best given in Peter Miller's own words, as shown from a manuscript in the possession of the present writer.

" The fear of God came upon the Gentlemen, who were their " Judges, when they saw six men before them, which in the " prime of their ages by penetential works had been reduced " to Skeletons, that they used great moderation, and granted " them their personal freedom, under condition, that they " should be taxed as one family for their Real-Estate."

ROM another contemporary source we learn that the judges finally asked the six brethren to say how much tax in their judgment would be just and fair; or, in other words, for them to assess their own rate. This the brethren refused to do, but finally after much persuasion suggested that a tax of forty shillings laid against the settlement as a whole would be fair. As this proved satisfactory to the board of judges the prisoners were discharged.

Great was the joy of the six brethren when free again and out of the toils of the law. It was with light hearts that they started on their long tramp through forest and field to the Cocalico. When they arrived in the settlement it was already after midnight and the night-watch was in full session. Fervent prayers were being offered for the release of the absent ones. During the invocation the six brethren silently filed into the Saal.

It was an impressive and picturesque scene; the large Saal, with its two galleries, shrouded in semi-darkness, the only light being the flickering tallow candles, one of which stood in front of each worshiper; the dark shadows in the corners; the six released brethren silently ranging themselves in front of the platform with heads bowed and hands crossed upon their breasts similar to the penitents of old; Conrad Beissel standing erect upon the platform, austere and immovable; and the various long-bearded solitary, sitting upon the hard wooden benches, listening to the invocation in behalf of their absent brethren.

With the entry of the party a hush at once came over the assembly. For a few moments the silence was painful; then it was broken by the stentorian voice of Brother Conrad [Weiser] intoning the grand old German chorale of Martin Luther, *Eine Feste Burg ist unser Gott.* Before the singing of the first line had been completed the hymn was taken up by all present, until the strains of the rugged melody reverberated throughout the large room. It was a spontaneous thank-offering emanating from the hearts of the assembled brethren. When the hymn was finished, thanks were offered, and the night-watch closed with an impressive address by Beissel on the power of the Beast upon earth.

As to the instigators of this persecution, the old record says: "Upon those neighbors, however, who had gloated over the misfortune of the brethren, there fell the terror of the Lord, so that they hurriedly left this region."

Shortly after the incident just related, Governor George Thomas made an official visit to the settlement. He was accompanied by a large retinue of "people of quality" from Virginia and Maryland. The fame of the settlement was not alone the result of the sensational trial just completed, but was mainly due to the professed holiness of the brethren and sisters, and the austere life of the solitary, together with their reputation for acts of charity, which had already spread over the country far beyond the bounds of the Province.

It was upon this occasion that Governor Thomas, who

declared himself well pleased with the institution, first offered to Conrad Weiser a commission as justice of the peace. Brother Lamech, in noting this act, says: " Having made a favorable impression on the brother, he now tendered him [Conrad Weiser] the office of a justice of the peace, which the brother would no doubt have gladly accepted if it were not against the principles of his people ; he did so, however, only on condition that the congregation would permit it. Thereupon at his request a council was held to decide the question whether a brother of this confession might be allowed to hold a government office. The fathers were of opinion that this could not be done. But the Superiniendent [Beissel] thought differently, and asked them whether they had a right to restrict a brother's conscience. And when he [Conrad Weiser] was asked about it, he declared that his conscience did not forbid him to accept ; upon which full liberty was granted him. The Governor also gave him the privilege to withdraw from court whenever such matters should happen to come up as were against his conscience."

This happened in the year 1736. As a matter of record Conrad Weiser was not commissioned until five years later, viz., 1741. Conrad Weiser at the time of Governor Thomas' visit was an active member of the Community, and with his family lived within the bounds of the settlement.

Another noteworthy incident of the year 1736 was the pilgrimage made by the Germantown Baptists to Ephrata, with the avowed purpose of combining the two congregations. This movement was directed by one of the Baptist leaders from Germany, Jeremias Naass, who eventually became the elder of the German Baptists in West Jersey.

As Beissel, Weiser, Miller and other prominent characters were absent on another revival tour in the Tulpehocken country, no definite results were reached as to the proposed union. The outcome of this movement will be related in a subsequent chapter.

We will now once again change the scene of our narrative and return to Germantown, to tell the story of the movement which led to the temporary settlement of a little secluded valley on the Wissahickon, a spot about which now cluster many tales of romance and fiction, one which has been immortalized by the artist's brush and the poet's pen, and which is known to the generations of the present as the MONASTERY OF THE WISSAHICKON.

THE GERMAN SECTARIANS OF PENNSYLVANIA.

CHAPTER XVIII.

THE MONASTERY ON THE WISSAHICKON.

HRONOLOGICALLY there now follows the awakening in Germantown. This was partly the result of the visit to Ephrata related in the previous chapter.

It will be remembered that after the death of the Patriarch Mack, the congregation of German Baptists in Germantown became more or less unsettled, with a strong leaning toward the stricter observance of the Ephrata movement. This feeling led to a closer intercourse between the two congregations, and culminated in an attempt made by a few of the more austere brethren at Germantown to establish a camp or settlement in that vicinity similar to the one on the Cocalico.

To carry out this purpose they settled upon a site on the land of Johannes Gumre. It was an elevated plateau, about one hundred and fifty yards east of the strip of land where the first baptism was held. This plateau is a little vale on the rugged hillside which forms the ravine of the Wissahickon. No more secluded scene can be pictured. It was an ideal spot, where these enthusiasts could retire from the outside world and yet remain in touch with it. It must be

ANCIENT PARSONAGE OF DUNKER CONGREGATION AT GERMANTOWN, BUILT 1756.

NOW 6611 MAIN STREET.

REPRODUCED FROM AN OLD SKETCH.

seen to be appreciated,—how it nestles among the tree-clad hills,—and the choice of the early enthusiasts will not be wondered at.

The leading spirit of this movement to establish a " Camp of the Solitary" near Germantown was Stephen Koch. He was one of the most austere members of the congregation, who fasted and prayed until he saw visions. He was known in the Community for his piety, and ended his days among the Brotherhood at Ephrata. He fortunately left some account of himself and his actions during this period giving us a few facts and dates, to which we will confine ourselves at present.

Stephen Koch notes that the immediate cause of his spiritual unrest was the death of Henrich Traut (January 4, 1733). Traut, who originally professed belief in the teachings of the Hermits of the Ridge, and took the vow of celibacy, subsequently fell a victim to the wiles and smiles of a widow whom he married. As the *Chronicon* states: "His Virgin [Sophia, the heavenly Wisdom, *i. e.*, saving faith] left him and he fell into earthly ways until finally, after many tears of penitence, she again took him up."

Koch relates the following incident, " how God finally regarded his misery" and came to his assistance : " On the third of May, 1735, at Germantown, as late at night I went behind the house into the orchard, it being bright moonlight, there came to me a delightful odor, partly from the blossoms of the trees, partly from the flowers in the garden, whereat I sobbing spoke to God : ' O, my God, everything is in its order and contributes to Thy glory and honor, save I alone ! For I am created and called by a holy calling to love Thee above everything, and to become a pleasant savor unto the glorifying of Thy name. Now, however, I behold the contradiction ; for I not only do not love Thee as I ought, but am also become an evil smell in Thy nostrils.

Alas, unfortunate that I am! Must I then pass my days in such misery? I gladly would love God, the highest Good, but I cannot. The world with all its glories cannot satisfy my sad spirit, for I ever see before my eyes spiritual and bodily death.'

" While I lamented thus to God it seemed to me as though suddenly a flame of God's love struck into me, which entirely illumined me within, and I heard a voice say to me: 'Yet one thing thou lackest.' I asked, 'What is it then?' The answer was, 'Thou dost not know God, and never hast really known him.' I said, 'Yes, that is so, but how shall I attain to it?' Then it seemed as though I were beside myself. But when I came to myself again, I felt an inexpressibly pleasing love to God in my heart; and on the other hand all anxiety, with all the temptations of the unclean spirits, had vanished. Yea, it seemed as if all my transgressions were pardoned and sealed, and day and night there was nothing else in my heart but joy, love and praise to God."

DIVINE INSPIRATION.
(From Kloster MSS.)

Upon another occasion, early in the year 1736, he "saw in a vision a beautiful virgin come into the meeting of the devout brethren, who preached wonderfully concerning sanctification and a life of virginity."

Koch at this time was much in company with Alexander Mack the younger. This intercourse had such influence upon the latter that he too became greatly disturbed about himself and the religious condition of the German settlers, so much so that he believed he would soon die, and made his testament accordingly.

N April 16, 1736, Stephen Koch, who for some time past had publicly exhorted the settlers whenever opportunity offered, took up his residence with Alexander Mack in the Pettikoffer house, the better to commune with the Spirit and contemplate the way to holiness. Shortly after they were joined by Heinrich Höcker. The three enthusiasts occupied one-half of the house, while Valentine Mack—who had married Maria Hildebrand, one of the original Spiritual Virgins living at Kedar in Ephrata—occupied the remaining part of the Pettikoffer house on the North Wales road.

During the summer of 1737 the three enthusiasts, Stephen Koch, Alexander Mack and Heinrich Höcker, concluded to retire into the solitude of the forest and live a life of holy seclusion, whence they could sally out among the German settlers and admonish them to repentance. The spot selected was, as before stated, a secluded valley on the grounds of Johannes Gumre the younger, who had bought the tract of 82 acres from his father. The ground was cleared by the three men, upon which they built a one-story log house[97] as a community house. This became known as the *Kloster*, which is the German word for monastery, a name which has adhered to the plot until the present time.

The eastern boundary of this secluded valley is a small rocky ravine, down which flows a little stream into the Wissahickon. Its source is a fine spring adjacent to the cabin built on the plateau. This spring gushes out from the rocks high up the hillside, and then leaps from crag to boulder until it mingles with the waters of the larger creek.

This ravine, a dark rocky dale, was called by the recluse

---

[97] According to Sangmeister, the cabin was built by Ulrich Hageman.

the *Felsen-schlucht*, and was used, as Kelpius used his cave, as a place for silent meditation and prayer. It was just such a spot as was used during the seventeenth century in the Fatherland for incantations and the conjuring of spirits. Weird, dark and ghostly even in midday, it was doubly so when the rays of the moon struggled through the foliage or were obscured by passing clouds. For our recluses, however, the dark nooks and fantastic shadows raised no fear; to them the little picturesque ravine became a place for prayer and silent contemplation, while the spring at the head of the stream furnished them with their only drink. The cabin was finished in the early fall and was occupied at once. The first religious service was held there upon October 14, 1737. The three recluses were now reinforced by another solitary brother, Johannes Riesmann, and a pious married couple. Thus was passed the winter of 1737–38. But on March 21, 1738, Alexander Mack, Heinrich Höcker and Johannes Riesmann left the Kloster on the Wissahickon, removed to Ephrata, and there joined the Solitary, while the housefather and his wife returned to their own piece of land.

This left Stephen Koch alone in the community house, he was, however, soon joined by another pious couple, Louis Höcker, with his wife and daughter Maria.

Shortly after the three first brethren left for Ephrata two deaths occurred in the German township, which excited more attention than any death since that of the Patriarch, Alexander Mack. This was the death of Johannes Gumre, May 16, 1738, and that of his wife upon the following day. It will be remembered that these two were among the party of Baptists from Germany who assembled at the house of Peter Becker, on that memorable Christmas Day in 1723, to organize the congregation; and it was at his humble home that the first love-feast was held immediately after the administration of the sacred ordinance.

Johannes Gumre, also spelled *Gumrie, Gomory, Gomorrie,*

THE HAUNTED RAVINE ON THE MONASTERY GROUNDS.

SEE PAGE 277-78.

Gumry, was a tailor by trade, and came to this country with Peter Becker in 1719. That he was not without means is shown by the fact that in January, 1719–20, he purchased from John Cunrads and his wife Alitic [*sic*] eighty-two acres of land fronting on the Wissahickon. This was a part of the Hugh Roberts tract, which Cunrads acquired on August 3, 1709.

Gumre, as he advanced in years, sold his farm to his eldest son, Johannes, and retired to a house which he had built on the North Wales (Germantown) road. Here he again worked at his trade as a tailor, and became a man of some estate and prominence in the German community.

His will is dated May 16, 1738, and was probated on May 24th of the same year. By a curious coincidence, his wife Anna died upon the following day. Considerable preparations were made for the double funeral. This was preceded by a great feast, at which, according to the account of the executors, there were consumed among other viands :

Bread & Cakes, at Sd Burialls	£1. 1. 0
Gamons, Cheese & Butter	15. 2
Molasses & Sugar	1. 14. 3

The last item evidently stands for rum and sugar.

The old couple were buried in the Upper Burying-ground near the Patriach, in the Gumre row, where they rest in unmarked graves. Johannes Gumre left three children : two sons and one daughter, viz., Johannes, who lived upon the plantation on the Wissahickon ; David, who inherited the house on the Germantown road ; and Catharina, who was married to William Johnson. Gumre's personal estate was appraised at no less than £290.03.0, a goodly sum for that day.

Stephen Koch, now alone with the Höcker family in the improvised Kloster, was far from idle ; he preached and exhorted almost incessantly during the summer among the

Germans in the vicinity, and his labors were crowned with success. The Kloster on the Wissahickon became, for the time being, the favorite place for revival meetings, which ended in a great awakening in and about Germantown. The most marvellous thing about these meetings was the number of young people who were attracted to them and professed religion.

Meetings were held in the grove surrounding the Kloster, and after the close the worshipers would walk back to Germantown and through the town, hand-in-hand, singing as they went, all of which attracted much attention.

Frequent meetings were also held at night within the borough, at which Rev. Peter Miller, Samuel Eckerling and Michael Wohlfarth were active leaders.

The presence of these three leaders of the Ephrata Community in Germantown at this time is accounted for by the fact that they were there as "correctors," supervising the printing of a new hymn-book for the Community on the Cocalico ; of which more hereafter.

This revival movement caused much discussion among the Germantown Baptist congregation. While some of the aggressive leaders— —spirits like Valentine Mack, Heinrich Kalckgläser and Johannes Hildebrand— supported it, the conservatives, led by Peter Becker, Jeremias Naass and others, opposed the movement and denounced it as merely "an outbreak of the Seventh-day Baptists of Conestoga."

Many were the heated discussions and recriminations between the two factions of the Germantown congregation. The chief contention was as to the true Sabbath and a a stricter observance of the Christian duties. The troubles of the congregation culminated in the summer of this year (1739) by a division, when twenty or more of the prominent members left the township and joined the settlement on the Cocalico.

During this agitation Johannes Pettikoffer, who still held title to the house built for the Patriarch and used for religious purposes, deeded it (August 22, 1739) in fee-simple over to Johannes Mack, stocking-weaver, eldest son of the Patriarch, and Andreas Bony, weaver, one of the original

SIGNATURES TO PETTIKOFFER-MACK DEED.

Schwarzenau Täufer, who was living as a hermit on the Ridge; after which act Pettikoffer with his wife joined the Sabbatarian party.

Among the people who left Germantown on this occasion and cast their lots with the monastic community at Ephrata were Heinrich Kalckgläser and wife; Valentine Mack and wife Maria (Hildebrand); Louis Höcker, his wife, Margretha, and daughter, Maria; Johannes Hildebrand and wife; Johannes Pettikoffer and wife Anna Elizabeth; the widow Gorgas and her children. Among the single persons who joined the celibates at Ephrata were Alexander Mack, Johannes Riesmann, Christian Eckstein, Heinrich Höcker, Martha Kinsing, Miriam Gorgas and Elizabeth Eckstein.

The chronicler, in noting this division, says : "At length the affair came to another separation, in which the Baptists a second time were made naked, and the flower of the congregation was lost. The separatists went together to the settlement of the Solitary, while the rest of this awakening gradually became extinct, extinguished like a straw fire."

This large secession sadly depleted the Germantown congregation, and proved a bad set-back for Peter Becker and his adherents. It was many years before the Germantown congregation recovered from this loss of membership, and then only by the efforts of some of the seceders who returned to Germantown in aid of the scattered congregation. Notable among these people was Alexander Mack the younger, who, after his return, it may be said, eventually placed the congregation upon a steady and firm foundation, and directed its fortunes, both spiritual and secular, until the end of his long and pious life, which did not occur until after the opening of the nineteenth century.

Stephen Koch, the real instigator of this awakening in Germantown, left the Kloster on the Wissahickon, March 27, 1739, and removed to Ephrata, leaving the Höcker family as its sole occupants. They kept it, until their departure for the Cocalico, as a sort of hermitage for any of the Ephrata Solitary who might come to the vicinity. With their departure in the fall of the same year the Kloster on the Wissahickon, so far as we know, was closed and left tenantless, and if used at all was, for the time being, put to the prosaic uses of an ordinary farm-house.

There is, however, a tradition, and in view of modern investigation evidently a true one, that, up to the time when Joseph Gorgas entered in possession of the tract, as well as during his tenure, the old Kloster, or at least a portion of it, was kept for the uses of the Ephrata Brethren when any came to Germantown. The same tradition adds that, even after the building of the stone mansion, the upper floor or loft of the new house was reserved as an asylum for any of the Solitary who sought its shelter.

It is never an agreeable task for an historian to turn inconoclast, especially in a case like the present, where so many romantic legends, weird stories and pathetic tales, which emanated from the fertile brains of Lippard, Fahnestock and others, were all founded upon this old stone mansion and the mystic monks who were supposed to have once lived here, but who, as a matter of fact, are the mere creations of the novelist.

ET us now trace the story of this particular spot, with its historic reminiscences, as they are to be found in the original records. As before stated, the land was originally a part of the Hugh Roberts tract. He sold eighty-two acres to Johannes Cunrads and wife, August 3, 1709. The latter held it until February 8 and 9, 1719–20, when they deeded it to Johannes Gumre, tailor. It will be recollected that the latter was one of the organizers of the Germantown congregation, and also that it was upon this ground, during his tenure, that the first baptism and love-feast were held.

At some time prior to his death, in 1733, Gumre sold the land to his eldest son, also named Johannes, he taking his bond therefor. The latter was evidently also in communion with the Brethren, as it was he who gave permission to Koch and his associates to settle in the little valley and there build their cabin or Kloster.

The younger Gumre and Sarah his wife finally disposed of the ground to Benjamin Shoemaker by an indenture dated October 29, 1742. Shoemaker, on March 2, 1746–47, sold it to Johannes Gorgas, a skindresser. He in turn sold it, on April 6, 1752, to

Joseph Gorgas, who was a miller or millwright. He appears to have occupied the land during the tenure of Johannes Gorgas, and to have developed the water-power of the creek at that place. It was Joseph Gorgas who built on the creek the first mills, which for over a century stood on its banks a few yards above the old Indian trail and ford. He also built the three-story stone mansion as a homestead, which has called forth so many legends and romantic tales.

By referring to the deed of Johannes Gorgas to Joseph, the following clause will be found, which, so far as the date of the Monastery goes, is final :

" Whereas the above named Joseph Gorgas has since [1746–47] at his own cost and charges built and erected a stone three-story house or messuage on a certain piece or spot of ground," etc. The property now became known as the " Mill Lands," and remained in possession of Joseph Gorgas until 1761, when he and his wife Julianna, under date of June 8, 1761, sold the property to Edward Milner. The indenture recites :

"A Grist or Corn Mill, with three pair of Stones under one roof, and a Saw mill thereon, also erected, unto the whole of which said Tract of land, with the Messuage or Tenement and the other buildings and Improvements thereon *erected by the said Joseph Gorgas,* etc."

Since this time it has gone through various hands. Of late years the Garseeds and the Kitchens were the most prominent owners, until now, at the dawn of the twentieth century, the property has been acquired by the Fairmount Park Commission, who are removing the remains of the old mills and out-buildings, together with the ruins of the former tenant- and mill-houses. The dam has also been opened and the stream unharnessed at this point, and henceforth the historic Monastery grounds will form a prominent feature in the greatest urban park in the world.

It will be apparent from the above recital that the present three-story stone building known as the " Monastery on the Wissahickon," has little or no connection with our band of mystic enthusiasts, or with the religious awakening in the German township during the years 1736–39, except that it was built between 1746–52 upon the site of the log cabin or community house erected in 1737 by the three austere revivalists, and which was called, partly by courtesy partly in derision, " The Kloster."

We will now say a few words about the Monastery. The house, when built by Joseph Gorgas, was perhaps the largest and finest private residence within the German township, if not in the immediate vicinity of Philadelphia, and appears to be the first three-story house of any pretensions in the outskirts of the city of which we have any record.

It was a large roomy house, practically square, the dimensions of the main building being thirty-three feet by a trifle over thirty-two feet; in addition there was an extension at the eastern end of twenty-five feet, which contained the kitchen offices. The main house was ornamented with an old-fashioned hollow cornice or pent-roof, which extended around the house between the second and third stories, as well as across the gable ends,—an ornamental feature which was still intact during the Garseed tenure.

At the same time it is well to consider that during the tenure of the various mill-owners, extending over a century and a half, the old mansion underwent numerous changes in its interior arrangement, which were modernized as the wealth of the owners increased. Among other changes the old fire-places were replaced with grates and hot-air appliances were introduced. These various changes also affected the doors and windows, in both its interior and exterior, from what it was when built by Joseph Gorgas. This will become apparent at a glance upon an inspection of the house and walls.   Formerly a balcony extended out from the north as well as the south front of the house, the supporting posts forming a porch below. Doors opened out upon both of these balconies.   Formerly the west wall was pierced for two additional windows in each of the three floors near the south front.   A door also opened out upon this side about where the cellar window now is, all of which are now closed.   In the north wall there were originally five windows, four of which are now walled up.   In the eastern end there was an additional one in each story, these are now also closed.

Just when these radical changes were made the writer has been unable to discover.   The painting in the possession of the Garseed family, made many years ago, shows the house as it now is.

However, these various changes do not affect our opinion in reference to the position we have taken as to the early uses of this old mansion.

The house, a fine specimen of colonial architecture, in its time, was a stately one, both in design and build, and with its many offices and out-buildings was a grand mansion, not only when in its pristine dignity, but even in later days when the hum of industry broke the silence of the romantic vale of the Wissahickon.

ERY naturally the question arises: How came it that Joseph Gorgas, a plain German miller, should build so elaborate and massive a mansion in this secluded spot?   Joseph Gorgas and wife, so far as known, had no issue, nor were they burdened with a surfeit of earthly riches. It is true that their mills once enjoyed the patronage of the German settlers, and became a profit to the miller; but this mansion was one far above their needs and wants.   Was it built with any other design in view than for a dwelling-house?   The style

THE "MONASTERY" ON THE WISSAHICKON SIXTY YEARS AGO.

FROM A PAINTING IN POSSESSION OF H. E. GARSED, ESQ.

would be against any such assumption. The large windows, high ceilings and bold stairway fail to harmonize with our ideas of narrow cells and cloistered monks; nor do they show any kinship whatever with the community buildings still standing at Ephrata.

Yet somehow all the old traditions, as heard by the writer in his youth, connect the Ephrata Solitary with the old mansion. Several even went so far as to say that Gorgas and his wife were wooers of the celestial Sophia. These traditions are independent of the many stories which for years have been accepted and printed without any proof as to their authenticity.

The *Chronicon Ephretense* and other Ephrata records are all silent upon the subject, neither is there any entry to be found in the Moravian diaries, usually so full of detail, that would shed any light upon it; no word or mention of the Gorgas mansion is to be found in any of the contemporary records.

Consequently the careful annalist of the present day would naturally assume that there was nothing in the old traditions susceptible of proof. This was exactly the position of the present writer, who was almost in despair in his attempt to harmonize the traditions with the dated records. In view of the latter, the investigation simmered down to the question: Whether the old stone mansion was ever used as a hospice for the Mystics or Solitary of Ephrata?

The finding of a diary kept by one of the Solitary, which fortunately came into the writer's possession, appears to give us a ray of light; and several entries, when taken together with the manuscript burial records, would seem partly to verify the old traditions, so far as showing a connection between Joseph Gorgas and his wife, on the one hand, and the Ephrata Brethren, on the other. They seem to substantiate the tradition that the Gorgas's sold the property to Milner in 1761 for the purpose of entering the

Community on the Cocalico. Joseph Gorgas, as is shown by the records just mentioned, died five years later as a Solitary, his identity being hidden under the kloster name of Brother *Chrysostomus*, and his wife, who outlived him many years, being disguised as Sister Julianna.

With these facts before us, we may well assume that the doors of the Gorgas mansion on the Wissahickon were ever open for the reception of the Solitary from Ephrata. There is, however, no word or mention to be found anywhere to show that any meetings or revival services were ever held on the grounds after the departure of Stephen Koch in the spring of 1739, possibly a decade before the stone house was built.

For over a century the mills of various kinds at the foot of the hillside were hives of human industry; rows of tenant houses, built for the operatives, skirted the road beside the creek; dye-houses and other industrial buildings were reared against the hillside; yet so secluded was this spot, that none of these buildings were to be seen from the old stone mansion built by Joseph Gorgas, the second of that family to own and develop the land, once the site of the Brethren's community house.

The past two centuries have dealt kindly with this historic spot; little or no change has been wrought by time in its immedate locality, and now, thanks to the Park Commission, it will once more be in its original condition, as all buildings, except the mansion proper, are to be removed. What the future of the old Monastery or Gorgas Mansion will be none can tell. A proposition has been made to restore it and use it for Park offices. May it remain for decades to come as a landmark, and in its romantic setting keep vigils unbroken by the inroads of time and recall to future generations the story of its immediate surroundings: how, at the foot of the hill, on the banks of the creek, the German Baptist Brethren completed their organization in America; and later, how some of the strictest and most austere members retired to this little vale, clearing the ground and building for themselves a humble cabin of rough logs, where they prayed for the conversion of their countrymen in this foreign land—from which fact it received a name which has clung to it through all the changes of time.

A REWARD CARD FOR CHILDREN, PRINTED AT EPHRATA AND USED IN THE SABBATH-SCHOOLS OF THE COMMUNITY DURING THE LATTER HALF OF THE XVII. CENTURY.

(Original in collection of Julius F. Sachse, Philadelphia.)

CHAPTER XIX.

THE UNITAS FRATRUM.

URING the summer of 1736 yet another religious element appeared in Pennsylvania in the form of a pioneer party of evangelists who arrived in the Province in April. Chief among them were the Rev. Joseph Spangenberg and Bishop David Nitchmann. Upon their arrival they at once joined with Christopher Wiegner, Christopher Baus and George Böhnisch at the house of the former on the banks of the Skippack. These three brethren had been sent to America with the Schwenkfelders, September, 1734, by Count Zinzendorf.

These new arrivals had come to our shores as missionaries with the avowed purpose of preaching the gospel of Christ to all persons, irrespective of color, race or condition; they were known as the *Unitas Fratrum*, or United Brethren,—the Moravians of the present day.

As soon as the arrival of Spangenberg and Nitchmann became known to Beissel, he sent three solitary brethren to Wiegner's on the Skippack to extend fraternal greetings to the newcomers, and invite them to visit the settlement on the Cocalico. As the awakening and successful revival movement instituted by Beissel and his followers was

AUG. GOTTLIEB SPANGENBERG.
Episcopus Fratrum.

already well known by report to Spangenberg and Nitchmann, they readily accepted the invitation to visit the settlement.

As the *Chronicon* states, "At first sight there was felt by
both parties a magnetic attraction between their spirits; for
both were yet in their first love." The visit and conference
between Beissel and Spangenberg proved satisfactory to both
parties. The visitors were greatly touched with what they
saw and heard in the settlement on the
Cocalico, as well as with the marvelous
success of the movement among the
Germans, together with the great show
of holiness and piety evinced at Ephrata
and the surrounding country. During
their stay they took part in the love-
feast instituted in their honor, as well
as in the nocturnal devotions, and were
deeply affected with the mode of ad-

SEAL OF THE
UNITAS FRATRUM.

ministering the sacred ordinance of baptism as practiced on
the Cocalico.

At the end of their sojourn, after special religious services,
the Moravian missionaries set out on their return to the Skippack. They were escorted by a number of the Ephrata
Brotherhood, who accompanied them for some distance on
their way; an old local tradition tells us that it was as far
as French creek in Nantmill, the stronghold of the English
Sabbatarians in Chester county. There amidst the wild
scenery and stupendous rock formation, at the spot known
as the "Falls," under the tall trees, where the silence is
only broken by the turbulent stream as it leaps from ledge
to ledge, or of the note of the feathered songster, a halt was
made. A circle was formed, and after certain mystic ceremonies a hymn was sung and an invocation offered in which
all were commended to Almighty God. Then hands were
joined, the sacred word was passed, and after mutual em-

braces the brethren separated, each party going its own way.

How much the visiting brethren were impressed with some of the observances at Ephrata is shown by the following entry in the *Chronicon:* "It has been reported concerning them that in St. Thomas, whither they went from Ephrata, they baptized the blacks whom they converted there by immersing them under the water, according to the Ephrata manner."

This was the first official meeting between the Sabbatarians and the *Unitas Fratrum.* The introduction was auspicious; the *denouement* came when the great leader, Count Zinzendorf, was in this country a few years later and sought to combine the two movements. This story will be told in its chronological place.

During the winter of 1736–37 Michael Wohlfarth, the irrepressible, published both German and English versions of his Testimony, which he delivered publicly in Philadelphia in September, 1734. To the English version were added some additional remarks upon the present state of Christianity in Pennsylvania. The booklet was printed by Benjamin Franklin and sold at four pence per copy. No specimen of this production has come down to us; the only positive evidence we have of its publication being the advertisements in the *Pennsylvania Gazette*, which set forth as follows:

Juſt Publiſhed,

THE WISDOM of GOD *crying and calling to the Sons and Daughters of Men for* REPENTANCE. Beiug the TESTIMONY deliver'd to the People in *Philadelphia* Market, *Sept.* 1734, by *Michael Wellfare* Together with ſome Additional Remarks on the Preſent State of Chriſtianity in *Pennſylvania.* To be ſold by *B. Franklin,* price 4d

The title to the German version reads :

Die Weissheit Gottes schreyende und ruffende den Söhen und Tœchtern der Menchen zur Busse, seynde das Wort des Herren, das Michael Wellfare, Verkündiget hat dem Volck. Zu Philadelphia gedruckt und zu Verkauffen bey Benjamin Franklin und Johannes Wüster in der Markt-strass, 1737.[97]

Such of the writings as were published in English attracted considerable attention among the Quakers and Sabbatarians in both this and the adjoining Provinces, and in some cases even were the means of bringing converts into the fold of the English Sabbath-keepers. This tended to strengthen the intercourse between the congregations whose bond of sympathy was the observance of the biblical Sabbath. Visits were made and returned between the leaders at French Creek and Ephrata, and great respect was always paid by the English Sabbath-keepers to the Germans on the Cocalico on account of their austere life and holiness.

Conrad Beissel also kept his pen active at this time. As the community increased in numbers and the awakenings in various parts of the neighboring country showed a long-ing for religious teaching and instruction, Beissel, to meet this want, proposed the collation of a new German hymn-book, not only for the use of the Ephrata Community, but for such other congregations as sought to be guided by the inner light and live a life of holiness. For this purpose he, with Wohlfarth and several others of his immediate supporters, composed a number of hymns, in which pre-vails a strain of inspiration and mysticism. To these hymns were added those contained in the three Franklin imprints of 1730, 1732 and 1736, which have already been described, and the manuscript collection of 1734, together with a large number of hymns used by the Inspired in

---

[97] Title from Hildeburn, *Issues of the Press in Pennsylvania.*

Germany, and which were printed in the "*Kleine David-ische Psalterspiel der Kinder Zions.*" These hymns, about seven hundred in number, were grouped under thirty-three separate headings. How this collection, which enjoys the distinction of being the first book to be printed with German type in America, was eventually brought out together with the controversies it engendered between the printer and publisher, forms one of the most interesting chapters in Pennsylvania bibliography.

SPECIMEN OF DISPLAY TYPE FROM THE KLOSTER FONT.
Made at Ephrata prior to 1748.

RADUALLY, as the Community on the Cocalico increased and mystic theology supplanted the plain Gospel teachings of the early Baptist and Sabbatarian movements, it became apparent that some other form of government was needed to ensure a permanent existence for the new community, which consisted of both sexes. As it was, the settlement was merely an aggregation of religious enthusiasts, most of the men living separately as hermits or anchorites. It will be recalled that an attempt was already made to organize the single women under a rule known as the Order of Spiritual Virgins. But all efforts looking toward the bringing about of a similar organization among the Brethren had thus far come to naught.

The only government of this peculiar settlement thus far consisted of the dictates of Conrad Beissel, or Brother Conrad as he was usually called, and even these were frequently ignored, as there existed no means of enforcing his commands. Now, however, the number of Brethren requisite to complete the mystic number of forty, the figure of Rosicrucian perfection having been reached, renewed efforts were made to change the solitary mode of life into a conventual one. This movement culminated in the estab-

lishment of a mystical monastic society.   Rev. Peter Miller
explains this step as follows :

" That a Monastic life was judged to be more inservient
to sanctification than the life of a Hermit, where many
under the pretence of holiness did nothing but nourish
their own selfishness.   For as the Brethren now received
their Prior, and as the Sisters their Matron, and we were
now by necessity compelled to learn obedience, and to be
refractory was judged a crime little inferior to high treason."

From the first formation of the congregation on the Mühlbach, its members realizing the vanities of the world in the
matter of apparel, had adopted the plain garb of the Friends.
This was also in accordance with the course pursued by the
Sabbatarian Brethren of Providence and Nantmill, a manner
in which they were later followed by the German Baptists
of Germantown and elsewhere.   There were, however, certain innovations which were gradually adopted by the Conestoga congregation—peculiarities in dress which are still
to a greater or less degree in vogue in Lancaster and the
adjoining counties.   Some of these peculiar features consisted in making as near an approach to man's original
state in costume as could be done under existing laws and
conditions.   The main features were the letting the beard
and hair grow, and going barefoot whenever the weather
permitted ; this, together with abstention from animal food
it was claimed, would restore man to his primitive state of
health [*Urgesundheit*], thus giving him the means of more
fully enjoying life and attaining a patriarchial age.[98]

---

[98] This was by no means a new theory ; in several German works of two
centuries ago it was propounded as a means of obtaining primitive health.
So late as the year 1851 a man named Mahner boldly advocated this theory
in Germany, and succeeded in gathering a large number of followers.
The chief congregation was at Naumburg, and flourished for some time
until suppressed by the authorities.   An account of this movement will
be found in the *Medical News*, Philadelphia, 1851, vol. ix, p. 98.

At the present writing a somewhat similar theory is again being widely

As to the growing of long beards, it was argued that, according to the Jewish literati, Adam was created in the fulness of manhood, and in the first hour of his existence upon earth disported himself in a luxurious black beard. In the East, even at the present time, oaths are taken upon the "beard of Moses," and even the Psalmist revels in a description of the venerable " beard of Aaron, which reached down to the hem of his garment." The Levital priests permitted their beards to grow, and had a definite law forbidding the trimming of the edges.[99] Among the ancient Jews long beards and trailing robes were held as a sign of honor and esteem. A cropping of the former or a curtailment of the latter was used as a severe punishment or as denoting the greatest humiliation.[100]

In the religious ceremonies incident to the love-feast and the Lord's Supper, the beard also played an important part ; for, when the kiss was passed, each brother would grasp his neighbor's beard with the right hand as he gave him the salute. This particular custom, which appears to have been confined to the Zionitic Brotherhood, was based upon the reference found in the second book of Samuel, verse ninth of the twentieth chapter, viz.: "And Joab took Amasa by the beard with the right hand to kiss him." No trace of this custom has been found to exist among the regular Dunkers or Seventh-day Baptists of the present day.

With the introduction of the monastic feature the dress of the members received renewed consideration. Much attention was given to this question by the leading brethren in council. Their avowed object was to approach as

---

exploited in several of the larger cities under the name of the "Kneip" cure ; it is claimed that going barefoot in the grass in early morn, while the dew is yet upon it, will cure all diseases flesh is heir to. An *Institute* with a *professor* (?) was lately opened in this city on Germantown avenue.

[99] Leviticus, xix, 27.

[100] II Samuel, x, 4.

nearly as possible to the life and customs of the first Christians. It was argued that to do this it was necessary to adopt a style of garment such as would muffle the mortal body, for its humiliation, in such manner that but little of it should be visible; they would thus be distinct from the material world, and would be recognized as persons who had renounced this world's vanities. To accomplish this object, the services of Martin Brämer (Bremer) the community tailor, were called into requisition. He proposed a habit somewhat after the style of the Capuchins or White Friars, yet modified so as to meet the ideas of Beissel and others of the congregation.

This distinctive dress was designed to be made of unbleached linen or wool according to the season of the year, and consisted, for the brethren, of a shirt, trowsers and a kind of vest, together with a long gown to which was attached a pointed cowl or monk's hood. The habit of the sisterhood differed only in the substitution of a narrow skirt for trowsers, and some little peculiarity in the shape of the hood or cowl, it being rounded in place of pointed. A belt or girdle was also used when the gown was worn. In addition the sisterhood, as a distinguishing mark of their spiritual betrothal, wore a large apron which covered them entirely in front and extended down the back as far as the girdle; this garment was somewhat similar to the Roman scapulary. When the different members of the Order attended public worship they wore in addition a special short cloak which reached well down to the waist; this garment also had a cowl attached which could be pulled over the head.

"The domestic householders," as the *Chronicon* designates the secular Sabbatarian congregation, soon after adopted a similar "Thaler" or gown of a gray color, as a distinguishing mark from the Solitary. This was to be worn at divine service as well as upon all public occasions, such as baptisms, processions and pilgrimages. In this habit there was also some distinctive mark for widows and widowers.

This special prayer costume was received at first with almost universal favor among the secular congregation, and the members vied with each other to be the first to discard their heathenish and Babylonian clothing, and long before the winter set in the faithful of the congregation when they assembled for worship upon the Bible Sabbath were equipped in the habit which they claimed was that of the primitive Christians.

The adoption of this distinctive habit gave rise to much gossip and unfavorable comment among the settlers not in sympathy with the Sabbatarians. Some said it was a mere revival of popish discipline and methods. Others, again, who were members of the congregation but did not feel kindly toward the movement, refused to assume the habit; they were men and women whom an old record designates as " extra holy" and " half-hearted" (*zwey-seeligen und halb-herzigen*), who gave as their objection that it were better to change the heart than the clothing. These and other arguments had their effect, and in the course of a few years the secular members gradually conformed themselves to the methods of the world in the way of dress as they did in many other respects.

This relapse, however, does not apply to the solitary orders, the members of which adhered strictly to their respective adopted habits, few or no changes being made in the peculiar costume during the existence of the monastic orders. Fortunately several contemporary sketches or drawings have come down to us which give an idea of the habits of both sexes, some of which are used as illustrations to this chapter.

An interesting account of the habit worn by the sisterhood, as well as of the immediate causes which led to the adoption of the peculiar dress, is recorded in the manuscript *Chronicon* or diary of the sisterhood.   This is written in that peculiar German phraseology and style used in the Theosophical epistles.   A translation of this chapter is here given, care being taken to preserve as much as possible the quaintness and construction of the original :

"As it came to pass that the Society of persons appeared to increase, and the Souls were attracted and called together by the only-begotten (*einigen liebes Geist*) loving Spirit of Jesus Christ ; as one came from here and the other from hence, so accordingly all kinds of fashions and manner of dresses were gathered together ; which did not accord with the only-begotten Spirit of Love, which was the cause for the Souls to resort to this our Spiritual-household or Family, that they might again obtain from God their support of the Spirit.

"As this did not seem to coincide, but appeared at variance, it happened that once upon a time, our by-God-elevated Father, or Spiritual leader, explained the circumstances of the many diversities of the clothing, as a matter entirely defective, and that could not exist according to the confined (*schrankenmassige*) rules of the Spirit.   He came to consult about this with several of us Sisters, and said that the matter was not to be continued, nor could it be concordant with a cloisteral or communal life according to Christian or Divine conduct with and among each other.

" While our comport (*betrag*) in clothing appeared to be entirely in contrast to the internal Spirit of Love, these speeches were well received by us.   And we soon accommodated ourselves after this conference to change the various hues of our clothing, inasmuch as we were still blended in a multitude of colors.   Thus were we then first assisted to take into hand the unity of color.   Therefore we accordingly selected what we thought was the most diverse ; we chose the black color for our clothing.   Thus was the multitude of color changed into a certain unity, but to an actual unanimity of the clothing itself, we were not helped; as such was a weighty matter, to find something between both [extremes], which the secular spirit had not previously applied in some other way. Therefor the matter was not to be reached quickly, but the instruction therein was to be obtained from God himself; so finally after a long embarrassment, and painful desire of the intimately-in-God-enamored spirits, it was given unto our God-blessed Father or Spiriual leader how to act in this matter.

" So it happened that there was found among the most venerated brethren one by the name of Martin Brämer, who now has passed from time into eternity; the Lord reward him on the day of Eternity for his pains and faithfulness which he demonstrated in this sorrowful struggle. This brother whom we have mentioned, at that time had the sewing for the brothers and sisters in his hands. With this brother our Spiritual leader consulted about the circumstances of the whole matter and how and what had happened.

" Then sundry of us Sisters were found who specially urged that the habit of the order should now be taken up and adopted. So with the consent (*handfüllung*) of our Spiritual Superintendent this brother was elected thereto, and at the same time was instructed by our Superintendent, how and in what manner he was to construct them. Consequently it was concluded to first fabricate the habits for the concordant Sisters. At first it was held that white woolen cloth should be taken therefor. And that the clothing should be arranged as follows: a long frock plain and straight (*schlecht und recht*), narrow sleeves without facing, so consequently the whole frock was to be narrow and close, so that it is more like unto a penitential robe than one for inciting worldly pomp.

" What further concerns the veiling or covering of the

A SPIRITUAL VIRGIN IN THE HABIT OF THE ORDER, SKETCH ON FLY-LEAF OF
MSS. HYMNAL, DATED 1745.

Original in collection of the writer.

countenance and the body, is this : Over the frock follows
a loose veil (*schleyer*) without hood, which is back and
front almost as long as the frock, only that there is a little
contrast in one from the other. After [upon] the veil follows a cover or hood (*kappen*) which back and front reaches
a little below the girdle, so that the shoulders and the countenance may by it be hidden and covered, and further, there
is still a wrap or mantle which is closed all around, wherein
the whole body can be muffied from top to bottom, and be
covered. This is not usually worn, except in wintertime,
and to the midnight masses and during the devotional
hours, also in the meetings of the general community, as
it is designed as a cover or protection against the cold of
winter, and all of these clothes were made from white
woolen cloth, therefore it was customary to wear them
only in winter. In the summer we wear even similar
clothing as is commanded, only that they are arranged to
the summer season, as the former are for winter, therefore
we usually use cotton cloth, or else take a light flaxen
cloth.

"To this habit belong shoes of uncolored leather, with
low heels, rounded front [toes?] plain and straight. This
now is the habit of our Order, which is worn for our bodily
[comfort] and separate uses.

" Further we are in all earnest intent, that in our whole
actions both outward and inward the unity of the Spirit shall
be felt and perceived. Therefore it is especially seen, too,
that this order of habit be assumed, wherefore it is ordered
and directed, some for the holy masstime, the other for
sacred duties [such as], going out to houses to break the
Bread, to proclaim the death of the Lord Jesus or otherwise
when visiting in a communal manner. For wintertime
it is unanimously agreed that the wraps or mantles be
usually worn to devotions, the masses, and general meetings. For going out, visiting or performing sacred offices

304 The German Sectarians of Pennsylvania.

it is ordered that the loose veil and clothing be worn, and it is not allowed as regular, that one robes herself in one way and another in a diverse manner."

Although the above habit called for leather shoes, as a matter of fact both orders usually went barefoot or wore sandals in summer, while during the inclement seasons heavy woolen stockings with either leather or heavy cloth soles gave the necessary protection.

How closely the Sisterhood of Ephrata clung to the adopted habit will appear in another chapter of this narrative.

ORNAMENTAL DESIGN IN KLOSTER SPECIMEN BOOK.

CHAPTER XXI.

THE ROSTER OF THE CELIBATES.

OW that the monastic feature was adopted by both orders of solitary, and the vain clothing of the world with its varigated hues, ornaments and furbelows had been renounced for the penitential robe of the early Christians, the next step was to sink their identity still further by dropping the Babylonian names given them by their parents at baptism and substituting therefor new spiritual names,—names by which many of the inmates became more or less famous and by which they are known in history.

There are quite a number of these religious enthusiasts whose former identity is irretrievably lost, as there is no clue to their baptismal names or former station in life. There is a tradition that originally a register was kept wherein the names, both baptismal and cloister, are said to have been entered. An extended search, covering a period of over twenty years, has failed to find any person who has ever seen such a book. The sisterhood, in connection with their diary, kept a register of such as became unfaithful (*Bundbrüchig*). This record unfortunately was destroyed about ten years ago to prevent its ever being published, as some of the descendants of these spiritual virgins who left the Kloster to re-enter the world and marry are now occupying high social positions in the community. In addition to the above records, mention is made in the sisters' *Chronicon* that there was kept, besides the diary, another book, *Ein Bürgerliches Stadt Buch*, wherein the names of all members of the Community were enrolled ; no trace of this, however, is to be found. No pains, expense or time has been spared upon this part of our narrative, as the identity of some of these persons is of considerable literary, genealogical and historical importance.

The interest in these names has been further increased by finding the fragment of a book, some fifteen years ago, written in the peculiar *mönchschrift* of the Ephrata Community, and giving a partial list of the monastic names, together with their meanings, of the celibates of both orders of the Kloster. Unfortunately this list is far from complete, and fails to give any clue to the secular names of the people. From several notes in this fragment the writer would infer that the different religious names assumed by the members were selected and applied according to their peculiar fitness to the recipient, and that it was not an arbitrary selection. The writer was permitted to copy this list at the time of its discovery, and it is incorporated in the present roster, the definitions being added in the original German.

The other names were gleaned from various sources, manuscripts, legal documents, records, private letters at home and abroad, diaries and printed books, together with the *Chronicon Ephratense* and the manuscript *Chronik* of the Spiritual Virgins of the Order of Saron. By a careful comparison and after long and laborious research the identity of many of these persons has now been positively established.

The list of names presented herewith is probably as nearly complete as it is possible to make it, unless some original registers or lists should be found.

The roster is as follows :

THE BROTHERHOOD.

AGABUS (*fürtrefflicher vatter*), Stephen Koch.

AGONIUS Michael Wohlfarth (Welfare).

[To his English letters he signs himself "*A mean Servant of Jesus Christ, and Pilgrim walking to Eternity.*"]

AMAZIAH [Amasias] (*des Herrn Last*), Hänsly Maÿer.

AMOS (*beschwerliche last*), Jan Meyle.

ABEL (*Klagort*) ——— ———.

ALBURTUS ——— ———.

ANTON, Anton Höllenthal.

AGRIPPA [Roman for Jaebez] (*Schwerlich geboren*), Rev. (John) Peter Miller.

ANDREAS, Andreas Erlewein.

BENEDICT, Benedict Jughtly.

BENNO [Benni] (*kindschaft*), ——— ———.

BENJAMIN [Ben Jamin] (*sohn der rechten*).

CHRYSOSTOMUS, Joseph Gorgas.

CONRAD, Johann Conrad Beissel.

DARIUS (*überwinder*), ——— ———.

DANIEL (*mein Richter ist Gott*), Daniel Eicher.

ELEAZER (*Gott helffer*) Jacob [Christian] Eicher.

ELIMELECH (*Gott König*), Emanuel Eckerling.

ELKANAH (*Gottes eiffer*), ——— Schäffer.

ENOCH [Henoch] (*ein geweiheter*), Conrad Weiser.

EPHRAIM (*Gewächs*), Jacob Höhnly.

EZECHIEL (*des Herrn Stärck*), Heinrich Sangmeister.

FRIEDSAM GOTTRECHT, Johann Conrad Beissel.

GOTTLIEB, Gottfried Haberecht.

GIDEON (*zerstörer*), Christian Eckstein.

GERMANN, ——— ———.

HOSEAS (*heiland*), Benjamin Gorgas.

HAGGAI (*feyertäglich*), ——— Kroll.

ISAIAH (*des Herrn Heil*), —— Lässly.

JAEBEZ (*mit Kummer geboren*), Rev. (John) Peter Miller.

JACOB (*füssentretter*), Jacob Zinn.

JEHOIADA [Jojada] (*des Herrn Bekenner*), Rudolph Nägele.

JEPHUNE [Jephuneh] (*Anseher*), Samuel Eckerling.

JEMINI (*gerecht*) —— ——.

JOTHAM (*gerechter Herr*), Gabriel Eckerling.

JETHRO (*fürnemlich*), Jacob Gast.

JOEL (*anfänger*), Peter Bucher.

JONADAB (*freigebig*), —— ——.

JONATHAN (*des Herrn gaab*), Jonathan Höcker.

JUST (*gerecht*), —— ——.

JOSEPH (*zunehmer*), —— ——.

JOHANNES (*gnadselig*) —— ——.

JAVADO, —— ——.

KENAN (*Erbnemmer*), Jacob Funck.

LAMECH (*arm*), —— ——.

LUDOVIC, —— ——.

MACARIUS, Hermann Zinn.

MANASSEH (*vergessen*), Martin Funck.

MELCHY [Melchi] (*des Herrn König*), —— ——.

MICHAEL (*Schlagender Gott*), —— ——.

MARTIN, Martin Brämer.

MANOAH (*gaabe*), —— Stattler.

NAANAM (*wohlgestalt*), Adam Konigmacher.

NATHAN (*geber*), Nathan Hagemann.

NATHANIEL (*des Herrn gaab*), Nathaniel Eicher.

NEHEMIAH (*tröstender Herr*), —— Hagemann.

OBED (*diener*), Ludwig Höcker.

OBADIAH [Obedja] (*des Herrn knecht*), Samuel Funck.

ONESIMUS [Leidselig] (*nützlich*), Israel Eckerling.

PHILEMON (*liebhaber*), Johann Conrad Reissmann.

PETER, Peter (?) Fahnestock.

RUFFINUS [Rufus, Rupinus] (*feuerroth*), Christian Reb.

SEALTIEL [Shealtiel] (*gottes begehrer*), Sigmund Landert.

SALMA [Salmon] (*friedmacher*), ——— Höffly.

SIMEON (*wacht*), Simeon Jacob?

Shontz.

SHABIA [Sheba] (*bekehrer*), ——— ———.

STEPHANAS (*gekrönt*), ——— ———.

THEOBALD, Philip Weiser?

THEODORUS, Thomas Hardy.

TIMOTHEUS (*gottes ehrer*), } Alexander Mack, Jr.
THEOPHILUS (*Gottlieb*), }

THEONIS, ——— ———.

WILHELMUS, Wilhelm Witt.

ZENNA [Zemah] (*gewächs*), ——— ———.

ZEPHANIA [Zephanja] (*schauender Herr*), Rudolph Nägele.

ZADOCK (*gerecht*), Peter Beissel.

THE SISTERHOOD.

ABIGAIL, Maria Hildebrand-Mack.

AMALIA, ——— ———.

ALBINA, Margaretha Höcker.

ANNA, Anna Eicher.

ARMELLA, ——— Fahnestock.

ARMELLA II, ——— ———.

ANASTASIA, Anna Thoma.

ATHANASIA, ——— ———.

ATHANASIA II, ——— ———.

BARBARA, ——— ———.

BASILLA, Elizabeth Höffly.

BLANDINA, Christina Funck?

BERNICE (*rein, unschuldig*), ——— Heyd [Heidt].

CATHARINA, Catharina Bohler.

CATHARINA II, Catharina Thomasin [Toma].

CHRISTINA, —— ——

CONSTANTIA, Valentine Mack's daughter.

DRUSIANA (*bethauet*), —— Höffly.

DEBORAH (*wohlrednerin*), —— ——.

EFFIGENIA [iphigenia], Anna Lichty?

ELIZABETH, —— ——.

ESTHER (*verborgene ärtztin*), —— ——.

EUNICKE [Eunice] (*guter sieg*), Widow Hanselmann.

EUFEMIA [Euphemia], —— Traut.

EUFRASIA, —— ——.

EUFROSINA, Catharina Gärtner or Gitter.

EUGENIA, Catharina Hagemann.

EUSEBIA, —— Beissel.

EUSEBIA II, Hildebrand-Nahor.

FOEBEN [Phœbe], Christianna Lässle.

FLAVIA, —— ——.

FRANZINA, —— ——.

GENOVEVA, —— Funck.

HANNAH (*hold selig*), —— Miller.

HANNAH II (*gnadenreich*), Veronica Funck?

JAEL (*die erhöcte*), Barbara Meyer.

JOSEBA (*des Herrn fülle*), —— ——.

JULIANNA, —— Gorgas.

KETURAH (*verbunden*), Elizabeth Eckstein.

LUCIA, Catharina Foltz.

LOUISA, —— ——.

MAGDALENA (*thurn erhöhet*), —— Hagemann.

MARIA (*bitter*), Maria Eicher.

MARIA II, Maria Baumann.

MAECHA (*zerstösserin*), —— ——.

MARCELLA, Maria Christina Sauer.

MELONIA, —— Brämin.

MIGTONIA, —— ——.

MIRIAM (*bitter meer*), Mary Anguas.

MARTHA (*lehrerin*), ———— ————.

MARIA MAGDALENA, ———— ————.

MARGARETHA, ———— ————.

NAEMY [Naomi] (*lieblich*) ———— Eicher.

PHŒBE [see Foeben] (*hell und klar*), ———— ————.

PAULINA, Maria Miller.

PELAGIA, ———— ————.

PERPETUA, ———— Zinn.

PERSIDA, ———— Schuck.

PETRONELLA, Maria Höcker.

PRISCAM (*alt*) ————, Graff.

RAHEL [Rachel] (*Shaaf*), ———— Landert.

ROSA, ———— Lassle.

ROSINA, ———— Schenk.

REBECCA (*feist dick*), ———— Gehr.

SARAH (*fürstin*), Salome Guth ?

SERAPHIA (*brenner*), ———— Jung.

SINCLETICA, Maria Stattler-Müller.

SOPHIA, ———— Gorgas.

SOPHIA II, Rosina Guth ?

SEVORAM, ———— Beissel.

SUSANNA (*Röslein*), Susanna Hartmann.

TABEA (*gütig*), Margaretha Thoma.

THEKLA, ———— Klopf.

THERESIA, ———— Stattler.

VERONICA, ———— ————.

ZENOBIA, Susanna Stattler.

H A L L E L U Ĵ A H,

Singet unſerm GOTTE und dem LAMM.

REDIT for establishing the first German printing office in America is universally accorded to Christopher Sauer of Germantown, whose acquaintance we have already made in our sketch of the Conestoga congregation.

Christopher Sauer, the Germantown printer, has been deservedly lauded for his enterprise in both prose and verse by speakers and writers of both German and native birth upon the platform as well as in the historical literature of the day.

Little has heretofore been known or written as to the immediate causes which led to Sauer's embarking in the printing business, and where the necessary funds were procured to successfully launch an enterprise whose first venture was to print what was thus far, with a single exception, the largest book issued in the middle colonies. Christopher Sauer himself is silent upon these points. Now, however, several documents, lately discovered by the writer, will shed some light upon this interesting question, and show the important part directly and indirectly borne by Conrad Beissel and his trusty supporters, such as Conrad Weiser, Peter Miller, Samuel Eckerling and others in the establishment of the Germantown press of Christopher Sauer. The connection, so far as Beissel was concerned, was one of short duration, owing to the firm stand taken by the printer and the equally unyielding course of his patron in reference to the meaning of one of the hymns.

It will be recalled that Sauer was by trade a journeyman tailor, from Germany, of humble extraction and with a common school education, whose early years in America were spent either at his trade or as a tiller of the soil in Lancaster county. Both employments were entirely foreign to the printer's art.

It further appears that Beissel and Sauer had been congenial spirits in Germany,[101] and when Sauer migrated to the Mühlbach and joined the congregation, all was well between the two men until Sauer's wife left her husband and family to follow the fortunes of the enthusiasts who longed for a stricter observance.

Christopher Sauer, now bereft of his housewife, upon whom so much depends in the rural districts, even down to the present day, was forced to give up farming; so he disposed of his plantation, and with his ten-year old son Christopher, journeyed in 1731 once more to Germantown, where he affiliated with the Dunkers under Mack and Becker. Here he worked at various trades, chiefly as a carpenter, wheelwright and cabinet-maker; and, being of an ingenious and mechanical turn of mind, he also repaired and cleaned the Schwartzwälder wall-clocks among the German settlers.

According to other accounts,[102] Christopher Sauer upon his return to Germantown lived for some time with Doctor Christopher Witt,[102] a former member of the Kelpius community and from him received some instruction in the mechanical and curative arts.

---

[101] *Chronicon Ephratense*, chapter xvii.

[101] *Thomas' History of Printing in America*, vol. i, p. 270.

[102] *Vide*, *German Pietists*, pp. 402–18.

THESE May Inform all Whom it might Concern That Mr John Kaighin of Ashfield in the Province of West New Jersey, hath Lived with me (here under named) a Considerable time, as a Disciple, to learn the Arts & Mysteries of [Physick] try, Physick, & the Abstral Sciences, whereby to make a more perfect Discovery of the Hidden Causes of More occult & uncommon Diseases, not so Easily to be discovered by the Vulgar Practice. In all which he has been very Diligent & Studious, as well as in the Administration of the Medecines, & in the Various Cases, wherein his Judgment may be Safely depended, upon all things, so far as he follows my Instructions. And Hope he may in all things answer the Confidence that may be reposed in him.

Germantown Febr: 20, 1758.   C. Witt.

FAC-SIMILE OF DIPLOMA GIVEN BY DR CHRISTOPHER WITT.

The above statement appears the most plausible, as it is known that Dr. Witt did give instruction in medicine, physics and the occult sciences, and to such of his students as made satisfactory progress he granted a diploma or certificate to that effect at the end of their term. One of these peculiar certificates is now in the collection of Hon. Samuel W. Pennypacker.

Incidentally it may be mentioned that among the students of Dr. Witt was a lad born of Jewish parentage, in Philadelphia, in 1720, who in after years became famous throughout Europe as "Jacob Philadelphia," one of the most renowned physicists and mechanicians of his day.[103]

There is nothing whatever to show that Christopher Sauer entered as regular student with Doctor Witt, or that he was ever granted any diploma by that erudite philosopher and student, in fact the evidences are against any such presumption, but being of an ingenious and mechanical turn of mind he was evidently employed by the versatile doctor as an assistant in his mechanical workshop, where he assisted among other mechanical pursuits in making and repairing clocks.

Christopher Sauer became proficient in this branch of mechanics, and when he left the employ of the mystic and mechanician he considered himself a capable clock-maker, and at once entered into competition with his late employer. For this purpose he took up his abode in Germantown on the land of John Adam Gruber. It was upon a lot containing six acres of land, which faced upon the northeast side of the main street opposite to Indian Queen lane; here he had a small house and workshop where he worked at various trades, chiefly as a carpenter, wheelwright and cabinetmaker. The sign, however, over his shop door bore the legend *Christopher Saur Uhrmacher*, etc. (clock-maker).

---

[103] See monograph on *Jacob Philadelphia*, read by the writer before the American Jewish Historical Society, December, 1897.

In addition to his trades he dealt in divers merchandise including medicinal remedies, religious books, etc.

From contemporary letters and documents, 1734–50, it appears that Sauer's ambition in that early time was to be considered a clock-maker, and that he was known as such for a decade after he had embarked in the printing business. This fact becomes even more apparent when he finally purchased in 1750, from John Adam Gruber and his wife Elizabeth, the six acres of land upon which he had lived for almost twenty years, and for the past eleven years had set up his printing office.

This deed, dated August 14, 1750, Recorded in Philadelphia, Deed-book H. I., p. 129, designates him as Christopher Sauer, *clock-maker*. The consideration for the land being thirty-five pounds Pennsylvania currency. This deed is the earliest record of Christopher Sauer as a landholder in Germantown or Philadelphia county. A subsequent deed in the next year (1751) mentions his son Christopher Sauer, Jr., as a bookbinder.

There is a strong probability that Sauer got his first ideas of a German press while he was yet in the Mühlbach valley. The relations between Beissel and Franklin, the Philadelphia printer, had proven more or less unsatisfactory, on account of the latter's antipathy to the " Dutch," as he called anything that was German. Consequently the lack of an independent German press was felt more and more as the German population continued steadily to increase in the Province.

To partly supply the wants of the Germans, Franklin, it is said, at the instance or suggestion of Beissel and the Eckerlings, started, as early as June 11, 1732, a German weekly newspaper in Philadelphia, *Die Philadelphische Zeitung*. The editor was Louis Timothee, language-master, who was a practical printer and scholar, and the first librarian of the Philadelphia Library. This paper purported to be a translation of the *Pennsylvania Gazette*, and was issued upon the Saturday following the English edition. This was the first German newspaper published in America. No specimen copy has been preserved, so far as is known, nor is it known how long the paper was continued. A fac-simile of Franklin's announcement of its publication is reproduced.

The Gazette *will come out again on* Monday *next, and conti-nue to be publißed on* Mondays.
And on the Saturday *following will be publißed* Philadelphi-fche Zeitung, *or Newspaper in High-Dutch, which will con-tinue to be publißed on* Saturdays *once a Fortnight, ready to be delivered at* Ten *a Clock, to Country Subfcribers.* Advervife-ments *are taken in by the Printer hereof, or by Mr.* Louis Timo-thee. *Language Mafter, who tránflates them.*

This venture of Franklin's may have been another incentive for Sauer to set up a German press. There was, however, one great obstacle : this was the lack of means to import the necessary outfit. It was about the time when Beissel was casting about for a printer for his third hymn-book, *Jacobs Kampff und Ritterplatz*. Sauer, it is said, requested him to delay for a year, as he might get a press, which would then be at the disposal or under the control of the congregation. This being acceded to, Sauer, for the time being again became a devout Lutheran, and posed, at least in his correspondence, as an extreme Pietist.

Letters were written to the Reverend Friedrich Michael Ziegenhagen, the celebrated Lutheran Court preacher at London, wherein representations were made as to the condition of the Lutheran Church in the Province. Warnings were also sent out regarding a committee sent by the Pennsylvania congregation to solicit contributions in Europe. In fact, Christopher Sauer constituted himself the confidential agent of the German Lutheran Church authorities.

The same course was pursued by Sauer toward the Rev.

Gotthilf August Francke, director of the Orphanage at Halle. There is still a letter in existence in the archives of that institution, dated June 15, 1735, wherein Sauer, after denouncing the committee from Philadelphia, then on a collecting tour in Europe, closes with a demand that a press and type be purchased for him and sent to America. Repayment was to be made some time in the future to Rev. Ziegenhagen at London. Francke, in communicating Sauer's request to Ziegenhagen closes his letter as follows :

" The before-mentioned Sauer has demanded in his letter that some type for printing be bought here and sent to him, and that he would refund the money advanced to your reverence. But, as we are overloaded here with other matters, we cannot adapt ourselves thereto. Further, I doubt whether any service would be rendered by a printing-press in the West Indies."

When Sauer learned that his well-laid plans had failed, he again became an outspoken Separatist, and whenever the opportunity offered expressed his opinion about the clergy of the orthodox faiths. This was especially the case as to such as were subsequently sent to these parts by the Halle institution.

The immediate result of Sauer's failure to interest the Halle authorities in 1735 was the printing of the Ephrata Hymn-book of 1736 by Benjamin Franklin.

ARMS OF THE PRINTERS' GUILD.

The embryo printer was not dismayed by the rebuffs from Halle and London. In less than two years after he received Francke's letter, we find him in possession of his coveted type. Sauer, in a letter to Büdingen, dated Germantown, November 17, 1738, and which was published in the *Geistliche Fama*, No. 25, p. 85, writes :

"Where can I find words to praise the good God! I am deeply indebted to Him. My all be at His service for the glorification of His name. This was in feebleness my desire and longing for the great benefits which I have enjoyed during my sojourn here as well as during my whole life. Therefore I longed to establish a German Printing establishment (*Buchdruckery*) in this land, which N. bought for me and has forwarded to this place."

Who this person was has thus far remained an impenetrable mystery. It has been repeatedly stated that this outfit was obtained from Jacob Gass (Gast), a Swiss Separatist, and a member of the Ephrata Community, of whom we shall speak a little later as Brother Jethro. The writer has not been able to verify this statement. All indications, however, point towards strengthening the tradition that Gass obtained the original outfit used by the Ephrata Community.

In regard to the Sauer press, there is a tradition, and no doubt a true one, that the printing-press was a home-made affair constructed by the printer himself.

After the type and press had been secured, an agreement was made between Sauer and the Ephrata congregation for printing a new hymn-book for the use of all Separatists in the Province. It was to be a duodecimo containing some six hundred and fifty hymns. There was, however, an obstacle in the way of its immediate execution. While the Germantown printer had his press and type, and was able to make his own ink, and the members of the Ephrata Community stood ready to aid in setting the type, working the press and correcting the proof, there was no paper. The whole stock of printing paper in the Province was controlled by Benjamin Franklin, and he refused to let Sauer have any except upon his own terms and for cash.

Here was an unlooked-for dilemma, as neither Sauer nor Beissel had the requisite amount of ready money. The situation was,—no cash, no paper ; and even then only at Franklin's price, who flatly refused " credit to the Dutch."

At this critical period Conrad Weiser came to the rescue of both the Community and Sauer. He made a journey from Ephrata to Philadelphia in the beginning of July, 1738, and pledged his personal credit for the amount of the paper bill. The paper was then delivered, and the *Weyrauchs Hügel* became an accomplished fact.

The title-pages of this book are as curious as its history. The chief title, by which it is generally known, reads :

Zionitischer | Weyrauchs Hügel | oder: | Myrrhen Berg, | Worinnen allerley liebliches und wohl riechen- | des nach Apotheker-Kunst zu bereitetes | Rauch-Werck zu finden. | Bestehend | In allerley Liebes-Würckungen der in Gott | geheiligten Seelen, welche sich in vielen und maucherley | geistlichen und lieblichen Liedern aus gebildet. | Als darin-neu | Der letzte Ruff zu dem Abendmahl des gros- | sen Gottes auf unterschiedliche Weise | trefflich aus gedrucket ist; | Zum Dienst | Der in dem Abend-Ländischen Welt-Theil als | bey dem Untergang der Sonnen erwecken Reiche —Gottes, und zu ihrer Ermunterung auf die | Mitter-nächtige Zukunfft des Bräutigäms | aus Licht gegeben. | Germantown: Gedruckt bey Christoph Sauer, 1739.

[Translation.—Zionitic Incense Hill or Mountain of Myrrh, wherein there is to be found all sorts of lovely and sweet-scented Incense, prepared according to the Apothecary's Art. Consisting of divers workings of effectual Love in God-awakened souls, which has developed in many and various spiritual lovely Hymns. Also therein the last Call to the Supper of the great God, in various ways is most admirably set forth, for service of those who, in this benighted part of the world, at the setting of the sun, awakened Church of God, and is given to the light for their encouragement, upon the midnight advent of the Bride-groom. Germantown : Printed by Christoph Sauer, 1739.]

ZIONITISCHER

Weyrauchs-Hügel

Oder:

Myrrhen Berg,

Worinnen allerley liebliches und wohl riechen=
des nach Apotheker=Kunst zu bereitetes
Rauch=Werck zu finden.

Bestehend

In allerley Liebes=Würckungen der in GOTT
geheiligten Seelen, welche sich in vieler und mancherley
geistlichen und lieblichen Liedern aus gebildet.

Als darinnen

Der letzte Ruff zu dem Abendmahl des gros=
sen GOttes auf unterschiedliche Weise
trefflich aus gedrucket ist;

Zum Dienst

Der in dem Abend=Ländischen Welt=Theil als
bey dem Untergang der Sonnen erweckten Kirche
GOttes, und zu ihrer Ermunterung auf die
Mitternächtige Zukunst des Bräutigams
ans Licht gegeben.

Germantown ; Gedruckt bey Christoph Sauer. 1739

TITLE-PAGE OF THE FIRST BOOK PRINTED WITH GERMAN TYPE IN AMERICA.

ALLEN
In der Wüſten girrenden
und Einſamen
TURTEL-TAEUBLEIN
Als
Ein geiſtliches Harffen-Spiel
In den
Mancherley Zeiten der Göttlichen
Heimſuchung.

✠✠✠✠✠✠✠✠ ✠ ✠✠✠✠✠✠✠✠

Apocal. 12. v. 1. 2. 5. 6.

Und es erſchien ein groß Zeichen im Himmel: ein
Weib mit der Sonnen bekleidet/ und der Mond
unter ihren füſſen/ und auf ihrem Haupt eine
Krone von zwölff Sternen.

Und ſie ward ſchwanger/ und ſchrye/ und war in
Kindes Nöthen/ und hatte groſſe Quaal zur
Geburt.

Und ſie gebahr einen Sohn/ ein Knäblein/ der
alle Heiden ſolte weiden mit der eiſern Ruthen.
Und ihr Kind ward entzückt zu GOTT und
ſeinem Stuhl.

Und das Weib entflohe in die Wüſte/ da ſie hatte
einen Ort bereitet von GOTT/ daß ſie daſelbſt
ernähret würde tauſend/ zwey hundert und ſechs-
zig Tage.

✠✠✠✠✠✠✠✠✠✠✠✠✠✠✠✠✠✠✠

REVERSE OF TITLE-PAGE OF WEYRAUCHS HÜGEL.

A partial explanation of the peculiar wording of this strange title will be found in Exodus, xxx, 34–36.

" And the Lord said unto Moses. Take unto thee sweet spices, stacte, and onycha, and galbanum ; these sweet spices with pure frankincense : of each shall there be a like weight :

" And thou shalt make a perfume, a confection after the art of the apothecary, tempered together, pure and holy :

" And thou shalt beat some of it very small, and put it before the testimony in the tabernacle of the congregation, where I will meet with thee : it shall be unto you most holy."

In the mystic cult *Weyrauch* is but a synonym for *Gebet*, prayer. It was taught that when ignited during supplication the prayer became corporeal and was wafted in fragrant clouds toward heaven. Upon this account the gum was kept exclusively for religious uses. A *hügel* or hillock also denotes an object held in special veneration by the mystics, as the rising sun first gilded the hill-tops when it rose in the east. Thus from time immemorial hills have always been designated as holy ground and became the chosen place for offering and sacrifice. To the adepts the chief line in the title meant more than a mere hill of incense. It typified the book as a volume of prayer, which, if properly used, would, like the visible fumes of burning incense, go direct to the throne of Grace.

Upon the reverse of the title-page it is dedicated to :

Allen | In der Wüsten girrenden | und Einsamen | Turtel-Taeublein | Als | Ein Geistliches Harffen-Spiel | In den | Mancherley Zeiten der Göttlichen | Heimsuchung.

[Translation.—To all cooing Turtle-Doves, alone in the desert as a spiritual harp-strain in the divers times of Divine visitation.]

Then follow four Scripture texts from Apocalypse xii, 1, 2, 5, 6.

The book proper has a preface of ten pages. This is dated: "*Ephrata in Pensylvanien, den 14. des 4ten Monats, 1739.*" Then follow 649 hymns on 736 pages. These are arranged under thirty-three different heads. To the complete book there is an appendix of 45 pages, containing 38 hymns, which are numbered separately but paged continuously.

The title of this appendix reads:

Die | Ehmals verdorrete, | Nun aber | Wieder grünende und Frucht-bringende | Ruthe | Aarons, | Bestehend in einem Anhang | Wichtiger und Erfahrungs-voller Lieder, | Darinnen | Die Tritte Gottes im innern-Heiligthum | umständliche vorgestellet sind; | Zur Aufmunterung | Den Wäysen und Verlassen zu Zion | Den Zionitischen Weyrauchs-Hügel | mit angehenckt. | Psalm 126, v. 5. | Sie gehen hin und weinen, und tragen edlen | Saamen; und kommen mit Freuden und bringen | ihre Garben.

[Translation.—The once withered but now re-quickened and fruit-bearing rod of Aaron, consisting of an appendix of weighty hymns, fraught with experience; wherein the steps of God in his inner Sanctuary are circumstantially presented, for the encouragement of the orphans and forsaken in Zion. Appended to the Zionitic *Weyrauchs Hügel.* Then follows Psalm cxxvi, 5.]

Upon the reverse of the title is a quotation from the Song of Solmon viii, 6, 7.

After the appendix follows an index of the thirty-three subjects and a general alphabetical index of the hymns.

The statement has been repeatedly made, and almost universally accepted, that all of the hymns in the *Weyrauchs Hügel* were original with Beissel and his followers. Such, however, does not appear to be the case. While it is true of the majority; a number of popular German hymns were included evidently on account of the familiarity of the tunes if not for the associations of the Fatherland. Among this

Die
Ehmals verdorrete,
Nun aber
Wieder grünende und Frucht-bringende

RUTHE
Aarons,

Bestehend in einem Anhang
Wichtiger und Erfahrungs-voller Lieder,
Darinnen
Die Tritte GOTTES im innern Heiligthum
umständlich vorgestellet sind;
Zur Aufmunterung
Den Wäysen und Verlassenen zu Zion
Dem Zionitischen Weyrauchs-Hügel
mit angehenckt.

Psalm 126. v. 5.
Sie gehen hin und weinen, und tragen edlen
Saamen; und kommen mit Freuden und bringen
ihre Garben.

TITLE-PAGE TO APPENDIX TO WEYRAUCHS HÜGEL.

list may be mentioned: No. 185, 510, Silesius; 49, Rembach; 14, 518, Frank; 158, 465, Schröder; 173, S. v. Birken; 187, Neander; 328, Dreius; 345, 482, Luther, 385, 397, Gerhard; 386, Dessler; 395, Justus Falkner; 495, Mentzer; 560, Schmidt; 568, Nicolai; 608, Trestrege; 610, Granmann; 617, Gotter; 627, Schutz.

The fact that Conrad Weiser was in any way instrumental in the printing of this remarkable book is shown by the entries in Franklin's account books, from which it appears that upon July 9, 1738, Conrad Weiser, on behalf of the Ephrata Community, bought of Benjamin Franklin 125 reams of paper for £62. 18. 6., upon which bill he paid on account £20. Some time afterwards he made an additional payment of £36, and an order on Caspar Wister for £10.16.6.

On the following eighth of September he ordered 52 reams more amounting to £32.10.0., which, with a ream of Post paper for £1.10.6., made the transaction amount to a total of £96.12.6., upon which a third payment was made of £13.4.6., making a total cash credit of £84.0.9. Another payment was made during the winter of £5.5.9. Franklin notes that on April 5, 1739, there remains due £7.6., which upon the opposite page is marked "Settled and Adjusted."

A fac-simile of these interesting accounts is here given:

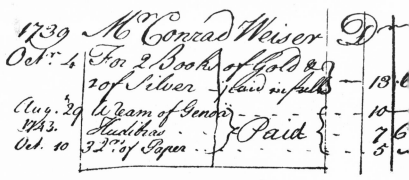

FAC-SIMILE OF ENTRY IN FRANKLIN'S JOURNAL.

Original in collection of American Philosophical Society.

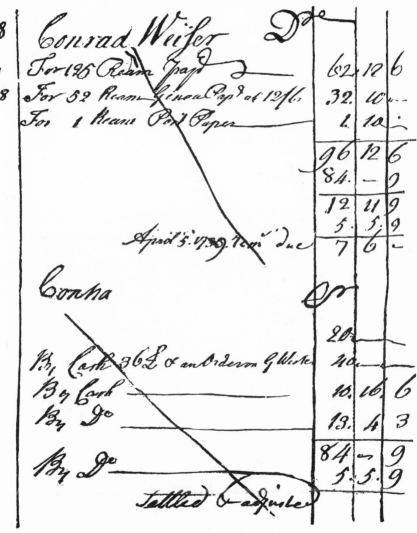

FAC-SIMILE OF FRANKLIN'S LEDGER ACCOUNT WITH CONRAD WEISER.

Original in collection of American Philosophical Society.

That Christopher Sauer, inexperienced as he was in the printer's art, had undertaken a task beyond his capacity may well be imagined. In a letter published in the *Geistliche Fama*, dated Germantown, November 10, 1738, we read :

" Sauer's newly established printing office is very irksome to him, and he must pay more dearly for his experience here than in any venture he has thus far tried. He must print for the Seven-dayers [*i. e.*, those who keep the seventh day holy] a large hymn-book. They are sharp and particular enough, as one hears : therefore it makes him much trouble."

The Ephrata Brethren, who were superintending the printing, as stated in the above letter, were exacting in their demands. The supervising brother and responsible proof-reader, or corrector, was Brother Jaebez (Rev. Peter Miller); he had for his chief assistants Brothers Jephune (Samuel Eckerling) and Agonius (Michael Wohlfarth).

After the paper was secured the printing of the book went forward without delay. All, however, did not go smoothly, as Sauer set himself up as a censor of the hymns. This from the first caused more or less friction between him and the supervising brethren, and finally when the 400th hymn was set up, a personal controversy arose between Beissel and the printer, which became exceedingly bitter, and ended in an estrangement lasting for fully ten years. Letters passed back and forth between the two men, which only tended to aggravate the controversy, and culminated in Sauer's publishing an account of his side of the story under the following title :

Ein abgenöthigter Bericht : oder zum öfftern begehrte Antwort denen darnach fragenden dargelegt ; In sich haltende : zwey Brieffe und deren Ursach."

Upon the reverse of the title Christopher Sauer printed the following pertinent Gospel verses, Matthew, xxiv, 24–26 :

Ein
Abgenöthigter
Bericht,

Oder:
Zum öfftern begehrte

Antwort,

Denen darnach fragenden dargelegt. In sich haltende; zwey Brieffe und deren
Ursach.

Dem noch angehänget worden eine Histo-
rie von Doctor Schotte/ und einige
Brieffe von demselben zu un-
seren Zeiten nöthig zu
erwegen

Germanton:
Gedruckt bey Christoph Saur 1739.

For there shall arise false Christs, and false prophets, and shall show great signs and wonders; insomuch that (if it were possible) they shall deceive the very elect.

Behold I have told you before.

Wherefore if they shall say unto you, Behold, he is in the desert; go not forth: Behold, he is in the secret chambers; believe it not.

But a single copy of this curious publication has come down to us. It is in the library of Hon. Judge Samuel W. Pennypacker, who has kindly placed it at the disposal of the writer.

Not the least interesting feature of this book is Sauer's explanation setting forth his objections to the spirit of hymn 400. This follows the preface, and is printed in heavy Gothic type. Both fac-simile and translation are inserted:

Die Anstöße so ich an diesem Liede hatte waren diese: Der Martialisch-und Mercurialische Geist wolte feuer-und Wolcken-Säule seyn; darum wollen fast alle Worte der 4. ersten Verse des Lieds soviel sagen; als hänget euch an mich/ und thut nichts als was ich euch sage/ sonderlich im 14. und 23 Vers. Im 25. klagt er daß er verachtet werde von seinen Brüdern sowohl als von den Sündern; und er hatte sie doch schon zu Gottes Licht gebracht/ wie im 31. Vers zu sehen. Im 33. und 34. macht er ihnen wieder Muth/ man solle ihn nur ohn verdrossen ansehn/ so würde man schon heil vom Schlangen-Biß. Im 36. will er sagen: dieses Liedgen hat gemacht der niemals will seyn veracht. Im 37. 38. und 39. vers springt Mercurius gar zusehr/ und schwingt sich auf den Thron/ und rufft: Sehet/ sehet ?c. Und dieses soll man auch noch singen; gewißlich die Haare solten einem zuberge stehn bey solcher Abgötterey/ wann man nicht bezaubert blind oder toll.

Translation.—" The objections which I had to this hymn are these : The Martial and Mercurial spirit [meaning Conrad Beissel] wanted to appear as a Pillar of fire and clouds. Therefore almost all the words in the first four verses say as much as : 'Join yourself unto me, and do naught but what I command you;' especially so in the 14th and 23rd verses. In the 25th [27?] he complains that he is despised by his brethren as well as by sinners, although he had already brought them to God's light, as is shown in the 31st verse. In the 33rd and 34th he again [attempts to] inspire courage. If one could only look upon him without loathing, he would be safe from the serpent's bite. In the 37th, 38th and 39th verses, Mercurius [Beissel] leaps entirely too high, and swings himself upon the throne and cries, 'See, see,' etc. And this we are also to sing. Verily, our hair shall stand upon an end at such idolatry, if one be not bewitched or mad."

The *Chronicon*, commenting upon this episode, states :

HE printing of the above-mentioned hymn-book now went forward. But towards the end there happened a matter which caused a great stir in the land, and which shall now be communicated. The printer Saur had already in Germany become acquainted with the Superintendent during the awakening there. He considered him indeed to be a God-fearing man; but when Providence placed him at the head of a great awakening in Conestoga, the good man held him in suspicion of seeking to become a pope, to which there came yet a secret dislike for the Superintendent because the latter received his wife, who had been separated from him, under his leading, and even made her sub-superintendent of the Sisters' House. At that time opinions concerning the Superintendent varied in the country. The great and coarser part of the people regarded him as a great wizard, whereto certain things that happened gave an appearance of plausibility. As has been mentioned above, the spirit under whose guidance he was, at times made him invisible, concerning which the following is yet to be mentioned in passing. A justice of the peace sent a constable after him with a warrant ; he took an assistant with him named Martin Graff. As they came towards the house, they saw him go in with a pitcher of water. They followed him, and while one stationed himself at the door, the other searched the house from top to bottom ; but no Superintendent was to be found. As they departed, however, and were quite a distance from the house, they saw him come out again.

"His brethren, however, who were daily with him, and may have seen much of this kind of thing, fell into the opposite extreme, and like the Jews concerning John, thought whether he might not be Christ. Even Brother Prior Onesimus said that such thoughts often came to him. Of all this the printer was aware. Wherefore when in printing the hymn-book he came upon the hymn : 'Since the pillar of cloud dissolveth,' etc., he wanted to force out the 37th verse a meaning as if the Superintendent intended himself thereby. He accordingly took the *corrector* to task about it, who, however, asked him, whether he then believed only in one Christ? This so outraged him that he wrote a sharp letter to the Superintendent, in which he reproached him for his spiritual pride. The Superintendent, who in such things never remained anyones debtor, sent back to him a short reply to the following intent : 'Answer not a fool according to his folly,' etc. 'As vinegar upon nitre, so is he that singeth songs to an heavy heart.' (Prov. xxv, 20.) This aroused the good man to a fiery heat, and he resolved to avenge himself for this affront. Therefore he published a document against the Superintendent in which he told under how strange a conjunction of stars the Superintendent was, and how each planet manifested in him its own characteristics: from Mars he had his great severity, from Jupiter his friendliness, from Venus that the female sex ran after him, Mercury had taught him the art of a comedian, etc. He even found in his name, *Conradus Beusselus*, the numbers of the Beast, 666. By this occurrence the good understanding between the printer and the Community at Ephrata was interupted for many years, and was not restored until the printer's wife, who had hitherto lived at Ephrata, went back to him again. From that time on until his death, he lived on good terms with the Superintendent and all the Solitary in the Settlement, and won for himself an everlasting remembrance among them by many deeds of love. May the Lord grant him to enjoy the fruits of this good seed in the resurrection of the righteous !''

Sauer's published statement, before mentioned, contains several of the letters alluded to in the above notice. On account of its extreme rarity and the light it sheds upon the publication of the first book printed in German tpye in America, a translation of such parts as relate to the controversy is incorporated. The translation is by Hon. Samuel W. Pennypacker, who first brought this curious work to the notice of historical students in a paper en-

PENNYPACKER ARMS.

titled "The Quarrel between Christopher Sauer, the Germantown printer, and Conrad Beissel, founder and vorsteher of the Cloister at Ephrata." [104]

Christopher Sauer to Conrad Beissel:

I have until within the last few days been in hopes that the work which I did, and caused to be done, upon the hymn-book

---

[104] *Vide* Pennsylvania Magazine of History and Biography, vol. xii, p. 76, *et seq.*

would redound to the honor of God, to whom I am under the greatest obligations for all that he has done for me and all creatures, and will still do through time and eternity, and I remain bound to Him even though I shall see no good day more. It is his way that when we dismiss all which is not from Him He fills us with that which more concerns Him. The result is that we love all that is from Him, and have a hatred and horror of all that does not please Him. In the beginning much remains concealed, while we are in the shoes of children as the saying is, which in years of youth and manhood become as clear as day. I have therefore with patience overlooked some hymns, which I had rather sacrificed to Vulcan by throwing them into the fire. I thought something might be given to the first alphabet scholars as it were according to their ability and which they could grasp and that it would not be wise to break down the first rounds of the ladder. I have willingly let go what the amateur poet through vanity and sentiment have brought together, especially since Brother Peter Miller said to me : "The worst soldiers are always put in the front rank." Taking this view of it I had nothing more to say. Afterwards so much of wood, straw, stubble, and trash came that it went pretty hard with me. It was very deeply impressed upon me that each work should be a birth to appear in eternity, not in the lightness of the mercurial pictures drawn by men, but to stand in the clean way. However I remained in hope that something better would come in the future. A still greater mercy befell me, to wit : In the beginning of the 16th Rubric or division there was placed a silly hymn which, on first reading through it, I considered to be among the stupid amature poetry and I wished that something better could be put in its place. In the 29th verse it runs :

> "Der doch träget deine Last
> Und dabei hat wenig Rast."

There I stopped and read the remainder over again, but while I was attending to some other business, it was printed. I was not at ease about it. I regarded it as among those great errors of which to-day the world is full and wished that it might still remain among those rejected. I thought if it should come,

either here or in Germany or any where else, before the eyes
of an enlightened spirit who has found and delights in God
and his Saviour as the true rest, he might be deceived by such
miserable stuff after such a magnificently brilliant title-page
and I should be ashamed because of my negligence.   I might
perhaps be able to find excuses that would answer before men,
but in my breast would burn a fire that would be quenched
by no excuses.   I thereupon asked Brother Samuel whether
he did not think a great mistake had there occured in writing,
since unskillful poets are often compelled for the sake of their
rhyme to use which destroy the sense.   He said to me, '' No,
I shall let it stand just as it is.''   I consented to do it then
because it suddenly occured to me, that in the pine forests the
industrious ants gather together straw, wood, earth, shells,
and resin, from the pines which they carry underneath into
the hill and that this is called '' Weihrauch.''   This pacified
me to some extent because it accorded with the title.   Still I
could not reconcile the word '' Zionitisch'' with it, because
upon Mount Zion no such collection can be found as I have
described.   There God is praised in silence.   There are there
only two hymns.   The one is the song of Moses running,
briefly, like this, '' Lord, thou and no other hast delivered
us from all of our enemies and dost protect us and lead us
through outer danger.''   Exodus, 15th.   There is no quarreling more, no time, no change of day and night.   It therefore
occured to me that you must have a wonderful idea of Zion
since you fix its nature but know nothing of and have not experienced real and actual death.   The second song is short.   It
is the song of the Lamb which is strangled.   It runs thus : ''All
is fulfilled.   There is nothing more to do.   Now praise we our
God in silence.''

But you said in the meeting when I was there that every
verse was suitable for Mount Zion.   That is easily said if a
man has a well smoothed tongue.   You will find out otherwise
however.   Meanwhile I regretted my lost time over the book
and that my hope which had something honorable for its object
should have so entirely failed.   I spoke with Brother Samuel
once more about it in what way it was to be understood.   He

answered me that I should not blame them for being Catholic, which I from my heart wished to be true since in the Community of Christ there are no others.   For instance we believe in the mediation of holy ones and truly of those who are afterward in life.   This caused me no scruple because it is my daily exercise notwithstanding I am still not holy.   What then will the holy do.   But when he asked me whether I believed only in the one Christ I would have been shocked into a cold fever if true quiet had not prevented.   I then read the whole hymn over again once more and saw the man who was intended and it gave great sorrow.   But I remembered how far the human race depart from God and that man is inclined to idolatry and easily moved to make images and to honor himself while the tendency to depart from the true way (found only in the ground of the spirit and by the abandonment of all creature things) is born in him.   He is therefore easily led to act with sects, parties, and like divisions, and one believes and receives from another that which is pleasant without real experience of what will be the outcome.   It may be therefore that it ought not to be taken amiss in the writer of the hymn, since as the eyes are so do they see.   Still I have no real peace about this affair.   I determined then to write to you and ask you whether you had not seen or read this piece or had not considered what a dreadful production it is ; to say that without serious difficulty it can still be taken out and in its place something to the honor of God, or for the good of weak souls, can be put in where the two pages are cut out which I will do at my own expense ; and to ask you whether on the other hand it was done according to your wish and inclination.   If so, I would remind you that the good Moses could not go into Canaan because he honored not the Lord when he said '' must we fetch you water.''   See what an afflicted burdenbearer and once true knight Moses was and where is such a Moses?   Herod may well have made such an unusually good address to the people that it caused them to say, '' That is the voice of God and not of man.''   The angel struck not the unwitting people because they were inclined to idolatry but him who accepted the Godly honor.

Already you suffer yourself to be called "Father."[105] Oh, would there were a single one who comprehended Christ and respected and carried out the commands of him who absolutely forbid that you let any one call you master and should call any man "Father" upon this earth! The misery is already great enough, as you yourself said to me significantly. You are the greatest God in the community. When you sat still everything fell back. You had once for sometime given up the meeting and everything fell away. Your dearest brethern hastened to the world. Even Brother N. had made a wagon in which to ride to the city. There were other instances which you told me. And did you not the other day in the meeting significantly and at great length speak of this idolatry and how they went whoring after you as is indeed the case. And now will they with full throats call and sing:

> "Sehet, sehet, sehet an !
> Sehet, sehet an den mann !
> Der von Gott erhöhet ist
> Der its unser Herr und Christ."

If Brother Samuel had not said to me concerning it that the hymn had a double meaning and one might take it as he chose, I should have considered the last as referring to Christ and looked upon the "God without rest" as a compulsion of the verse. Are there not already molten calves enough? Is not the door of Babel great enough that they should build another little door through which they call loudly, "See here is Christ" in order to entice souls to themselves? Do not misunderstand me. I value highly the favor of returning to you. But I fear God will play his own part in it and leave the beautiful vessel empty lest otherwise upright souls might suffer an injury which certainly would cause no single child of God pleasure. Much more where it to be wished from the innermost heart that all the might of the stars were entirely lost and that Christ were indeed the ruler in you and the whole community. This would give me great joy to look upon through my whole life long. There is nothing more to say except that, with the permission

---

[105] His Kloster name was Father Friedsam.

of Brother Michael,[106] I should like, if I might, to take out this
one hymn and put another in its place because it concerns the
honor of God.   It is easy to see that I have no earthly concern
in it and that the influence of no man's interest has anything
to do with it.   There are still as many as a hundred hymns
with which you can feed the senses that they die not.   I am
sure that a thousand pounds would not persuade me to print
such a one, for the reason that it leads the easy way to idolatry.
If it were my paper it would have been already burned.   But
my suggestion was met by the brethren only with scornful and
mocking words, and at last they said, " Now we will pack up
the paper."[107]   I thought " they have still better right to it than
the Hussars." With such disposition of the matter for my own
part I can be at peace.   God will find a way to protect his honor.
As to the rest, I love thee still.   CHRISTOPH SAUR.

Thereupon I received the following letter instead of an
answer :

[CONRAD BEISSEL TO CHRISTOPHER SAUER.]

In some respects the subject is entirely too bad for me to
have anything to do with thee about it, since it has been
written : " Answer not a fool according to his folly, least thou
also be like unto him."

" Answer a fool according to his folly, least he be wise in
his own conceit."   This is the reason that I have been moved
and thou needest not think that thou hast made a point.   But
that I should be like unto thee from having to do with thee
will not happen, since we already before made the mistake of
having too much to do with thee.   Thou wast not fit for our
community.   Therein also was fulfilled what has been written :
" As he that taketh away a garment in cold weather, and as
vinegar upon nitre, so is he that singeth songs to an heavy
heart."

If thou hadst not always acted in this way it might perhaps

---

[106] Michael Wohlfarth, who in the Cloister was Brother Agonius.

[107] This is another proof that the paper did not belong to Sauer, *vide*
pp. 320, 326, 327, J. F. S.

have been thought that there was some reason for it, but since thy whole heart is always ready to blame what is above thy conceited Sophist—Heaven, it is no wonder to me that thou comst now puffed up with such foolish and desperate conceits : through which thou layest thyself so bare that any one who has only ordinary eyes can see that thou art indeed a miserable Sophist. If thou hadst only learned natural morality thou wouldst not have been so puffed up. A wise man does not strive to master or to describe a cause of which he has neither comprehension or experience, but it is otherwise with a fool. Thou ought first to go to school and learn the lowly and despised way of the Cross of Jesus before thou imaginest thyself to be a master. Enough for Thee. This may inform thee that henceforth I will have nothing to do with thy two-sided, double-hearted, odious and half-hypocritical pretensions of Godliness, since thy heart is not clean before God, otherwise thou wouldst walk upright in the way and go not the crooked way thou dost.

One almost springs aloft when he sees how shamefully the name of God is misused.

The world sings its little song and dances straight and without hesitation to hell, and covers it over with the name of God so that the deception and wickedness may not be seen. Believe me, thy way is sure to come before God, thy juggling tricks and spiritual slight of hand which thou, from the natural stars and not in the true fear of God, hast learned will come to judgment : and I say to thee as the word of truth that if thou dost not make atonement and change thy heart thou mayest expect a wrathful and terrible God, since the Lord is hostile to all that is double-faced and false. Indeed, the paths which lead out from thee run through one another so wonderfully that the wonder is that God does not punish it at once as he did the rebellious pack,—Korah, Dathan and Abiram.

Thou hast also in thy letter to me said that a fire burned in thy breast over this or that. It would be a good thing if that fire, if there is one, should consume thee until there should nothing remain but a soft and sweet spring of water in which thy heart might be mollified to true repentance. Then indeed couldst thou for the first time learn to know rightly what is from God and what from nature, what from God and what from the stars in the heavens.

When I know of a man that he does not bend before God but still walks in his own highway, I accept absolutely no judgment as in Godly affairs, but say to him freely that he wash and clean himself before I can have anything to do with him.

As concerning those other things in which one man has to do with another it has also come to an end. Further and lastly it is my determination to remain as I have said above. I am so tired of the untruth of men that if I were not under the greatest necessity, if God did not plainly intend and it were not His will that I must be needed for the cause of conscience, I would rather be dismissed into the still everlasting. On that account I would have prayed that I might henceforth be spared from such defamation, but should it give pleasure to load me with more of it I shall bear myself as one who knows not that there are such things in the world. I will at the last be separated from all and will no further participate pro or con. Still will I in some measure continue my writing and do it again if circumstances require it.

What I have still further to say is this : that henceforth all right over my person shall be taken entirely out of thy hands, since thou for many years hast gone to work so wonderfully about it as if thou hast bought it for a sum of money in order to do with it according to thy pleasure. Thou must not think that one is blind and foolish and dost not see what thou hast in mind. It does not even please me that I could write German to thee, since thy envy and falsehood are so great that it is not easy to measure them. Therefore I consider thee entirely unfit to be a judge in Godly affairs, and for this reason I have little or nothing to answer to thy letter. Thou hast no experience in the way of God, for thou all the time walkest thine own way.

COMMENT [BY CHRISTOPHER SAUER].

We have here now heard a voice, whether it came from Zion or Mount Sinai may those judge who know the difference. I am inclined to make a comment upon each word, but every one may make his own as he chooses. I wish him only the soft and sweet spring of water which he needs instead of the fiery zeal of Sinai. Otherwise when he goes forth soon will he make fire fall from heaven, which we always hear crackle in his letter, and do signs and wonders. If I had thought he would take the trouble to describe my propensities and his, I would have sent him a great register of the old Adam in me which I could describe much better than he. Since I for a long time have besought God to enable me thoroughly to discern their enormity, and since I have found so much to do with myself I am ready to say the simple truth so that no man need be disturbed about me. And this is the reason for my long silence, and also for my thinking seldom of his person, not that it is too bad for me but because it can neither aid nor hinder me. If I were in such a position as he, to give my natural possession I should need only the princes and powerful who still to a considerable degree have rule over the conceited Sophist-heaven, since they desire so much to rule upon earth and to fasten their throne there. I could have also given him certain information that I have been beloved by spiritual persons who truly were more beautiful and purer than those whom he holds above Christ. God has also so willed it that I for the same time cannot otherwise believe than that all is good to which the same spirit impelled me. I blame not the spirit which impelled him. He is God's creature. I only say : he is not clean and is still far from the spirit of Christ. I rejoice that he praises God the Lord as all good spirits do, and in that respect I love him. I hate only the untruth which he brings to light and wishes to lay in the hearts of men. And when he as that one which through a maid had its pleasure in telling only the truth pointed out the Apostles to men, and sought to further their happiness (Acts, xv, v, 17), I should leave him in the place for which he is good, and as for myself rather hunger until death for the completeness of my Jesus. In that I make myself entirely clear. In like manner I make a distinction between Conrad Beissel as he stands in his still well-proportioned attributes derived from the old-birth or birth of the stars—♄ ♃ ♂ ☉ ♀ ☿ ☽.

When one approaches him he shows first the complaisance of Jove ; when one bends, rises, and heeds well he finds his sweetness and lovingness from Venus, his solar understanding and mercurial readiness. If one fails a little he shows the gravity and earnestness of Saturn. If one attacks only a little his spiritual pride he shows the severity of Mars with thunder and lightning, popely ban, the sword of vengence and fiery magic. What can induce a weak soul in sorrow and need to come and lay itself humbly at his feet, when the unclean spirit, which takes pleasure in the fact, triumphs in this way. Therefore would I counsel no one upon whom he has laid his hands or who has been baptized by him or by another Father, since all those who have given up the world and the gross fleshly life are prepared to be the habitations of a spirit, and through their own freed spirit and its suggestions and help of other spirits they have the power to torture a deserter and to put him in pain of body and soul, and also those who have little strength and do not depend with their whole hearts upon the true living God, but rely particularly upon their own virtues. Conrad has subjected me to this proof. He has intruded upon my etheral past, which has taught me how it goes with others, and how I have need of the support of my Saviour and to press into the centre of love or heart of Jesus where this aqua fortis cannot reach. Therefore, as I have said, I would not counsel no one without higher strength to oppose this Spirit. It is very powerful. And yet they are not bound by this strong magic, they have a free will. God has for many years shown me how many good and beautiful spirits there are which still are not clean. Already in the time of the Apostles there were many spirits which had gone beyond their limits in this our world. I therefore do not believe all that every one tells me, even when they speak through a spirit and speak only what the spirit says. The moon goes through many phases, and this is also his nature. It has happened because of his beautiful and well-proportioned nature that he would like to be something great. He looked upon the dumb creatures in their deformity and wanted to bring them to the right. For this purpose he takes the means, method and way which pleased him. So that now all must dance according to his will and do what through the power of his magic he compels. But I also want to say that I by no means overlook what he has in him which is good, and I freely recognize that he has much that a true Christian cannot be without, and this many innocent people see and they are drawn to him by it. But for myself I can never be attached to him for the reason that I know that his teaching hitherto has been a compound of Moses, Christ, Gichtel and Conrad Beissel. And no one of them complete. The spirit of Moses stood up boldly and prayed for the people who had disobeyed him and done wrong. Should his people oppose him how soon would Mercury spread his wings. Christ was an entirely different disposition. He knew his betrayer long before, and when the latter came to take his life he was such a gentle lamb that he said, " Friend ! wherefore art thou come ?" He received his kiss. He cured the ear of Malchus. Our dear Conrad is very far from anything of that kind. In many points he is very close to Gichtel and still closer to the little beast, described in Revelations, xii, 11, which represents his peculiarity in spiritual things. His figure is such that if one beseeches him he has the horns of a lamb, but if one touches his temper only a little he speaks like a dragon and is indeed not to be regarded as the first great beast, whose number is 66. He is not indeed so beast-like, but is also not clean Godly, but is humanly peculiar and no other than CVnraDVs BeIseLVs. DCLVVVI—666.

If he had not for the future entirely taken out of my hands all right to his holy person, I could and would have opened up to him the inner ground of his heart a little between me and him alone, but I must now be entirely silent for I am bound hand and foot. It seems to me that during the two weeks which he took to write to me he did not remember Him who suffered an entirely different opposition from sinners, who, although He was in the Godly image, held it not for a wrong to be like God but lowered Himself and became as a man. But this one must be regarded as a God, and therefore the little calf should and must remain upon its place. When my Saviour had done a noble deed He desired it should be unknown. See

to it that no man learn of it.   But to this God we must sing to
his folly.   If I had ten hymns in the book and had been
requested I would have taken them out, but Conrad is not
accustomed to having his will broken.   I could have overlooked it in silence out of natural morality and as a printer,
but it concerned the love of God that I should not be silent.
The spiritual harlotry and idolatry would have been increased
and confirmed my support.   I would rather die of hunger than
earn my bread in such a way.   It would go worse with me
than with the primate in Poland who proclaimed a king upon
the throne and could not keep him there.   I have, without
baptizing myself and letting myself be baptized four times
(like him), placed myself under the standard of my Saviour
and loved him, and still have not had the freedom to ask of
him that he make an officer of me ; but I gave myself to him,
as he best knows, as poor clay to be formed in his hand as by
a potter, or to be thrown into a corner as clay which is worth-
less.   He has nevertheless appointed me as the least beneath
his standard as a sentry to watch my post, a watchword has
been given to me which reads "love and humility."   When I
then upon the dark nights call out "who goes there?" and
this parole is not answered me, I know that it is no good friend
and no man of ours.   I must then fire my piece so that each
upon his post may be warned.   But since the Commander is
not far away he will himself have a care.   To him only the
honor.   For me willingly the shame.

This interesting controversy with Beissel did not, however, estrange Christopher Sauer from the Ephrata Community, as we find a constant intercourse between the Germantown printer and some of the mystic brethren on the
Cocalico, especially with the faction opposed to Beissel.

Before dismissing Christopher Sauer, it may be well to
mention a few items about the earliest issues of his press :

The first issue of the Germantown printer was a broadside, printed on one side, it bore the following title :

Eine | Ernstliche Ermahunng, | An Junge und Alte :

Eine

An Junge und Alte:
Zu einer

Ernstliche Ermahnung,

Angeheuchelten Prüfung

Ihres Herzens und Zustandes.

Kürzlich aus England nach America gesandt, und wegen seiner Wichtigkeit
Aus dem Englischen ins Deutsche treulich übersetzt: Von einem Liebhaber der Wahrheit.

NUn noch einmal, spricht der HERR, will Ich erschüttern nicht allein die Erde, sondern auch den Himmel: und dieses Wort: Noch einmal/ bezeichnet eine Hinwegnehmung der Dinge, die beweget sind oder

und mercket, auf welchem Grunde ihr stehet; daß es wird euch nicht helfen, wann die Reihe an euch kommt, daß ihr die Heilige Wahrheit bekennet: wenn ihr nicht auch darein gegründet seyd, so werdet ihr gewiß Schaden leiden. Darum bitte und

schon werden auf die Probe kommen, auch so gar die Auserwehlten, und die nicht auf dem rechten Grunde stehen, werden Schaden leiden. Seyd daher gewarnet alle, denen dieses mag vors Gesicht kommen: nehmet euer selbst wohl wahr.

Dis ist das inbrünftige Verlangen seines geringen und bekümmerten Knechts, und treuen Wolwollers seiner Kirche.
Gegeben den 3ten Monath des Jahrs 1738.

Benjamin Lay.

Germanton Gedruckt und zu finden bey Christoph Sauer. 1738.

THE FIRST ISSUE OF SAUER'S PRESS.

Zu einer | Ungeheuchelten Prüfung | Ihres Hertzens und Zustandes. | Kürtzlich aus Engeland nach America gesandt, und wegen seiner Wichtigkeit | Aus dem Englischen ins Deutsche treuliche übersetzt; Von einem Liebhaber der Wahrheit.

This was a translation from the English, who the "lover of truth" was does not appear, the typography and press-work, however, shows the work of a practical printer, whoever he may have been. The heading and imprint of this broadside, the "first issue of the German press in America," is presented in fac-simile. But two copies of this imprint are known.[108]

It will also be noted that the printer's name is spelled with an "E." In the early days of his sojourn in Pennsylvania he always wrote it "Saur."

Again referring to his letter in the *Geistliche Fame*, he writes that he knew of no better *vehiculum* to spread the news of the establishment of a German press throughout the land than to issue an almanac.

Der Hoch-Deutsch | Americanische Calender | auf das Jahr | nach der Gnaden-reichen Geburth unsers | Herrn und | Heylandes Jesu Christi | 1739 | Eingerichtet vor die Sonnen-Höhe von Peunsylvanien; Jedoch an denen angrenzenden Landen ohne merklichen Unterschied zu gebrauchen. Zum ersten mahl herausgegeben. Germanton, Gedruckt und zu finden by Christoph Saur, wie auch zu haben bey Joh. Wister in Philadelphia.

No perfect copy of this almanac is known, the specimen in the Pennsylvania Historical Society lacking the title-page.

After the completion of the *Weyrauchs Hügel*, Sauer put into execution his plan for a German newspaper, the first successful German periodical on the continent.

---

[108] One in the collection of the Historical Society of Philadelphia and the other in that of Judge Samuel W. Pennypacker.

Der Hoch-Deutsch

Pensylvanische
Geschicht-Schreiber,

Oder:

Sammlung

Wichtiger Nachrichten, aus dem Natur- und Kirchen-Reich.

Erstes Stück August 20 / 1739.

Geneigter Leser

Nter andern Abgöttern, denen die grobe und subtile Welt der sogenanten Christen dienet, ist nicht der Geringste der Vorwitz, öfter und Begierde gerne offt was neues

hen, in Hoffnung es werde nicht ohne einigen Nutzen, wenigst der Aufweckung und des Auffschauens bey einigen, die es lesen, schaffen. Auch möchten wohl künfftig einige Anmerckungen und der Zeit dienliche Sagen ernstlichen Gemüthern zum Nach-

The initial number bears the date August 20, 1739. It was a small sheet of four pages, with double columns, the size was thirteen inches by nine inches, and bore following title :—

Der | *Hoch-Deutsch* | *Pensylvanische* | *Geschicht-Schrei-ber,* | *Oder :* | *Sammlung* | *Wichtiger Nachrichten, aus dem Natur- und Kirchen-Reich.*

The paper was issued monthly at a subscription rate of three shillings per year. Subscribers had the further privilege of having advertisements inserted gratis.

The heading of the first page of this issue of Sauer's newspaper is reproduced in fac-simile on page 347. So scarce have these specimens become, that one hundred dollars were paid for the page here reproduced. An even greater sum is offered for a perfect copy of the Almanac of 1739.

As a matter of interest we also present on page 349 a reduced fac-simile of Sauer's specimen sheet and price-list for printing and the various sizes of type. This unique specimen, supposed to have been issued as early as 1740, undoubtedly the first typographical specimen sheet issued in America.

After the German printing house at Germantown was firmly established, the two publications *Der Hoch-Deutsch Americanische Calender* and *Der Hoch-Deutsch Pensylva-nische Geschicht-Schreiber* were used by the printer as a vehicle to give expression to the Separatist views, and at the present day give us an interesting insight into the religious condition of the Province from a non-orthodox standpoint, of which more will appear in the course of the narrative.

Alle Menschen sind Erde

Grobe Canon.

Unschuld wird die Frommen leiten.

Kleine Canon.

ehüte dein Hertz mit allem Fleiß.

Roman Fractur.

in Bogen von die-
r Schrft hält in sich
00 Buchstaben: Für
etzen, Corrigierë und
ie erste 500 Bogen zu
rucken 19 Schilling.

Text Fractur.

on dieser sind 6690 Buch-
aben im Bogen N.K. und
ägt das Setzen, Corrigierë
nd die erste 500 Stück zu
rucken 20 Schilling

Mittel Fractur.

Ein Bogen N.K. von dieser Schrift be-
ht aus 14650 Buchstaben; Und kost
r Bogen zu setzen, corrigieren und 500
tück zu drucken 25 Schilling·

Cicero Fractur

Von dieser Schrifft begreift ein Bogen N.
K. gemeiniglich 18944 Buchstabz; Und thut
das Setzen und Corrigieren nebst den ersten 500
Stück zu drucken, dreyßig Schilling.

Cicero Fractur.

Dieser so genanten Cicero Schwabacher
Schrift begreifft ein Bogen NK. ohnge-
or 18000; Fürs Setzen und Corrigieren
ebst der vor-gedachten Zahl zu drucken,
neun und zwantzig Schilling.

Garmont Fractur.

Von dieser Schrift verfaßt ein Bogen N.K. ohnge-
fehr sieben und zwantzig tausend und fünf hundert
Buchstaben; und beträgt das Setzen, Corrigieren und
die vor-gedachte fünf hundert Stück Judrucken. sieben
und dreyßig Schilling.

Garmont Schwabach

Diese Garmont Schwabacher ist in der zahl
von der Garmont Fractur nicht sehr unterschie-
den/ und also auch im Preyß nicht.

Petit Fractur.

Ein Bogen von dieser Petit Schrift, hält insich auf klein
Papier sechs und vierzig tausend, sieben Hundert und sechzig
acht Buchstaben; und beträgt das Setzen, Corigiren und die
erste 500 Bochen zu drucken drey Pund und was über die
erste 500 Bogen mehr gedruckt wird, da kostet sebs 100.
2 Schilling und 6 Pens, und das Papier apparte zu bezahlen.

Petit Schwabacher.

Die Schwabacher Petit ist nicht viel unterschieden
von der Fractur/ darum ist auch wenig unterschiedt
im Preyß.

· Jeses ist nun der Preiß von den obgemelten Schriften, neinlich, wie schon
zum öftern gemeldt: Für das Setzen. Corrigieren und jederzeit 500 Bogen
drucken.   Das Papier muß aparte bezahlt werden: Und trägt ein Rieß
der vorgedachten Sörte N.K. 10 Schilling; Ein Reß hat 20 Buch, darunter
2 Buch die gemeiniglich nicht wohl zu brauchen sind: und beträgt also das
pir zu 500 Stück 1 ſch. und 6 p.   Für jede 100 Bogen, so über die vurge-
hte 500 gedruckt werden sollen, werden 2 ſch. und 6 p. gerechnet, ohne das Papier.

CHAPTER XXIII.

THE ZIONITIC BROTHERHOOD.

 ET us now return once more to the peaceful vale on the Cocalico. The year 1738 opened sadly for the solitary orders, ushered in as it was with a sad bereavement for the Community.

It was during the night of Friday, March 3d, the midnight services being over and the Solitary having returned to their respective *kammers* to rest their weary heads again upon the hard blocks which served as pillows, that suddenly the stillness of the night was broken by the notes of the Kloster bell. Clear and loud the ringing sounded forth in the quite night. From Ephrata mountain to Zion hill the echoes reverberated the metallic sound. Awakened from their slumber, Solitary and settlers, irrespective of faith, rushed to door and window seeking for the cause of the unusual alarm. Suddenly the pealing ceased, to be followed by a solemn tolling of the bell until a certain number was recorded. It was the public announcement that the grim Reaper had invaded the Kloster confines and had claimed his first victim from among the Solitary. To Brother Martin (Bremmer) the lot had fallen. He had wrought as the Community tailor, and in that capacity had designed the habits for both the male and female organizations.

The ringing of the Kloster bell at the death of any member of the Community was practiced for many years, and as it took the popular fancy it was followed by both Lutheran and Reformed churches, while in the Moravian congregations public announcement of the death of members was made from the roof of the church by trombonists, special melodies being played according to the class and station of the deceased. Among the Seventh-day Baptists of the present day the custom has for many years fallen into disuse, yet in many of the other churches in the vicinity, and it may be said throughout Lancaster and the adjoining counties, this usage still obtains, particularly in the rural communities. It is customary when a death occurs among the members of the congregation for the pastor to notify the sexton, who immediately rings the church bell to attract the attention of the community, and then tolls a knell to indicate the age of the departed, giving one stroke for each year of age. It happened to the writer to be in the vicinity of the old *Bergstrass* Evangelical Lutheran church during such an announcement. No more solemn publication of a death could be made, if we except the trombonists of the Moravian church. Upon the occasion referred to the mournful strokes that wafted their notes over the still November air numbered forty-eight.

Martin Bremmer's death caused much sadness in the Community, as he was universally beloved, and his funeral was made the occasion for considerable ceremony. Among the strange customs observed in the case of Brother Martin, transplanted from the Fatherland, was the opening of the window as soon as the breath had left the body, so that the soul could take its flight heavenward unhindered and unobstructed. Upon the night of the funeral, as the body was carried out of the Berghouse, a bucket of water was poured upon the door-sill and swept outward, after which the door was immediately closed. This was done to prevent the spirit of the departed from returning to its old habitation. With the same purpose in view three crosses were marked upon the door-jamb with red earth or clay.

Brother Martin, who in the Ephrata register is called "a peculiar spiritual person," was buried in the meadow, between where the Saal and the Brotherhouse now stand. The interment took place by torchlight during the midnight hour, with the full mystic ritual of the order. Not a vestige of his tomb remains at the present day. An old manuscript before me records as follows:

"At the beginning of the year 1738, on the third or fourth day, did Brother Martin Bremmer gently and quietly pass from time into eternity. He left a goodly testimony, and remained true unto his profession and brotherhood even unto death. He was an earnest, zealous warrior who for almost nine years abided with the Community."

Among the important events of the year 1738 was the formation of the Zionitic Brotherhood and the erection of a large building for the uses of this mystic society, the organization of which was completed at this time, its origin and aims will now be explained. As before stated, members continued to flock to the settlement from all parts of this and other provinces; thus the secular congregation at Ephrata soon became the largest Sabbatarian settlement in the Province. Among the more notable accesions to the Community at this time were Brothers Sander,[109] Höcker and Rismann; they arrived a few days after the funeral of Brother Martin. Brother Jonathan Höcker was the first to be consecrated with a monastic ritual. Shortly afterward, another character of some importance, of whom unfortunately little or nothing is known, came to the settlement. This was Ludwig Blum, a musician, who virtually introduced the system of music peculiar to the Ephrata Kloster, specimens of which will be presented in a future chapter.

---

[109] Alexander Mack, Jr.

In April of this year Jacob Höhnly [Ephraim] arrived, followed in September by Christian Eckstein [Gideon]. On September 20th the number was increased by Valentine Mack, who was accompanied by his wife and his father-in-law, Johannes Hildebrand, whose acquaintance we have made in previous chapters. They were joined in November by the erratic Gottfried Haberecht, who for a time poses as Brother Gottlieb.

Apart from the arrivals mentioned, the brethren of the Berghouse found their habitat becoming the rallying-point for all the mystics in the Province; and as their number increased they clamored for better accommodations, similar to those of the sisters' house, Kedar. The matter, however, seems to have been held in abeyance on account of a lack of necessary funds. These were eventually supplied by one of their number, Brother Benedict (Benedict Jüchly), a young Swiss, from Kilchery-turnen, a scion of a rich family in the district of Berne, who had joined the Community some time previous to the adoption of the monastic feature. The *Chronicon* states that:

"Inflamed by the love of God he resolved to devote his fortune to the erection of a convent; which was accepted as coming by divine direction, and his proposition granted. There was in the settlement a pleasant elevation from which one had a beautiful view of the fertile valley and the mountains lying opposite; of this height the brethren in the hill-house at that time held possession. When now it came to the selection of a site, the most held that the valley along Cocalico creek was the most desirable on account of the water; the Superintendent, however, went up the hill until he came within the limits of the property of the hill-house, and there was the site chosen. By this the spirit of wonders indicated at the very beginning that the Brotherhood would at first build its structure on the heights of reason, and thus soar aloft until at length by a great storm they would be cast down into the valley; all of which was afterwards fulfilled in the minutest detail."

EFORE describing this building it will be well to state that these brethren in the Berghaus passed their time in speculations as foreign to the pure and simple Sabbatarian teachings as they were to the Rosicrucian tenets; the rites which they practised were similar to what are now known as the "strict observance," or the Egyptian cult of mystic Freemasonry. It is not known that Beissel or Wohlfarth or Miller, were either in sympathy with or took part in the movement; the leading spirits among these votaries were the brothers Eckerling, one of whom, Israel, held the patent for the 239 acres of land occupied by the *Lager.* The four brothers of this name—Israel, Samuel, Gabriel and Emanuel —of whom we shall have more to say later on—were all prominent among the members of mystic tendency of the community. In direct contrast to Beissel and Miller, who were both religious and retiring men. They were, to say the least, ambitious and overbearing, and this difference in character led, after the introduction of the monastic system, to more or less friction between the leaders, and eventually resulted in the expulsion of the Eckerlings from the community. The speculations and mystic teachings of Beissel and Miller were nothing else than the Rosicrucian doctrine pure and undefiled, while the *Zionitische Brüderschaft* or "Brotherhood of Zion," of whom Gabriel Eckerling was the first "Perfect Master" or prior, was an institution with an entirely different tendency and constitution, in fact, it was one of the numerous rites of mystic Freemasonry practiced during the last century. The professed object and aim of the members of the Zionitic Brotherhood was to obtain. physical and moral regeneration. To accomplish this object it was deemed essential that "Zion" be built in accordance with plans duly set forth in the teachings of the ancient rite.

There was always more or less distrust and suspicion felt by the adherents of Beissel toward the four brethren, the charge even being made that they were Roman Catholics and were in fact still in accord and secret communication with the authorities of that church, to which, however, they were wrongly accused of holding fealty. However, at this time, notwithstanding the opposition of Beissel, they had adherents enough, with the aid of Juchly's funds, to build the house and organize a chapter of the "Brotherhood of Zion."

That the love for mysticism in Lancaster county was not confined to the German religious enthusiasts in the Conestoga valley is made manifest by the fact that during the earliest days of Lancaster's history a Masonic lodge was organized among the wealthier English residents. This was undoubtedly the first Masonic lodge organized in the Province outside of Philadelphia, and was one of the lodges alluded to by Franklin in his note in the *Pennsylvania Gazette*, No. 108, Dec. 3 to Dec. 8, 1730, where he states:

"As there are *several* Lodges of Free-Masons erected in "this Province [Pennsylvania], and People have lately "been much amus'd with Conjectures concerning them; "we think the following Account of Free-Masonry from "London, will not be unacceptable to our readers," etc.

All regular records of this lodge appear to have been lost. Now, however, from the Journal and Ledger of Benjamin Franklin, lately discovered by the writer in the archives of the American Philosophical Society, confirmatory evidence is assured, as Franklin in his account with the parent or Grand Lodge of Philadelphia makes the following charges:

LODGE OF MASONS at B. HUBARDS.

1734 August 31, For three Constitutions by John Catherwood,
Lancaster County   o. 7. 6.
August 15, For 6 by Rennells to Lancaster   o. 14. o

It will be recollected that in this year, 1734, Franklin printed by special order of the Pennsylvania Grand Lodge;

The | Constitutions | of the | Free Masons, | Containing the | History, Charges, Regulations, &c. | of that most Ancient and Right | Worshipful Fraternity, | For the Use of the Lodges, London Printed; Anno 5723. | Re-printed in Philadelphia by special Order, for the Use | of the Brethren in North America. | In the year of Masonry 5734. Anno Domini 1734.

As these Constitutions were charged to the Grand Lodge of Philadelphia and were sent to Lancaster and elsewhere, the inference would certainly be that there was a lodge at Lancaster, as none of these books were furnished by the Philadelphia lodge to individual members. We have here another fact of which Franklin's Ledger offers ample proof. Again subsequent charges in the above account show that the lodge paid for seventy copies sent to Boston and twenty-five copies sent to the Carolinas (Charleston, S. C.), where Masonic lodges had been set up. In connection with this subject, it may be well to state that both John Catherwood and (John) Rennells were well-known Lancaster residents. Then again the above entries in Franklin's Ledger go far to substantiate the statement made in a letter written November 17, 1754, to Dr. Thomas Cadwalader, wherein it is stated "That the writer, Dr. Henry Bell, of Lancaster, was instrumental in organizing, in the fall of the year 1730, at the Tun Tavern in Water street, the first regular Masonic lodge in America.[110]

Nothing, however, appears to show any connection between the regular English Freemasons and the German mystics on the Cocalico.

To return to the affairs of the Zionitic Brotherhood:

---

[110] See Franklin's account with the "Lodge of Masons," 1731–1737. Proceedings of the Right Worshipful Grand Lodge F. and A. M. of Pennsylvania, December 27, 1898.

preparations were once begun to erect a building for the brotherhood, this work went on so rapidly that in May, 1738, the timbers were all framed, and the building was raised [111] with much ceremony of ritual and prayer; five months later it was ready for occupation, although it was not entirely finished until five years afterward. This unique structure was erected on an elevation or hill within the bounds of the Lager, which became known to the brethren as "Mount Sinai," while the Chapter-house itself was called "Zion." This curious house was three stories in height, the lower floor consisted of one large room, known as the refectory, connected with which were three small ante-chambers (*kabinettchen*), two of which served as pantries for storing the provisions and necessaries for use during the forty days' seclusion, and the remaining chamber constituted the receptacle for such paraphernalia as was used by the brethren in their ceremonial. The second floor was arranged so as to form a circular chamber, without any window or means of admitting external light. In the center of this chamber there was a small table or pedestal, on which was placed a lighted lamp, which, during the practice of the rite, was kept burning continually.

Around this pedestal were arranged thirteen cots or pallets, like the radiating spokes of a wheel. This chamber was used by the secluded votaries as their sleeping-room, and was known as "Ararat," typifying that heavenly rest which is vouchsafed by the Almighty exclusively to his chosen few, visibly instanced when the Ark of Noah settled down on the mount of that name, there to rest forever. The third or upper story was the mystical chamber where the arcana of the rite were unfolded to the secluded. It was a plain room measuring exactly eighteen feet square,

---

[111] The operation or work of setting up the frame of a building, a full account of a Pennsylvania "raising," will be found in a subsequent chapter, "Bethania."

with a small oval window in each side, opening to the four cardinal points of the compass ; access to the chamber was obtained through a trap-door in the floor.   It was in here that the ceremonies of the rite was performed by the thirteen brethren who were striving for their moral regeneration and seeking communication with the spirit world.

Thirteen adepts who had passed through the physical regeneration were necessary for this latter ceremony, which lasted forty days.

The structure was no sooner advanced far enough for occupation than the necessary provisions and paraphernalia were obtained, and preparations were made by the thirteen votaries to undergo the ordeal, viz. :

1. Gabriel Eckerling, Perfect Master or Prior, known as Bro. Jotham.[112]

2.	Jacob Thoma	Bro. ———.
3.	Benedict Juchly	Bro. Benedict.
4.	——— ———.	Bro. Jemini.
5.	David Lässle	Bro. Isai.
6.	——— ———.	Bro. Benno.
7.	Peter Bucher	Bro. Joel.
8.	Peter Gehr	Bro. ———.
9.	Jacob Hönhnly	Bro. Ephraim.
10.	Nathaniel Eicher	Bro. Nathaniel.
11.	Christian Eicher	Bro. Eleazer.
12.	——— ———.	Bro. Just.
13.	Emanuel Eckerling	Bro. Elimlech.

At the conclusion of certain religious services, among which was the saying of the 48th Psalm, a procession was formed, and the thirteen elect were escorted up the hill to the portals of the building, which, as soon as the adepts had entered, were securely locked to prevent any intrusion or interruption during the forty days of their retirement

---

[112] The elder brother, Onesimus, who was intended for this office at that time yet held back, *Chr. Eph.*, chapter xviii, also chapter xxvi.

from the outside world. These days were spent as follows:

six hours of each day in silent reflection; three hours in public or common prayer, in which each votary offered his body and soul as a living sacrifice, or offering to the glory and honor of God; nine hours were devoted to the study and practice of the esoteric problems of the ritual; lastly, six hours were spent in communion among themselves looking toward the regaining of the lost or ineffable word.[113]

The ritual further states that at the end of the thirty-third day of seclusion a visible intercourse commenced between the brethren and the seven archangels, viz.: Anaël, Michael, Raphael, Gabriel, Uriel, Zobiachiel and Anachiel; this visible communion lasted until the end of the fortieth day, when the labor was finished, and each of the adepts received from the senior archangel a parchment or scroll, on which was the seal, or the sacred pentagon, containing the ineffable name. The attainment of this great treasure completed the "moral regeneration," or, as it was known among the *Brüderschaft*, the "state of primitive innocence" (*unschuld*). The fortunate adept who had thus successfully completed the ordeal, with physical body as clean and pure as that of a new-born child, his spirit filled with divine light, with vision without limit, and with mental powers unbounded, would henceforth have no other ambition than to enjoy that complete rest while waiting for immortality, when he should finally be able to say to himself,—

I AM, THAT I AM.

The ordeal which the neophyte underwent for the physical regeneration, prior to the moral regeneration as above

---

[113] The name of God—as declared unto Moses from the burning bush on Mount Horeb, Exodus, iii, 14—according to the Rosicrucian theosophy "The power which eminated in the beginning from the eternal centre."

described, was as follows: the candidates for the state of perfection (*vervollkomung*), accompanied by a single attendant, is to retire to a hut or cave in the forest, on the night of the full moon in the month of May, and for the following forty days is to live secluded, according to the strictest and most austere rules of the order, mortifying the flesh and passing his time in fasting and prayer, his meals consisting merely of broths deprived of fatty substances, comprised mainly of laxative and sanative herbs, and no other drink being used than rain-water which had fallen during the month of May. A piece of hard ship-biscuit or dry bread-crust was allowed, but the repast invariably commenced with a liquid. On the seventeenth day of this abstemious life, the recluse, in order to further reduce to subjection the physical nature, had several ounces of blood taken from him, after which certain white drops were administered; six drops of this elixir were taken at night and six in the morning, increasing the dose by two drops a day until the thirty-second day. The composition and preparation of this elixir was a secret known only to such adepts as were admitted to the highest mysteries, and so securely was this secret guarded that the component parts were never even revealed to the votaries on the Cocalico. On the thirty-second day, as the first rays of the rising sun gilded the horizon, a further quantity of blood was drawn from the brother who was undergoing the ordeal, who was then to retire to his couch and there remain until the end of the quarantine. At sunrise on the thirty-third day the first grain of *materia prima* [114] was to be taken.

This *materia prima* is the same substance which God created to confer immortality upon man when he was first made in paradise, but which, by reason of man's wickedness, was lost to the race, and at the present time was only to be obtained through or by the favor of such adepts as

---

[114] *Materia prima* (primordial matter), A' Wâsa: A universal and invisible principle, the basic substance of which all things are formed.

were within the highest circle of the Rosicrucian Brotherhood.

The effect of this grain of elixir was that the moment it was taken the neophyte lost his speech and power of recolection ; three hours later convulsions and heavy transudation set in ; after these had subsided, his bed was changed by his attendant or serving brother, and a broth made from lean beef and sundry herbs was given. On the next day the second grain of the *materia prima* was taken in a cup of this broth ; the effect of this dose was that, in addition to the above-described symptons, a delirious fever set in which ended with a complete loss or shedding of the skin, hair and teeth of the subject. On the thirty-fifth day a bath of a certain described temperature was taken. The following day the third and last grain of the *materia prima* was taken in a goblet of precious wine, the effect of which was a gentle and undisturbed sleep, during which a new skin appeared, the hair and teeth, which had been shed two days before, were also miraculously renewed. On the awakening of the subject he was placed in an aromatic herb bath. On the thirty-eighth day of the ordeal an ordinary water bath in which saltpeter had been dissolved was taken, after which the votary resumed his habit and exercised his limbs. The next (thirty-ninth) day ten drops of the elixir of life, also known as the " grand-master's elixir " or balsam, were administered to him in two large spoonfulls of red wine.

With the end of the fortieth day, which ended the period of perfection, the votary completely rejuvernated and restored to the state of innocence of which mankind had been deprived by reason of original sin, now leaves his cell with the power to lengthen his earthly existence to the limit of 5557 years, and live in a state of health and contentment until it should please the almighty Ruler of the Universe to call the perfect adept to the grand chapter above the skies.

This process of physical regeneration had to be repeated

every forty years, as before stated, during the full moon of May.

Little authentic information has come down to us from the Zionitic Brotherhood itself, as for obvious reasons the chronicler as well as other writers are silent as to the ritual. A little insight, however, is gleaned from the MSS. of Johann Frantz Regnier, who was one of the first to attempt to gain physical and spiritual regeneration at Ephrata according to the mystic ritual of the *Zionitische Brüderschaft.* This was published by Fresenius, Frankfurt a. M., 1747. To other actions of this erratic, if not insane enthusiast, we have already referred in another place.[115] In his written account he states:

"In July, 1734, I came to the Beisselianer, on the Cocalico, and spoke to them [about the way to grace]. They answered that by a strict life and bodily denial one may grow and increase in sanctification, and the Eckerlings offered to practice therein with me, and described the rite and observance as we would have to pass through it, if I concluded to enter into the matter. They thought that I would not submit myself to the severe ceremonial. As for myself I had now found food for my taste and scattered senses, and answered 'Yes' to all their demands, and asked leave to commence that very day. They marveled at my willingness, but postponed the commencement from one day to another, in the hope that I should lose my desire.

"However, as I had the countersign that belongs to the brotherhood, I was at last acknowledged by all as a true brother, without anyone even asking me if I considered myself converted, nor did they ever examine me to see if I was in fact or not. It was not long ere I was counted among the most important brethren, and they were willing that I should keep the Sacrament with them, Conrad Beissel and the Eckerlings even extended the offer to me several times before they had an opportunity to baptize me,

---

[115] Pp. 192–5, *supra.*

But all this could not satisfy me; I asked daily, 'When shall we commence to live as you have taught me?' At last I found that they were not in earnest to undertake the ritual, and that they only sought to throw dust in my eyes. ! I said to them, I will now commence the observance of the ritual even if I have to carry it through alone. I, however, depended upon their promise to help me to erect a cabin or hut wherein to obtain physical regeneration; all that I asked was for them to keep this part of their promises.

" When they saw that I intended to undertake the matter in earnest, they were very unwilling [for me to do so], and attempted to dissuade me. I asked if they would acknowledge that it was not right [*i. e.*, the ritual or process as communicated by him]. The reply was that it was correct, and one should live a just life if they wish to be sanctified, but that no one could endure the trial [*i. e.*, the rigorous requirements of the ritual]. They themselves had tried it. I answered that they had been unfaithful, because, as they acknowledged the correctness of the ritual, they should have endured it even at the expense of their body and life. I told them I shall endure it if I can thereby gain sanctification.' I then commenced to build myself a hermit hut or cabin, in which several aided me, to redeem their promise, only unwillingly, however, and with displeasure. We then broke off all intercourse. I subjected myself in my cabin to all the rules and requirements of the ritual, even more strictly than they had been communicated to me. This went on without my attaining anything of that which I sought; until I at last lost my reason and became delirious. When I was completely mad, and without reason, they took me from the hut, demolished it, and confined me in a cell (*kammer*) guarding me day and night,[116] but as they could not accomplish anything they removed me to a dark cell, and beat and lashed me so that

[116] This must have been in the Berghaus.

I might recover my reason. As all proved for naught and I only became worse, they removed me to another place;[117] then again to another where I had more liberty, after which I again became sane—however, not without many relapses. Although my reason had been entirely gone, everything remained in my memory, and I can readily recall all, so long as nothing else crosses my mind. Thus I recovered and came gradually to my sound senses, but whenever my will was opposed, the *turba* [frenzy] and confusion again appeared. After I eventually recovered my intellect I endeavored on three or four occasions to return to my brethren; but I was not received, because I would not acknowledge that I had done wrong, in so far that I did not permit them to lead me step by step. When they rejected me the third time, I left them, and on July 15, 1735, started for Georgia in the hope of meeting Count Zinzendorf and through him learning the way to perfection and sanctification."

Thus the Brotherhood of Zion, with its peculiar teachings and ceremonies, had become an established fact on the hill-side overlooking the settlement on the Cocalico. The austere religious ascetics were looked upon with awe and veneration by the secular members, and it was not long before the ambitious prior attempted to use his position to undermine the power and usurp the authority of the *Vorsteher*.

Beissel and Wohlfarth from the beginning were not in accord with the Eckerlings and their followers in establishing this peculiar feature within the settlement; but as a matter of fact neither the *Vorsteher* nor the foremost men of the secular membership offered any serious objection to the undertaking, and during the building of Zion, when all indications pointed to success, Beissel brought out an enlarged hymn-book known as the *Weyrauchs Hügel* for the use of the Brotherhood as well as for general circulation among the Germans in the Province.

---

[117] Probably to one of the individual cabins.

CHAPTER XXIV.

THE AMWELL DUNKERS.

UDGING from the records, the year 1738 was a most eventful one in the life of the Mystics of Ephrata. The organization of the Brotherhood of Zion and the influence of the Eckerling brothers built up in the infant community a force which for a time threatened to overturn the whole policy of the settlement, and to successfully oppose which took all the power of Beissel, Wohlfarth, Miller and such others as represented the conservative element.

That Beissel was not always far-sighted enough for his shrewd rivals will appear from various incidents occurring during the next five years, the end of which period marked the time of their final overthrow.

The first radical innovation was a proposition to have one's self baptized for the dead. This scheme originated in the fertile brain of Emanuel Eckerling, who managed to convince Alexander Mack that his father, the patriarch, had never been properly baptized. This effected, the two men went to Beissel and requested him to baptize them for their deceased relatives.

Beissel, after some hesitation, acquiesced, having been won over by Elimelech's subtle arguments. This decision of the superintendent quickly spread throughout the settlement.

No efforts were spared by the Zionitic Brotherhood to make the ceremony an impressive one. Upon the day set a procession was formed of the Zionitic Brotherhood, the Spiritual Virgins and the secular congregation. They wended their way down the hill past the various buildings, across the meadow, to a pool in the Cocalico, about opposite to where the Brother House now stands. Special hymns were sung and fervent invocations ascended when the banks of the stream were reached.

Beissel was the administrator, and the first subject, Emanuel Eckerling, who presented himself to be immersed for his deceased mother. He was followed by Alexander Mack, the younger, who was baptized for his deceased father, the sainted patriarch of the Dunker Church. Both of these parents had been baptized in Germany. An attempt was made to justify this questionable proceeding by the supposition, deduced from the words of Paul, that the first Christians did the same.

The idea of thus securing immunity for deceased or absent kinsfolk and friends struck the popular fancy, and notwithstanding the contention of so clear headed a theologian as Peter Miller, the custom obtained a firm foothold and was practiced for many years. This movement was not confined to the Ephrata Community, as there were many cases where even members of other faiths had themselves baptised by proxy for relatives and friends. Indeed, this peculiar custom actually outlived the Community, and there are traditions of children having become substitutes in baptism for parents, or *vice versa*, as late as the fourth decade of the present century.

Another interesting incident of the year was the conferring of the title of *Vater* (Father) upon Beissel ; heretofore he had been plain Brother Conrad. This change of title was an innovation which only became an accomplished fact after much controversy and rancor among the members, the subject not being finally settled until three years later. This matter came about as follows: with the increase of the congregation and the establishment of the two celibate orders, the name Brother Conrad appeared too commonplace for the position of the *Vorsteher*. So he expressed his wish to several house-fathers who went to great trouble to find a name for him that would harmonize with his present surroundings; but none of all the titles suggested seemed fitly to express the actual relationship. He therefore suggested "Brother *Friedsam*" (peaceful), this met with their approval, and it was at once adopted by the congregation.

A few days after this approval, Brother Onesimus (Israel Eckerling) felt concern that it was not meet and right for the solitary brethren to call the *Vorsteher* simply "brother," "since to many of them he had been, next to God, the cause of their salvation. Therefore they concluded to call him "Father." A council of the Zionitic Brotherhood was called to deliberate upon the question, at which it was resolved to call him *Vater;* of this action they notified him through two deputies. According to the *Chronicon*, "He accepted without contradiction; for he was so instructed from above that he would not readily have refused the good intentions of anyone, even though he might therefor reap the greatest reproach."

When this new departure became known among the congregation it caused much unfavorable comment. It was not, however, until the next regular love-feast that official notice of the change was given. To make this announcement fell to Brother Agonius (Michael Wohlfarth), who stated to the worshipers that "It would be too commonplace to designate Brother Friedsam merely as 'Brother.' Methinks it were well to resolve upon how we should address him, namely, 'Fater Friedsam.'" This proposition occasioned various conferences, resulting in the decision that the Solitary should call him "Father," while those of the secular congregation should call him "Brother." Thus the matter rested until the year 1741.

N December of the year under consideration (1738) a second pilgrimage was organized, having as its objective point the Dunker set‌tlement at Amwell in New Jersey. This community centered around a " cross roads " now known as Baptisttown or, in older records, as Dunkertown. It is in Delaware township, Hunterdon county, about a mile northeast of the Washington Headquarters.[118]   The congregation in Amwell was then under the leadership of Jeremiah Naas, and was supposed to be in full accord with the Becker party in Germantown, the elder was seconded by Johann Naas, Anthony Deerdorf, Jacob Mohr, Rudolph Harley and Johann Peter Laushe, all resident settlers of Amwell. This was not the first attempt made to introduce mystical theology and Sabbath-keeping in the Baptist community ,beyond the Delaware. It will be recalled that two years previously a similar effort was made, in which Conrad Weiser was a prominent actor. The visit in 1736 had opened up more or less intercourse, both social and commercial, between the Germans in Lancaster county and New Jersey, and had resulted in several members moving from Ephrata to Amwell, among whom was Heinrich Landis, who in 1737 married Elizabeth, daughter of Elder Jeremiah Naas.

With this intermingling of the Sabbatarians and regular Dunkers the same partisan feeling arose in Amwell as in Germantown, and resulted in frequent visits to Ephrata by such of the Jersey brethren as adhered to the teachings of Beissel. These visits, seconded by reports from the resi-

---

[118] At first the meetings were held in the different houses. It was not until about 1750 that a church, a plain frame structure, was erected, which served its purpose for more than a century ; it was replaced in 1856 by the present house of worship, which is known as the German Baptist church.

dent Sabbatarians, had induced Beissel to organize the present movement, his companions for the visitation were chosen from among the most austere of the Zionitic Brotherhood.

Upon its arrival in New Jersey, the second pilgrimage at once gave evidences of material results. Revival meetings were held, and an outpouring of the Spirit took place at which even one of their local preachers, Bechtelsheimer, felt constrained to approve Beissel's course. So favorable an impression was made by the Solitary, that resolutions were passed by the German Baptists of Amwell looking more distinctly than before toward the establishment of similar orders and discipline to those flourishing at Ephrata.

This induced Beissel upon his return home to convene a church council, at which Brother Elimelech (Emanuel Eckerling), who already held the degree of Melchisedek in the Zionitic Brotherhood, was selected as the teacher at Amwell, and ordered to be publicly consecrated to the secular priesthood. This took place upon the appointed day, in the large Saal, both orders of Solitary and the congregation at large being present. The event excited much attention among the people, and the ceremonial was administered under the personal direction of Beissel, who, after repeating several solemn charges and admonitions, consecrated Emanuel Eckerling to his office by the laying on of hands, after which a Bible and a large key were handed to the new incumbent, and he was publicly proclaimed Elder of the Amwell congregation.

At the close of this ceremony a large blank book was produced, and all present—celibates, householders and visitors—were asked to pledge themselves by signing their names, thus recognizing Elimelech as head of the Amwell church. This many refused to do, and to others the proposition gave so much offence that they left the congregation for a time.

Beissel now handed a missive to Elimelech. This, as

the records state, was full of priestly unction, cautioning him to " Continue steadfast in prayer and with watchfulness of spirit for the flock of Christ, that thou mayest rightly divide the Word of Truth which hath been sown in you." A cotemporary copy of this curious missive has fortunately come into the possession of the writer, and as it offers us an insight into the spirit which animated Beissel and his followers in their efforts at evangelization among the early Germans, as well as having an interest from the fact of its being the rule for guidance given to the elder upon his departure for his new field of labor, a translation is here given :

" BELOVED BROTHER IN THE LORD.

" The dew of God, begotten out of the Celestial and divine Sun, spread itself out over you, and the fire of the most refined Love of God excite a holy desire within you, that your whole house be filled therewith, and the flames bursting out into a blaze, may ascend before God in a holy flame of Love, such as neither water can quench nor streams extinguish.

" Let the true sanctifying and saving grace be your guide in all matters, and that wisdom, which is the master of all things, enlighten you, and be your light upon your course ; and may the word of Life spread itself within you to divine fructuosity.

" Let nothing separate you from God and his love, so that you may become qualified as a holy example and guide for the believers, over whom you are placed as an eye, by which the whole body is ruled and kept in order, so as accurately to go in its way.

" Preserve carefully what is intrusted to you, in sacred and divine supervision, and in all matters have a penetrating love toward the chief Overseer of all things, whose fulness will be proffered unto you, sufficient to a devout leadership and course of life.

" Keep on in prayer and in watchfulness in spirit for the flock of Christ, which is intrusted to you by loyal hands, so that you may justly impart the word of Truth which is sown in you.

" Have constantly before your eyes the great redemption work and Mediator's office of Jesus Christ ; thereby gauge all your work, that in the end and departure the same may be obtained. Accept nothing that befalls you and others, if you cannot reconcile it at the end and departure with the spirit of the New Covenant and the grace which is in the sacrifice of atonement. For the eye of our Chief Overseer hath no other design upon death and hell than that eventually they may be dissolved, appeased, assuaged and subjugated.

" In this spirit you will at all times find divine instruction, and know how to approach every one for his own betterment, and you will to many prove an incentive to their own Salvation. To some be a closed garden ; but unto others an open fountain, by grace and love, for the Salvation of their souls.—Be sober and lowly, and keep watch over yourself. Beware of the in and out goings of your heart, not only toward those who esteem you in an inordinate manner, but to such as wrongfully hate you as well ; thus you will secure God's favor and the esteem of man.

" Love, suffer, endure, hope, in equal paces, for where there is much love, there is suffering, and where there is much patience, there hope establishes itself. Patience and hope must endure until the end.

" Lead a life without fear, and you will have a clean heart and conscience. Lead a life undaunted before God, and he will make a holy abiding-place within you, for such a life weakens sin and causes it to flee, seeing that fear, anguish, and pain come out of darkness, and consequently are a sustenance of sin. Therefore be bold and fearless in all your actions, and you will not do wrong, but always that which is right, and you will have joy upon the day of judgment, when He will come.

" Lastly, in all things let the hope of an everlasting life be your only purpose, object, and anchor. You will then have much peace, and your hope of future felicity will make you an heir in the new world, and you will receive the life without end.

" The Lord continue to bless you and your walk, and make you acceptable to Him in everything that you purpose or execute. May nothing separated you from God and his love; thus you will be blessed in time and eternity."

This epistle was handed to the new elder as his rule and guide. He took it with him to Amwell and there presented it to the congregation as his credentials.

Elimelech was well received by the Amwell brethren. A log cabin was built for him on the grounds of John Peter Laushe, and he at once assumed charge of the evangelistic services. So successful was he at the outset that seven candidates, male and female, were baptized shortly after his arrival. His popularity, however, was of short duration. Whenever he began to preach, he kept on and never knew when to stop. This habit he carried to such an extreme that his hearers were eventually tired out by the length of his discourses. The present writer has seen the manuscript of one sermon preached by Elder Elimelech which took no less than five hours to deliver.

The climax was reached when the elder proposed holding midnight watches, such as had been introduced on the Cocalico. Here he met with much opposition, and when finally he ordered all members, male and female, to appear at these midnight services, the matter culminated in the austere elder receiving his passport to return whence he came. The old record states that the Amwell brethren feared that offences might arise from these midnight meetings, and therefore dismissed him ; whereupon he returned to the settlement on the Cocalico in disgrace.

The dismissal of the elder, however, failed to allay the strained feeling among the congregation, which only ended when a number of the influential members of the Amwell church, who were deeply convinced of the truth of the Sabbatarian doctrine, shortly afterward determined to follow the discarded teacher to the Cocalico. Prominent among these settlers who migrated from Amwell to Lancaster county were Dietrich Fahnestock, Conrad Boldhausen, Johannes Mohr, Bernhard Gitter and several others, all being married men accompanied by their households. The first-named upon his arrival in Lancaster county lived with his family for some time in or near the Kloster confines. But shortly afterward he obtained 329 acres of land by patent from the proprietors, at a cost of one hundred and forty dollars. The land was located on a branch of the Cocalico, about two miles distant from the Community grounds, and one mile south of what is now known as Lincoln. Here he lived a consistent Sabbath-keeper until 1775; his death occurring October 10 of that year. In his family were two sisters, who accompanied him from Germany and thence to Lancaster county, where they both joined the sisterhood at Ephrata. One, however, relented and married into the Laushe family;[119] the other remained steadfast, and lived and died in the Kloster as Sister Armella.

Among the Solitary who accompanied Beissel on the Am-

well pilgrimage were Prior Onesimus and Brother Timotheus. These two men, who appeared to be drawn so closely together, notwithstanding that they were so different in disposition, had frequent conversations with the Vorsteher as to their spiritual course, and bewailed the fact that there was still something wanting to complete their consecration. They were satisfied that they were properly baptized, also that they had taken the vow of celibacy, yet there was nothing to prevent them from re-entering the world and marrying, so they concluded upon a new covenant, with the Virgin Mary as the patroness of their order.

This was at first kept very quiet, but as it became noised abroad it raised such a storm of indignation that a

---

[119] They settled in what is now Annville, Lebanon county.

three-hour reproof was administered to the offending prior and brother in public meeting. This admonition, however, failed to have any effect upon the two enthusiasts. So shortly after the return from New Jersey, Onesimus and Timotheus (according to another account it was Eleazer and Timotheus), went to the Vorsteher and asked him to renew their vow of perpetual chastity, and in token thereof to cut the tonsure, as a visible sign of their betrothal to the Virgin ; so that "the world might know that they had devoted themselves to God in the priestly office." The Vorsteher, who always counseled chasity and celibacy, entered into the spirit of the movement and complied with their demand. This was no sooner done than the prior convened the Brotherhood in the Chapter, and after the meeting was opened he ordered every brother in turn to kneel down, repeat his pledge, and, after renewing his vows, have his hair cut and his crown shorn.

After this ceremony in the Chapel on Mt. Zion, the Vorsteher, not to be outdone by the prior, convened the Spiritual Virgins in their Saal. When they had assembled Beissel entered, presumably with the brother shearer, and after re-consecrating the assembled sisters he proceeded to have their hair cut "after the manner of the primitive Christian Church ; " after which he ordered their crowns likewise shorn. When this piece of idiotic vandalism was completed the Vorsteher gathered up the shorn tresses and carried them to the Chapter of Zion, where he laid them upon the Altar, with the wish that he might live until their (the sisters') heads were gray. It was further resolved and ordered that the tonsure should be renewed every three months, and in the meantime no one was to put shears to their heads.

The prior from this time forth continued to exalt himself in his priesthood. He caused the sisters to make for him a robe or costume, such as is described in the Bible as having been worn by the high-priest in the Temple. This regalia, of which more hereafter, he was wont to assume when he presided at the agapes and baptisms.

Night watches or vigils, and processions were also introduced by Onesimus; and it was not long before the Vorsteher, Conrad Beissel, was virtually superseded by the cunning prior. However, when these actions, so foreign to the simple Sabbatarian precepts originally promulgated by Beissel and Wohlfarth, became known to the Community at large, they brought additional ridicule upon the religious enthusiasts. Among their German neighbors of other denominations they thenceforward became known by such opprobrious appelations as *Glatzköpfe*, *Vollmonde*, *Bettel-Mönche*, *Pfaffenmucker*, etc.[120]

Another effect of this aping of the monastic customs of the Roman Church during the Middle Ages was to arouse the ire and increase the antogonism of the Scotch-Irish, a sturdy race of unyielding Presbyterians who had settled in Chester and Lancaster counties between the Octoraro and the Susquehanna. These settlers from the start looked upon the Mystic Community and its peculiar practices with suspicion; and when finally the tonsure was adopted and the Solitary appeared in public with the shaven crowns, the worst fears of the Scotch-Irish seemed to be realized, and the charges that the settlement on the Cocalico was merely a nest of Jesuit emissaries appeared to be substantiated beyond any doubt.

Nothing that could be said or written to the contrary could change these sturdy Covenanters in their opinion;

---

[120] These opprobrious epithets were common *Schimpfworte*, used in Germany in derision more against the friars than the regular clergy. Rendered into English, the two first would be bald pates, shaven crowns, full moons, these have reference to the tonsure—a round bare spot on the crown. The two latter terms, "medicant friars," "Popish double-dealers," were applied to all such members of monastic institutions as mingled with the Community.

consequently, the "croppies," as they called them, were decried from the pulpit, as well as held up to scorn by the individual members wherever the opportunity offered. The result of the sectional agitation thus engendered was widespread and far-reaching, and in course of time, on account of the fancied similarity of their institutions, the opposition extended to the Moravians, who were then making a successful effort to Christianize the Indians within the Province. This feeling eventually was responsible for the massacre of the Christian Indians at Conestoga and in the jail at Lancaster, whither they had fled for refuge.

The belief that at least the Eckerlings and their followers were Popish emissaries was not confined to the Scotch-Irish, but was shared by many of the Germans in Philadelphia and the surrounding counties, who declared that the prior and his brothers had originally been brought up in the Romish faith in their native city of Strassburg.[121] Even in official circles it became the accepted belief that the Community was governed by Popish laws and principles, if not directly subject to the dictation of the Church authorities of France or Rome. When the situation of the Province became serious during the French and Indian troubles, these insinuations and suspicions against the Community, together with the refusal of the whole congregation of Sabbatarians to bear arms against the common foe, induced the Government to appoint a special commission to visit the settlement and investigate the common charges. Beissel and Peter Miller, who were then the leaders of the Community, easily convinced the committee that they were a Christian institution, founded upon the Word of Life and the Gospel in its truth and simplicity, although maintaining a monastic order.

---

[121] The Eckerlings were of Reformed parentage, as will be shown in the course of this narrative.

CHAPTER XXV.

THE HOUSE OF PRAYER.

QUITE a number of important accessions marked the advent of the year 1739. Early in March, Brother Simeon Jacobs came to the settlement with his wife. They immediately separated; he joined the Zionitic Brotherhood and the wife entered Kedar as a spiritual sister. Toward the end of the month Stephen Koch arrived from the Wissahickon and entered Zion as Brother Agabus. On the 6th of April the Community ejected from his cabin one Ludwig Benter, who, to the great mortification of the Brotherhood, had renounced his vow of celibacy and taken a wife unto himself. Upon the following day this cabin was turned over to Ludwig Höcker with his family, of whom, as Brother Obed, we shall have more to say in the course of this narrative. About this time Brother Johannes Höffly and his family also came from Coventry on the Schuylkill and settled at Ephrata; other prominent accessions during the spring and summer months were the Kalcklöser (Kalckgläser) family from Germantown, and the return, after an estrangement of ten years, of Johannes Hildebrand with his wife, daughter and son-in-law, Valentine Mack, a son of the patriarch.

As was stated in a previous chapter there was no provision or room for congregational gatherings in the house built for the Zionitic Brotherhood. Consequently the assemblages and love-feasts were all held in the " House of Prayer" adjoining the Sister House, "Kedar." This not only caused more or less inconvenience to the Zionitic Brotherhood, who had to traverse the intervening distance in all kinds of inclement weather ; but the nocturnal processions wending their way toward the habitation of the Spiritual Virgins called forth all sorts of unfavorable comment from outsiders, who did not hesitate even to question the integrity of the brethren or their adherence to their vows.

AMONG the neophytes at this time were two young men, Rudolph Nägle and Samuel Funk. They were the sons of two of the house-fathers, as the heads of the secular congregation were called. These two men were received into the Brotherhood of Zion in October, 1739, and after their period of probation was over they were invested with the dress of the Order, the first one receiving the name of Zephaniah, the other that of Obadiah. Upon the investiture of these two brethren, their fathers, to put an end to the rumors of scandal caused by the nocturnal processions to the prayer-house, offered, in the name of their two sons, to build a prayer- and school-house. This chapel was to adjoin Zion and be large enough to accommodate the secular congregation of the Sabbatarians, as well as all of the recluse and enthusiasts within the bounds of Ephrata. This proposition of the two house-fathers was received with great favor, and permission for the work was given without objection. Active preparations were commenced without delay ; trees were felled, timber was squared, stone was quarried, sand was hauled, and lime was burned. In the midst of this activity, a new tower clock and bell arrived from Europe, a present from the father of Brother Jaebez (Peter Miller).

This it appears was the second clock and bell acquired by the Community. The first one was made for them by no less a person than Dr. Christopher Witt, of Germantown, as early as 1735. It was rather a small and crude affair as compared with some of a later date. It showed two dials upon opposite sides, with an hour hand only; there was no minute hand. The hour was struck upon a bell in the cupola above the clock.

[This curious clock, bearing the legend "C. W., 1735," may still be seen in the cupola surmounting the old academy facing the turnpike. It is said that when in running order the clock keeps excellent time. This is, without any doubt, the first tower clock made in America of which we have any knowledge. The works now, after the lapse of over a century and a half, are still in fair condition, and if they were put in order and received proper attention there is no reason why they should not mark the passing hours for many years yet to come. The original bell has latterly been replaced by a large modern one. After the demolition of the houses upon Zion hill subsequent to the Revolution, this clock and bell were removed to one of the smaller houses or cabins in the meadow near the Saal, where it remained in use until the school-house or Seventh-day Baptist Academy was built in 1837, when it was placed in its present position, since which time it has done duty for both the academy and township school. At the present writing the clock movement is sadly out of repair; an effort, however, is now on foot looking to its repair and preservation.]

So rapidly did matters progress in the gathering and preparation of building material, that by October, 1739,

KLOSTER BUILDINGS ON ZION HILL ABOUT 1750.

BERGHOUSE
PRAYER-SAAL.

CONVENT, ZION AND SAAL.
KEDAR.

FROM AN OLD SKETCH FOUND AFTER CHAPTER XVI WAS PRINTED, VIDE PP. 256-57.   THE FIGURE IS SUPPOSED TO BE PRIOR ONESIMUS.

the ground was broken for the new Saal of Zion. The two brethren who are named as the originators of the project were both men of family ; they furnished all of the building materials, while the Brotherhood performed the manual labor. It is said that the mason work was done in six weeks, during which time not a drop of rain nor flake of snow fell to retard the brethren.

The work was no sooner well under way than an order was issued by the Vorsteher (Beissel) to demolish the " House of Prayer" adjoining the Sister House, Kedar, which had been erected but a little over three years before and the completion of which had been effected only after much toil and privation upon the part of the Community. After the first surprise, evoked by this unaccountable order had passed, the brethren in blind obedience to their Superior set to work, and in a short time the beautiful and ornate building, with its double galleries, was razed to the ground. The *Chronicon*, commenting on this episode, states :

" The cause for which [the destruction of the building] " can scarcely be comprehended by human reason ; the " standard is too limited. . . . It is probable that a hidden " Hand made use of him, in this wise symbolically to rep- " resent the wonders of Eternity, after which the veil was " again drawn over the affair ; for there is a likeness in its " history to that of the Temple at Jerusalem, which after " it was scarcely finished was plundered by the King of " Egypt."

Most of the traditions which have come down to us in relation to this curious episode place the blame for this piece of vandalism, which caused so much dissatisfaction among all of the members, wholly on Beissel, but probably the parties who were really the instigators of the scheme were none other than the Eckerling brothers, who for some sinister purposes of their own influenced the Vorsteher to issue the edict which caused so much comment. This explanation is further strengthened when the fact is taken into consideration that but a few months prior to this, on August 13, 1739, they had caused a deed or conveyance to be made by Jan Meÿle and Barbara his wife to them for 180 acres of land, which covered the whole settlement of Ephrata, with all of the buildings, improvements, water rights, etc., the consideration being £27. 18*s.* [about $75], this purchase was made without the knowledge or consent of either Beissel or the Community.   The deed was in fee-simple to Samuel Eckerling, Israel Eckerling, Emanuel Eckerling and Jacob Gasz; the subscribing witnesses were Gabriel Eckerling, Johann Grippel and Conrad Weiser. The acknowledgment was taken before Zacheus Davis, Esq., justice of the peace.   Not a single word or sentence appears in the document to indicate any trust or trusteeship for the Community.

It may be further noticed that all parties to the conveyance, either as principals or witnesses, were antagonistic to the Vorsteher.   This transaction was carefully guarded from the knowledge of Beissel; even the very existence of the deed did not become known until many years afterward, nor was it placed upon record until June 16, 1764.

HE strangest part of this transaction was that Meÿle and his wife did not own the ground. One hundred and twenty-five acres of the land on which the settlement of Ephrata stands was originally warranted to one Ulrich Carpenter, January 10, 1733, while the adjoining tract of one hundred and fourteen and three-quarter acres was surveyed to George Masters, November 10, 1737.   After the surveys were completed, Carpenter and Masters both declined to comply with the conditions and pay for the land, for the reason that it was already settled upon and they did not wish to dispossess or distress the Community.

This fact by some means came to the knowledge of Israel

Eckerling, when he at once petitioned Governor John Penn individually,—it will be noticed that this was two years after the date of the Meÿle deed,—to grant him the said lands, under the same metes and bounds, for the same consideration money. This petition is still on file in the Land Office of the Commonwealth.

In response to this petition Governor Penn issued a warrant under the lesser seal of the Province to Israel Eckerling for the said 239¾ acres of land, which also grants the property to Eckerling in fee-simple, viz. :

BY THE PROPRIETARIES.

PENNSYLVANIA. *ss* :

Whereas by virtue of a Warrant under our lesser seal bearing date the tenth Day of January, Anno Domini 1733, a Survey of one hundred and twenty-five acres of land situate on a branch of Cocalico Creek in the Co. of Lancaster was made unto Ulrich Carpenter of the same County. And whereas by virtue of one other Warrant under our lesser seal bearing date the tenth day of November Anno Dom : 1737 one other survey of One hundred and fourteen acres and three quarters of an acre of Land Adjoining the tract aforesaid was made unto George Masters, of the said County, which said warrants being granted under certain Conditions, that have not been complied with by the said Ulrich Carpenter and George Masters, nor either of them, the same together with the Surveys made in persuance thereof, are become utterly void. AND Israel Eckerley having requested that WE would be pleased to grant him the said Land. Under the same Metes and Bounds and agreed to pay to our use the Consideration Money, which ought to have been paid by the said Ulrich Carpenter and George Masters for the same,

THESE are therefore to authorize and require Thee to accept and receive the said Surveys. And make return thereof for the Use and Behoof of the said Israel Eckerly into our Secretary's office in order for further Confirmation and in so doing this shall be thy Sufficient Warrant. Given under my Hand

and the Seal of our Land office at PHILADELPHIA. This sixteenth Day of May in the Year of our Lord 1741.

JOHN PENN.

To BENJ. EASTBURN, SURV'R GEN'L.
    ENDORSED
        Lancaster
  1741
May 16 ISRAEL ECKERLY 239¾a.

Ret. 16 May 1741.
WM. BRIGDALE.

The Vorsteher, being in total ignorance of the secret actions of the scheming Eckerlings, did not swerve from his course, but kept on in the even tenor of his way, notwithstanding the fact that many of the secular members of the congregation openly charged Beissel with making fools of his people.

There was at this time, without doubt, much local jealousy between the Zionitic Brotherhood and the Order of Spiritual Virgins, which worked to the detriment of the Sabbatarian congregation at large. The brotherhood, to further injure the sisterhood and undermine Beissel, as soon as the chapel, or House of Prayer, adjoining Kedar had been demolished, erected in its place a small house or cabin for the use of the Vorsteher, in which they caused him to take up his abode, after which for a time he devoted himself wholly to the sisterhood.

All of the buildings erected up to this time had been built without any definite plans for the future, but were merely designed and erected under the spur of whatever motive influenced the projectors at the time being, without concern as to what might be the eventual relation of one building to the others.

Fortunately for the brotherhood the winter of 1739–40 proved to be an exceedingly mild one, no severe storms or frosts appearing until the 10th of January; consequently the work upon the new chapel went on without intermission or hindrance. Everything, even the elements, seemed

GOVERNOR JOHN PENN,
(THE AMERICAN)

WHO GRANTED THE PATENT TO THE ECKERLINGS.

PHOTO. BY J. F. SACHSE FROM ORIGINAL CANVAS AT HIST. SOC. OF PA.

to favor the brotherhood in their undertaking, and by Christmas-day, 1739, the mason work was completed, and the frame of the great structure was raised and pinned in place. The brotherhood naturally felt themselves specially favored by Providence, and likened their undertaking to the restoration of the Temple at Jerusalem in the days of old.

This building, "Zion's Saal," was projected upon an extensive scale; it was three stories in height, and when finished was a large and sightly structure. The lower story was a large hall, designed to accommodate the whole congregation, secular as well as mystic or recluse, when assembled for public worship. The walls were adorned with texts in ornamental script, such as are still to be seen in the Saal, and with which this book is illustrated. At one end of the hall [most likely in the east] a platform and choir with a gallery were built, the lower part for the Zionitic Brotherhood and the gallery for the sisterhood. In front of this choir or chancel the Vorsteher had his seat and desk or table, while the entire body of the hall was furnished with chairs and benches for the secular congregation. In the second story was a large hall, or Saal, arranged and furnished with all conveniences and appliances for holding the agapes, or love-feasts, as well as performing the service of the "pedelavium" or washing of feet. The third story was divided into a number of cells or *klausen* for the Solitary brethren of the Zionitic rite.

On the Sabbath, July 5, 1740, the last joint divine services were held in Kedar, after which the building for the time being fell to the uses exclusively of the sisterhood or Order of Spiritual Virgins. On Wednesday, July 16, 1740, the new Prayer-house of Zion was dedicated to its pious uses with great religious and mystic ceremonies. To the former all Sabbatarians from far and near were invited, not excepting the Welsh and English brethren of the faith in Nantmill and Newtown, in Chester county; invitations were also scattered broadcast among the Germans beyond the Schuylkill. The hospitalities of the Community were extended to all who came ; love-feasts were held and pledges of faith renewed. The expenses attendant on this dedication were borne by one Henry Miller, a wealthy secular member of the Lancaster congregation.

Of the mystic rites and occult ritual with which the Zionitic Brotherhood dedicated their Temple, in the ghostly hour after midnight, we have nothing but faint traditions which tell of processions, incantations, prayers, and mystic ceremonies, said to date back to the ages of the Pharaohs.

From this time forward the congregation as well as the orders held their devotions in the new building. The *Chronicon*, commenting on the house, states that " In this house many wonders of God were manifested forth, so that its future fate was much lamented." [It was this building that was converted into a military hospital for the sick and wounded during the Revolutionary war shortly after the battle of Brandywine.]

After the dedication, the next noteworthy ceremony of which we have any record that took place within the new chapel was during the following August, when Beissel, by virtue of his office, as Vorsteher of the whole settlement, in the presence of the whole congregation solemnly consecrated Brothers Onesimus (Israel Eckerling), Jaebez (Peter Miller) and Enoch (Conrad Weiser) to the priesthood, by the laying on of hands ; after which they were admitted to the ancient Order of Melchizedek by having the degree conferred on them in ancient form.

After the ceremony the Vorsteher, assuming the rôle of Grand Master of the Zionitic Brotherhood, deposed Prior Jotham and appointed in his place the newly-ordained Brother Onesimus as prior or perfect master of the Zionitic Brotherhood. This act called forth an energetic protest from the deposed prior, seconded as he was by a number of the brethren present. The *émeute* was, however, of but short duration, and ere the Chapter closed Beissel's author- ity was acknowledged by all present. This action of the Vorsteher was the result of differences which had arisen in the congregation incident to the controversy with Chris- topher Sauer over the hymns in the *Weyrauchs Hügel*.

In these internal troubles Beissel and the other heads of the congregation did not interfere, as Peter Miller states, "as long as the Prior stood to him (Beissel) in subordina- tion." The new prior, however, was even more ambitious than his predecessor, and further he applied the discipline so severely as to be almost unbearable ; Peter Miller writes that "Now was between the poor devotees of Ephrata and "the wool-headed African Sclaves (*sic*) no other difference "than that they were white and free Sclaves."

Unfortunately for the Sabbatarians throughout Lancas- ter county, the completion of this large and elaborate house of worship did not stop the bickerings between the two orders of the Solitary, or equalize the interests of the secular members with the peculiar ideas and actions of the mystics. Two months had hardly passed since the solemn dedication and love-feasts, when the differences between the two mystic orders became so great that a separation took place, and each held their religious services independently of the other. It was on the 21st of September, 1740, that the Brotherhood held their first midnight prayer-meeting in the new chapel. The secular congregation now regu- lated their services independently of the others, and at such times as suited themselves without any reference to either of the recluse orders.

Just prior to this division (seventh month, 1739), the Zionitic Brotherhood obtained permission to place in a steeple over the roof of the Saal the new clock and bells which were donated to the Community by the father of

Peter Miller. This clock contained an attachment for chiming the bells and rung them at different times during the day and night, calling the devotees to their religious exercises. This was an innovation which was not received with much favor by the settlers at large outside of the Sabbatarian congregation. In regard to the latter the *Chronicon* states :

"When this was rung at midnight, not only did all the "settlement arise, but as one could hear it for four English "miles around the settlement, all the families also arose and "held their home worship at the same time ; for in those "days the fires of the first love still burned everywhere. The "brethren attended their services clothed in the garb of "the Order, wearing in addition also a mantle with a hood "like that of the Capuchins."

That these innovations, together with the rites and ceremonies of the two orders, interfered still more with the worship of the secular congregation was not to be wondered at, and before another month had passed several prominent members commenced a vigorous protest against their exclusion, or the curtailment of their rights and privileges. This matter culminated at a general meeting, when the Vorsteher declared—

"That it was not yet a settled thing for the congregation "to hold its meetings in this house, and it would be to its "disadvantage if this should continue for any length of "time. The congregation must build itself an own house "of prayer ; thus is it ordained in the divine order of the "work, and I will render aid thereto in the spirit."

A heated discussion now followed, and ended by a number of prominent members of the congregation withdrawing from the Community, among whom were Johannes Mergel, Heinrich Gut and Abraham Paul. The Vorsteher, however, equal to the emergency, consoled the congregation regarding this loss with the statement that "Thus God

"ever purged the fold of such persons as loved their own
"life better than the leading of God."

The Zionitic Brotherhood, now seeing that their scheme
for obtaining the new chapel for their own uses showed
promise of success, at once set to work to prepare the frame
and timbers for another prayer-house, this time nominally
for the exclusive uses of the secular congregation.

It is stated that the timber for the proposed structure
was donated by Benedict Juchly, who had bought a tract
of land in the "swamp" between seven and eight miles
north by east of Ephrata.[122] All of the timbers used in
this new meeting-house were cut and squared on the ground,
and after the winter had set in were sledded to the settlement, a labor in which the brethren were assisted by such
of the secular congregation as were not disaffected. The
site for the new building was staked out within the graveyard in the meadow, some distance from the other structures, which were all upon the higher ground on the hillside. In size the new prayer-house was to be forty feet
square and forty feet high, thus symbolizing the number
of perfection.[123] As a matter of fact, however, whilst
actual measurement proves the length to be correct, the
width is two feet narrower than the perfect number calls
for, and in height to the top of the extreme gable it measures some feet in excess of that number. The good fortune
attending the Brotherhood during the building of the Saal
upon Zion hill failed them in the present instance, as they

---

[122] It was a few rods west of Reinhold station on the R. & C. railroad.
During the XVIII century and this there were two principal roads lead-
ing to Reading : commencing at the Kimmel House south of Ephrata—
one leads by *Erbs* (*Old Miller Hotel*), *Black Horse*, *Vera Cruz* (*Schmolz
Gasse*). The other by *Ephrata* (*Gross' Corner*), *Reamstown* (*Zoar*),
Muddy Creek, *Adamstown.*

Black Horse is ¼ mile from Reinhold's Station and is the old landmark.

[123] *Vide, German Pietists*, pp. 39, *et seq.*

were doomed to experience much disappointment and many delays during the performance of the task.

It appeared as if all the elements were against the completion of the work. The weather during the fall season of 1740–41 was of exceptional severity, and the winter proved phenomenal for its severe storms and extreme cold. During the first week in January, the thermometer fell lower in Lancaster county than was thus far recorded in the Province. In the Conestoga valley the snow was over three feet deep on the level. To this difficulty must be added that of the extreme cold and biting winds. The severity of this winter was so great that many cattle died from want of fodder; even deer were found dead in the woods, and frequently they came to the runs about the settlers' houses, and in some cases came tamely to the plantations and fed on hay with the domestic cattle. The inhabitants in remoter districts suffered much from want of bread, and many families of new settlers had little else to subsist upon but carcasses of deer they found dead or dying in the swamps about their cabins. Even the Indians suffered on account of the lack of the game upon which they were wont to subsist. Notwithstanding these drawbacks our religious enthusiasts were not to be deterred from their undertaking; neither the severity of the season nor the sufferings incident to the extreme cold hindered them in completing the preparations for a "raising" as soon as the weather permitted a resumption of outside labor. When the spring once more opened, the Brotherhood, being now joined in their undertaking by the congregation at large, preparations went on rapidly.

Before a month had elapsed, however, they received another severe check. This was the death of Michael Wohlfarth, the faithful assistant and unyielding supporter of Conrad Beissel.

BROTHER AGONIUS.

Brother Agrippa, in editing the diary of the Community, adds a special foot-note in reference to this bold evangelist, wherein he says:

"This remarkable man, otherwise called Michael Wohl-farth, was born at the fortress of Memel, on the Baltic sea. How he first became acquainted with the Superintendent, when the latter yet lived in solitude, has already been recounted. All his life he was a faithful assistant of the Superintendent; and not only was he his companion on all his travels when he declared to the people in Pennsylvania the counsels of God concerning their salvation, but he also sat by his side at all meetings and followed him in speaking. Otherwise, according to the manner of the time, he was in pretty close agreement with the Inspirationists, and at Philadelphia spoke prophetically both in the market-place and at the Quaker meetings, so also at other places, though he never received therefor more than a prophet's reward. In the difficulty between the Superintendent and the Baptists he incautiously proceeded too far in judgment with those people, which rose up against him on his death-bed. This was expressed by the Superintendent as follows in the last verse of his funeral hymn:

> "This in time my error was,
> Wherefore it must be the cause
> Why so sore my strife must be,
> Ere by death I was set free.

"His great merit," continues Agrippa, "which stood by him in every temptation, was this, that he was a man after God's own heart, like David, who knew how to humble himself when brought into judgment. For, especially in the beginning, he often stood in the way of the Superintendent's spiritual work, and because a hidden hand always protected the Superintendent the good brother was often thereby brought into severe condemnation, when he might,

THE LONDON COFFEE-HOUSE.

NORTHWEST CORNER FRONT AND MARKET STREETS, SHOWING SLAVE SALE IN PROGRESS. UPON SUCH OCCASIONS MICHAEL WOHLFARTH WOULD ADMONISH THE POPULACE.

like others did, have parted from him in anger; but as he walked in David's footsteps he humbled himself, and accepted the judgment, even as his hymns bear witness. When, contrary to his and others' supposition, the large houses were built in the settlement, he was sore confounded, especially when he saw that great churches with bells were being procured, abuses against which he and others had so earnestly striven. This tempted him not a little to mistrust whether the Superintendent had not perhaps forsaken his post. And although he never broke the bond of brotherly love between them, these temptations yet brought him so far that he again became a hermit, though without withdrawing from fellowship. To this end the brethren built a solitary dwelling in the mountains of Zoar, some five miles from the settlement. Finally, however, he was especially strengthened in the faith that God's hand was in the work, by considering that there were already seventy persons, of both sexes, and mostly young people, dwelling together in the settlement, who had renounced all their earthly happiness for the sake of the kingdom of God. Wherefore he again renounced his seclusion and removed to the convent of Zion, where he led a very edifying life until its close, being subject to all the rules of the Order. His decease was greatly deplored, because, as has already been mentioned, he brought about great changes."

The death of Brother Agonius at this time proved a serious loss not only to the recluse on the Cocalico, but to the Sabbath-keepers, German and English, throughout the Province. Bold and aggressive, fearless and sincere, as he was, Michael Wohlfarth may well be called an apostle of Sabbatarianism. Believing it to be his duty to preach the keeping of the seventh day, he, as has been shown in the course of this narrative, was wont to travel on foot from place to place, staff in hand, dressed in pilgrim's garb; and no matter where he was, on the roadside or in the market-place, in meeting-house or church, in town or country, he boldly and fearlessly proclaimed his doctrine and admonished his hearers ; being oblivious to taunts or persecution, wherever he could find an audience there was his voice heard admonishing to penance and obedience to God's command as to the Sabbath-day.

OHLFARTH, or Welfare as he was known among the English, was one of the earliest religious leaders among the Germans in Pennsylvania to employ the printing-press to reach the populace both of German and English nationality, versions of his works being published in both languages. One of his earliest pamphlets, printed by Bradford, referred to in a previous chapter, is being now first brought to the notice of bibliographers and students through the efforts of the present writer.

His dealings with Benjamin Franklin have already been noted upon these pages in the course of our story. Franklin in his autobiography, pp. 272–273, makes following mention of the Ephrata pilgrim, after eulogizing the Sabbatarian Dunkers, he goes on to mention :

" I was acquainted with one of its founders, Michael Welfare soon after it appeared. He complain'd to me that they were grievously caluminated by the Zealots of other persuasions, and charg'd with abominable principles and practices, to which they were utter strangers. I told him this had always been the case with new sects, and that, to put a stop to such abuse, I imagin'd it might be well to publish the articles of their belief, and the rules of their discipline. He said it had been propos'd among them, but not agreed to, for this reason : ' When we were first drawn together as a society,' said he, ' it had pleased God to enlighten our minds so far as to see that some doctrines, which we once esteemed truths, were errors; and that others, which we had esteemed errors, were real truths. From time to time He has been pleased to afford us further light, and our principles have been improving, and our errors diminishing. Now we are not sure that we are arrived at the end of this progression, and at the perfection of spiritual or theological knowledge ; and we fear that, if we should once print our confession of faith, we should feel ourselves, as if bound and confin'd by it, and perhaps be unwilling to receive farther improvement, and our successors still more so, as conceiving what we, their elders and founders, had done to be something sacred,—never to be departed from.' ''

So much for Brother Agonius' explanation why no confession of faith was ever promulgated or published by the Ephrata Sabbatarians.

Franklin, in his comments upon Wohlfarth's statement, says :

'' This modesty in a sect [the Sabbatarian Dunkers of Ephrata][124] is perhaps a singular instance in the history of mankind, every other sect, supposing itself in possession of all truth, and that those who differ are so far in the wrong ; like a man travelling in foggy weather, those at some distance before him on the road he sees wrapped up in a fog, as well as those behind him, and also the people in the fields on each side, but near him all appears clear, tho' in truth he is as much in the fog as any of them.''

According to the *Chronicon*, Brother Agonius' departure into eternity was as follows :

'' This important change was made known to him some time before, though he did not think it was so near. Though a weakness overcame him a short time before, he yet recovered so far that on the Sabbath before his death (May 16, 1741) he was at meeting, and the following evening at the brethren's table, so that there were good hopes of his entire recovery. But his malady returned with such violence that when the brethren came from their midnight devotions they

---

[124] The creed or confession of faith of the regular (first-day) Dunkers or Baptists was published by Hochman as early as 1702. It was reprinted in America by Christopher Sauer in 1743.

found him in such a condition that they saw that now his eager desire to depart would soon be fulfilled."

His illness was brief and very severe, lasting only four days, in which "God's hand lay heavily upon him, and fulfilled the remainder of his sufferings until his sacrifice on the cross was complete, wherefore also he said that he did not know whether any saint had ever endured such martyrdom." On the following second day (Monday) at night, just as the brethren were at their service and about singing the hymn, "The time is not yet come," etc.,[125] their intercessions were asked for that God might open to him his prison door.

As Agonius' sufferings increased and his condition became critical, he asked that certain psalms and parts of Tauler's *Last Hours* be repeatedly read to him, and when he felt his end approaching he asked to be anointed according to the usage of the first Christians. This request was complied with, Beissel personally applying the chrism. Thus he lingered in great pain until the close of the ninth hour of the fourth day of his illness (Wednesday, May 20), when his soul took its flight to the realms beyond to reap, let us trust, the full reward due to the faithful pilgrim.

The circumstances surrounding his final departure are as follows:

"It appears as if it had been revealed to him that his end would come at the ninth hour of the day; therefore he looked keenly toward the hour-glass, whether the eighth hour was not soon to pass. As soon as it struck nine he had himself set upright and thus he expired, but when again let down, he once more revived and asked whether he had not yet died. After that he expired at the end of the ninth hour."

On the following day, Thursday, May 21st, his mortal

---

[125] *Zionititcher Weyrauchs Hügel*, hymn No. 322.

remains were interred in the "God's acre" adjoining the settlement,[126] as the *Chronicon* states, "in a coffin neatly prepared for the occasion." The last rites were not alone attended by the Sabbath-keepers but by settlers of all denominations for miles around, who came out of respect for the deceased exhorter. The services were performed with much ceremony. As his body was lowered into its last resting-place the Sabbatarians sung a special funeral hymn, composed for the occasion by his friend the Vorsteher, of which the following is a stanza :

> See all the anguish, trouble and pain
> I suffered before death in vain,
> Until the oil of grace so mild,
> Refreshing my soul,
> Was poured upon my head.
> Oh, comfort rich which I enjoyed !
> The brother-balm, it entered me
> And caused my heart at rest to be.

The funeral was closed with the mystic rites of the Zionitic Brotherhood.

---

[126] The old graveyard of the Community, dating from about 1737, was situated in this meadow, and the intention, no doubt, was that the prayer-house or church of the congregation should be in the centre of the grave-yard as was the custom both in Europe and America. This, however, was not the first place of burial of the Community. When Sigmund Landert's wife died in 1728 she was interred in the corner of a field on her husband's plantation. In the following year the old widow Eckerling, the mother of the four brothers who played so important a part in the early days of the settlement, also found her resting-place there, together with her daughter-in-law, Catherine, the wife of Samuel (Brother Jephune). This place was used as the regular burial-place by the Conestoga congregation until about 1737, when a part of the meadow was selected for the purpose ; this in turn was used until about 1750, or perhaps a few years later when the present graveyard on the turnpike was laid out. So far as the writer has been able to discover no mark or vestige of either of the two former places of sepulchre remains at the present day. This is the more strange when we consider the number of interments there must have been in the meadow around Peniel prior to its abandonment.

By the direction of Beissel a tombstone[127] was placed over the grave. It is said to have been in the meadow a little to the eastward of where Beissel's cabin still is. It bore the following inscription written by Conrad Beissel:

" Hier ruhet der gottselige Kämpfer

AGONIUS

starb Anno 1741.

Seines Alters 54 Jahr, 4 Monat, 28 Tage.

Der Sieg bringt die Kron,
U. der Glaubens -Kampf den Gnaden- lohn
So Krönet der segen den seligen kämpfer,
Der allhier ein Sünden- und Belials-
        Dämpfer
Im Frieden gefahren zu seiner Ruh-kammer,
Allwo er befreyet von Schmertzen und
        Jammer."   (Chron. Eph. pp. 121.)

Translation :

Here Reposes the Godly Warrior

AGONIUS.

Died Anno 1741.

Aged 54 years, 4 months, 28 days.

Victory brings the Crown
In the fight for faith, grace and renown.
Thus blessings crown the warrior true
Who bravely Sin and Belial slew.
Peaceful he passed to his chamber of rest,
Where now he is free of all pain and distress.

---

[127] A careful search as late as the fall of 1898 failed to reveal any trace of this tomb.

THE SAAL AND SISTER HOUSE AT EPHRATA.

SOUTH FRONT OF SISTER HOUSE.
ANGLE OF SAAL AND SISTER HOUSE FROM N. E.
THE SAAL (PENIEL).

N. W. PROSPECT OF THE SISTER HOUSE (SARON).
SOUTH GABLE OF THE SAAL.
ANGLE OF SAAL AND SISTER HOUSE FROM S. W.

PHOTOGRAPHED BY J. F. SACHSE, 1886.

CHAPTER XXVI.

PENIEL.

WING to the many draw-
backs which the Commu-
nity experienced during
this building operation, it
was not until September
that the new structure was
enclosed. A curious fea-
ture of the building is the
extreme pitch of the roof.
This was occasioned by
the fact that the winter
of 1740–41, as has already
been stated, was a pheno-
menal one, with an extraordinary snowfall. This induced
the brethren to raise the angle of the frame so as to shed
the snow the more readily in case the succeeding winters
should prove as severe.

It was only by hard work and persistent effort that the
new structure was made tenantable for the congregation by
the following December (1741), when it was consecrated to
its pious uses with a general meeting and love-feast, upon
which occasion the Vorsteher named the new building
" Peniel," for, according to the *Chronicon*, " upon this spot
had he wrestled in the spirit and prayed, and had a vision."

As a matter of fact, it was the name which Jacob gave
to the place in which he had wrestled with God (Gen.,
xxxii, 30).

After the dedication, Brother Elimelech (Emanuel Eckerling) was inducted as Intendant or Vorsteher of the new

house of prayer, after which divine services were held under his direction at stated intervals for the congregation at large.

The arrangement of the Saal at first was entirely different from what it is at the present time. As originally designed and built, it was double the height of the present room; it was light and airy, with two broad galleries running north and south, supported by a single post in the centre. The high ceiling was supported by two heavy beams set at right angles, thus forming four panels. They in turn were supported by a massive chamfered pillar; this is still in place. The general entrance for the Brotherhood and congregation at large was by the door in the west. This has the same peculiarity as have all the doors leading into the prayer-halls of the Community, in being very narrow, so as to carry out the scriptural injunction, that "narrow is the road that leads to God." [128] In the east, directly opposite the door and upon a slightly raised platform, stood the preacher's bench and table.

The two galleries, or *por-kirche* as they were called, were screened with lattice work, and were for the use of the women of the settlement, the north gallery being reserved for the sisterhood of Spiritual Virgins. In this arrangement they also followed the custom observed in the Holland and German synagogues, wherein the women were relegated to the screened galleries. The entrance to these galleries or *por-kirche* was by a door which opened upon a narrow staircase in the northeast corner of the building, which in turn led to a corridor running the length of the building at the eastern end. A narrow door, twenty by sixty inches, gave access to the north and south galleries. By this arrangement the sisters and the women of the congregation could enter and depart from the services without coming into contact with the male worshipers. Each of these galleries

---

[128] Straight is the gate and narrow is the way that leadeth unto life, Matt., vii, 14. See also Luke, xiii, 24.

was lit by three windows, while the west wall was pierced for four windows. The plan of the Saal as here described was continued until after the adjoining convent became the home of the sisterhood.

PECULIARITY about these unique Ephrata buildings is the almost total absence of iron in their construction. Wooden pins were used in place of spikes or nails wherever it was possible to do so. Even the split oak laths which hold the plaster in place are fastened without the use of nails. A channel or groove was plowed in the upright timbers, and the laths were cut to proper length, the ends pointed, and then slid down in grooves in the posts, after which the grout or plaster was filled in on both sides of the laths ; thus a solid wall was built up impervious to either vermin or weather, and to the present day these houses are cool in summer and warm in winter.[129] Even the chimney flues were built of plank lined inside with a thick coating of a mixture of clay and fine chopped grass or straw (*hecksel, häckerling*). The absence of iron is explained by the fact that in the Cabalistic as well as in Rosicrucian theosophy and Biblical teachings, iron was the metal which represents and was symbolical of night or darkness.[130] It was the antithesis of gold, the symbol of purity and light. Iron was held to be the product of the powers of darkness, and to be the medium by which all physical and moral evil was brought into the world. That this belief existed far back in the dim ages of the past may be seen by reference to Exodus, xx, 25, where the Lord says to Moses, "If thou wilt make me an altar of stone, thou shalt not build it of hewn stone, for if thou lift up

---

[129] The same construction was applied to the floor of the Dunker church in Germantown in 1770, the split oak lath and mortar are still visible from the basement under the floor of the church.

[130] Zoar, ii, 24, a and b.

thy tool upon it thou hast polluted it.   An altar of whole
stones, over which no man hath lifted up any iron." [131]

Another prototype of the Ephrata theosophists was the
Temple of Solomon, into the construction of which great
edifice no iron whatever entered,[132] the scriptural injunction
given by Moses[133] being literally obeyed, "Thou shalt not
lift up any iron tool upon them."

By reference to the interpretation of Nebuchadnezzar's
dream[134] it will be seen that even in Babylon iron was
known as the symbol of destruction.   Coming down to
later years, it was taught by the Rosicrucians that the so-
called Iron Age or the dark Medieval period was the epoch
during which the destroyer reached his greatest power,
when vice, ignorance, superstition and priestcraft had full
sway and reigned supreme.[135]   It was in obedience to these
Biblical commands, reinforced by the teachings and traditions of the Order, that little or none of the proscribed metal
was used in the construction of the buildings intended for
sacred purposes; the furniture of the Saal was put together
entirely with wooden pins, while the boards which formed
the altar were carefully scoured with fine sand to eradicate
every sign of a tool mark before they were put together for
the pious uses in the east.

They even went farther and eschewed the metal utensils
at their love-feasts; their plates or platters were made of
poplar wood, as were the candlesticks used in the religious
meetings; their knives and forks were made of the harder
hickory.   The sacred vessels, the paten and chalice used in
the administration of the holy communion were also of
wood, made by the brethren, it is said, without the use of

---

[131] Joshua viii, 31.

[132] Kings, vi, 7.

[133] Deutronomy, xxvii, 5.

[134] Daniel, ii, 40.

[135] *Molitor Philo. d. Hist.*, IIIn 389.

iron tools; [136] and, strange as it may seem, the snow white altar-cloth, or linen cloth used to cover the table, even to the present day, after being washed is smoothed or ironed with square wooden blocks which are used in place of the ordinary flat or sad irons, so that none of the proscribed or unholy metal may touch the altar or its belongings. [137]

In the interior arrangements, however, there have been some radical changes. The most important one was made some years after the adjoining convent was handed over to the sisterhood, and the large Saal adjoining the Brother House (Bethania) was built. It was the division of the large Saal into two separate rooms. For this purpose the centre pillar was morticed and two beams were introduced to carry joists between the two galleries, these were then floored over, thus closing the open space. The effect of this change was to make the Saal the low dingy room that we now see it.

In the upper part the lattice work was removed from the former galleries, and these, with the intervening space now floored over, formed a large light room of corresponding size to the one below (about thirty-six by twenty-seven feet). This room was broken by a single obstruction only, viz., the large central pillar. Entrance was gained to the halls upon both floors from the adjoining Sister House by narrow doorways (twenty by sixty inches) in the extreme north-west angle of the room.

After this radical change was consummated, the lower room was continued in its original uses for public worship and occasional love-feasts. The upper room, however, became the private chapel (if the term be permissible) or prayer-room (*bet-saal*) of the Sisterhood of Saron.

---

[136] A local tradition states that the goblets were turned with a hardened bronze chisel or tool.

[137] Two of these wooden sad irons, if the term is permissible, are still in use at Ephrata at the present time, where they were shown to and examined by the writer.

The public entrance to the lower Saal is by a hooded door in the west front; this door is flanked by a small window upon either side with nine panes of glass. The private entrance from the adjoining convent or Sister House, Saron, is, as above stated, by way of a narrow door at the northwest corner of the room. This door with its wooden latch and hinges is low and narrow, a peculiarity which is further accounted for, beside the scriptural injunction already mentioned, by the fact that all of the celibates were supposed to be thin and spare, a physcial condition brought about by the mode of living and the mortification of the flesh as practiced within the Kloster. Any one who preferred feasting to fasting, or physical comforts to a life of absolute self-denial had no place within the Community. Then, again, the entrance was made low, so that the worshipers were forced to bow the head or bend the knee as they entered the house of prayer.

As we step into this venerable sanctuary the visitor is at once struck with the extreme plainness of the room and its furnishings. The walls are wainscoted about half way up the sides with unpainted boards, above which they are as white as lime can make them, and for purity in color vie with the linen cloth spread upon the communion table. No decorations or ornaments greet the eye, except the old scriptural texts and allegorical compositions in ornamental penmanship (*fractur-schrifft*) hanging against the walls, and which were placed there over a century and a half ago. There are still to be seen within the Saal twelve of these large illustrations of ornamental Kloster penmanship. Once upon a time they were choice specimens of the sister's writing-room, examples of patient toil and artistic handiwork, unsurpassed in the delicate tracery of flourish and detail, but now yellow and discolored,—the paper disintegrating and crumbling, with ink brown and faded, while some of the wording is hardly decipherable. Yet they are

priceless mementoes of the past, showing the present generations to how great an extent education and culture flourished among the early German settlers in this valley.

Light is admitted to the Saal by six windows in addition
to the two in the west wall; three of these are in the north
and south walls respectively. To keep out the sun these
are shaded with a piece of plain white linen, having a hem
at the top, through which a cord is drawn and fastened at
either side of the casement. The furniture of the Saal
consists of four long tables in the body of the hall, flanked
by wooden benches devoid of backs upon either side of the
table. Along the sides of the room are ranged regular
benches with backs, while against the south and west walls
a shelf is fastened, high up near the ceiling, for the hats
and wraps of the worshipers.

In the east end, upon a small raised platform, is the
preacher's bench and the communion table; this is a plain
unpainted wooden affair covered with a fair linen cloth,
upon which usually is placed the Bible, hymn-book and
an old hour-glass, whereby in olden times the length of the
preacher's sermon was regulated. This was a common
custom with some of the German congregations in Lancaster county, and was one that acted in the interest of
both the clergyman and his hearers. In the former case
the minister knew that he was not unduly lengthening his
discourse with his "thirdly's" and "lastly's." Upon the
other hand, as the hour-glass (*sanduhr*) was always turned
at the beginning of the sermon, the worshipers were assured
that they were receiving the full quantity of religious discourse to which they were entitled.

There is still in existence a petition from a congregation
in Lancaster county to Synod, wherein complaint is made
to that body that the minister's discourse was not long
enough, and did not last until all of the sand had run
down. The result of this action was that another "quarter

hour of sand" was put into the *kanzel uhr*, and pastoral relations were not severed.

A door to the left of the preacher's platform leads into the kitchen offices, this department consisting of a long narrow room extending the whole length of the house. In this room are still to be seen the appliances for preparing the viands and baking the unleavened bread used in the love-feasts. Here is still the old dough-trough in which the flour was mixed, and the plain oaken table upon which the dough was worked until it was ready to shove into the large brick oven, the door of which opened directly into the room. Here is still to be seen the *reiser*, an ingenious tool with which the loaves were scored before baking so that the bread would break evenly. Access to this department was also gained by the door, which opened to the private staircase already described, whereby the sisters in charge of the kitchen could enter and depart without being seen by the other worshipers.

Returning to the Saal of to-day, we find the girders or beams of the ceiling supported by two heavy posts in addition to the morticed pillar; these posts are directly below the beams which formerly supported the galleries. The ceiling between the heavy timbers is made of yellow poplar boards, with narrow laths covering the joints, and, similarly to all other woodwork in the Saal, is unpainted and kept as scrupulously clean as when the Sisters of Saron here reigned supreme.

The portion of this ceiling beneath the old gallery is said to be in its original condition. If the visitor to the old sanctuary will cast his eyes aloft toward the northwest corner of the room, directly under the old north gallery, and look carefully at the boards forming the ceiling, he will plainly see at regular intervals the impression of the naked human foot upon the boards, marks that have remained here during all these lapse of years, notwithstanding repeated attempts to eradicate them with soap and sand and an application of muscle such as only a Pennsyl-vania-German matron is capable of.

Several explanations of these mysterious footprints have been given to me in the course of the years covering my investigations of these people. The first story, by an old inmate of the Kloster, was as follows: Far back in the days when yet the Eckerlings were the ruling spirits, and the Brotherhood of Zion practiced their mystic teachings and occult rites, some question was raised at one of the mid-night meetings as to the truth of the claims made for the esoteric and mystical rites and practices of the Zionitic Brotherhood. There was a great outpouring of the spirit upon that occasion, and the discussion finally grew into a challenge to the mystic brotherhood to produce some proof of their supernatural or occult power. With that the seventh hour pealed forth from the tower of Zion hill; this hour corresponds with our midnight. Hardly had the sound died away when two of the Zionitic brethren accepted the challenge. Throwing off their long robes and taking the sandals from off their feet, they mounted one of the long tables, and supporting themselves for a few seconds by their hands, raised their feet to the ceiling, and thus walked in this reverse order among the brethren. One of these men was the prior, and wherever his feet touched the ceiling they left their impression upon the unpainted wood. Thus was manifested a double miracle. Such is the legend as told to me many years ago. In later years, the venerable Sara Bauman told me a similar tale, and further said that she had repeatedly tried to scrub the marks off the ceiling. These traditions appear to be further strengthened by re-ferences to be found in both *Chronicon* and contemporary manuscripts, wherein it states that in the prayer-houses of the celibates "were manifested forth many wonders of God."

Another explanation of the mystery, as given by persons who deny any mystical origin of the footprints, declares that while the boards were being sawed down at the Kloster *säg-mühle*, and it being customary to work barefooted in summer one of the brothers became sore in his feet, greased the soles during the day and in the course of his duties walked over the freshly sawed yellow poplar boards, thus leaving the imprint of his naked feet upon the fresh lumber. The advocates of this theory, however, fail to state how it was that the subsequent planing failed to remove the marks. However, be this as it may, the footprints upon the ceiling of the Ephrata Saal will always remain an interesting mystery.

In the centre of the room stands a relic in the shape of an old cannon stove, such as were made early in the century and intended to consume anthracite coal; specimens of this kind are now seldom met with.

Thus we find the old Saal of Ephrata upon the verge of the twentieth century. It forms a span or link with the past, when yet the red man roamed over our fair domain and we owed allegiance to the Hanoverian Georges, who were then upon the throne of England. The great march of improvement, modern methods and the longing for ease and luxury during the hours of worship and for ornate services have found no foothold within this venerable sanctuary. The room, as well as the services held therein, is still as in the days of yore,—in appearance as plain and unadorned as were the first Quaker meeting-houses,—with services as fervent as when led by the austere Prior Jaebez. Long may the old Saal be preserved and remain in its primitive simplicity as a reminder of the religious pioneers who settled here and kept alive the fires of mystic theosophy in these western wilds!

Mention was made of the large specimens of Kloster

WITHIN THE SAAL.

ENTRANCE FROM SISTER HOUSE.   FACING TOWARD NORTHWEST.
GENERAL VIEW.   THE PREACHER'S TABLE.
SOUTHWEST CORNER.   NORTHWEST CORNER.

penmanship hanging against the walls of the Saal. These examples of early caligraphic art are worthy of an extended description. Our wonder and admiration for them increases when we consider that the same hands that executed such exquisite penmanship wrought the finest kind of embroidery and needlework and even wove fine laces, at the same time during a part of the day performed laborious farm work in both field and stable, besides attending to the menial duties of house and kitchen.

AVING to greatly reduce our chapter initials they give but a faint idea of the beauty of the original drawings, which fortunately still exist. The specimens upon the walls of the Saal are now fast going to decay; the paper is discolored and stained by age, and where covered with ink is disintegrating and crumbling into dust. This is the case with all of the Ephrata manuscripts. The explanation given is that the ink was a decoction of gall-apples and copperas and that the irretrievable damage which they have sustained is due to the latter ingredient. Photographs and faithful copies of these placards have been made by the writer and are reproduced in this history.

We will now walk around the Saal and examine these curious tablets with their strange inscriptions. Commencing with the one over the door leading into the Sister House. This consists of six lines:

Die Tür zum eingang zu das Haus
Wo die vereinte seelen wohnen
Last keines mehr von da hinaus
Weil Gott tut selber unter ihnen frohnen
Ihr Glück blüth in Vereinten Libes-Flammen
Weil sie aus Gott und seiner Lib herstammen.

Which I translate:

> The door for entering into this house
> Where the united souls reside
> Lets none from hence depart,
> As God himself among them doth abide
> Their fortune blooms in united flames of love
> As they from God and his love descend.

Upon the west wall, almost joining the narrow door, is a tablet of five lines, two of which are in large capitals, while the three lower lines are in lower case and capitals:

> CHRISTUS
> DER HIRTE
> dieser Schaar tuth sie als Schäfflein
> weiden, drum gehen sie bey Paar u Paar
> Und rühmen Gott mit Freuden

Translated:

> CHRIST
> THE SHEPHERD
> Of this flock doth them as Lambs
> Attend, thus they go pair by pair
> and glorify God with joy.

The tablet on the north wall, to the right of the narrow entrance, consists of eight lines:

> So lebt denn die reine Schaar
> Im inneren Tempel hier beysammen,
> Entrissen aller Weltgefahr
> In heiss verlibten Libesflammen
> Und lebet dann in Hoffnung hin
> Nach der beglückten Freiheit die dort oben
> Da sie nach dem verlibten Sinn
> Ihn ohne Zeit und End wird loben.

Translated:

> Thus lives the pure company
> In the inner sanctuary here together,
> Rescued from all worldly harm
> In burning flames of love enamored

And living now on in hope
toward that happy freedom, which there beyond
They according to the enamored sense
Him without time and end will praise.

Upon the east wall, over the door leading into the kitchen offices, we find a tablet of four lines:

Die Lib ist unser Kron und heller Tugend Spiegel,
Die Weisheit unsere Lust und reines Gottes-Siegel
Dass Lamm ist unser Schatz, dem wir uns anvertrauen
Und folgen seinen Gang als reinste Jungfrauen.

Translated:

The [divine] Love is our Crown and bright mirror of Virtue,
The [divine] Wisdom is our joy and pure signet of God,
The Lamb is our Bridegroom, to whom we trust ourselves
And follow in his lead as the purest vestal virgins.

To the left of this, in the northeast corner of the room, is another inscription consisting of nine lines, three of which are in capital letters:

UNSRE KRONEN DIE WIR TRAGEN
HIER IN DIESER STERBLICHKEIT,
Werden uns in Trübsals Tagen-Durch viel Leiden zubereit
Da muss unsre Hoffnung blühen-und der Glaube wachsen auf
Wenn sich die Welt und Fleisch bemühen uns zu schwächen
in den Lauf
O Wohl dann, weil wir gezählet. In der reinen Lämmer Heerd
Die dem keuschen Lamm vermählet. Und erkauffet von der Erd
Bleibet schon all hier verborgen. Unser Ehren Schmuk und
Kron
Wird uns doch jenem Morgen, Krönen Jesus, Gottes Sohn.

Translated:

OUR CROWNS WHICH WE WEAR
HERE IN THIS MORTALITY
Were for us in Afflictions days, in great sorrow prepared.
Here our hope must bloom and our Faith grow on high
When the world and the Flesh endeavor to weaken us in our
cause

Oh, what joy ! for we are numbered among the flock of pure
  Lambs,
Who by the immaculate Lamb espoused, are redeemed from
  the world,
  Although here are hidden our sacred jewels and crowns,
Yet upon yonder morn will crown us JESUS, the Son of GOD.

Directly over the preacher's bench is a tablet of five
lines, the two upper ones in large capitals :

GOTT UND
DAS KEUSCHE
Lamm muss stetig in uns wallen
Und uns in Ewigkeit nicht lassen mehr
ERKALTEN.

Translated :

GOD AND
THE IMMACULATE
Lamb must continually within us abide,
Nor must He forever let our
ZEAL ABATE.

Immediately to the right of the tablet is one of mystical and allegorical import. This is about three feet square, but is so discolored that it is almost undecipherable. It represents the "Narrow and Crooked Way," and is a most curious and ingenious composition. The chief feature is a labyrinthine path, filled up with texts of Scripture, admonishing the disciples of their duties and obligations which their profession impose upon them. This specimen of Kloster art is rapidly crumbling into dust.

Upon the south wall another allegorical subject attracts the eye; unfortunately this is also in a dilapidated condition, even more so than the last one described.

This tablet upon the south wall represents the "Triple Heaven" and is divided into three unequal sections; all are filled with innumerable figures and Bible quotations [Sprüch].

In the first section, Christ the Shepherd is represented gathering his flock together. In the second, over three hundred figures in the habit of the Order are represented with harps in their hands, singing praises to the Saviour. In the third is seen the throne of the Almighty Ruler of the Universe surrounded by over two hundred angels and archangels, the whole being divided by almost innumerable *Sprüche* or Bible quotations.

In the southwest angle of the room there are two large tablets, almost filling the space between the wainscoting and ceiling. The tablet upon the south wall consists of five lines, two of which are in large ornate capital letters:

BITT U. FLE-

HET DAMIT

Seinem Geist, und tuht in Libe wallen

Dass jedes seine Wunder preisst ohn einiges

VERALTEN.

Translated :

ENTREAT and SUPPLI-
CATE THEREWITH
His Spirit, and then in Love abide,
That each his wonders praise, without any
Zeal abating.

The tablet upon the west wall contains a quotation from the Apocalypse xxi, 23 :

UND DIE
STADT DARF
Keiner Sonnen noch des Mondes dass
Sie ihr scheinen ; den die Herrlicheit Gottes
Erleuchtet Sein Ihre Leuchte ist dass Lam. Off. 21, 23.

Translation :

And the city had no need of the sun, neither of the moon, to shine in it ; or the glory of God did lighten it, and the Lamb is the light thereof.

Another upon the south wall contains a quotation from the Apocalypse xxi, 24, 25.

Lastly we have one of two lines.

Wo Filadelfia blüht als a ein grünes Feld
Da sihet man aufgehen die Frucht der neuen Welt.

Translated :

Where Philadelphia [138] blooms as a verdant field
There one sees arise the fruits of the New World.

The historic Saal now serves as a meeting-house for the local German Seventh-day Baptist congregation, who since 1813 are the legitimate successors to the old Community. Religious services are held upon the seventh day whenever a preacher can be obtained, as they divide their time between the congregations of Ephrata, Snowhill, Salemville and Morrison's Cove.

---

[138] Used in the sense of brotherly love.

For some years past the upper portion of Peniel was divided off into rooms and used as tenements. Now, however (1899), under the guidance of the present intelligent board of trustees, the different tenants have been dispossessed, and the building is being restored to the same condition as when occupied by the old sisterhood, and at the same time is being put into complete repair, so that it may withstand the ravages of time, and together with the two other houses it will remain, we trust, for many years to come a prominent landmark and reminder of the German Sectarians in Lancaster county.

CHAPTER XXVII.

A CELESTIAL VISITANT.

ITHIN a few weeks after the dedication of Peniel a celestial phenomenon appeared in the shape of a beautiful comet. The coming of this erratic visitor, unheralded or announced, wrought great consternation among the German settlers throughout the Province. The memory of the fiery comets that appeared in the sky prior to the French invasions and devastation of the Palatinate was yet fresh in the minds of the older people, and so firmly rooted was the belief that comets were the precursors of war, famine and pestilence that fears were expressed by even those of sober thought that the flaming star foretold similar scenes of bloodshed in the New World. The beautiful visitant in the sky especially affected the superstitious residents of Germantown, to make no mention of the remaining hermits on the Wissahickon, who looked at it as a possible harbinger of the celestial Bridegroom whose coming they so long and earnestly expected. To the mystic enthusiasts on Mount Zion at Ephrata the flaming tail typified a bunch of switches,[139] with which the divine forces were about to punish the unrepentant and unregenerate of mankind. According to the old tradition, it was on Monday, February

---

[139] *Feuerige Ruthen.*

22, 1741–42, as the midnight bell was being tolled as usual, just as its sharp tone ceased to reverberate among the wooded hills and valleys of the Cocalico, that the Brotherhood of Zion in response to the summons, cloaked and cowled, slowly filed out of their narrow corridor and *kammers* and silently took up their march toward the hall of prayer on Mount Zion, as was their custom to keep their vigils (*nacht-metten*) during the ghostly hour of midnight (*geister-stunde*). The night was moonless, cold and clear, the air frosty, the stars sparkled in their settings of deep azure; not a leafless twig stirred, all were silent; Kedar and Zion loomed up darkly on the hillside, while in the meadow below the sharp angles of Peniel nestling amidst the silent graves were outlined dimly against the horizon; the only sound heard after the notes of the monastery bell had died away was the creaking of the brethren's wooden sabots on the icy ground. Half the distance to the "*Bethaus*" had hardly been traversed by the drowsy brethren when suddenly a bright light was seen, and to their great surprise the brethren saw in the eastern heavens a blazing star, with a bright fiery tail, which had suddenly flashed upon the sky. That the mystics were struck dumb with fear and amazement may be surmised. Prior Onesimus at once fell upon his knees on the frosty ground and commenced to pray for mercy, and that the great calamities portended by the fiery messenger in the heavens might be averted and that the Deity would hear their prayers and penance. After the first surprise was over, the Vorsteher, who was sent for, ordered the bell rung to alarm the Community, with orders to assemble in Peniel for religious services, which were held under his personal direction.

The sudden appearance of this erratic celestial visitant naturally had a marked effect upon the peculiar temperament and superstitious minds of these Germans, wrapt as they were in their religious enthusiasm and speculations.

With them the comet for the nonce engrossed all their time and attention, as it was supposed to be the forerunner of war, pestilence and other dire calamities; some even thought that it augured the end of the world; and that the long-looked for millenium, which had been so earnestly prophesied by Brother Agonius before his death, was near at hand.

After the first surprise had subsided, the prior ordered the reciting of the special prayers or liturgy for such occasions, as set forth in the Cabalistic ritual of the Zionitic Brotherhood. Brothers were also detailed to read the prayer at the services of the sisterhood and the congregations of the households at Peniel. This special liturgical services consisted of the reading of the IV Psalm, closing with the invocation :

"O great and mighty Lord, whose ineffable Name is contained within this Psalm, Thou that hearest the supplications of those who repeat this Psalm, have mercy upon us, and heed our supplications on this the third day of the week, whose heavenly signs are the Ram and the Scorpion, its Angel 'Sammeal' and servant 'Moadim' (Mars). Amen."

The signs, guardian angel and planets were varied each day, according to the table provided by the secret ritual of the Zionitic rite, viz. :

	SIGN.	ANGEL.	PLANETS.	
SUNDAY	LION.	RAPHAEL.	CHAMMA	SUN.
MONDAY	CRAB.	GABRIEL.	LEWANNA	MOON.
TUESDAY	RAM AND SCORPION.	SAMMEAL.	MOADIM	MARS.
WEDNESDAY	TWINS AND VIRGIN.	MICHAEL.	CHOCHAB	MERCURY.
THURSDAY	ARCHER AND PISCES.	ZADKIEL.	ZEDEK	JUPITER.
FRIDAY	BULL AND SCALES.	ANNAEL.	NOGAH	VENUS
SABBATH	WATERMAN AND GOAT.	CHEPHZIEL.	SABBATHAI	SATURN.

According to Brother Jephune, who was the astronomer of the Community, the comet was supposed to be near the equinoctial of the heavens. On the next night he

observed the celestial portent to be in the tail of the
Eagle; on the following nights the heavens were obscured
by heavy clouds, and when it was again seen on Saturday
night it stood near of Lyra, having taken a northward
course; on the next night it was seen in the tip of the
Swan's wing. So rapid was its flight that it had traversed
five degrees northward within twenty-four hours. The
night following it was just entering the head of the Dragon,
after which it vanished again into space. It was a long
time before the fear inspired by this celestial visitant was
forgotten. From this period date a number of hymns,
which were afterward incorporated in the collection known
as the *Paradisches Wunderspiel.* These hymns were full
of prophecy, and, as the *Chronicon* states, belong to the
"Evening of the sixth time-period, that is, the holy Ante-
Sabbath." These hymns represented the mysteries of the
last times so impressively that it seemed to the religious
enthusiasts as though the kingdom of heaven was already
dawning. These were followed by the *Wunderschrift*, a
mystical disquisition by Beissel upon the fall of man. It
was delivered and then written in German.

*Mystische Abhandlung | über die | Schöpfung | und von
des | Menschen Fall und Wiederbringung | durch des |
Weibes Samen | von einem | Friedsamen | Nach der stillen
Ewigkeit wallenden | Pilger | Ephrata: Typis Societatis,
Anno MDCCXLV.*[140]

This essay, which is perhaps the most remarkable of
Beissel's many productions, was one of the first pamphlets
to be printed on the Ephrata press. For some reason this
work is one of the scarcest of the Ephrata imprints. The
only known copy is in the library of the writer, and this
unfortunately lacks the printed title-page. A fac-simile of
the first page of this curious work is shown upon page 420.
According to the *Chronicon* it was at once translated into

[140] Title from a MS. copy of the *Wunderschrift.*

Eine tiefe Angelegenheit meines Geistes hat mir Ursache gegeben diese Wunder-Schrifft aufzusetzen: u. etwas wehniges davon an den Tag zu geben, nemlich: durch welche unbeschreibliche Angelegenheiten ich daran gekommen bin. Und ob sich schon die Schrifft zur vollen Gnüge selbst anpreißt: so will doch, als zur Vorrede, etwas anmercken, um einen Eingang zur Sache zu machen.

Ich habe zwar in den Tagen meiner Göttlichen Jugend gemeinet, es könte mir nicht fehlen, wann ich mich würde auf das sauberste üben, um meinen Wandel im H. Verliebt-seyn und Göttlichen Lichte zu führen. Allein dieses hat so viele harte und schwere Gegensprüche erwecket, daß mich offt Entsetzen und Grausen ankam: wiewohl ich daneben mein H. Verliebt-seyn fortsetzte, in der Meinung es im Sieg zu gewinnen. Allein, je mehr Fleiß ich anwandt, desto eine heftigere Rebellion ich in mir erweckte: welches mich freylich so geübet und gesiebet, daß offtmal die Steine, wann sie hätten eine Empfindlichkeit gehabt, mit mir hätten schreyen müssen, sonderlich weil der grose Fleiß und die allerreinste Brunst der Liebe allezeit das Feuer geschürt zu einem neuen Allarm. (1) Dieses hat mich freylich in gar

A　　　　　　　　　　　　tiefes

(1) Der Sinn dieser Reden ist folgender: Je mehr wir uns lassen das Gute angelegen seyn, desto mehr wird das Uebel in uns rege. Es ist dieses eine aus langer Erfahrung bestätigte Warheit: dahero, wann wir　　　　　　　　　　　　　　Gutes

FIRST PAGE OF BEISSELS' WUNDERSCHRIFT (DISSERTATION ON MANS' FALL).

A
Diſſertation on
MANS FALL,

Tranſlated from the High-German Original.

INVENIT HIRUNDO NIDUM, JEHOVA ALTARIA TUA

DELICIÆ EPHRATENSES

Printed: *EPHRATA* Anno MDCCLXV.
old at Philadelphia by. Meſſieurs CHRISTOPH
MARSHAL and WILLIAM DUNLAP

TITLE-PAGE OF ENGLISH VERSION OF BEISSELS' WUNDERSCHRIFT
Original in Historical Society of Pennsylvania.

English, and printed, "on account of its excellence," with the following title :

A | Dissertation on | Mans Fall, | Translated from the High-German Original. | Printed: Ephrata Anno MDCCLXV. | Sold at Philadelphia by Messieurs Christoph | Marshal and William Dunlap.

According to Peter Miller the English version was originally printed in the *Edinburgh Magazine*, a statement which the writer has not been able to verify. An English edition of one thousand copies was reprinted at Ephrata in 1765, but even this extraordinary edition was soon exhausted, as appears by a letter written in 1790 by Prior Jaebez (Rev. Peter Miller), the successor to Beissel as leader of the Community, wherein he states that he has not even a single copy left for himself. A curious circumstance in connection with this book is that toward the close of the Revolutionary war a copy was sent by Peter Miller to Italy, with the request to translate it into Italian and publish the work in that country, dedicating the volume to "His Holiness the Pope." The Ephrata records tell us that while Beissel was compiling this work, "Because he thereby disregarded nature too much, he contracted a severe illness." Brother Agrippa further says: "Unless the reader is versed in the spirit of the Virgin-estate, it is somewhat unclear in its expressions. In it, however, he had opened up a far outlook into eternity, and has gone further than even the holy Apostles in their revelations, bringing glorious things to light concerning the Mother church, and how the Father finally shall deliver his office to the Mother; similarly concerning the Sabbatic Church in the time of the bound dragon; what God's purposes are with this Church; and why he permitted her to be so severely tried by Gog and Magog."

CHAPTER XXVIII.

THE SKIPPACK BRETHREN.

ENTION was made in a previous chapter of the Wiegner homestead as the headquarters of the Moravian pioneers who paid a visit to the Province and the Ephrata Community in 1736. This house was in northeastern extremity of Philadelphia (now Montgomery) county. The place is still known as the Wiegner farm, and lies two miles south of Kulpsville, a post-town a short distance west of Lansdale on the North Penn railroad. The old stone house which sheltered the first Moravian missionaries has long since been demolished.

Christopher Wiegner, who was a religious enthusiast from the Fatherland, and who came over with the Schwenkfelders, held devotional services at his house whenever opportunity offered; and his home was always open to all comers who sought spiritual advice or comfort, and thus it was that his place became somewhat of a hospice. It was not long before a number of German settlers gathered around him and met regularly at his house for the worship of God and religious edification. Most of these men had become Separatists at home, and having severed their relations with the orthodox faiths came to this country to escape religious persecution.

These gatherings resulted in the organization of a religious society irrespective of any denominational creed, under the name of VEREINIGTE SKIPPACK BRÜDER (Associated Brethren of Skippack). The leading members of this new sect, the acquaintance of some of whom we have already made, were Heinrich Frey, Johann Kooken, Georg Merkel, Christian Weber, Johann Bonn, Jacob Wenzen, Jost Schmidt, Wilhelm Bossen and Jost Becker, of Skippack; Henry Antes, Wilhelm Frey, George Stiefel, Heinrich Holstein and Andrew Frey, of Frederick township; Matthias Gemaehle and Abraham Wagner, of Matetsche; Jean Bertolet, Franz Ritter and Wilhelm Pott, of Oley; Johann Bechtel, Johann Adam Gruber, Blasius Mackinet and Georg Benzel, of Germantown.

Nearly all of the above brethren eventually ended their days within the Moravian fold,—some, however, only after gravitating between Ephrata and Bethlehem.

Of the tenets or mode of worship of the Skippack Brethren there is little or nothing known; the organization appears to have been a non-sectarian one, whose members strove to impart religious instruction to all settlers irrespective of creed; and when Count Zinzendorf arrived in 1742 they were among his most earnest supporters in his early efforts to bring about an evangelical union by means of what are known as the Pennsylvania Synods or Conferences.

It has been claimed by some investigators that the services at Wiegner's were Moravian, pure and simple, and that from the start he organized his neighbors into a Moravian congregation,—a claim which appears to be without any foundation in fact. However, be this as it may, the humble farm house became a rallying point not only for the Moravian missionaries, but for all other separatists and evangelists as well.

Thus it was that the celebrated Whitefield held a service

at Wiegner's on the afternoon or evening of May 5, 1740. He states that he preached there to about three thousand people; as he notes in his journal, "at a Dutchman's plan- "tation, who seemed to have drank deeply into the conso- "lations of the Holy Spirit, we spent the evening in a "most agreeable manner. I never saw more simplicity; "surely that house was a Bethel." [141]

The curious part of this incident is that but few of the people present were conversant with the English tongue; so after Whitefield had finished, Peter Böhler, the leader of the advance party of Moravians who came from Savannah to Philadelphia, April, 1740, preached in German, or, at least, was supposed to render Whitefield's sermon into German.

The occasion of Whitefield's visit to this part of the Prov- ince was the building of a house he designed to erect on his land (Nazareth) as a school for negroes. He came to Wiegner's with the purpose of making a proposal to Peter Böhler and to engage the brethren who had accompanied him from Georgia to do the carpenter work for him. A contract was entered into between the two parties and two houses were commenced upon the land where Nazareth now stands. One, a small wooden house, known as the "First House," the other the fine stone mansion known as the "Whitefield House."

During the following winter Whitefield and Böhler had a controversy about some pecuniary matters, which ended by the former discharging the brethren, the large stone house being no farther advanced than the foundations. Eventually, however, the whole property came into the possession of the Moravians, who finished the large house and there established the Nazareth economy.

The Moravian party in the Province were reinforced December 15, 1740, by the arrival of Bishop David Nitsch-

---

[141] *Whitefield's Journal*, London, 1761. Evidently one of the so-called forest sermons.

THE WHITEFIELD OR EPHRATA HOUSE AT NAZARETH.

A MISSIONARY HOUSE OF THE MORAVIAN CHURCH.

COURTESY OF THE PENNSYLVANIA-GERMAN SOCIETY.

man, his uncle of the same name, also Christian Fröhlich, and two sisters, Johanna S. Molther and Anna Nitschman. The headquarters of this party was established at Wiegner's, and the Moravian diaries note many meetings held there at that time. When the Brethren at Ephrata learned of the Nitschman party, three of the Solitary brethren were at once sent to Wiegner's to welcome and greet them, as the *Chronicon* states, "because at that time the fire of first love was still burning."

Early in March of the next year (1741) a larger party of Solitary made a visit to Nazareth, and, as the diary notes, "expressed admiration at the industry and contentment of "the former in their indigent circumstances."

A few months later, a return visit was projected by the Moravians to the Ephrata settlement. This was planned with two objects in view,—one relating to a possible union of the two evangelical movements ; the other, to thoroughly investigate the monastic feature of the Ephrata settlement. For the latter purpose Anna Nitschman and David Zeisberger the elder, set out for the Cocalico on the 12th of July, and arrived there two days later. Anna Nitschman at once quartered herself with the sisterhood, while Brother Zeisberger took up his abode in Zion.

Among the brethren who greeted the two evangelists upon their arrival at the Kloster was Brother Gottlieb (Gottfried Haberecht), one of the Zionitic Brotherhood. Haberecht, originally a Moravian, was one of the party who came over with Spangenberg to Savannah in 1735. He was a native of Piela, Silesia. He left Georgia in 1737 and came to Germantown, but after a short sojourn in solitude on the Ridge, he drifted to Ephrata, was baptized by Beissel and entered the convent of Zion.

Sister Nitschman spent several days among the sisterhood, "during which time she enjoyed much love." Upon one point, however, she differed from her entertainers, viz., on the question of justification and the marriage state. This led to considerable argument between the visitor and her hosts, and caused the prioress to detail a sister to be always about her visitor so as to give her no chance to interview any sister privately. Notwithstanding this precaution, Sister Nitschman afterward stated that "most of the sisters in the settlement would like to throw off the yoke if they but knew of another retreat."

This report led to some correspondence between the parties, and letters were even received from other persons asking for information. Thereupon one of the sisters, who was detailed to keep a watch upon the visitor while at the Kloster, wrote a detailed account of Anna Nitschman's visit, wherein she stated that she had always been about the person mentioned, but she never heard any of the sisters say the like of it to her. This interesting missive was published; no original copy, however, is known to the writer. It was reprinted at Frankfurt (Germany), a copy of which is in possession of the writer. It will be noticed that in this reprint the name of the Countess Benigna was substituted for that of Anna Nitschman, or else the latter represented herself as the Count's daughter during her visit to Ephrata, viz. :

Brief einer Sieben-Tägerin an eine ihrer Verwandten, betreffend den Besuch, welchen des Herrn Grafen von Zinzendorf Comptesse Tochter bey ihnen abgelegt, und den Eingang, den sie unter diesen Sieben-Täger-nonnen gehabt haben soll. Frankfurt u. Leipzig, MCCLXVIII.

Translation :

Letter of a Seven-dayer to a relative, concerning the visit paid to them by Count Zinzendorf's noble daughter, and the entrance she claims to have had among the Seven-dayer nuns :

" What Zinzendorf's daughter is reported to have said about us, and as you desire to have a true report of our behaviour toward her, I will now from love to you, according to your desire, write you in as few words as possible, how she demeaned herself towards us, and what the connection was from the very beginning.—That (we) to them are as poison, and that they carry in their hearts a great enmity toward our Community, is not unknown to you, neither is it to us.—But as we in all our actions strive to emulate our teacher Jesus Christ, who at all times loved His enemies, and who blessed such as cursed Him, yea, He even gave unto Judas a kiss, after he had betrayed Him. Accordingly we received this person with due honor.

"She arrived toward evening, and went to Kalcklöser's house, and at the command of her Father sent word to the Prioress or Mother, to come and call for her there : But as she was just away from the house (convent) it happened that I and another Sister called for her, and brought her unto the chamber, wherein I live, and the same evening took her to table before the whole sisterhood.—Upon the second day we showed to her our whole habitation, and went with her into all the rooms of the Sisterhouse. Towards evening the Mother (prioress) returned, who she desired to meet, and was therefor received by her, in the same manner as we had, as if we were an innocent child, who knows neither good nor evil ; and out of discretion was merely spoken to about ordinary subjects after her own liking ; as it is not our habit to speak to such persons, about our private life, or about divine matters, as our conscience does not permit us to misuse the word of God, nor to cast our pearls at the feet of such as would crush them. We rather approach such persons heartily with our outward goodness, in such a manner not to offend the good God.—And now to continue my story. It so happened, that on the same night we kept a Love feast, and permitted her to look on, thereafter on the third morning [of her visit] according to our custom, we took her with us as we went to keep our hour of prayer, at which meeting she said a parting word to all sisters, which was quickly done. When we took her again to the Brother's house whence we had found her.

"So I can tell you truthfully, that she did not speak confidentially or privately with any sister in such manner as she claims, as I was with her continually, and spoke more with her than any one else.—Consequently she cannot say, that it was specially I, who would like to have gone with her—which was furthest from my thoughts.—I trust that I may forever be preserved from such seductive teachings, and not take upon myself a worse state, than I was in prior to my conversion. So much I can give you in a concise and circumstantial account of our demeanor toward the Count's daughter.

"And now again, shortly afterwards another of their sisters came to us,—intending to visit us in the same way, and perhaps thought that we sat there, waiting for one of our doors to open.—But she found it different : as we at once closed our portals, as they came running one after another. They must have been out on a tour of speculation or spying, so they were plainly told that we had enough of them, and that our community was entirely distinct from theirs, and that in the future our hearts and habitations would be closed against them, and all intercourse would be interdicted.

"In this manner we disposed of them, and believe that henceforth they will not bother about us : as it is meet and right. Further I will now close."

THE NEW MOONERS.

HEN the visit of the two Moravian evangelists to Ephrata drew to an end, they journeyed to the house of Johannes Zimmermann in the Conestoga valley, a short distance from Ephrata. He was the high priest of another religious sect which had of late grown spontaneously upon the fertile soil of Lancaster county. This sect was known as the "New Mooners" (*Neumondler*), as they only held their meetings for religious worship during the growing or increase of the moon.

The chief day for worship and prayer was the first day

of the new moon. It was based upon the divine command given to Moses as recorded in Numbers xxviii, 11. One of the curious features of their worship was the use of trombones upon that day, so as to comply with the scriptural injunction in Numbers x, 10. Other passages upon which they founded their faith and ceremonies are recorded in 2 Kings iv, 23; Samuel xx, 5, 6; and Amos viii, 5.

Among the claims set forth by these people was one that all prayers and supplications made during the early phases of the lunar orb increased and magnified as they were wafted towards heaven; while such as were offered during the declining quarters of the satalite were apt to remain within the terrestial atmosphere, and fail to ascend to the celestial throne. Therefore the regular services and celebrations were always held during the first quarter. It was from this peculiarity that the sect became known as " New Mooners."

Another of their peculiar teachings was the disposition of the soul after death. It was taught that the spirits of the departed were wafted into space and there separated, *i. e.*, the good from the bad. These souls were disposed of four times every month. In the growing moon when the horns were up, forming a boat as it were, the souls of the good went aboard and were thus carried into the realms of everlasting bliss. Upon the two last of the monthly trips, when the moon was in its third and last quarter, the souls of the wicked were gathered upon the now convex side, and the spirits not being able to maintain any foothold would slide off into space and thus fall into the bottomless pit, where there was the rattling of dry bones and the gnashing of teeth.

This was really a survival of an ancient belief, which was founded upon an old heathen saga and had its inception in pagan times, long prior to the introduction of Christianity into Germany. It was an old folk-tale which had obtained a hold on the popular fancy and may well be classed among the many similar varieties of *Aberglaube* brought to our shores by the early settlers.

From the Bethlehem diaries we glean a few additional items in relation to this curious sect of Pennsylvania Christians. An entry, dated January 4, 1748, states that the Moravian party on their way from Muddy creek to Mill creek visited the house of Hans Zimmermann—" The New Mooners have their meeting with him. They meet the first Sunday after the new moon, and De Benneville preaches to them." This De Benneville was Dr. George De Benneville, an eccentric character who claimed to have visited, while in a trance, the realms of bliss and departed spirits. He was a close friend to Brother Ezekiel (Heinrich Sangmeister), the disgruntled member of the Ephrata Community, who wrote out an account of De Benneville's wonderful trance, which was found among his papers after his death. Bishop Spangenberg, under date of March 11th of the same year, writes: that he left Muddy creek for Hans Zimmermann's, where he preached to an audience of " bearded men "—Mennonites, Dunkers and seceeders from the Mennonites. Zimmermann himself was glad and helpful to Spangenberg. " He is as he was ten years ago, no better and no worse."

The New Mooners never gained much strength in the outside community, and even before the death of their high priest, Johannes Zimmermann, the sect ceased to be a distinctive body. The members were rapidly absorbed by other faiths, and the New Mooners soon passed into history.

————

Brother Zeisberger and Anna Nitschman returned from their Ephrata trip to Nazareth, July 21 [1741]. One of the effects of this visit to the Cocalico was that while at Ephrata, Anna Nitschman had an interview with Gottfried

Haberecht and tried to prevail on him to return to his old communion. He refused, however, to entertain the suggestion; but as time passed and the abstemious mode of life bore hard upon him, he longed over again to meet his old friends, and in the following September he journeyed to the Forks (Bethlehem). Here he remained, and at the end of a month concluded to withdraw from the Zionitic Brotherhood. Bishop Nitschman wrote them respecting his decision, and dispatched Johann Böhner to Ephrata with the following letter.[142] (Translation :)

" Gottfried Haberecht, who in a mental confusion, was received and instructed by you with great patience, now humbly and repentantly knowledges before you, that he withdrew both untimely and irregularly ; mainly in so far as he arbitrarily demanded to visit his Brethren, and thereby set a bad example for others. I thank you that you have thus far sustained me, and according to your ability have laboured for my soul. This has not been without blessing for me. Now I should have returned unto you, according to the wish and expression of my Brethren ;[143] but as you to me personally and at the two public religious conferences granted me a dismissal, with a forgiveness of all previous happenings, so I now thank you therefor and wish heartily that the Brethren may again receive me."

The Bethlehem diaries contain the following entries on the Haberecht episode :

" September 13th, 1741. On the road we met Gottfried Haberecht, who had joined the Baptists at Ephrata. Haberecht appeared depressed, and was desirous of seeing the brethren.

" September 26th. Gottfried Haberecht and Augustine Neisser arrived. The former had met with ill treatment at Ephrata and came here for refuge.

" Sept. 29th. Gottfried Haberecht remained at the Forks.

---

[142] Moravian MS.

[143] By the term Brethren, Haberecht here means the Moravian Brethren.

"October 12th. As Gottfried Haberecht had withdrawn from the Baptists at Ephrata, and had concluded to remain in the Forks [Bethlehem], David Nitchman, Episc., wrote them respecting his decision, and dispatched John Böhner to Ephrata with the letter."

This case of Haberecht's caused much bad feeling between the two communities, the Ephrata people openly charging that Anna Nitschman was the real cause of Brother "Gottlieb" leaving the Brotherhood.

The *Chronicon* openly blames Anna Nitschman for his defection, who, it states: "when she visited the settlement, drew him back to her communion." Henceforth the career of Haberecht was cast with the Unitas Fratrum.

Gottfried Haberecht,[144] came with Spangenberg, Anton Seyffert and other, to Savannah, Georgia, on the "Two Brothers," Capt. Thompson, March 22, 1735. He was born in May, 1700, at Schoenheide, Lower Silesia, of Lutheran parents. He was reared a tailor, and came to Herrnhut in 1732. He was married, and lost his wife in Georgia. In 1736 he came to Pennsylvania, and for three years was an inmate of the Kloster at Ephrata. He returned to Bethlehem in 1741, and accompanied Count Zinzendorf on his return to Europe in January, 1743. In 1747 went to Algiers to aid Carl Notbeck in his labors of love among the Christian slaves, was there ten months. In 1749 went to London, and between 1754–1759 assisted Brother Caries in Jamaica, thence he returned to Bethlehem, and died February 28, 1767, at Christian Spring, whence he had gone to superintend the weaving shop of the economy.

Upon the arrival of Count Zinzendorf in America, December, 1741, and the establishment of the Moravian settlement at the Forks of the Delaware (Bethlehem), the congregation of the Skippack Brüder gradually declined, as most of the

---

[144] Extracts from Moravian diaries kindly furnished by John W. Jordan, Esq.

members affiliated with the Moravians, a course which by no means ended their usefulness, as the names of a number of these same Skippack Brethren will be found among the most active evangelists in the Province. Wiegner's house remained a preaching station for some time after the founding of Bethlehem ; the meetings, however, soon lost their individuality, and the members were absorbed by the more active movements of the Unitas Fratrum.[145]

It is not to be wondered at that after the establishment of the Moravians at Bethlehem and Nazareth, both of these somewhat similar Communities should have become the objective point for the various crack-brained religious enthusiasts and adventurers who had come to the colony to ventilate their dogmas, and at the same time better their fortunes. Where some of these enthusiasts were successful in imposing upon the succeptible Germans, others at once came to the Ephrata or Bethlehem communities, but, finding that a strict discipline was maintained, soon left the one to go to the other, finally to leave both, and again enter into the whirlpool of sin in the outer world. There were exceptions, however, where after changing from one to the other, they returned to their first choice and remained steadfast unto the end,—even if they did not remain in the " single " houses of their respective communities. Of these cases, that of Brother Theodorus is of special interest.

This brother was an Englishman of gentle if not noble birth, who, when he came to Ephrata, gave the name of Thomas Hardie and asked to be received into the Brotherhood. He was well educated in both the languages and the law. Of his lineage and family he revealed little or nothing, except that his father had lived in London and his mother was a lady from Normandy, further that his grandfather had been English Ambassador in Spain.

---

[145] *May 27, 1747.* " Old widow Born, of Skippack, has sold her plantation, & with her two sons John & Herman, has come to Bethlehem." (Bethlehem diaries).

While yet at home he became interested in some of the mystical religious societies of his native country, and thereupon expressed an intention of going to Pennsylvania, as he had heard that the mystical theories were there carried into practice. This his father attempted to prevent. The young theosophist, however, disguised as a sailor embarked on a vessel leaving for America, and while at sea destroyed everything that might lead to the identification of himself or family, the last thing to be consigned to the deep was his emblazoned seal ring.

Upon his arrival in Philadelphia, the captain, as was usual with the unscrupulous mariners of that day when they had a friendless passenger, offered him for sale for a term of years, ostensibly to reimburse him for passage money claimed to be still due. Rather than disclose his identity the young man permitted himself to be sold as a redemption servant. His purchaser was a German from Maxatawny, named Siegfried, who wanted an English teacher for his children. Siegfried realized considerable profit from his servant, as the latter beside teaching school acted as conveyancer and legal adviser of the neighborhood. So well pleased was the German with his bargain, that he made him an offer of his daughter and 100 acres of land. The Englishman refused the seductive offer, and upon the expiration of his term of bondage he wandered about among the Germans, as he stated, "in order to find agreement to his holy calling."

Hardie first went to Bethlehem, but soon found the strict discipline under which he was placed there was irksome. Then his ideas of mystic theology were confronted with the sound gospel doctrine of the Moravian Brethren. This led to many disputes and finally unsettled his reason. After his recovery he came to Ephrata, and "as soon as he got sight of the person of the Superintendent, the celestial Venus in him became so eager to embrace the heavenly

Virgin, that he soon after entered into the *Actum* of betrothal in the water of baptism." [146]

After his immersion he joined the Zionitic Brotherhood and entered the convent, when he was given the name of Theodorus. He was at once installed as translator from German into English. However, after a sojourn of about six months, the confined life affected his health to so great an extent that he was obliged to leave the settlement. Thereupon he was sent by the Brotherhood to various parts of the back settlements of the Province in the capacity of a schoolmaster, to give instruction to the neglected children of the settlers, no matter whether they be German or English. He led an humble life and loved poverty, he frequently preached and held religious services. His life was often so austere that it had to be forbidden him by his superiors at Ephrata. [147]

This pious evangelist lived until 1784 when his death was marked by the following curious incident, which is also recorded in the *Chronicon:* When taking leave from his friends in Pittsburg, intending to visit his brethren in the settlement, one of his friends told him that he had seen in a dream that he would die there; he, therefore, delayed his journey for another week; but a hidden hand moved him to take up the project again, for it was decreed that his body should be again delivered to his brethren as a pledge. As soon as he arrived at the settlement he was seized with sickness, and recollecting what had been prophesied of him, he prepared for his decease and departed after a short illness. So much for the old legend. Thomas Hardie was buried among the brethren in the old God's acre by the roadside, where he rests in an unmarked grave.

The following interesting letter written by him to Conrad Beissel has been preserved.

---

[146] *Chronicon Ephretense,* chapter **xxiii.**
[147] *Ibid.*

Translation:

FATHER FRIEDSAM:

I thank thee for all the acts of love done to me, for all thy innocent suffering on my account, for all thy faithfulness. My friend, my Brother, how beautiful thou art in priestly adornment when thou enterest the sanctuary with the golden censer, on the days of atonement, with many priests, when the bride Sophia, in a column of clouds, with many thousand saints, fills thy hand with incense. Praised be thy God, who elected thee. May he bless thee with everlasting comfort, from his loving heart, and be this the reward for all the affability thou didst show to the children of man. Now, my good heart, soul living in God, I wish thee inexpressibly much good, my dear prophet, thou servant of God, pray incessantly for me to thy and my God, and the God of us all. High priest of God, in whom dwelleth his parental love, to whom he delivered the kingdom in order that he might keep me from evil!

Now, my dear one, receive from me, in spirit, a hearty, mutual, loving kiss, and enter the sanctuary in peace. Love the Lord in his holiness, praise the work of his hands, for his grace abideth for ever and ever.   THEODORUS.

P. S. Now I depart from thy presence with a weeping heart, the heart tells more than the pen. I shall greet thee above in the garden of him who has loved thee and me.

COUNT LUDWIG VON ZINZENDORF

BORN, MAY 26, 1700 ; DIED, MAY 9, 1760.

CHAPTER XXIX.

THE PENNSYLVANIA SYNODS.

INZENDORF, the noble missionary and evangelist, mystic and theologian, who came to our shores with the avowed purpose of spreading the Gospel among all human creatures, irrespective of race or color, looms up before us at this period as one of the most heroic characters in our history. Nikolaus Ludwig, Count of Zinzendorf and Pottendorf,—in America, Brother Ludwig or Ludwig von Thürnstein,—was a descendent of a noble family of Austria, born in Dresden, Saxony, May 26, 1700, and was grand commander of the theosophical fraternity, known as *Der orden des Leidens Jesu* (the Order of the Passion of Jesus), and also the founder of the order of the Mustard Seed, as well as of the revived sect of the *Unitas Fratrum* or Moravians. He landed at New York on the second day of December, 1741. Eight days later he arrived at Philadelphia ; the nineteenth and twentieth he spent at Wiegner's on the Skippack, and four days later he held the festival of Christmas Eve in the settlement at the Forks of the Delaware. It was upon this occasion that the Brethren's settlement received the name of Bethlehem.

The following day, Christmas, the Count and his followers set out for the Conestoga valley by way of Oley. One of the chief objects of Count Zinzendorf, in undertaking this journey in the inclement season, was to interest the Ephrata Community in his proposed union of all denominations. The strong hold which the Sabbatarian doctrine had obtained upon the German populace in Pennsylvania was an unexpected surprise to the noble evangelist, and more so, when he found that the question of the true Sabbath had even been raised previous to his arrival amongst his followers, the scattered brethren at Bethlehem, who, for the double purpose of conciliating the Sabbath-keepers and conforming strictly to the Holy Writ, for a time had also kept the seventh day as well as the first.[148] This action was officially approved at the council held at Bethlehem on June 24, 1742, at which Zinzendorf was present when this important resolution was passed :

" To observe as a day of rest not only Sunday, the day of the Lord, but also Saturday, the Jewish Sabbath."

This was partly in order to avoid giving offense to the Seventh-day Baptists at Ephrata, and partly on account of the Indians and missionary laborers among them, as not a few at that time supposed that the Indians might be descendants of the ten tribes of Israel, which had been led into the Assyrian captivity.

The above resolution in a manner decided the character of this congregation for a number of years.[149]

For some unknown reason Count Zinzendorf appears not to have extended his visit to the Ephrata settlement at this time. The *Chronicon* mentions that " he undertook a journey up the country, even before the conference, but visited only the door-sill of the Ephrata House." From the Bethlehem diaries it appears that on Christmas Day he

---

[148] Bethlehem Diaries.

[149] Rev. Levin Theodore Reichel : *Zinzendorf at Bethlehem.* Nazareth, 1888.

THE HISTORIC FIRST HOUSE IN BETHLEHEM, BUILT 1741. NO LONGER STANDING.

preached in the house of Jean Bertolet at Oley, and five days later (December 30th), we find him in Germantown where he issued a call for a synod or religious conference, irrespective of denomination, to convene, on the twelfth of January next, at the house of Theobald Endt, at Germantown.

Zinzendorf's object in calling this conference was not with the view of uniting all denominations with the Moravian church, as has been repeatedly stated. As a matter of fact, there was none in America at that time.[150] The Count's idea was for all to agree in essentials, and thus form "*one congregation of God in the Spirit*," though outwardly divided into different denominations and communities. The magnitude of the task which he imposed upon himself may be comprehended when we glance over his list of the different sects flourishing in the Province at the time of his visit. He there states : "All shades of Sectarians exist here down to open infidelity." Besides the English, Swedish and German Lutherans, and the Scotch, Dutch and German Reformed, there were Armenians, Baptists, *Vereinigte Vlaaminger en Waterlander*, Mennonites from Danzig, Arians, Socinians, Schwenckfelders, German Old Tunkers, New Tunkers, New Lights, Inspired, Sabbatarians or Seventh-Day Baptists, Hermits, Independents and Free Thinkers. Spangenberg adds still one more class to this number, where he says : " Many thousands of these people cared so little for religion that it became a common saying in reference to such, who cared neither for God nor His word, that they had *the Pennsylvania religion*."

---

[150] It will be noted that the preliminary steps toward organizing a Moravian congregation were taken but a week before this call for the first conference was issued. Among the Moravians present at the council we find, besides Zinzendorf, John Jacob Müller, Bishop David Nitschman, Andrew Eschenbach, Pyrlaeus, Büttner and Rauch. The solemn organization of the Congregation was not complete until June 25, 1742. See also *Reichel's Early History of the Church of the United Brethren*. (Nazareth, 1888, p. 109.)

Im Namen Jesu! Amen.

Mein lieber Freund und Bruder, etc.

Dieweil in der Kirche Christi ein entsetzlicher Schade geschiehet unter denen zum Lamme gerufenen Seelen, und daß meißt aus einem Mißtrauen und Argwohn einer gegen den andern, und daß vielmal ohne Grund, wodurch der Zweck zu etwas Gutem allemal abgeschnitten wird; und ist uns doch die Liebe geboten: So ist man schon wohl zwey Jahre oder mehr damit umgangen, ob nichts möglich wäre eine allgemeine Versammlung anzustellen, nicht der Meynung mit einander zu zanken, sondern in der Liebe zu handeln, von den wichtigsten Glaubens-Artikeln, um zu sehen, wie nahe man einander im Grunde werden könnte, und im übrigen in Meynung die den Grund der Seligkeit nicht stürzen, einander in der Liebe zu tragen, damit alles Richten und Urtheilen unter denen obmeldeten Seelen möchte gemindert und aufgehoben werden, wodurch man sich doch der Welt so blos stellet, und Ursach gibt zu sagen: Die den Frieden und die Bekehrung predigen sind selbst widrig gesinnt,; So hat man diese so wichtige Sache nun wieder mit vielen Brüdern und Gottsuchenden Seelen in Bedenken genommen, und vor dem Herrn ge- prüfet, und beschlossen den künftigen Neujahrs-Tag in Germantown zusammen zu kommen; So wirst du auch herzlich gebeten, mit noch etlichen deiner Brüder die Grund haben und geben können von ihrem Glauben, mit beyzuwohnen, wo es euch der Herr zuläſſet: Es ist auch meißt allen andern durch eben solche Briefe bekannt gemacht. Es wird vermuthlich eine große Versammlung werden, aber laß dich das nicht abhalten, es wird alles ohne großen Rumor veranstaltet werden. Der Herr Jesus verleihe uns seinen Segen dazu.

Von deinem armen und geringen doch herzlich gesinnten Freund und Bruder

Henrich Antes.

Friederichs Township in Philadelphia Co.
   ben 15. Dezember 1741.

CIRCULAR LETTER SENT BY HENRY ANTES TO THE EPHRATA COMMUNITY.

When the circulars of the proposed convention were received at the Ephrata settlement a general church council was at once called, wherein it was resolved that one Zionitic Brother, together with several fathers, should attend it. Prior Onesimus demanded that, by virtue of his office, he should represent the Zionitic Brotherhood and take charge of the delegation. This was granted, and upon the appointed day, January 12, 1742, the Ephrata deputation, consisting of Prior Onesimus, Johannes Hildebrand, Heinrich Kalcklöser and another brother, appeared at the first Pennsylvania synod, presented their credentials, and took their place in the conference.

This meeting was held at the house of Theobald Endt, which stood on the west side of Germantown avenue, near the corner of what is now Queen lane. It was a stone house, of two stories, with a quaint penthouse overhanging the door and windows of the lower floor. The heavy sash, set with small lights, and the solidity of the inside woodwork, showed that it was built at an early day.

Among the men who attended this meeting, all kinds of opinions were represented. Beside the four mystics from Ephrata, there were several apostates of the settlement, also Dunkers, Mennonites and Pietists, with a few Lutheran and Reformed. Prominent among these present were the Rev. Samuel Gulden, George Steifel [151] and a few other old Separatists. Then there was Conrad Weiser, the only German justice within the Province, and who but a short time before, as Brother Enoch, was one of the most influential members of the Ephrata Community. Conrad Matthäi, now living as a hermit on the Ridge ; Schirwagen, an Inspired from Germany, and Blasius Daniel Mackinet, with another Quaker who was conversant with the German language, completed the list. Of all this assemblage, the Ephrata delegation was accorded the place of honor, and it

---

[151] See *Reichel's Moravian History*, p. 49.

appears that Count Zinzendorf took special pains to ingratiate himself with Prior Onesimus.

He spoke a good deal with the Prior about the economy of the Solitary in the settlement, and foretold that he would be the Superintendent's successor in office, which was an easy prophecy, for Tacitus says : *Cupido dominandi cunctis affectibus flagrantior est.* "The lust to govern surpasses all passions." [152]

Owing to the result of this intimacy between Prior Onesimus and Count Zinzendorf, it was resolved to issue a call for another synod to be held at Ephrata two weeks later.

When the Prior and his companions returned home and reported what had been done, great opposition was at once aroused against the holding of the proposed conference at the settlement and the arbitrary conduct of the Prior. Beissel wrote forthwith to Henry Antes, asking him to revoke the decision upon holding the conference at Ephrata, as under no circumstances would it be permitted.

Enclosed in this letter was a theosophic epistle, bearing the following title :

Von der himmlischen Weiblicheit, und der Vergestaltung unserer in derselben Bild durch die in der Paradisischen Libes-Flamme entzüdete u. von dem Treiben des Feuermännlichen Selbst-Willens gereinigte Magia unsers Geistes. Nicht weniger von einer zweÿfachen Seligkeit des Gesetzes und Evangelii.

The epistle closed with this allusion to the Moravian Brethren : "Regarding the matter with which we together have been concerned, through the management of several brethren of our Community, I shall remain your devoted patron and well-wisher. But in regard to the matter itself I stand still, and will neither further nor oppose it, but seek with my people and God to maintain the peace of Christ Jesus, together with all who are children of the same peace.

---

[152] *Chronicon*, chapter xxiii.

Salute for me, in addition all salvation—bringing souls whom you know to be such. Fare you well, my beloved, and be unto God and His love truly commended." (Translation.)

As a result, the second conference was not held at Ephrata but assembled at Falkner Swamp. According to the Bethlehem diaries it was at George Hübner's on January 25, 1741–42. But by the Ephrata accounts it was at the house of Henry Antes on January 29th. It does not appear just who represented the mystic community on this occasion. The following item, taken from the printed proceedings, is interesting :[153]

"Query XXII. Is it true that the Moravian Brethren make too much of the matrimonial state and those of Ephrata too little?

"Answer. It has seemed as if the congregation at Ephrata and the Brethren at the Forks, in the matter of matrimony, were in direct contradiction. But when the Brethren publicly stated their position, the latter said they had nothing against this. We have here upon the one side acknowledged that the suspicion of a carnal necessity, for the sake of which matrimony is exalted, is unfounded, until the contrary is found and acknowledged. Upon the other side we declare the congregation at Ephrata in the future to be innocent

---

[153] DIE XXII FRAGE.—Ist's wahr, dass die Mährischen Brüder zu viel, und die von Ephrata nichts auf der Ehe halten ?

ANTWORT.—Es hat geschienen als wenn die Gemeinde zu Ephrata und die Brüder in den Forks, in dem artikel der Ehe einander direct wiedersprachen als aber die brüder ihrem grund öffentlich darlegten, so sagten jene dawieder hätten sie nichts. Wir haben also hiermit den argwohn von einer fleischlichen noth, um deren willen die Ehe erhaben werde auf der einen seite vor unbegründet erkant, bis man das gegentheil siehet und findet, und auf der andern seite sprechen wir die Gemeinde zu Ephrata, in zukunft von dem verdacht der lehre des Teufel frey ; und niemand der zu uns gehört soll sie ihnen schuld geben, und wer in künftig etwas dergleichen höret, soll die person nennen, die es gesagt hat, und nicht die Gemeinde beschuldigen.

from any suspicion of spreading the teachings of the Devil. And no one belonging to us is to accuse them thereof; and whoever in the future hears similar tales is to name the person who said it, and not accuse the congregation." (Translation.)

The third Pennsylvania Synod was called at the house of John de Turck at Oley, February 21, 1741–42. Here the Zionitic Brotherhood were represented and gave their testimony against the Beast, the Whore and False Prophets, after which a considerable discussion was indulged in regarding the matrimonial state, infant baptism and the Eucharist. The arguments eventually ran so high that the Sabbatarians withdrew before the close of the meeting.[154]

In the printed report of the third Synod the following note was introduced, thereby making it appear as if their departure was upon religious grounds:[155]

" Whereas, the Brethren from Ephrata can neither reach their own nor any other suitable place before the Sabbath, and it is the wish of our entire gathering that this respectable submission of the church before the law appear not to be transgressed by us, although we have not yet received any Divine admonition looking toward the universal introduction of this doctrine: therefore we have given their matters precedence over all others, and devoted thereto the first day of the conference, and willingly permitted the aforesaid Brethren to depart upon the evening of the second day thereof." (Translation.)

---

[154] Fresenius: *Americanische Nachrichten*, Band iii, p. 159.

[155] XV Wiel die brüder von Ephrata weder ihren noch sonst einen bekanten ort vor Sabbats halten erreichen können; unzer ganzen versamulung aber daran gelegen ist, das diese respectable praxis der kirch vor dem Gesetz von uns nicht übertreten zu werden scheine ob wir gleich zu deren algemeine einführung noch nicht keinen Göttlichen wink sehen; so haben wir nicht nur ihre sache dis mahl allen den übrichen vorgezogen, und den ersten Conferenz tag dazu ganz angewendet sondern auch willig geschehen lassen, dass die vorgemeldete brüder am zweiten tage der Conferenz gegen abend wieder abgereist.

Immediately after the adjournment of the Synod, Count Zinzendorf, with several companions, among whom was Rev. Jacob Lischy, set out for Ephrata by way of Tulpehocken, and arrived upon the same day at the settlement on the Cocalico, where he was hospitably received by Prior Onesimus and lodged in the convent Zion. The following morning Count Zinzendorf presented himself to the Prior and told of his intention of having an official interview with the Vorsteher, further, that he was going to use the lot to advise him whether to present himself before Beissel or summon the latter to appear before him. Onesimus advised against this, and announced him officially to the Vorsteher.

The latter, however, who regarded himself as of a higher rank in the theosophical fraternity, considered it against his dignity to call on Zinzendorf, and issued an edict for the Count to come to him and in open Chapter acknowledge his superior authority. This the Count naturally refused to do, probably being more or less influenced in his action by his entertainers —the Eckerlings. So he, too, stood on his dignity, and eventually left the Community without meeting Conrad Beissel.

The *Chronicon* in commenting upon this episode, says: "Thus did two great lights of the Church meet as on the threshold, and yet neither ever saw the other in his life."

What effect the union of these two forces would have had upon the German population of this and the adjoining counties, had the two leaders met and agreed to work in unison, is hard at the present day even to surmise. The similarity of some of their ideas is apparent from the fact that the Moravians, as well as the Ephrata Community, erected and maintained separate brother and sister houses. Moreover, after the Moravians came into possession of the Whitefield house, now Nazareth, they for a long time used the name first given to the projected institution, Ephrata, while the Brethren themselves were known as "the Community of St. John" (*Johannische Gemeinde*).

Upon Zinzendorf's return to Germantown he wrote a letter to Beissel to the purport that he should descend from his spiritual height, that others might sit alongside of him without danger to their lives, of which the Vorsteher remarked :

"If I were as great as he supposes, he would not have been afraid of me."

Beissel subsequently answered the Count's letter by the following missive :

"Abundant salvation and blessing from God and His rich Spirit, together with the communion of the holy Divine power, and in all that furthers the holy and internal growth of the secret life of Grace hidden in God.

" I hardly know what power induces me to issue this mite unto you, without perceiving some inner deep and very secret draughts of love, which urge and challenge me. Should it strike in the Spirit, it would be well, if in future the heavens would make truth and justice drop down from above, and honesty grow upon the earth, and the children of man be taught the truth. Then there would be some hope of recovery. Alas! wither shall we turn, that the universal evil and corruption be constrained? Is it not the rock of our salvation, Jesus Christ the Son of God, who came down from heaven, whom the Father gave all authority in heaven and earth, and made Him Heir and Lord over all? So necessarily now our only salvation, and the treasures of His wisdom, lie in Him and concealed in His counsels, in and out of which all fulness of grace is derived.

" It would certainly mean an entire new church reformation, and indeed, primarily, one with an entire outwardly healthy natural morality ; in which certainly the teachings, which the Son of God brought down from heaven, would be kept back and behind a mountain : for instance, when one deals with the mysteries of the love which Jesus entertained toward His disciples, and refused to trust to the world.

" In this sense, can much good be in truth accomplished in our times, that is, so long as the Gospel remains free. It is also acknowledged by most true theologians that there is no more dangerous matter than when a man without proper knowledge touches upon the meaning and intent of the Gospel.

" N. B.—The object of the Gospel is not the punishment, but the remission, of Sin.   So if we avow the Gospel without an internal conversion of the heart (where first an outward conversion must take place by works of righteousness) it is of no service to man.

" Then, even as there are two Testaments, so there is also a two-fold application of the same.   And each hath its own manner and time, in the Divine worship, with the appointed time of the Father, etc.   So there are also in these two Testaments two kinds of births : one, that in servitude ; the other, which is born in freedom, etc.

" It is therefore perceived in a strong degree of light that almost all outward Divine worship, as the same appears outwardly, and even what Christ suffered outwardly, was of the Old Testament, and born in the servitude.

" Even for this reason there are so few essential Christians. As the Jew with his righteousness is not sufficient, and consequently needs a conversion, so the lawless heathen places himself in the Gospel, wherefrom such a lawless anti-Christianity is born as we now have at the present day.

" In this sense I can, in a certain measure, stake not a little : when to wit, give us one still better, as in this our time much can be wrought and accomplished among us, provided, however, God be the cause, albeit not necessarily present.   For my own part, I have never felt the presence of God so near in sacrifice or in worship as in the mortal life of Jesus, or when I must hang with him upon the cross between two malefactors.

"Even in the same manner have I, in Him, lost my fair features, so that they are now less comely than those of others. This sun of tribulation has already burned into me so strong that its fire can hardly ever be extinguished within me until the day of eternity, when God will wipe away all tears from our eyes."

Ephrata, the 9th of
Eleventh month, 1741.

> This trifle from me, Friedsam, Fr., otherwise called Conrad Beissel, at present a stranger and pilgrim in this world.

P. S.—This little missive is an outcome of a very secret and intimate epitome of the Spirit. Pray proceed in this so far as practicable, according to the utmost rules of love.

The fourth Synod was again scheduled to be held at Ephrata (March 21, 1741), but the episode and resulting correspondence just related made a change in Zinzendorf's plans desirable, and the meeting was called at Germantown, to meet in the house of John Ashmead, near the market house, and almost opposite the German Reformed church. Nothing of note occurred relative to the Sabbatarians at this gathering.

April 18th. The Synod met for the fifth time, and in the Reformed church in Germantown. This meeting was chiefly conspicuous for the quarrel between Count Zinzendorf and Christopher Sauer.

The sixth Synod assembled on May 16th at the house of Lorentz Schmelzer, also at Germantown.

June 12, 1741. The seventh and last of the Pennsylvania Synods met at the house of Edward Evans, on the north side of Race street, above Second street, in Philadelphia.

But little was accomplished by the various conferences toward bringing about an evangelical union of all the Germans in the Province, irrespective of creed or denomination. The chief result was a flood of vituperative literature, much of which, fortunately, was not printed. Sauer, in a letter to Germany, dated March 26, 1742, writes:

"I have had no time yet to print for them [156] except "when he [157] arrived here, a little hymn book of six sheets "for beginners, which I judged to be harmless. Since "then I have cut off his correspondence. If I had printed "all that was offered *pro* and *con*, it would have been a "comedy; for here the people are mostly children of Adam "and know naught of the count."

This hymn-book, a duodecimo of 95 pages, printed by Christopher Sauer, was entitled:

Hirten Lieder | von | Bethlehem, | zum Gebrauch | vor alles was arm ist, | was klein und gering ist.

It was prepared for publication by Count Zinzendorf within six days after his arrival in the Province, and contained a small selection of old and new hymns suitable for the use of all denominations. This was the first literary outcome of the Moravian missionary movement in America. This book is so scarce that even the Pennsylvania Historical Society does not own a copy.[158] The fac-simile of the title-page and advertisement upon its reverse is from the copy in the collection of Hon. Samuel W. Pennypacker.

Among the earliest issues of the Ephrata Brotherhood was a printed broadside written by Onesimus. It is not known to a certainty whether this sheet was printed upon the first press of the Community or that of Christopher Sauer. It gave a short account of the reasons why the Ephrata Community refused to affiliate with the Moravian

---

[156] The Moravians.

[157] Count Zinzendorf.

[158] *Proceedings of the Pennsylvania-German Society,* vol. vi, p. 9, *et seq.*

Hirten Lieder

Von

Bethlehem,

Zum Gebrauch

Vor alles was arm ist,
Was klein und gering ist.

Germantown, gedruckt bey C. Saur, 1742.

Dieses Büchlein ist zu haben in Philadelphia, bey Benjamin Franklin. In Germantown, bey Christoph Saur, oder Johannes Bechtel. Im Falckner Schwamm, bey Henrich Antes. Und in Canastoge, bey Johannes Hildebrand.

Brethren. Both German and English versions were printed for distribution. In these we find a new and interesting account of the visits and reception of Zinzendorf and some of his followers at Ephrata.

From this account it would appear that Count Zinzendorf made two visits to the Kloster, followed by one from his daughter Benigna, and still later another from a Moravian Elder and his wife:

"Now it so happened that the Count came to us a second time, and we felt it our duty to receive him in the most cordial manner, especially as they had already passed their judgment upon us in the most hostile way, as at all times enviers of God's truth have done. It would, therefore, not be meet for us to retaliate in the same manner, but rather to the contrary. For that was our watchword, whereby we gained the complete separation in our hand, so that we may now with our holdings stand apart from them. Consequently we are entirely free and liberated. Upon our side, as we in a modest manner can demonstrate, notwithstanding that they had attempted to prove the contrary.

"But as they, to all appearances, were entirely ignorant about us, they attempted to find further entrance among us, and if possible, to incite a longing after a foul doctrine. Therefore shortly afterwards they made another visit to us, to wit, the Count's daughter [159] with her Vorsteher and his wife came to us. We received them in the same manner, as we held it unnecessary to say a single detrimental word either in their presence or absence.

"We took special pains to meet them upon every occasion with all discreetness, and without showing the least intention of entering into any intimacy with them, as they had already placed the full proof in our hands, wherefrom we easily perceived that they did not wish to reach the good in our Community.

---

[159] See page 428 supra.

"Furthermore, we felt complete freedom, as honorable persons, to extend all courtesy to them. Notwithstanding all this, the matter did not end here, as they could not desist from spying into our affairs and troubling themselves further about us. It seems as if they did not know us rightly, or they would have saved themselves this trouble.

"It is to be added that shortly afterwards, another visit was made to us. This was from two persons, a woman and a man, who was said to be one of their teachers, and who came to us in Zion Convent, felt in duty bound to receive him as our guest, and after the evening meal-time several of our brethren came together to welcome him, and show him our good will; when all at once certain words were spoken, which caused a very bad feeling within us. As he soon let us know what his intentions were; he also told us of the woman who went to the Sister House, and how she was inclined to remain there for some time. But as the matter continued more unclean to us, and caused considerable pressure, so we made cause to speak further with them, especially about their strange work, whereby they sought to draw so many young people unto them; and when they had them in their hands, they made men and women out of them.

"We told them that to us this appeared very strange and absurd, as we did not know of a single instance of a saint in the new dispensation from whom it could be shown that, by such a carnal increase of the Church of God, it would profit. On the contrary, we see it as clear as sunshine that Christ and his apostles built the Church of God upon an entirely different foundation, and continued it by other means," [160] etc.

---

[160] "Ein kurtzer Bericht von den Ursachen, warum die Gemeinschaft in Ephrata sich mit dem Grafen Zinzendorf und seinen Leuten eingelasssen. Und wie sich eine so grosse Ungleichheit im Ausgang der Sachen auf beyden seiten befunden." No original copy is known, as what was left

Several efforts were subsequently made by Zinzendorf to induce the secular brethren of the Ephrata Community to leave the fold of the Sabbatarians and unite with the Moravians; but the scheme was always foiled by the influence of Beissel, or the actions of his deputies who attended the conference. The explanation given in reference to this non-agreement of the two leaders is in an old German MSS., seen by the writer some years ago, and probably offers the correct solution: "They were both hard unyielding stones, and two hard burrs grind no grain."

of these broadsides were burned together with the Eckerling papers by order of Beissel at the time of their expulsion from the settlement, *Chronicon Ephratense*, chap. xxv.

The translation is made from the reprint in *Fresenius Nachrichten, III*, pp. 462–474.

PICTURE OF ST. JOHN ON FLY-LEAF OF
BRUDER AMOS' "MARTYR SPIEGEL."

CHAPTER XXX.

THE ORDER OF THE MUSTARD SEED.

KEEN and eager to carry the Gospel to all people, Count Zinzendorf extended his excursions into the Indian country beyond the Blue Ridge and personally supervised a plan for its civilization.

The decade between 1740 and 1750 presents a period of religious awakening, excitement and enthusiasm,—call it what what you will,—unparalleled in the history of the Province. Within this period is embraced the establishment of the monastic feature of the Ephrata Community; the advent of the Moravian Brethren; the thorough organization of the German Dunker Church; the visit of Whitefield and its attendant excitement; the bitter feud and schism among the Presbyterians; the advent of Mühlenberg and his efforts to firmly establish the Lutheran Church in this country; the coming of regular clergy of the Reformed faith; and the numerous revivals in the Baptist Church; together with the decline of the Society of Friends, both politically and religiously; all of which falls within this short period of time.

Thus far but little attention has been given by writers on Pennsylvania history to the influences exercised by the various mystical, theosophical and cabbalistic societies and fraternities of Europe in the evangelization of this Province, and in reclaiming the German settlers from the rationalism with which they were threatened by their contact with the English Quakers.

Labadie's teachings; Boehme's visions; the true Rosicrucianism of the original Kelpius party; the Philadelphian Society, whose chief apostle was Jane Leade; the fraternity that taught the Restitution of all things; the mystical fraternity, led by Dr. Johan Wilhelm Petersen and his wife Elenora von Merlau—both members of the Frankfort company—all found a foothold upon the soil of Penn's colony, and exercised a much larger share in the development of this country than is accorded to them. It has even been claimed by some superficial writers and historians of the day that there was no strain of mysticism whatever in the Ephrata Community, or, in fact, connected with any of the early German movements in Pennsylvania. Such a view is refuted by the writings of Kelpius, Beissel, Miller and many others, who then lived, sought the Celestial Bridegroom, and awaited the millennium which they earnestly believed to be near.

With the advent of the Moravian Brethren in Pennsylvania, the number of these mystical orders was increased by the introduction of two others, viz., the Order of the Passion of Jesus (*Der Orden des Leidens Jesu*) of which Count Zinzendorf was grand commander, and the Order of the Mustard Seed (*Der Senfkorn Orden*).

These two fraternities differed somewhat from those just enumerated, as there was a missionary feature connected with them. The object of the members was not confined to seeking the inner light; to attaining spiritual or physical regeneration and perfection; to studying mystical speculations on the divine essence, to revelling in the embraces of the celestial Sophia; or to gazing anxiously at the skies for the appearance of the expected harbinger who would announce the millennium. Their chief aim was a far more practical one, for, in addition to theosophical belief, it was incumbent upon every member of both fraternities to go willingly to any part of the globe to spread the Gospel of Christ.

The relation of these two orders to each other was somewhat similar to that of the Blue Lodges of Free Masonry to the Grand Lodge. The Order of the Mustard Seed was the lower body, while the Order of the Passion of Jesus was formed of such of the bishops and clergy of the Unitas Fratrum as had passed through the various degrees of the lower order. To the latter organization the laity of both sexes were eligible for membership, but not for advancement to the higher body, as the elective offices were almost always restricted to the clerical members.

ARMS OF HALLE.

The history of these orders dates back to the early years of the eighteenth century; they owe their inception to Count Zinzendorf, when he was attending the Pädagogium at Halle, being then fourteen years of age. Here five lads banded themselves together, under certain principles, based upon the teachings of Jesus, looking toward extending the Kingdom of God upon earth. The little band of embryo missionaries called themselves "Slaves of Virtue" (*Die Tugend Sclaven*).

The insignia of the order, when first constituted, was a medal with an "Ecce Homo,"[161] surrounded by the inscription *Nostra Medala*. The interest and enthusiasm of these few was not permitted to flag, and by the activity of Zinzendorf rapidly increased. After an existence of several years some changes were made in the ritual, when the fraternity became known as "The Society

---

[161] "Behold the man": a picture which represents the Saviour as given up to the people by Pilate.

of the Professors of Jesus Christ" (*Die Gesellschaft der Bekenner Jesu Christi*). The influence of the fraternity was now extended to aristocratic circles, and in the year 1724 was again reconstructed, and regular rules and statutes of the Order were issued under the name of " The Order of the Mustard Seed " *Den Orden vom Senfkorn*). This had reference to the parable of the Mustard Seed (Mark iv, 30–32).

In the reconstruction of the Order these original rules, formulated in 1714, were adopted for the government of the fraternity.

THE ARTICLES OF THE ORDER OF THE MUSTARD SEED,
    FROM A TRANSLATION (ABOUT 1744) FROM THE
        LATIN ORIGINAL OF 1714.

The view with which the members of our Society from its beginning till the year last past have bound themselves, may be seen from what follows :

I.—The members of our Society will love the whole human race.

II.—They will seek to further the welfare of the same by all ways and means.

III.—They will seek to unite souls to their Creator, and also to their Redeemer, as soon as they know any thing of Him.

IV.—They will act uprightly, and though circumspectly and guardedly, yet always without dissimulation.

V.—They will not hurry anything, but after due consideration first had, proceed in it with certainty.

VI.—They will not long consider about entering in at ye doors, which the providence of God shall from time to time open for the furtherance of his work, and which is for them to do therein, cheerfully and undauntedly to do it : But they will take the utmost care ; that in the Prosecution of this, no pass already open may be caused to be shut.

VII.—Should any one have an Adversary, who oppresses him, and who is hurtfull to him in his person.   But the work of our Common Lord prospers in his Hand : He shall not hinder him, but shall afford him all imaginable Assistance. That his work may succeed, and great profit accrue therefrom.

VIII.—To the casting off of some good Things, altho' they may not be agreeable to us, yet no one shall lay a hand to it, without the Strictest and Exactest Examination made, but much rather assist the Re-establishing of ye same.

IX.—We will all avoid that exceeding pernicious (but in our Times grown a quite natural) principle, of introducing Innovations in Doctrine, Moral, or Ceremony, but much rather Strive and help to restore the old, wch has of all preeminence, where it can be done without the suspicion of a Renovation, and what is once introduced, rather Sanctify, than cast off.

X.—We will according to our Saviours advise, not mix new Regulations with the ye old and superannuated Ones, that the Breach be not made worse.

XI.—The works of the Lord wch have of long Time been cover^d over with Darkness, but thro Divine Marvelous Grace preserv'd and restor'd to their former Brightness. We will be studious to maintain, and keep in their Lustre.

XII.—If any one acts Uprightly, and has a good Intention, such a one we will with all our power, Assist, Admonish and Help forward, & if he has an uncertain, or as yet an unsolved plan, we will not therefore despise him, but help him into it, that our common Lord may be served with united powers.

XIII.—When these and such like things are happily compleated according to the Lord's good pleasure, Then we will lay us down to Sleep, We shall have deserv'd nothing, we will tho' lay us cheerfully down to Sleep, when we have done the Lord's Will here in Time, pray for Mercy, Hope in the Grace which the Cross of Christ has Purchased.

After Labouring, Rest is Sweet.

It will be noticed that in neither the ritual of the Zionitic Brotherhood, nor that of the Order of the Mustard Seed, does there appear any penal oath or affirmation; the obligation must have been a moral one. As a matter of fact, nearly all the Pennsylvania Sectarians objected to taking an oath, judicial or extrajudicial, under any consideration or in any form.

We have here an interesting problem for the students and members of the oath-bound secret societies of the present day ; as in no case, so far as known to the writer, were the secrets or esoteric rituals of these societies ever exposed or communicated to the outer world.

The reconstructed society now rapidly increased in membership.   Among the patrons of the Order were Christian VI of Denmark ; John Potter, Archbishop of Canterbury ; Thomas Wilson, Bishop of Sodor and Man ; the Cardinal of Noailles ; General Oglethorpe, Governor of Georgia; and numerous other notables of the time.

One of the peculiar features of this fraternity of the Mustard Seed was the arrangement by which members were often kept unknown to each other, and their connection with the Order carefully concealed from all.   This feature was but similar to the ritual of the Rosicrucian fraternity, where the candidate never knew the *frater* who received him at his profession.

Shortly before Zinzendorf's journey to America the Order was extended into England and Holland, and a proposition was made to publish the names of the patrons and members of the society.   This called forth a reply, which later appeared in the *Büdingische Sammlung*.   This sets forth " that the Order was one which also admitted private persons of civilian condition as an incentive to virtue and advancement of righteous knowledge.   It was established during the early years of the present [XVIII] century, and flourished in laudable quiet and secrecy, so that many a worthy member of the same has already passed away from this world without being known to all his fellow-members.   As from that time until now persons of such quality and conditions have been connected therewith, it has not been found advisable to incorporate their names upon our registers, nor would it be policy to publish them at the present time, as a number of the Seniors of our Society have neither call nor inclination to cut any figure in the material world. Then again there are persons who would count it a great indiscretion if, by our fault, what to them is held as a great secret should become a matter of speculation to the general public," etc.

The grand insignia of the reconstructed Order of the Mustard Seed was a gold cross[162] with green enameled edges. A large oval in the centre of the cross was enameled blue, upon which a mustard tree (?) was painted in the natural colors, surrounded by the inscription in gold: *Quot fuit ante nihil.* In the angles of the cross were represented sprouting grains of mustard, in which three seeds were seen. The remaining space between the arms of the cross was filled in with golden rays. These insignia were worn by the grand commander, suspended around his neck by a golden chain, the links of which typified sprouting mustard seeds and were symbolical of the Order. For the officers of secular grade the insignia were suspended from a piece of sea-green (*Meer-gruen*) silk ribbon in the place of a gold chain. The clerical brethren used a white silk ribbon with sea-green edges.

All persons upon their initiation into the Order received a gold ring,[163] which, during the ceremony, was placed on the third finger of the left hand. This ring was to be worn at all times. It was enameled white with green edges, and the inscription was in Greek characters: $Οὐδεὶς ἡμῶν ἑαυτῷ ξῇ$ (Rom. xiv, 6).

A number of this confraternity were among the early Moravians as well as a few in the Ephrata Community;[164] but who they were, or how many, is a matter which is lost in oblivion. Neither the numbered breast-stones nor the

---

[162] The original was about double the size of the engraving. A single specimen only of this decoration is known to be in existence.

[163] Five of these rings are known.

[164] Gottlieb Haberecht is an example of the latter.

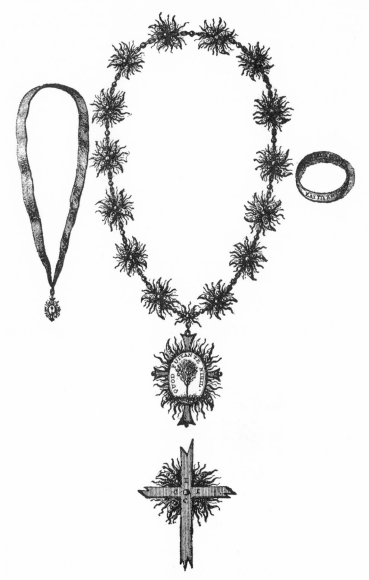

JEWELS AND INSIGNIA OF THE ORDER OF THE MUSTARD SEED.

burial records of either community, so far as known to the
writer, makes any mention of the Order. How many of
these rings there may be in the numbered graves of Bethlehem, Nazareth, Lititz, Philadelphia, or the other God's
acres of the Moravian and Sabbatarian Brethren throughout the Province will perhaps never be known.

The third insignia of the Order, the Mantel-Cross (*Das
Mantelkreutz*), was a large cross worn over the heart upon
the left side of the purple cloak which formed a part of the
regalia, after the manner of the Knights Templar and St.
John. The shape was that of a Latin cross, and was formed
of silver braid. In the centre was fastened a single grain
of mustard, encircled by the embroidered monogram :

This denoted *Crescit Christo in immensum*, doubtless in
allusion to Ephesians iv, 13. The members of this fraternity, irrespective of sex, willingly went to any part of
the globe, wherever sent by the superiors, to enlighten the
benighted or the heathen with
the glorious truths of the Gospel
of Christ.

INSIGNIA OF THE ORDER OF
THE PASSION OF JESUS.

The insignia of the higher fraternity consisted of a gold medal,
in the centre of which was the
manifestation of Christ with two
kneeling figures upon each side,
the whole surrounded by the inscription in Latin type : *Wir
Halten Über der Bekenntnis vom
Leiden Iesu.*

The grand cross was a Latin cross of gold. Upon the
upper limb was a full length figure of Christ in relief,
representing his manifestation. Upon the arms of the cross

were portrayed a number of prostrated figures, also in relief, adoring the risen Christ. Upon the lower limb appeared a chalice, surmounted by a passion cross. This jewel was worn upon the breast, suspended by a ribbon around the neck, and is shown upon the portrait of Bishop John Nitschman.

The first practical results of the teachings of the Order of the Mustard Seed in America culminated on February 22, 1742, during the last session of the second Pennsylvania Synod, when three Indians, from Shecomoco, as the Diary states, were " baptized into the death of Jesus." The scene was an impressive one, even though it was not celebrated in a vaulted cathedral, with organ, trombone and kettledrum, accompanied by the voices of trained choristers, and all the churchly surroundings of medieval pomp. The ceremony which marked the commencement of the Moravian missionary work in America was held upon the plain humble barn-floor of John de Turck at Oley, to which the attendants of the synod adjourned, because it was larger than any room in his house, where the synod was held.

The Indian converts had come by appointment from Schecomoco to be admitted into the Christian church. For this purpose the barn was improvised for a meeting-house, and a large tub of water was placed upon the floor. After prayer and invocation, the three Indians knelt around the tub, and leaning over the edge, were solemnly baptized by missionary Christian Rauch, in the presence of the assembled synod and of Bishops David Nitschman and Zinzendorf ; the former Bishop wearing the Rosy Cross ; the latter, the *Crux Aurea* of the Order of the Passion of Jesus, prominently displayed upon the front of their snow-white and crimson-girdled surplices.

Thus were the first three Indian converts of the Moravian Church ushered into the Christian faith in the presence of two grand commanders of our Mystic Brotherhood.

BISHOP JOHN NITSCHMAN.

BORN, 1703; DIED, 1772.

WITH GRAND CROSS OF THE ORDER OF THE "LEIDEN JESU."

The names given to these converts were Abraham to *Shabash*, Isaac to *Seim* and Jacob to *Kiop*. In the course of time, as the number of Indian converts increased, they were divided into classes or degress, somewhat similar to the *Senfkorn Orden;* viz., apprentices, candidates, baptized and communicants; and an effort was made to incite a love for theosophic mysticism among them, thus to establish an aboriginal American branch of the Order of the Mustard Seed—a scheme which, however, soon had to be abandoned, owing to the character of the material from which it was proposed to recruit.

MYSTIC SEAL OF THE EPHRATA CLOISTER.

ROM the facts presented in the preceding chapters it will be seen that the theosophical enthusiasts, both male and female, were by no means allowed to idle away any of their time, for, when not at their devotions or taking the rest necessary to maintain their strength, they were kept employed in the various departments of the Ephrata economy under the able management of the Eckerlings; and when, finally, the communal life was formally instituted, all private ownership of property was, as the *Chronicon* states, declared an "Ananias sin." This, however, only referred to the Solitary. The Sabbatarian congregation at large, or "domestic households," accumulated property as best they could, but were supposed to make daily offerings in the shape of tithes, such as vegetables or other produce suitable for the sustenance of the Solitary members.

Owing to the success of their plans, the Eckerlings now conceived a scheme for inducing such members of the secular congregation as occupied land adjoining the settle-

---

[165] This chapter, as well as that of Saron and Bethania are grouped together somewhat out of their chronological order for the purpose of bringing the description of all of the various Kloster buildings into this volume.

ment to bring themselves to a still higher spiritual condition. The plan was to erect a large building to be divided into two parts, one for the fathers the other for the mothers; and upon their entering this establishment their farms and landed estates were to be handed over to the Brotherhood, thus becoming convent property. This cunningly devised scheme to possess themselves of the settlers' lands and improvements was presented to the Vorsteher, with arguments based upon the fact that several couples had of late followed the example set by Jephune in the autumn of 1730, and Simeon in 1739, who separated from their wives, the men entering Zion the women Kedar, the most prominent among these late divorcees being Rudolph Nägele (Jehoiada) and Sigmund Landert (Shealtiel). Further, they represented that there were many others prepared to take the same course. Beissel's consent to the scheme was thus secured.

It was several years, however, before the Eckerlings could perfect their plans, consequently it was not until the spring of 1744 that they were warranted in building a house for this express purpose. This new structure was built at right angles with Peniel, and was called Hebron.[166] The name was selected for this structure, as according to the mystical theosophy it signified the common tomb of the Patriarchs. In Ephrata it symbolized the end of conjugal life. The mystical speculations regarding Hebron date back to the earliest ages; they are probably a relic of the Moloch fire cult. Hebron, the place or city of fire (*Uro*, to burn up), was under the rule of Ephron the son of Zohar (Gen. xxiii, 8), and was selected by Abraham as a burying place, and so became the sepulcher of the Patriarchs, and it was believed that the place at the end of time would be consumed with celestial fire together with all of the remains interred there.[167]

---

[166] Also called Das Haus der Gemeinschaft.

[167] *Zohar*, Gen. f. 124, Amsterdam edition.

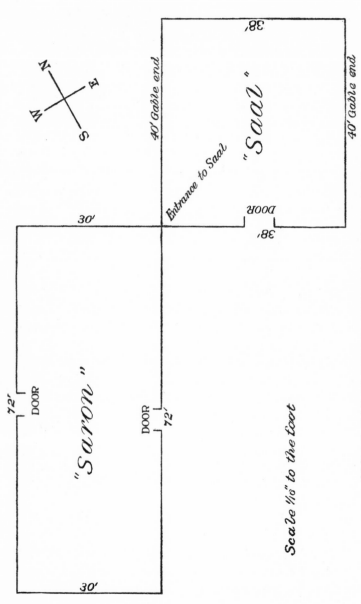

GROUND PLAN OF HEBRON (SARON) AND PENIEL (THE SAAL).

By Christmas, 1743, the new house was ready for occupation. Its dimensions were seventy by thirty feet. It was divided into two parts, one of which was to be occupied by the men, with an entrance on the north side. The other part was for the matrons, their entrance being from the south side. It was so designed that each division was a counterpart of the other. In addition there were rooms, chambers and a hall for love-feasts, similar to those in Zion and Kedar, and in order to fully introduce the monastic discipline, several of the Zionitic Brotherhood moved into the house and took charge of the services. Johann Sensemann was installed as *Bruder Schaffner* or general steward.

Upon the day set for the dedication, January 12, 1744, the whole community assembled at Peniel. After impressive services a procession was formed, and wended its way toward the stream amidst the pealing of the Kloster bells and the chanting of hymns. When the pool was reached those of the brethren and sisters who were to enter Hebron were re-baptized in the icy flood of the Cocalico. At the close of the ceremony the party again wended its way toward the prayer-saal. After dry clothing was assumed, religious services were resumed in Peniel, during which the letters of divorce, that had been prepared by Onesimus and which had been previously signed by the interested parties, were handed to the house-fathers and matrons who had voluntarily divorced themselves with the intention of improving their spiritual condition by living separate lives in Hebron.

The *Chronicon*, in describing this peculiar arrangement, states :

"This new institution was for some time richly blessed
"by God, for these good people were not only very simple-
"minded, but bore a great love toward God ; they also were
"very benevolent, and harbored many poor widows whom

"they maintained out of their own means, so that their "household resembled a hospital more than a convent."

That a condition of affairs so foreign to a sound public policy could not succeed in the new Province might have been foreseen. Even the promoters of the scheme found that although a number entered the convent and nominally divorced themselves, they still held on to their landed property. This was just what the Eckerlings did not intend them to do. Then, as many of these couples had left their children in charge of their farms, or in the care of other members of the congregation, parental feelings gradually commenced to assert themselves, and it soon became evident that the scheme was destined to end in failure.

Another danger which threatened the new institution was the action of the civil authorities, who took steps to investigate these extra judicial divorces, proceedings which according to one account, were first instituted by Conrad Weiser, who it will be recalled was for a time an active inmate of the Ephrata institution, but as his ambition for worldly honors was greater than his religious fervor, he made use of the Community for his personal advancement,[168] and finally accepted a commission as justice of the peace, which at that time was equal to a Common Pleas judge. As soon as this became known he was sharply reprimanded by Beissel, which naturally led to a rupture between the two men, and caused much feeling between the new justice and his former brethren. Another force that influenced Weiser at that time was the intimacy which had sprung up between him and Rev. Mühlenberg, and resulted in the latter marrying Weiser's daughter, Anna Maria. Mühlenberg, as in duty bound, did his best to bring his prospective father-in-law and his family back into the Lutheran faith,

---

[168] Conrad Weiser's letter of resignation from the Ephrata Community will appear in the next volume.

and at the same time used all of his persuasive powers against the Ephrata Community and their peculiar rites and observances.

So even before the new Community in Hebron was fairly settled in its habitation legal processes were issued against the leading members of the Zionitic Brotherhood, a proceeding for which Weiser was held responsible by the Kloster authorities. It is stated in an old manuscript that Conrad Weiser claimed, in his own defence, that the information against the Community was not instigated by him, but was lodged by one Abraham Paul and one Merkel; further, that he thereupon wrote to Beissel in reference to the matter. Beissel's letter-book, however, is said to contain nothing in reference to this correspondence.

Subsequently Onesimus and Jaebez went to Weiser and induced him to discontinue the suit. This he promised to do, but it seems that notwithstanding this promise the case was reported to Governor Thomas and a process issued. At the hearing, however, the two prosecutors failed to appear and the case against the Community fell. The problem was now left to work out its own solution. For this they had not long to wait. The first trouble arose among the house-mothers, who naturally longed for their children who had been left at home in charge of the farms, and were subject to all the allurements and temptations of the world. Others, again, suffered from neglect and the want of maternal care,—facts that were not slow in reaching the ears of the matrons in Hebron; so it was not long before one after the other demanded that her husband should again rejoin her and return to their old home. When this feeling was brought to the notice of Beissel, he without hesitation advised every house-father to again receive his helpmate and return to his former condition,—advice which was acted upon and resulted happily in every case.

After the last couple to renounce their solitary state had

reunited, a special convocation was called of all the orders. An altar was erected in the angle formed by Peniel and Hebron,. upon which, after an impressive divine service, the divorces or articles of separation were solemnly cremated. Thus ended this remarkable episode in the history of the Ephrata Community. Hebron, now vacant, was handed over for the use of the widows and poor of the settlement, which had been sheltered by the Hebron Community, and were now supported by the labor of the Zionitic Brotherhood.

A new complication, however, arose shortly after the final reunion of the households. Some of the late inmates, who had contributed largely toward the erection of the building, under the impression that it was to be their permanent home, now demanded the return of their contributions. The largest of these creditors, Heinrich Miller, who had given his whole property to the fund, was reimbursed with one hundred acres of Community land. To pacify the others Zion Prayer-Saal was handed over to them for the uses of the secular congregation. By these measures all claims against Peniel and Hebron were released.

THE SAAL AND SISTER HOUSE IN 1898.

CHAPTER XXXII.

SARON.

FTER the failure of what may be designated as the Hebron project, a proposition was made to hand over to the uses of the Sisterhood the two buildings in the meadow. This suggestion meeting with the approval of Beissel and other leaders, steps were taken forthwith to carry it into effect.

The proposition was that the Order of Spiritual Virgins should be reorganized into an order similar to the Zionitic Brotherhood, and that thenceforward the female celibates should be known as the "Roses of Saron." This designation was based upon the mystical interpretation of the second chapter of the Song of Solomon. Hebron was to become Saron, and Peniel the "Schwester-Saal," and these two names, Saron and Saal, have remained until the present day. Kedar was to be handed over to the uses of the widows who had been temporarily quartered in Hebron.

Efforts were immediately begun to prepare the two houses for the purposes of the reorganized Sisterhood; it was not, however, until the first week in July, 1745, that the necessary repairs, alterations and renovation were completed.

The dedication took place July 13, 1745, and as usual

was made an occasion of more or less ceremonial. Not the least interesting of the inaugural solemnities was a midnight procession of both orders from Mount Zion to Peniel, or the Schwester-Saal as it was henceforth called, where the sisters with an elaborate ritual dedicated themselves afresh to the heavenly Bridegroom. They also took the vow of allegiance and obedience to their spiritual mother and superintendent, "Mutter Maria" (Maria Eicher). It was upon this occasion that Beissel composed a special dedication hymn, which contained a prophecy respecting Ephrata, a prophecy which has been verified. This hymn, in elegant terms, invoked steadfastness of purpose among the brethren and sisters of the Kloster, and prophetically laments the downfall, contingent upon declension therefrom, in most affecting strains. Following is a stanza from this hymn of the Vorsteher :

> Auch Ephrata, wird hier so lange stehen,
> Als Jungfrauen darinn am Reihen gehen ;
> Wann aber dieser Adel wird aufhören,
> So wird die Rache dieses Ort verstören.

Translation :

> Even Ephrata will here endure, so long
> As virgins therein in order stand ;
> But when this nobility shall decline,
> Then shall vengeance this spot destroy.

Thenceforth the Sisterhood became a separate order, entirely independent of the Brotherhood ; Father Friedsam Gottrecht (Beissel), however, was acknowledged as the spiritual director and leader.

The celibates were now divided into seven classes, each class having its own special duties. The arrangement of Saron was such that several cells or *kammern* opened out upon a common room containing a fireplace and other conveniences. Each of these common rooms was used by the respective class for their own special economy,—thus there was one for spinning, another for writing, and so for singing, for basket weaving, for quilting, sewing and embroidery, etc. Each class was under a sub-inspectoress, who was alone responsible to the Mother Superior.[169]

A separate house-diary or *Schwester-chronic* was commenced. This curious manuscript was still in existence a decade ago, and was then copied by the present writer.

The first of the Sisterhood to leave this transitory life and go forth to join the celestial Bridegroom beyond the skies, was Bernice, who died of consumption, while the Sisterhood were yet in Kedar, November 30, 1743, in the thirty-second year of her age. She was Leonard Heidt's daughter, a beautiful girl, who lived with her parents at Oley, and after a visit from the Solitary Brethren to her father's house was so enraptured with the thought of a spiritual life that she followed them to the settlement and became one of the founders of the Sisterhood.

During her illness she suffered great pain; longing for release, she, while in despair, would ask to be struck in the head with an axe, and thus be relieved from this world's suffering.

After death had come to her relief, her burial was made the means of an imposing ceremony, at midnight by torchlight. The corpse was carried upon a bier by six cowled monks from Zion, followed by the Sisterhood and brethren, carrying rushlights and chanting a dirge composed for the occasion. Weird and ghostly was the procession as it wended its way slowly over the frozen ground from Mount Zion to the new God's acre by the roadside.[170] The footfalls upon the hard ground; the sighing of the winter winds; the mournful tolling of the convent bells; the doleful chant of the two orders; with the darkness of the night

---

[169] The various changes made in Peniel, upon being handed over to the Sisterhood, have already been described in a previous chapter.

[170] There is a tradition that sister Bernice was the first interment in the God's acre by the roadside.

broken only by the flickering torches,—all added to the solemnity of the occasion, and formed a scene fit for portrayal by the pencil of a master artist or the pen of a poet.

The body was consigned to the earth with the full ritual of the Zionitic Brotherhood. The room which Bernice had occupied in Kedar was now closed for a time, and the following *segenspruch* was placed upon the walls of the kammer to her memory.   It was composed by Beissel and executed by the sisters in ornamental *fractur-schrift :*

"*Bernice, Freue dich in ihrem gang unter der Schaaf-weide, und sey freundlich u. huldreich unter den Lieb-habern.*"

Translation :

" Bernice, enjoy yourself in your sojourn among the sheep-pastures, and be affable and gracious among the suitors."

THE GERMAN SECTARIANS OF PENNSYLVANIA.

THE OLD BROTHER HOUSE—(BETHANIA).

CHAPTER XXXIII.

BETHANIA.

HE Eckerlings, while yet in the zenith of their power, conceived a plan for building a large addition or wing to the Zion Convent. This house was to contain no less than one hundred *kammern* or cells for that number of male celibates, together with the necessary community rooms and offices requisite for their comfort. The plan of this house in many respects was formed after that of the old monasteries in the Fatherland, and if it had been erected as originally designed would, together with the other houses on Zion hill, have formed a most unique group of buildings, and offered ample accommodation for the anticipated arrivals of novices that were expected to come from both at home and abroad.

Most extensive preparations were made for the early completion of this new monastery. The foundations of the new structure were laid, the timbers were prepared, and the needed boards were seasoning in piles down by the saw-mill.

In the midst of this activity, however, an event occurred which not only changed the plan for building this house, but affected the general policy of the Community as well. This was no less than the expulsion or dethronement of the Eckerlings,—an episode which will be fully described elsewhere in this work.

After the departure of the Eckerling party, all work upon the new building ceased. It was then proposed that the Community erect a brother house in the meadow near to the Sister House, Saron, and thus utilize the building material which had been prepared for the monastery. This proposition, which came from Brother Jaebez, who in the meantime (viz., on March 23, 1746) was appointed as Prior, met with general favor. A week later (March 31, 1746) the building of the new Brother House in the meadow was commenced under the direction of Brother Shealtiel, an experienced carpenter, and so energetically was the work pushed that the framing was completed within thirty-five days, The raising of the frame was commenced May 11th, and it took three days to raise and key the large and heavy timbers in place. This work, as the Diary states, was accomplished without accident, the record saying, "at which dangerous task Providence took care of the work, so that nobody was hurt."

This as well as the former "raisings" within the settlement were occasions to which were invited the sturdy neighbors for miles around, and partook somewhat of a social gathering. A raising was one of the customs of the day, when house, barn, or mill was to be built. Help was scarce and labor-saving machinery as yet unknown, so it was necessary to place the heavy timbers in place by main strength. On such occasions, great and sometimes herculean feats of strength, in lifting heavy timbers, were displayed by the men, among whom rivalry prevailed; and sometimes wagers of nominal value were laid as to who should prove the stronger.

Invitations to a raising were generally accepted, not only by the men, but the women and young folk, boys and girls, would gather to have a good time, the women folk taking care of the culinary department.

At the Ephrata raisings, while the men wrought at the

heavy timbers, the Sisterhood aided by the visiting women prepared meals for the Community, as well as for their guests both male and female. It is needless to say that after the heavy labor of the day the appetite of the men was extremely good, and full justice was done to the out-come of the sisters' kitchen.

Another peculiarity about these Ephrata raisings, a feature wherein they differed from all other barn-raisings, log-rollings, husking-bees and harvest-homes, was that there was no strong drink furnished to the participants, as the Ephrata Community was strictly a temperance organization, it being the first regularly organized community in America wherein the use of spirituous and malt liquors was strictly prohibited.

Toward the end of September, after the large posts, beams and joists were up and in place and the building was under roof and enclosed, it was found that there was enough heavy hewn timber and other material left over to build an even larger house than the one just being completed. It was then proposed to utilize this material by building a chapel or saal adjoining the new Brother House, The frame of this Brother-Saal was raised in November, all of the timbers being prepared and put into place within five weeks. This was the most stately building thus far erected by the Community. As a diarist writes, "its equal was not to be found in North America."

We now come to one of the strangest episodes in the history of the Mystic Community which has come down to us; this is the curious controversy relative to the lineal dimensions that should be adopted for the projected Brother-Saal. Bishop Cammerhoff, who was in the vicinity of Ephrata at the time, has left us an account of the dispute, of which the substance is given in the following paragraphs:

Bishop Cammerhoff says: "That in the spring of 1747 he visited Ephrata and was kindly received by Brother

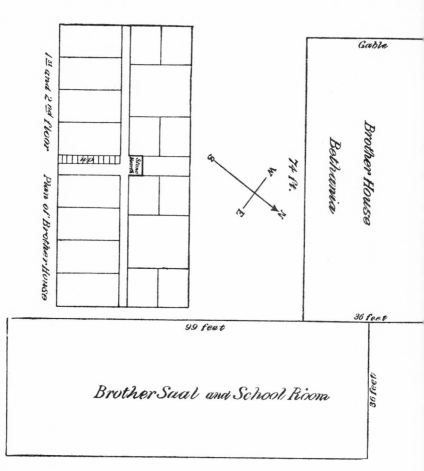

GROUND PLAN OF BROTHER HOUSE.

DIMENSIONS OF SAAL ACCORDING TO THE CAMMERHOFF ACCOUNT.

SCALE 1-16 INCH TO FOOT.   PLANS BY DR. JOHN F. MENTZER.

Jaebez; further, that some time before his visit the largest
of the three houses had been finished, and that a disagreement about its size or dimensions led to a withdrawal of
some of the fraternity. There were some of the Brotherhood who suggested 66 feet, some 99 feet and 100 feet as
the length for the new Saal. The contention ran high, and
it was feared that the building of the much-needed structure
might be postponed indefinitely.

"The solution of the difficulty was effected by those who
insisted upon 99 feet, they having one night received a
divine token that there was a cabalistic meaning attached
to the component parts or elements of figures; and the next
night they were instructed, too, in the mystery of the occult
science. It was after this fashion, said Brother Jaebez, that
the cabalists argued.

"Those who proposed 99 feet said they were right, in so
far as O (zero) signifies God and the downstroke man
$\left\{ \begin{array}{l} \text{God oo} \\ \text{Man 11} \end{array} \right\}$; hence if sixty-six feet was adopted it would
place God under man $\left\{ \begin{array}{l} \text{Man 11} \\ \text{God oo} \end{array} \right\}$, and if 100 feet it
would place man before God. Hence 99 feet was adopted:
God was above man.

"Cammerhoff says that upon arriving at the Kloster his
party were welcomed in an extremely cordial manner, as
they had come from Bethlehem. Peter Miller was very
complaisant. 'He stands,' continues Cammerhoff, second
only to Conrad Beissel. They said they had not kept any
meetings for six months. Back in Zion live the old worn-
out or fossil widows and widowers; lower down, in the
large house, live the single sisters. In front of this they
have erected one of three stories. In it are eight rooms,
and in each room eight chambers, besides a kitchen and
refectory. Their kitchen they would not exhibit. On
asking them whether they had many accessions, they
made no answer."

If we are to receive the above account of the interior arrangement of the Brother House literally, the original arrangement must have been similar to Saron. It is, however, very improbable that any such radical changes were ever made in the old monastery as this account would seem to indicate. In writing out his story, the good bishop evidently confounded the Brother House with the Sister House, Saron.

The new chapel was placed at right angles with the Brother House, the north gable end commencing about in the center of the eastern end of the Brother House, and, according to the evidence here presented, must have extended southward for a distance of ninety-nine feet. The main entrance to the Brother-Saal was by a door in the west front. The Brotherhood of Bethania, however, had a private entrance upon each floor. These doors were at the end of the corridors which divided the monastery, and opened into the extreme northwest corner of the Saal. It will be noticed that the salient features of the Sister House and adjoining chapel were reproduced in this instance.

Traces of the position of the old Brother-Saal and the doors opening into the monastery can still be seen by a close inspection of the east end of the old building; they also show plainly in the photographs illustrating this paper. There are still some persons living who remember the old Brother-Saal, and whose parents attended the academy held in the second floor. For, in the course of years, the Brother-Saal underwent a similar change to Peniel, in so far that the *porkirche* was turned into a hall on the second floor, and this large room was utilized by the brethren as an academy or classical school.

It is the third floor of the old Brother-Saal, however, that is of more than ordinary interest to us, as here was set up, after its completion, the enlarged printing establishment of the Ephrata Society. Here the type was set, the levers of

INTERIOR VIEWS OF BROTHER HOUSE.

(A) INTERIOR OF ATTIC, SHOWING WOODEN CHIMNEY FLUE.　　(B) NARROW CORRIDOR ON SECOND FLOOR,
SHOWING ENTRANCE TO THE KAMMERN.

the presses pulled, the sheets printed and hung up on long poles to dry, of the Ephrata imprints, some of which, on account of their scarceness, have since become almost priceless. Here also the sheets were folded, glued and stored until the demand warranted the binding.

An interesting story is told of one of the methods of punishment as applied by Brother Obed to some of the unruly boys who attended the academy. This was to lock them up for a certain time in one of the huge fireplaces. The chimney flues in this building were also of generous dimensions, formed of planks covered upon the inside with a thick coating of clay and *hexel*. The fireplaces were merely hearths for burning large pieces of wood, and were closed with doors during the season when not in use. One of these fireplaces was utilized by Brother Obed as a place of punishment wherein he was wont to confine his obstreperous scholars when all other means of discipline failed. Upon this occasion, when his pupils were more unruly than usual, he relegated four of them to the chimney and barred the door. When the hour of release was at hand, as no sign or word of complaint had come from the improvised cell, Brother Obed went to the door to release the culprits, intending, as was his custom, to first exact a promise of good behavior in the future.

As he opened the door, what was his surprise to find the apartment empty. The birds had flown. All that greeted the surprised schoolmaster was an extra amount of soot upon the hearth. A look up the wide chimney flue also failed to disclose the missing boys. As the door had not been opened since their incarceration, their absence could only be accounted for by a possible escape up the flue on to the roof, from whence there could be no escape. Three of the boys were sent down to look and see if the missing ones were upon the steep roof; but they returned in a few minutes without having seen any sign of the absent ones.

The mystery was finally solved when the four students, as sooty as chimney-sweeps, were led into the school-room by two of the brethren, by way of the door from the Brother House. They had found the footholds in the chimney used by the sweeps during their annual visits, and thus clambered up the flue. Once upon the roof, they, by some means, performed the dangerous feat of swinging themselves on to the adjoining Brother House, and then coming down through the trap-door, when they were discovered by some of the brethren, who led them back without ceremony.

The Brother-Saal was used for school purposes for many years after the decline of the Community, until, finally, for some unexplained reason, it was demolished about the year 1837. No picture of this old sanctuary is known.

We will now take a look at the old Brother House as it is at the present day. Time has dealt kindly with the old landmark, and when the writer first visited it about twenty years ago, but few changes had been made in its interior arrangements.

One of the peculiarities of this building is the recession of the third floor. Just why this is has never been explained ; nor is it known just how the timbers were framed. There is also a slight projection between the first and second stories. There have been many changes in the window openings of the old monastery, and they now present an irregular appearance, as but a few of the original frames remain.

As we step into the old house by way of the south door, the visitor is attracted by the narrow and steep staircase, with a rope affixed to the one side, by the aid of which the mystic recluses ascended the steep and narrow flight of steps. Just how the lower floor was originally arranged is difficult to surmise, in view of the changes made in late years, since the rooms were used for tenement purposes.

Originally, the lower floor was undoubtedly used as a refectory and for culinary purposes.

On the second floor one yet sees the long corridors upon which open the small cells or *kammern* of the religious votaries. The doors are but twenty inches wide, and even the passage-way emphasizes the scriptural path to heaven. According to one of Bishop Cammerhoff's letters, the brethren cast lots for the cells after the monastery was finished.

The loft or garret of this old building is well worthy of a visit, as here may be seen intact the original wooden chimney flues, a photograph of which feature is presented.

Some years ago several of the interior partitions were removed and the rooms utilized as tenements. Of late, however, steps have been taken to make all necessary repairs, to ensure the preservation of what remains of the old Kloster, Bethania, which, like its companion, the Sister House Saron, across the meadow, forms a unique setting within the old Kloster confine.

Darum O HErr! öffne den Menschen-Kindern die Augen! aufdaß sie sehend werden/ und lernen: rein und unbefleckt durch die Welt hindurch wandeln/ damit Dein REJCH bald offenbar werde/ und Dein WJLLE geschehe wie im Himmel/ also auch auf Erden/ Amen!

INVOCATION FROM AN EARLY EPHRATA IMPRINT.

END OF VOLUME I.

INDEX.